Regulating Competition in Stock Markets

Regulating Competition in Stock Markets

Antitrust Measures to Promote Fairness and Transparency through Investor Protection and Crisis Prevention

LAWRENCE R. KLEIN

VIKTORIA DALKO

MICHAEL H. WANG

EDITORS

WILEY

John Wiley & Sons, Inc.

Published by John Wiley & Sons, Inc., Hoboken, New Jersey.
Published simultaneously in Canada.

For general information on our other products and services or for technical support, please contact our Customer Care Department within the United States at (800) 762-2974, outside the United States at (317) 572-3993, or fax (317) 572-4002.

Wiley also publishes its books in a variety of electronic formats. Some content that appears in print may not be available in electronic books. For more information about Wiley products, visit our web site at www.wiley.com.

Library of Congress Cataloging-in-Publication Data:
Regulating competition in stock markets: antitrust measures to promote fairness and transparency through investor protection and crisis prevention/Lawrence R. Klein, Viktoria Dalko, and Michael H. Wang, editors.
    p. cm. – (Wiley finance series)
  Includes bibliographical references and index.
  ISBN 978-1-118-09481-5 (cloth); 978-1-118-22344-4 (ebk); 978-1-118-23686-4 (ebk); 978-1-118-26186-6 (ebk)
  1. Stock exchanges–State supervision. 2. Stock exchanges–Government policy.
  3. Financial crises. 4. Competition. I. Klein, Lawrence Robert. II. Dalko, Viktoria.
III. Wang, Michael H.
  HG4551.R384 2012
  332.64'2–dc23

                                                                      2011046012

Printed in the United States of America

10 9 8 7 6 5 4 3 2 1

To Our Inspiring Teachers

Lawrence R. Klein, Viktoria Dalko, and Michael H. Wang

Contents

CHAPTER 5
Preventing Stock Market Crises (III): Regulating Earnings Manipulation   113

Xin Yan, Lawrence R. Klein, Viktoria Dalko, Ferenc Gyurcsány, and Michael H. Wang

CHAPTER 6
Preventing Stock Market Crises (IV): Regulating Trading by Corporate Insiders   133

Xin Yan, Lawrence R. Klein, Viktoria Dalko, Ferenc Gyurcsány, and Michael H. Wang

CHAPTER 7
Preventing Stock Market Crises (V): Regulating Information Manipulation by Sell-Side Analysts   165

Xin Yan, Lawrence R. Klein, Viktoria Dalko, Ferenc Gyurcsány, and Michael H. Wang

CHAPTER 8

Preventing Stock Market Crises (VI): Regulating Information-Based Manipulation

Xin Yan, Lawrence R. Klein, Viktoria Dalko, Ferenc Gyurcsány, and Michael H. Wang

CHAPTER 9

Preventing Stock Market Crises (VII): Principles of Regulating New Reporting That Cultivates Long-Run Manias and Triggers Short-Run Panics

Xin Yan, Lawrence R. Klein, Viktoria Dalko, Ferenc Gyurcsány, and Michael H. Wang

Foreword

Franklin Allen

The Great Crash of 1929 was followed by the Great Depression and the failure of many banks. Given the terrible impact of the Great Depression on the economy, there was a widespread and strong desire to understand the causes of the calamity. In 1932 the Senate Committee on Banking and Currency set up an inquiry that became known as the Pecora Investigation to look into the causes of the Great Crash. The investigation uncovered a wide range of abuses in the banking and securities industries. This led to the passage of three major pieces of legislation to curb these abuses. The first was the Glass-Steagall Act of 1933 to separate commercial and investment banking. The second was the Securities Act of 1933 to regulate securities issues. The third, the Securities Exchange Act of 1934, set up the Securities and Exchange Commission (SEC) to regulate the securities industry.

These acts were followed over time by five other acts administered by the SEC that completed the framework of securities legislation in the United States. These were the Public Utility Holding Act of 1935, the Trust Indenture Act of 1939, the Investment Company Act of 1940, the Investment Advisers Act of 1940, and the Securities Investor Protection Act of 1970.

As mentioned, the Securities Act of 1933 was concerned with distributions of securities. It specified what information companies must provide when issuing securities in the public markets. It requires prospectuses with a significant amount of affirmative disclosure.

The Securities Exchange Act of 1934 was concerned with publicly traded stocks after they were issued. It has been amended on numerous occasions. The main regulations are concerned with the following.

- Publicly traded firms are required to file accounting returns periodically. Directors, officers, and holders of 10 percent or more of the shares are also required to provide information on a regular basis.

- Solicitation of proxies is controlled.
- Regulation of tender offers was added in 1968.
- Oversight of the stock exchanges and over-the-counter markets. Self-regulation is encouraged through self-regulatory organizations such as the New York Stock Exchange (NYSE), the National Association of Securities Dealers (NASD), registered clearing agencies, and the Municipal Securities Rulemaking Board. In 2007, the NASD merged with the NYSE regulatory committee to form the Financial Industry Regulatory Authority (FINRA).
- Prevention of market manipulation.
- Prevention of insider trading.
- Control of credit to purchase securities by the Federal Reserve System.
- Regulation of clearance and settlement processes.
- Regulation of markets in municipal securities.

The third statute chronologically was the Public Utility Holding Company Act of 1935. This was concerned with the regulation of electric and gas holding companies.

The Trust Indenture Act of 1939 supplemented the Securities Act of 1933 for situations where debt is being issued. It required the filing of an indenture with the SEC. The indenture provides information on the obligations of the trustee in the event of default and various other situations.

Customers of investment companies were perceived to be especially susceptible to unscrupulous behavior by the managers of these companies because of the liquid nature of their assets. The Investment Company Act of 1940, which was subsequently amended in both 1970 and 1980, was designed to prevent some of these abuses. Regulatory provisions were designed to ensure the following:

- Honest management
- Participation in management by security holders
- Adequate and feasible capital structures
- Effective financial disclosure
- Prevention of selling abuses
- Desirable incentives for managers through restrictions on forms of compensation

The Investment Advisers Act of 1940 required all investment advisers to register with the SEC.

Finally, the Securities Investor Protection Act of 1970 was designed to protect investors in the event of a broker going bankrupt. All brokers and dealers registered with the SEC are required to be members of the Securities

Investor Protection Corporation. This provides protection up to prespecified limits in the event of bankruptcy.

This framework of regulation served the United States well for many years and improved the operation of the securities markets significantly. As a result, it was widely copied around the world.

The crisis that started in the summer of 2007 has raised concerns that the regulation of the banking and securities industries has become flawed once again. This book contributes significantly to the debate on this issue. It provides extensive documentation that the securities markets have been subject to many abuses. The authors' focus is on the desirability of competition. It is usually claimed that financial services is a competitive industry. However, one of the most important tests of this claim is the extent to which firms in the industry make profits. Figure F.1 contrasts profits in manufacturing and financial services. It can be seen that in 1960 financial services' profits were about 1.5 percent of gross domestic product (GDP). By the middle of the 2000s they had risen to 3 percent of GDP and overtaken manufacturing profits.

The book documents in a very accessible way that in fact the securities industry is not competitive. The authors show monopoly can take many different forms, most of them quite different from standard notions of monopoly in other industries. They also lay out an agenda for regulatory change to remove this monopoly and restore competitive markets. This is an extremely important agenda and they are to be congratulated on it.

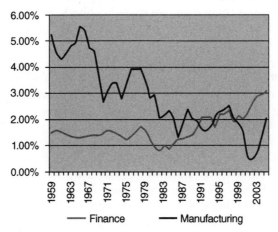

FIGURE F.1. Profits as Percent of GDP
Source: Economic Report of the President: 2007
Report Spreadsheet Tables, Tables B-1 and B-91.

Not content with providing a new framework for thinking about competition in financial markets, Part 1 of the book contains two chapters that outline new ways of measuring the costs of financial crisis. The existing literature on the costs of crises focuses on fiscal costs and lost output (see, for example, Allen and Gale (2007) pp. 18–19[1]). Chapter 1 points out that there are other significant costs arising from the crisis. They conduct a survey and document that crises have an important cost in terms of damaging health and happiness. In particular, people's emotional health suffered at the start of the crisis and physical health followed with some delay. Chapter 2 considers the suicide rate in industrial countries during the crisis as an extreme indicator of unhappiness. Persuasive evidence is presented that the economic situation of industrialized countries is the primary determinant of their suicide rates.

Part 2 of the book contains seven chapters and focuses on imperfect competition and antitrust regulations in stock markets. Chapter 3 presents evidence from a data set hand collected from securities regulatory agencies in the United States, China, India, Japan, and Hong Kong, that stock price manipulation is widespread in secondary markets. The authors focus on the *Accumulation-Lift-Distribution* (ALD) scheme for manipulation. In the accumulation stage, the manipulator acquires a large proportion of the supply of the stock in order to have monopolistic pricing power. In the lift stage, some form of deceptive activity is used to raise the price. This can be trade-based like wash sales or fake trades, or information-based such as the spreading of rumors. Once the price has risen, the manipulator sells the shares acquired in the first stage. The first suggested regulation to prevent this type of monopolistic manipulation is to eliminate the accumulation stage by preventing large concentrations of shareholdings. Chapter 4 is a continuation of Chapter 3 in that it focuses on regulations to prevent trade-based price lifting in the second stage of ALD schemes. The authors develop an anatomy of a manipulator's activities and identify nine variables that regulators can focus on to improve daily monitoring and regulatory operations.

Chapter 5 focuses on regulating earnings manipulation. There is a long history of earnings manipulations in the United States going back many years. Enron, WorldCom, and Lehman Brothers are just the most recent extreme examples of this type of manipulation. Numerous studies in the accounting and finance literature have documented that many U.S. corporations engage in less-extreme manipulation. The Sarbanes-Oxley Act attempted to curb this type of earnings manipulation, but the authors argue that it was unsuccessful in achieving this aim. They suggest that reducing earnings manipulation requires a focus on the factors that lead managers to undertake these activities. Examples are reducing external pressure that arises from sell-side analysts by regulating them, improving auditing efficiency, enhancing effectiveness in enforcement of existing restrictions, and regulating trading by corporate executives.

The focus of Chapter 6 is on improving the regulation of trading by corporate insiders. While the existing regulations are powerful, they are typically not strongly enforced. A number of new measures are suggested to improve this state of affairs. The first is to impose a daily limit on trading volumes of corporate insiders. The second is to give the right to regulators to investigate any abnormal price movements prior to information releases. The third is to impose responsibility for abuses on the chief executive officer.

Chapter 7 considers regulating information manipulation by sell-side analysts. The authors argue that the information sell-side analysts produce has investment value for informed investors mainly because it assists them in their manipulative trading strategies. Sell-side analysts effectively have an information monopoly similar to that of managers with earnings announcements. The chapter suggests measures to reduce this information monopoly.

Information-based manipulation is considered in Chapter 8. The basic idea behind information-based trading is to release information that is deceptive and then trade in the opposite direction. In the ALD schemes, this involves releasing information that is false and then, after the price has risen, selling to uninformed buyers. The authors suggest that the way to detect this type of manipulation is to look for inconsistencies between the information released and the investment position of the person or institution releasing it. Regulations to prevent this kind of behavior should focus on these kinds of inconsistency.

Finally, Chapter 9 develops principles for regulating news reporting that triggers short-term panics and cultivates long-run manias. The basic problem is that news can be a form of information monopoly just like the other ones discussed in previous chapters. Many examples of this kind of manipulation are provided, such as prosecution of a journalist writing the *Wall Street Journal*'s Heard on the Street column. They also provide evidence that business news reporting is frequently upward-biased. The main way to regulate the effects of dramatic news is to impose trading halts, circuit breakers, and price limits in securities markets. These methods can be effective, but they also have limitations, and the authors suggest various ways that they can be improved.

The editors and authors are a very distinguished group of economists. The book lives up to the expectations generated by their past work. It represents a fundamental contribution to how the competitiveness of financial markets can be ensured. The book is likely to stimulate a whole literature on this very important topic.

NOTE

1. Allen, F., and D. Gale (2007). Understanding Financial Crises, Oxford and New York: Oxford University Press.

Introduction

The primary question that will be explored and studied in this research series is how the functioning of the economic institution, and in particular the financial institution, affects human health and happiness. In order to gain some insights into this question, we studied the most recent financial crisis, asking whether the global financial crisis of 2007 to 2009 had measurable consequences on broadly defined health and happiness. It is important to consider whether its impact was minor and transitory, or significant and long term. If there is found to be such an impact, the most critical factors for determining the level and change of health and happiness in times of crisis should be examined. Our study is among the first to link a financial crisis simultaneously with both health and happiness, and even with the most extreme conditions of unhappiness.

Once we establish that financial crises can result in major losses in indicators of health, happiness, and even life, we turn our attention to the stock market, as a primary example of a financial market, to study the origins of these problems. We focus especially on those characteristics that may cause unfair losses to investors, market instability, and financial crisis, as these are the main characteristics that are related to the loss of human health and happiness. We identify certain monopolistic practices, especially as monopoly power is exercised through market manipulation, to be the key source of the problems.

BACK TO THE ORIGINAL QUESTION

In response to the recent global financial crisis, G-20 leaders led a call to build a stronger supervisory and regulatory framework for the future global financial sector, a global financial system that will avoid future systemic risks such as financial crises. The call serves as the main motivation for us to conduct research on systemic risk factors to financial markets and corresponding regulatory proposals. To gain a better understanding of these systemic risk factors, we start with a more fundamental question, that is, the question raised at the beginning of the Introduction.

For the stock market's 400 years of existence, no comprehensive research has been undertaken to diagnose how human health and happiness are affected by the real functioning of the financial system. In recent history, per capita income has enjoyed substantial growth, especially in developed countries. Life expectancy has increased steadily since the end of the Second World War, many diseases can now be cured, and many symptoms can be reduced, and so on, thanks to public health campaigns, modern medicine, and social advancement. As individuals can afford more amenities, and enjoy improved access to information, they live longer and healthier, and thus demand better health.

Demand for health and happiness improvement is a global trend. Therefore, it is natural to consider the implications of this global trend in the academic study of the functioning of major financial and economic institutions. This is why we provide the first diagnosis of how well the financial system, and the stock market in particular, fits into the current social trend of health and happiness. We find monopoly power in the stock markets that is exercised through market manipulation, causing a lack of objective information, excess volatility, unfair losses to smaller investors, and even financial crisis. We provide recommendations in an antitrust spirit, in order to reduce the impact of monopolistic power in the stock markets, and therefore to improve the quality of stock markets so that they are more supportive of human health and happiness.

OUR EXPECTED CONTRIBUTION

Before elaborating on our expected contribution to the literature on this topic, we briefly describe our approach. We collect evidence to establish the existence of a persistent and widespread phenomenon—market manipulation in stock markets in selected economies. The facts in securities litigation cases and empirical research form the foundation of our discovery of the key areas of various manipulation tactics and corresponding regulatory proposals. We do not form a hypothesis or build a theory; thus, not many assumptions need to be made. Comprehensiveness is another feature of our approach. Details can be seen in the following.

This work, out of our research series, marks five unique features in our expected contribution to the understanding and prevention of stock market crises that may originate from market manipulation.

1. Our research series is the most comprehensive study to date on stock market manipulation. It is the first to bring together three layers of

information—namely, empirical literature, theoretical models, and securities litigation cases.

(1.1) We review a wide range of empirical studies on market manipulation and information bias from multiple disciplines, beginning from the 1930s. The disciplines include finance, economics, accounting, legal studies, criminology, psychology, public health, medicine, and media studies, among others.

(1.2) We include theoretical advancements on health and happiness (Chapters 1 and 2). We review the theoretical contributions to the existence of market manipulation without superior information (Chapter 3), the price impact of large trading volumes (Chapter 4), herding by investors (Chapter 9), and media cultivation (Chapter 9).

(1.3) We present hundreds of securities-litigation cases that we have collected from the securities regulatory agencies of many countries over decades that cross the century. These cases provide solid evidence that manipulations, in various forms, exist, and have been frequent, widespread, and occasionally rampant in the stock markets of both developed and developing economies.

2. Our research series is the first to provide comprehensive and thorough micro-level regulatory proposals related to trading, with the goal of investor protection and crisis prevention. It differs from macro prudent regulation, and from single policy suggestions. We identify key areas of various manipulative practices before proposing effective regulatory measures. The proposed measures are practical and implementable; most are measurable, quantifiable (and thus can be converted to a computer algorithm), adjustable, and cost-effective. In many cases, implementation may not require legal changes, depending on the particular country's current laws.

3. Our research series is the first attempt to collect evidence, especially from market manipulation litigation cases, on an international scale. It is the most comprehensive study in terms of geographical coverage. It includes individual cases based on news media reports and case studies from numerous economies around the world. The majority of the litigation cases are found on the official web sites of the securities regulatory agencies in the United States, China, India, Japan, and Hong Kong. Press reports of individual cases are from developed economies such as the United Kingdom, Germany, France, Canada, Australia, Taiwan, Korea, and Greece, and developing economies including China, India, Brazil, and many others.

4. This research series is also the first to provide comprehensive evidence on the multiple methods used by stock market investors for market

manipulation. In trade-based manipulation, these methods include accumulating large percentages of shareholdings often using numerous accounts (Chapter 3), fictitious trading such as self-dealing (wash sale) or cross-dealing (matched orders) (Chapter 4), fake trading or placing orders without actually executing them (Chapter 4), and advancing the bid or bidding at a price repeatedly and substantially deviated from the previous market price (Chapter 4). In information-based manipulation, before and on the time of information release to the investing public, these manipulative methods include earnings manipulation (Chapter 5), especially in conjunction with trade in stocks by corporate insiders (Chapter 6), analyst information distortion for proprietary trading teams and favored large clients to support distribution of shares (Chapter 7), pump-and-dump or information-based long manipulation (Chapter 8), trash-and-cash or information-based short manipulation (Chapter 8), high-frequency trading with flashed orders (Chapter 8), and frontrunning (Chapter 8). We also analyze the role of the media in triggering short-run mini-bubbles, precipitating panic selling, and cultivating long-run mania (Chapter 9).

We consider in this book numerous media outlets and publishing platforms that are used for information-based manipulation. They include print and electronic media—for example, newspapers, magazines, TV, investment advice web sites, Internet bulletin boards, e-mail spamming, and personal communication tools such as massive newsletter mailing, fax blast, auto-dial equipment, instant messaging, and investment conference presentations.

5. In addition to finding predatory pricing in the stock market, we propose the new concept of information monopoly. Analyzing millions of observations from empirical literature and litigation cases, we find a common core underlying successful market manipulation. We call this core *information monopoly,* and identify three components of information monopoly, that is, potentially price-moving information, publicity, and credibility. Information monopoly, our new category, is related to information asymmetry. Information asymmetry means that different people know different things (Stiglitz 2002). This has far-reaching consequences, as is proven by the success of the economics of information. Information monopoly in the stock market includes potentially price-moving information that is generated or obtained only by certain market participants. From this perspective, it is specific asymmetric information relevant to stock price movement. However, only when those participants have access to publicity and credibility in addition to potentially price-moving information can they then turn this information into an information monopoly.

Information monopoly is exercised in market manipulation. Market manipulation is primarily the manipulation of perception of other investors, with the goal of taking advantage of them through inducing them to trade in a way desired by the manipulator. The market manipulator, subsequently, obtains unfair trading profit at low risk.

While the concept of information monopoly is extracted from thousands of market manipulation practices in the stock market, it has the potential to be tested more broadly, such as in the futures market and other financial markets. It is expected to have more general implications for the market economy and even other aspects of life.

DETAILS OF THIS RESEARCH SERIES

This research series has nine chapters in Part 1 and Part 2. Part 1 contains two chapters, Chapters 1 and 2. Chapter 1 provides empirical analysis of the impact of the current financial crisis on broadly defined health—including emotional, physical, and relationship health—as well as happiness on a small but innovative sample. Chapter 2 contains an econometric analysis of the association of the ongoing recession with the most extreme unhappiness—suicide—in 30 countries. We observe that profound unhappiness, as measured by suicide, is directly linked to loss of economic welfare.

We establish that the stress caused by the financial crisis has an impact similar to that of traumatic events such as the terrorist attack of 9/11 and Hurricane Katrina. Therefore, prevention of a financial crisis should be considered with attention similar to that for the prevention of other major traumatic events to society.

Part 2 contains the remaining seven chapters, Chapters 3 through 9, in which we find monopoly in all forms of manipulation analyzed. Thus, monopoly is the key concept for piecing through all chapters in Part 2. Significant concentration, or quantity monopoly, underlies trade-based manipulation, which is analyzed extensively in Chapters 3 and 4. Information monopoly is seen in all forms of information-based manipulation where monopoly power is used for trading strategies. Trading by corporate insiders involves an information monopoly when such individuals trade around public announcements (Chapter 6). Trading by proprietary traders against recommendations published by their own sell-side analysts necessarily involves an information monopoly (Chapter 7), as does trading by rumor-mongers against publicized false rumors (Chapter 8). Trading by information-based manipulators on the Internet involves an information monopoly if their schemes work (Chapter 8), and an information monopoly can also be exercised for the individual or collusive trading profits of business journalists (Chapter 9).

In addition to unfair trading profit, information monopoly can be used to advance other business or individual interests. It can be used for corporate earnings manipulation, mergers, and acquisitions, as well as a variety of other corporate business interests (Chapter 5). It can be used for marketing for issuers by sell-side analysts (Chapter 7), and for maintaining strong relationships between brokerage firms and client institutional investors (Chapter 7). An information monopoly can also be used for rent-seeking by a private stock exchange (Chapter 8), and by journalists and media firms to enhance their reputation or market position (Chapter 9).

We propose corresponding regulatory measures and principles to prevent the utilization of monopoly power in illegal or unfair trading strategies. The multiple measures proposed in Chapters 3 and 4 target large concentrations of shareholding and various trade-based manipulation tactics based on the nine variables at a trader's discretion. The proposed measures are primarily aimed at preventing high trading speed, which may lead to crises. Chapters 5 and 6 deal with corporate insiders. Several proposals are presented in Chapter 5 to reduce external pressure and internal temptation for managers to manipulate earnings and other corporate information. In Chapter 6, four measures are recommended to substantially prevent corporate insiders from exercising their information monopoly in their illegal profit-seeking or loss-avoidance trading strategies.

Sell-side analysts an generate information monopoly once their recommendations are publicly disseminated. This information monopoly is utilized in a distinct way toward their own employers, client issuers, client institutional investors, and public investors. In Chapter 7, we propose six regulatory measures targeting trading prior to scheduled public release of the analysts' research, enforcing mandatory transparency and uncertainty in their publicity. Chapter 8 treats information-based manipulation in general and provides a comprehensive analysis of the concept of information monopoly. Eight proposals are advanced based on anti-inconsistency around public announcement of potentially price-moving information, using preannouncement abnormal price behavior as the trigger for regulatory action. Since the Internet is poorly regulated, more enforcement is suggested for inclusion in monitoring and regulation. The last chapter, Chapter 9, proposes multiple principles to prevent media from publicizing biased business news reports that may cause short-run mini-bubbles and cultivate long-run mania. It also suggests two principles to deal with the market impact of breaking news that may trigger marketwide panic selling.

DISCLAIMER: NOT AN INVESTMENT GUIDE

This research series is not an investment guide. The goal is to propose stock market regulatory principles that can enable the market to achieve a more fair and transparent competitive equilibrium. The research series does not provide recommendations for trading strategies, and it should not be used for trading purposes. There are many books available that are focused on advising investment strategies; our series is not one of them. The authors of this research series do not endorse any trading strategy, and are not responsible for anyone's trading results.

SCIENCE, HEALTH, AND CIVILITY

The current reality is that financial crises remain hard to predict. The public's savings can be suddenly lost due to repeated and unexpected financial crises. From this perspective, it seems that the current functioning of the stock market is not very scientific—it has a tendency to collapse, the timing of which is very hard to predict.

A more scientific trading environment would require not only somewhat predictable results by all participating investors and relative certainty that savings will not be abruptly lost, but would also be expected to provide access to objective information for all market participants, so that decisions can be made based on reliable sources. In this research series we find that it is difficult to decide if the trusted information sources studied that influence small investors' decisions are objective or not. This is not a surprising result, given the findings by Stiglitz (1974) that markets do not provide appropriate incentives for information disclosure, thus there is a role for government. We have found a lack of objectivity in each information source studied, including corporate earnings reports, sell-side analyst recommendations, business media news, and even the auditor opinions—all can be used for manipulating the perception of induced small investors. Therefore, the information available for small investors' trading decisions is hard to consider as scientific, as it is frequently manipulated.

We find that during the most recent financial crisis, in addition to material losses there are more subtle but important effects. The loss of predictability, combined with many other rising uncertainties in times of financial crisis, results in a multitude of financial, social, and emotional burdens to individuals that eventually erode their physical and mental health. In the process, happiness is also negatively affected. Therefore, financial crisis prevention has a special significance in preventing any kinds of crisis-related disease and human suffering.

Our recommendations aim at less volatility and avoiding severe financial crisis, and, as such, would protect investors from experiencing unfair losses and other consequences of financial crises. Subsequently, implementation of these proposals would improve people's health and benefit their happiness.

Manipulation violates the basic rules of civility in the stock market, as it creates the perception of false reality in the minds of the uninformed in order to take advantage of them. Hence, preventing manipulation would improve civility. Trust would also be improved once investors no longer feel the need to suspect that someone is intending to take advantage of them. Without the constant threat of severe financial losses, investors would be able to become more civilized toward their family members, their colleagues, and society in general.

Acknowledgments

We thank the many researchers, practitioners, and regulators at a number of universities, securities firms, and stock exchanges in the United States, European Union, China, Hong Kong, and Taiwan, in alphabetical order, for their helpful feedback and support: Clark Abt, Philippe Aghion, Franklin Allen, Messod D. Beneish, Anana Black, Rainer Böhme, Derek Bok, Roger C.Y. Chen, Daniel Cohen, Raymond Comeau, David Cutler, Sheng Dai, Sanjiv Das, Mark L. DeFond, Ed Diener, Richard Easterlin, Hadi Esfahani, Jill Fisch, Bruno S. Frey, Laura Frieder, Robert Frosch, Xavier Gabaix, Deborah Gregory, Michel Habib, Kathleen Hagerty, Saling Huang, Imre Janosi, Robert A. Jarrow, Daniel Kahneman, Janos Kertesz, Asim Khwaja, Imre Kondor, Janos Kornai, Albert (Pete) S. Kyle, Larry H. P. Lang, Richard Layard, Erik Lie, Xiaodong Liu, Chunlin Lu, Hai Lu, Adair Morse, Terrance Odean, Zoe-Vonna Palmrose, Thomas Philippon, Stephen Craig Pirrong, James Poterba, Jay Ritter, Asani Sarkar, Oliver Schnusenberg, Martin Seligman, Nejat Seyhun, Douglas J. Skinner, Richard Sloan, Jeremy Stein, Rafael Di Tella, Judy Tsui, Jiang Wang, Robert F. Whitelaw, Peter D. Wysocki, Leslie Young, Amy Y. Zang, and Jonathan Zitrain.

For able research assistance and general help, we also thank (in alphabetical order) the following: Richard Chen, Adam Demos, Georgios Deves, Iryna Dolan, Tom Glasberg, Jennifer Lin, Simon Lukyanchyk, Katie Orr, Siobhán O'Shaughnessy, Santiago Suarez, and Blessing Tawengwa. We give special thanks to the survey participants who have made Chapter 1 possible.

We thank the organizers, discussants, and participants of the following conferences: the Western Economic Association International 86th Annual Conference, San Diego, California, June 29 to July 3, 2011; the Asian Finance Association 2011 International Conference: "Frontiers in Finance: Asia-Pacific and Beyond," Macau, China, July 10 to 13, 2011; the 16th World Congress of the International Economic Association, Tsinghua University, Beijing, July 4 to 8, 2011; the 9th NTU International Conference on Economics, Finance, and Accounting, Taipei, May 25 to 26, 2011; the 6th Annual Seminar on Banking, Financial Stability and Risk, Sao Paulo, August 11 to 12, 2011, hosted by the Banco Central do Brasil; the 8th

International Conference on Advances in Applied Financial Economics, Samos Island, Greece, June 30 to July 2, 2011; and the Third Annual Meeting of the Academy of Behavioral Finance and Economics, UCLA, Los Angeles, September 21 to 23, 2011.

We thank Pamela Van Giessen, Bill Falloon, Kimberly Bernard, Judy Howarth, Stacey Fischkelta, and all other friends at John Wiley & Sons for their trust and support. Their high-quality work has made it possible for this book to be in your hands.

Regulating Competition in Stock Markets

Happiness, Health, and Longevity during the 2008 Global Financial Crisis

CHAPTER 1

Does the Recent Financial Crisis Impact Health and Happiness?

Xin Yan

Lawrence R. Klein

Viktoria Dalko

Ferenc Gyurcsány

Michael H. Wang

Christine Huang[1]

Has the global financial crisis of 2008 had measurable consequences for broadly defined health and happiness? Is its impact minor, transitory, or significant? If there is an impact, what are the most critical factors in determining the level and change of health and happiness in times of crisis? Our study is among the first to link a financial crisis simultaneously with both health and happiness. For our longitudinal study we designed a survey and collected semiannual survey responses from spring 2008 to spring 2010—five data points over two years, from 335 young professionals, who were mainly working professionals, and were former graduate students of the authors. The statistical analysis of the small and unique panel data reveals that the current global financial crisis has had a measurable and detrimental impact on health and happiness. In particular, there has been an immediate loss of happiness. Emotional health deteriorated at the onset of the crisis, and physical health followed after a delay, resulting in loss of happiness due to the financial crisis. We compare the impact of the financial crisis on happiness and health with that of the terrorist attack of 9/11 in the United

States and of Hurricane Katrina on direct survivors. Such traumatic impact on people calls for financial-crisis prevention.

CONCEPTS OF HAPPINESS

Happiness and governance were intrinsically linked by Aristotle in his *Nicomachean Ethics* (2011). According to Aristotle, the goal of governance is to create the conditions in which citizens can be happy. In the contemporary era, the Stiglitz Committee (CMEPSP 2009), as well as Derek Bok (2010), reaches the same conclusion. Bruno Frey announced that economics "is—or should be about happiness" (2008). Happiness is certainly a very close—some argue, the closest—construct to what economists traditionally mean by utility and welfare. We use Aristotle's standard as a reference for our approach to defining the objectives and the methods to apply in dealing with financial crisis.

The happiness concept we use in our research is based on our understanding of Aristotle's *Eudaimonia,* and as such it includes a notion of deep self-awareness as to the consequences of change in the comforts of life as well as the implications for one's ability to accomplish the most important goals in life—in work, family, friendships, and ultimate contribution to society. The concept of happiness we focus on is not a momentary mood or a brief experience of pain and pleasure—and therefore we did not collect instantaneous reports of feelings of pain and pleasure as it is done by contemporary hedonic psychology (Kahneman, Diener, and Schwartz 1999). Rather, we asked survey respondents about their happiness experience over a longer time horizon, such as the previous one month. Even though our aim was to measure happiness similar to Aristotle's *Eudaimonia,* we recognized the difficulties it poses, especially the challenges of surveying the level of virtue and frequency of virtuous acts of other people. Therefore, at this stage of our research we did not incorporate questions regarding virtuous actions into our survey. When interpreting the survey results, we relied on the millennia-old tradition of Chinese medicine and the progress made during the last several decades in positive psychology, the appraisal theory of emotions, stress research, and the economics of happiness.

To the best of our knowledge, our research is among the first to connect a financial crisis simultaneously with health and happiness. We approach the question of health and happiness using a defensive orientation; that is, unlike most of the current literature, we do not look for factors in the private or public domain that could contribute to more happiness of the public but take the opposite logic to address what should be avoided so people do not lose happiness. In so doing we aim to build a stronger defense against unhappiness on a national and international level since we identify a condition for the deterioration of happiness: financial crisis.

In our study, health has a very specific meaning, inspired by the World Health Organization (WHO): "Health is a state of complete physical, mental, and social wellbeing and not merely the absence of disease or infirmity" (1948). When we talk about *health,* we mean this kind of comprehensive health. Accordingly, the *domains of health* we distinguish in our study are emotional health, physical health, social relationship health, and economic health. When we refer only to a particular domain of health, such as physical health, we specifically say so.

Our key contribution is that, based on our unique survey results, we can answer the questions on whether the global financial crisis of 2008 had measurable consequences for broadly defined health and happiness. We are also the first to define the most critical health domains determining the level and change of health and happiness in times of crisis.

THE HISTORY OF MODELING HEALTH AND FINANCIAL CRISIS

The statistical and theoretical modeling of how crisis impacts health, which has a history going back to the Great Depression of the 1930s, focuses on three areas: crisis impact on mental health, morbidity, and mortality.

Crisis Impact on Mental Health, Morbidity, and Mortality

Pollock (1935), in describing the Great Depression, and later Brenner (1973), in a study of 127 years of history, firmly established the relationship between health and the state of the economy, especially between the level of unemployment and mental illness as measured by mental hospital admission. Eisenberg and Larzarsfeld (1938), and later Wecter (1948), also focused on the mental health impact of the Great Depression. Dooley and Catalano (1980) provided a survey of the field. In particular they reviewed all previous individual-level longitudinal studies on the connection between unemployment and subsequent psychological problems including suicide, depression, anxiety, and psychopathologic symptoms. They propose a model of intervening variables that may causally link changes in the economy with subsequent changes in treated mental disorders. Ganzini, McFarland, and Cutler (1990) documented that mental health deteriorates as a result of catastrophic financial loss, while Stuckler et al. (2009) pointed out the long-lasting effect of fear and anxiety that is due to crisis. In terms of its mechanism, mental health has been found to deteriorate as a result of stress (Dohrenwend 2000; Turner, Wheaton, Lloyd 1995; Cui and Vaillant 1996; McGonagle and Kessler 1990). Das et al. (2009) and Friedman and Thomas (2007) documented the impact of the recent financial and economic crisis and find persistent increased psychological distress as a result of the crisis.

Social and economic determinants of health are widely accepted today (Wilkinson and Marmot 2003). As such, crisis also has a measurable impact on morbidity. Studies have linked unemployment and economic crisis to health (Catalano and Dooley 1983; Rayman and Bluestone 1982; Musgrove 1987). Bloom, Canning, and Jamison (2004) discussed the "vicious cycle" linking deteriorating health and slower economic growth. Burazeri et al. (2008) documented a case of a financial crisis affecting physical health: six to nine years after the collapse of a widespread pyramid scheme,[2] which resulted in severe and unexpected loss to a large part of the population of Albania, hospital admissions that were due to acute coronary syndrome significantly increased. Based on results obtained by stress researchers, we would also expect to see a negative impact of financial crisis on health; as House (2002) pointed out, there is considerable evidence that negative life events, including major economic losses or setbacks, are risk factors of morbidity. Kasl and Jones (2000), Pearlin et al. (1981), and House (1987) provided additional evidence on the contribution of crisis to morbidity. *The financial crisis and global health,* the WHO Report (2009), Frankenberg, Thomas, and Beegle (1999), and Cutler et al. (2002) documented the impact of a more current financial and economic crisis on health globally, in Indonesia, and in Mexico, respectively.

Mortality has been linked to economic crisis through either recession (Colledge 1982) or unemployment (Brenner 1979), although with a considerable time lag. Stuckler et al. (2009) warned against the potential mortality consequences of the current global crisis. Even though there is mounting evidence for the existence of a negative effect of financial crisis on physical health, Cutler et al. (2002) reached the conclusion that "no studies have systematically examined the link between economic crisis and health, or considered the mechanisms through which economic crisis affects health." Our research aims to add to the understanding of how the current economic and financial crisis is influencing health.

Crisis Impact on Happiness

Statistical analyses of and theoretical arguments about happiness in general are active research fields in psychology (Kahneman, Diener, and Schwartz 1999; Seligman 2002), summarized for economists by Frey and Sultzer

(2002); as well as in economics (Easterlin 2010; Layard 2005; Graham and Pettinato 2002; Bruni and Porta 2005). The sources of happiness mentioned in psychology and economics are generally accepted to be one's level of living, family, health, job/work, and social values/character (Cantril 1965). The same types of dimensions have been listed by Easterlin (2003) as income, family, work, health conditions, and friendship. Layard (2005) provided a list of prerequisites to happiness: family relationships, financial situation, work, community and friends, and health. These categories correspond well to the list Aristotle provided as the prerequisites of happiness (or rather *Eudaimonia*): adequate health, food, and other care for the body; friends; wealth; and power (*Nicomachean Ethics* 2011). Therefore, if financial crisis destroys any of these prerequisites of happiness, we expect happiness to decline.

Impact of Declining GDP, Unemployment, Financial Loss, and Financial Strain on Happiness A short-term relationship has been demonstrated to exist between life satisfaction and gross domestic product (GDP) growth. Life satisfaction declines during economic contraction/collapse and increases during expansion/recovery as documented in 25 developed countries (DiTella et al. 2001), in 17 developing Latin American countries, and 3 transition economies (Easterlin, et al. 2010). Empirical studies using cross-sectional data showed that subjective wellbeing is negatively affected by personal financial loss and the loss of employment as an individual event (Clark and Oswald 1994; Turner, Wheaton, and Lloyd 1995; Frey and Stutzer 1999; Layard 2005), as well as unemployment over time (Winkelman and Winkelman 1998). In addition, DiTella et al. (2003) measured the impact of macroeconomic slowdown and growing unemployment on those who did not lose their jobs, a feature that they refer to as the "important psychic cost of recession," and Wolfers (2003) demonstrated the measurable impact of macroeconomic volatility on happiness. With these findings in mind, we expect to find that the impact of the financial crisis on happiness at least to some extent *directly* results from personal unemployment, financial loss, and the "psychic cost of recession."

Health and Happiness

Kahneman et al. (2004) and Stone and Shiffman (1994) found that measures of emotional experiences are correlated with life satisfaction. Argyle (1999), Blanchflower and Oswald (2004), and Frey and Sultzer (2002) demonstrated that healthier people are happier. Okun et al. (1984) found that self-reported health and happiness correlated by 0.32 on average. Graham (2009) provides evidence that around the globe, across cultures and countries (the United States, Latin America, Russia), self-reported health has the strongest coefficient among all (otherwise sociodemographic) variables explaining happiness.

The relationship between health and happiness is not one-directional. Blanchflower and Oswald (2004) point out that there is a self-reinforcing cycle: (Un)happier people are (un)healthier and (un)healthier are (un)happier. On the other side of causality, Roysamb et al. (2003) and Takkouche, Regueira, and Gestal-Otero (2001) found that happier people reported better perceived health and fewer physical symptoms. Diener and Chan (2010) provide a comprehensive review of the field. Their notion of subjective wellbeing contains three factors: high-level positive emotions (including happiness), low-level negative emotions (including anger and fear), and life satisfaction. Diener and Chan (2010) establish that especially in originally healthy populations, subjective wellbeing has predictive power over physical health and longevity. Happy people are healthier and live longer, and unhappy people have more diseases and live a shorter life.

Psychologists repeatedly find that good relationships are important for happiness. Friends, family, and other social connections have been long recognized as sources of joy, happiness, and personal satisfaction (Campbell, Converse, and Rodgers 1976; Buss 2000; Seligman 2002). In fact, relatedness has often been found to be the most or close to the most important factor in subjective well being (Argyle 1987; Myers 1999). Stress research often considers the quality of relationship with friends and family as a buffer for coping with stress, so a good relationship can shelter one from the negative consequences of chronic stress (House 2002).

Theory: How Emotions Impact Physical Health

There is ample empirical evidence on the physiological pathways from emotional to physical health (Kiecolt-Glaser et al. 2002). There are also numerous population studies documenting the same regularity (Hemingway and Marmot 1999; Williams and Schneiderman 2002). This time we are concerned about the theoretical progress in explaining these transmission mechanisms from emotional to physical health. Two schools of practice and knowledge help to explain how individuals are affected when faced with major life events. The first, Traditional Chinese Qigong and its application in Traditional Chinese Medicine (TCM), has been practiced continuously for more than 5,000 years. The second, stress research applied to emotions, has its intellectual roots in Aristotle's work but has developed in its current form mainly since 1990.

In Traditional Chinese Qigong, and its application in TCM, the central concept is Qi (usually translated as *life force*). According to TCM, the experience of extreme negative emotion causes immediate damage to a person's Qi. If not treated, the accumulation of negative Qi in the body over time manifests as physical diseases. (See more in *The Medical Classic of the Yellow Emperor* 2001.) It is not only an ancient theory; such practice of healing and prevention has been present through thousands of years.

Growing contemporary literature in stress research applied to emotion also testifies for the association between emotional health and disease (see reviews of the literature in Booth-Kewley and Friedman 1987; Herbert and Cohen 1993; Krantz and McCeney 2002; Watson 1988). It is rooted in the works of Hans Selye (1956).

David Lazarus created the analytical framework he called "appraisal and coping" to understand stress (Cooper and Dewe 2004). A contemporary summary of appraisal theory of emotions can be found in Sceerer, Schorr, and Johnstone (2001). Lazarus proposed that emotions are generated in the process of "appraisal" of environmental change, the same process that generates stress (2001). The word *appraisal* in common language invokes a conscious decision process; however, emotions arise as a response to changes often instantaneously, such as being startled by a clap of thunder.

Happiness Is a Good Measure of Welfare and Utility

The concepts of utility and welfare are cornerstones of economic theory. Neoclassical economic theory employs an *objectivist* approach, measuring utility according to the individual choices related to the consumption of goods, services, and leisure. However, there is a long history of challenges to this view (Frey and Stutzer 2002). Instead of relying on observed consumption (*decision utility*), a subjective approach has been shown to be useful in complementing the measure of wellbeing more directly ("experienced utility" as coined by Kahneman et al. 1997). Today individual wellbeing is measured by asking people about their self-reported happiness or life satisfaction in surveys, and the results are consistent and reliable (Ehrhards, Saris, and Veenhoven 2000; Sandvik, Diener, and Seidlitz 1993).

OUR THREE OBJECTIVES

This chapter has three objectives. The first objective is to establish whether the financial crisis has had a significant impact on the happiness of a well-educated, highly motivated, middle- and high-income group of international managers and business students. The second question we want to answer is whether the crisis has impacted these people's broadly interpreted health. The third research question follows naturally: How are health and happiness related during times of financial crisis? We approach the third question in cross section and in time series. In a cross-sectional model, the question becomes: What is the role of health domains in shaping happiness during a crisis? In a time series setup the question is: How do changes in different domains of health contribute to the gain or loss of happiness? Our aim is to illuminate the discussion about the causal model (Diener et al. 1999) by conducting a longitudinal study that highlights the impact of health indicators on happiness during a time of severe financial crisis.

We Created Our Happiness and Health Domain Indices

We examined three major databases—the World Values Survey database, the Eurobarometer database, and the Gallup-Heathway database—that are commonly used for happiness research. We found that none of them were suitable to address our research questions; therefore, we designed our own survey.

The question on happiness we asked was: "Rate your current level of happiness during the last month as Poor (1), Fair (2), Good (3), or Excellent (4)." We asked for a one-month period because we wanted to collect information that was sensitive enough to capture changes during the crisis. People who are surveyed actually do consider the time frame asked in the question (Diener and Larsen 1984; Watson, Clark, and Tellegen 1988); so, by requesting an answer for a one-month period, we hoped to avoid having respondents average out the crisis and noncrisis time periods and answer a lifetime satisfaction level.

As mentioned earlier, we took inspiration from the famous WHO definition of health as "a state of complete physical, mental, and social well-being and not merely the absence of disease or infirmity" (WHO 1948). Whenever we use the word *health,* we mean this *comprehensive* health. Accordingly, the *domains of health* we distinguish in our study are emotional health, physical health, social relationship health, and economic health. Emotional health: Extraordinary reactions of human beings to unexpected health-related events are categorized by the ancient Chinese as seven emotions: excessive joy, anger, worry, deep thought, grief, fear, and shock. These particular emotions are widely utilized in China and some other parts of Asia and have been important practical tools in Traditional Chinese Medicine for preventive, diagnostic, and healing purposes (*The Medical Classic of the Yellow Emperor* 2001; Kaptchuk 2000). In TCM, any of these emotions—when they are excessive—can bring about diseases in the

TABLE 1.1 Comparison between the Terms of TCM's Extreme Emotions with the Negative Affect of the Positive and Negative Affect Scale (PANAS)

TCM	PANAS Negative Affect
angry	hostile, scornful, grouchy
worried	distressed
lost in deep thoughts	blue, drowsy
grief-stricken	sad, sorry, apologetic
fearful	fearful
shocked (startled)	astonished, nervous, jittery

organs to which they correspond. The list of extreme emotions from thousands of years of TCM corresponds closely with the list of negative effects from modern psychology, as measured by Watson, Clark, and Tellegen (1988) and displayed in Table 1.1. Emotional health and negative affect are concepts similar to that of psychological distress used by other researchers. We measured the emotional health index of an individual as the intensity of six emotions, without excessive joy.

Physical health: We measured physical health using the self-reported perceived health status in terms of rating of fitness, pain or discomfort, quality of sleep, frequency of doctor's visits, and overall rating of health. According to TCM, pain, difficulties with sleeping, and lack of fitness are all signs of imbalance in the Qi circulation and quantity and quality of the Qi in the body, so these are all signs of physical disease formation or progression. (See more traditional literature on the Four Examination Methods of Traditional Chinese Medicine attributed to Bian Que in *Shi Ji* (1995) and *The Medical Classic of the Yellow Emperor* 2001). Contemporary stress research also recognizes these signs as stress symptoms (Benson and Klipper 2000; House 2002). The perceived physical health symptoms we used in our survey are similar to the symptoms of clinical depression defined by modern psychology. According to the American Psychiatric Association (1994), symptoms of depression include changes in weight, insomnia, fatigue, and diminished interest or pleasure. Our concept of physical health is similar to the notion of intensity of physical symptoms, somatic symptoms, level of physiological distress, physical health complaints, and reported physical symptoms—categories used by other researchers.

Social relationship health: We collected data about the quality of participants' social relationship health in three realms of their lives: at work, with family, and with friends. Our construct of social relationship health is related to the content of friendship (Graham 2009), quality of interpersonal relationships, social support, and social affiliations (Stansfeld 2006), and might be linked to social capital (Putnam 2000).

<u>Economic health:</u> The reason we use the terminology *economic health* is to distinguish it from income and wealth variables that are often used in literature. We included an individual's work status and level of difficulty with paying the bills in our index. Economic health is a concept close to the ideas of economic hardship (Ahnquist, Fredlund, and Wamala 2007), material wellbeing (Csikszentmihalyi 1999), and financial fitness used by other researchers.

In addition to the variables that combine to create these four health domain indices, we gathered multiple sociodemographic data.

OUR FINANCIAL CRISIS–IMPACT MODEL

Many studies of happiness struggle to disentangle causalities from reverse causalities (CMEPSP 2009). Since we are documenting the impact of an external event—the global financial crisis of 2008—as a "natural experiment," changes in the domains of health and happiness are clearly due to the initial external shock of the financial crisis.

Usually in similar studies, researchers have great difficulty entangling the emotional and physical disturbances, since these phenomena can form a mutually reinforcing cycle. This results in technical problems of econometric modeling and the calls for simultaneous equations, due to the problem of endogeneity. However, in the case of our study, the financial crisis is certainly an external event; the crisis outbreak is not influenced by any survey participants' emotions or physical health. Hence, everything we measure is caused by the financial crisis. It is true even though we cannot exclude the ignition of self-reinforcing mechanisms over time; for example, it might happen that the crisis causes emotional problems, and in turn emotional disturbances later on lead to physical symptoms, like pain that will, in turn, further worsen emotional conditions.

Our Model of Happiness Consists of Two Equations

$$\text{Happiness}_{it} = \alpha_t * \text{Emotional health}_{it} + \beta_t * \text{Physical health}_{it} + \gamma_t \\ * \text{Relationship health}_{it} + \delta_t * \text{Economic health}_{it} + \varepsilon_{it}, \quad (1)$$

where Happiness$_{it}$ is the value of happiness of person i in period t; and Emotional health$_{it}$, Physical health$_{it}$, Relationship health$_{it}$, and Economic health$_{it}$ are the values of the respective health index variables for person i in period t. We estimated Equation (1) for each of the five periods separately, using the entire data set of all survey responses at each period t. We did not make any restrictive assumptions about the levels of the coefficients and allowed the coefficients to change over time.

The second equation expresses changes in happiness as a function of change in any or all of the health indices between period t and period t-j:

$$\Delta\text{Happiness}_{it,t-j} = \acute{\alpha}_{t,t-j} * \Delta\text{Emotional health}_{it,t-j} + \acute{\eta}_{it,t-j}$$
$$* \Delta\text{Physical health}_{it,t-j} + \acute{\iota}_{it,t-j} * \Delta\text{Relationship health}_{it,t-j}$$
$$+ \acute{\upsilon}_{it,t-j} * \Delta\text{Economic health}_{it,t-j} + \varepsilon_{it,t-j},$$

$$(2)$$

where $\Delta\text{Happiness}_{it,t-j}$ is the change in happiness level of person i between period t and t-j; and $\Delta\text{Emotional health}_{it,t-j}$, $\Delta\text{Physical health}_{it,t-j}$, $\Delta\text{Relationship health}_{it,t-j}$, and $\Delta\text{Economic health}_{it,t-j}$ are the changes in the levels of the respective health variables for person i between period t and t-j. We estimate Equation (2) from the subset of the full database and include only the answers of those who provided a complete set of answers both in period t and in period t-j. We also allowed the change in coefficients between different pairs of periods.

We estimated the two equations from two databases, where the second database is a subset of the first. We treated happiness as a latent continuous variable; however, we can observe only a discrete choice, the participants' selection of happiness out of four possible answers (coded as one to four, the higher number meaning more favorable conditions always), so we used the ordered Probit model to estimate Equations (1) and (2). For more on similar model setup, see Di Tella and MacCulloch (2008).

Survey Participants and Timing

We surveyed people who at some point took graduate-level finance or economics courses from the authors. The large majority of these former students were in the past part-time master's of business administration (MBA) or other business-related graduate-degree students. By the time of the survey most of them had completed their degree and thus they were working professionals. These participants were selected because we wanted to ensure high-quality data and we wanted to conduct a longitudinal study by asking the same people the same questions over time, and we felt it was more likely that our former students would submit to multiple surveys. The surveys did not include any of our current students, even though some were still at school.

Over the two years, starting from 247 e-mail invitations, and adding an average of 75 new e-mails every six months as students graduated from our classes, overall we had 471 valid e-mail addresses. We sent all potential participants an invitation via e-mail asking for their voluntary participation in this survey. Willing respondents were directed to an online survey web site where they filled out the questionnaires anonymously, although there was an option to provide their name. As a result, the survey participants never filled out the questionnaires in each other's presence so they could not influence each other in any foreseeable or likely way. We collected data over four different time periods: The first survey was sent on October 14, 2008, followed by surveys sent on May 9, 2009, October 18, 2009, and May 14, 2010. Therefore, we collected information about five time periods:

- Spring 2008: Pre–financial crisis
- Fall 2008: September 14 to November 10, 2008
- Spring 2009: April 9 to June 9, 2009
- Fall 2009: September 18 to November 16, 2009
- Spring 2010: April 14 to June 6, 2010

Spring 2008 information was collected retrospectively, together with information about fall 2008, to establish a benchmark. In our first survey we asked the participants when they thought the financial crisis began and asked them to answer the questions to the best of their recollection of certain experiences at that time. The participants' answers that defined the beginning of the crisis varied between the summer of 2007 and the fall of 2008, with both the mean and the median time April 2008. Therefore, in the following we refer to precrisis as spring 2008. It is customary to ask questions retrospectively (Snyder and Park 2002; Kessler 2006; Kaiser 2007). We use our retrospective data with caution, remembering that respondents may underreport spring 2008 happiness (Miron-Shatz, Stone, and Kahneman 2009). The survey questions for all other periods, other than spring 2008, asked about the participants' experience in the most recent month. The demographic characteristics of respondents are shown in Table 1.2.

The typical survey participant is a 34-year-old male. More than half of the participants live in the United States, European Union, and Canada combined; the rest reside mainly in the Far East: China, India, Hong Kong, Indonesia, Malaysia, Singapore, Taiwan, plus a few other (mainly Middle Eastern) countries.

Table 1.3 shows that the survey participants are highly educated, with most (80 percent) having completed a master's or doctoral degree. Family sizes are small, as an average of only 1.4 dependents live in the same household with the survey participants. Among the respondents, 34 percent

TABLE 1.2 Geographic Location, Gender, and Age Distribution

Country of Residence	Percentage
The United States	48.49
Non–United States	51.51
Country of residence in the West (the United States, Canada, European Union) or in the East (China, India, Hong Kong, Singapore, Taiwan, Indonesia, Malaysia) or Other (mainly Middle Eastern countries)	
East	29.10
West	58.19
Other	12.71
Gender	
Female	22.82
Male	77.18
Age group	
20–29	35.45
30–39	45.48
40–49	13.04
50–60	6.02

TABLE 1.3 Education, Family Size, Mortgage Obligation, Business Ownership, and Perceived Relative Financial Position

Highest Degree Earned	Percentage
Bachelor's degree	19.73
Master of science in finance	25.75
Other business master's degree	41.47
Other master's degree	10.37
Doctoral degree	2.68
Number of dependent family members	
0	31.10
1	26.76
2	20.07
3	14.38
More than 3	7.69
Participant has a mortgage	
Yes	34.11
No	65.89
Family owns a business	
Yes	28.52
No	71.48

currently pay a mortgage, and the families of 28 percent of the participants own a business.

RESULTS

The survey shows a highly significant shock in the happiness distribution between precrisis spring 2008 and the most intensive time of the crisis, fall 2008, as shown in Figure 1.1. Happiness greatly deteriorated from spring 2008 to fall 2008 for our survey participants. Fall 2008 saw the dramatic rise of those who were very unhappy, and the disappearance of those who were very happy. As we mentioned, this is probably an underestimation of the negative impact, due to asking the questions retrospectively. On a medium term, from spring 2008 to spring 2010, the percentage of those who reported the lowest degree of happiness increased 37 times. The overall distribution of happiness, however, seems to have largely recovered its precrisis form by fall 2009. This is the first major finding from our data.

Next, we considered the behavior of the four health domain indices over time. First, their average values clearly changed over time (see Figure 1.2). Though we used sum values of the survey questions to form indices, average values are used in this figure for a better illustration. The highest value (four) represents the best condition in each variable that contributes

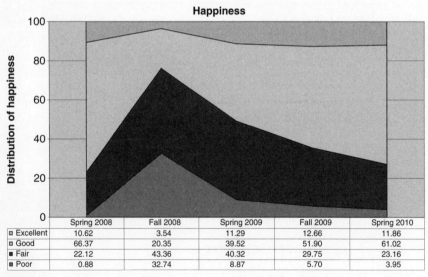

	Spring 2008	Fall 2008	Spring 2009	Fall 2009	Spring 2010
Excellent	10.62	3.54	11.29	12.66	11.86
Good	66.37	20.35	39.52	51.90	61.02
Fair	22.12	43.36	40.32	29.75	23.16
Poor	0.88	32.74	8.87	5.70	3.95

FIGURE 1.1   Change in the Distribution of Happiness Level Over Time

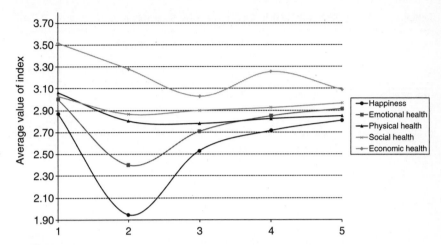

FIGURE 1.2 Average Happiness and Average Level of Health Indices
Note: Higher values denote better conditions. Maximum value is four, and minimum value is one.

to the index, and one represents the worst possible case. For example, if the emotional health index of person *i* at period *t* is one, this person frequently experienced each of the six emotions (excessive anger, worry, lost in deep thought, grief, fear, and feeling shocked) during the last month prior to the *t*th survey. An emotional health index of four would mean that this person never experienced any of these six emotions during the same month.

Figure 1.2 shows the immediate negative impact of the initial shock of September 2008 on all four health domain indices as well as on happiness. Afterward this negative impact began to diminish on some but not all health domains, although none of the average health domain values returned to their precrisis levels (spring 2008), even after two years (spring 2010). The economic health index had a temporary boost in fall 2009, which may be related to the sample characteristics: Those graduating in the summer get a job in the fall. It is important to note that physical health declined for an entire year and never recovered.

Therefore, the answer to our first and second questions is a resounding yes: The 2008 financial crisis has had an obvious immediate and medium-term impact on people's happiness as well as on their comprehensive health—including emotional, physical, social relationship, and economic health.

Estimates of Happiness Equations

In order to answer the third question, the relationship between health and happiness during and after the crisis, we used our microlevel happiness

TABLE 1.4 Happiness and Health, Ordered Probit Regression

Independent Variable	Dependent Variable: Happiness				
	Period 1	Period 2	Period 3	Period 4	Period 5
	Spring 2008	Fall 2008	Spring 2009	Fall 2009	Spring 2010
Emotional health	0.070	0.085***	0.072**	0.099***	0.105***
	(0.044)	(0.033)	(0.034)	(0.032)	(0.032)
Physical health	0.227***	0.130***	0.144**	0.001	0.159***
	(0.066)	(0.049)	(0.055)	(0.042)	(0.048)
Social health	0.078	−0.051	0.374***	0.377***	0.262***
	(0.080)	(0.064)	(0.073)	(0.067)	(0.057)
Economic health	−0.133	0.123*	−0.086	0.142**	−0.046
	(0.099)	(0.070)	(0.061)	(0.063)	(0.054)
Pseudo-R2	0.1574	0.1169	0.2694	0.2408	0.2340
Number of observations	112	112	124	158	177

Statistics in the cell: regression coefficient (standard error)
Boldface: ***Significant at 1 percent level, **Significant at 5 percent level, *Significant at 10 percent level

equation, and estimated the latent variable coefficients with ordered Probit regression analysis. First, we estimated the happiness equations in the extended form of Equation (1). Table 1.4 summarizes the results. The signs are all as expected (positive when statistically significant), and every health domain variable enters the equation significantly at some time period. Emotional and physical health are important determinants of happiness in four out of five periods. Social health is significant in three out of five, and economic health emerges in two periods as an explanation of the level of happiness. Therefore, we can conclude that health domains do influence happiness, so Equation (1) does in fact provide a useful framework with which to analyze the determinants of happiness in times of crisis.

Table 1.4 further reveals that, as the financial crisis was unfolding, different health domains became important over time, influencing happiness. Physical health, which was the most important determinant of happiness precrisis, remained almost consistently important. Emotional health became important after September 2008, and remained critical throughout. Social health became important during spring 2009, and remained important afterward. Economic health is cyclical, which may be due to the placement of new graduates in the fall.

We estimated Equation (2), the change in happiness over time, with an ordered Probit model using only the data from those participants who filled out multiple rounds of surveys to estimate the regression coefficients for the appropriate period-to-period changes. Table 1.5 reveals that happiness changed due to shifting factors as the crisis unfolded. These internal dynamics seem to be nonlinear, since the financial crisis had a differentiated impact on each health domain, and each health domain affected the change in the happiness level at a different time. For each period, there was only one, and usually a different, health domain responsible for the changes in happiness level. The major decline in happiness from spring 2008 to fall 2008 was due to the instantaneous damage of the crisis to emotional

TABLE 1.5 Change in Happiness Due to Change in Health, Ordered Probit Regression

Independent Variable	Dependent Variable: Change in Happiness				
	Period (1–2)	Period (2–3)	Period (3–4)	Period (4–5)	Period (1–5)
	Spring 2008 to Fall 2008	Fall 2008 to Spring 2009	Spring 2009 to Fall 2009	Fall 2009 to Spring 2010	Spring 2008 to Spring 2010
Change in emotional health	**0.111***** **(0.036)**	0.021 (0.042)	0.064 (0.040)	0.038 (0.050)	0.035 (0.062)
Change in physical health	0.087 (0.065)	**0.138*** **(0.074)**	0.060 (0.059)	0.009 (0.057)	**0.172∗∗** **(0.079)**
Change in social health	−0.036 (0.078)	0.029 (0.076)	**0.169**** **(0.085)**	**0.454***** **(0.098)**	0.113 (0.130)
Change in economic health	0.130 (0.092)	−0.049 (0.114)	−0.120 (0.088)	−0.102 (0.088)	0.100 (0.148)
Pseudo-R2	0.0838	0.0522	0.0916	0.1549	0.1368
Number of observations	112	52	65	83	37

Statistics in the cell: regression coefficient (standard error)
Boldface: ***Significant at 1 percent level, **Significant at 5 percent level, *Significant at 10 percent level
Note: Columns 2 through 5 of Table 1.4 refer to the change between two particular time periods, as expressed by Equation 2, as t = {2, 3, 4, 5} and j = 1. Column 6 refers to Equation 2, as t = 5, j = 4.

health. From fall 2008 to spring 2009, the main reason for the change in happiness level was the change in physical health, while some health domains improved and some further declined. From spring 2009 to fall 2009, as well as from fall 2009 to spring 2010, social relationship health played the key role in explaining the change (or, rather, the lack of further decline) in happiness.

Taking a medium-term view, when we compare the beginning of our observation period with the end, over the course of two years, we find that physical health deterioration is the key and the only variable responsible for the loss of happiness over the entire observation period (see Table 1.5, column "Period (1–5)").

Since not every participant filled out every survey, we tested whether those who responded to consecutive surveys represent well all of the contemporaneous survey respondents. We found that between consecutive periods, repeat respondents gave similar answers to their nonrepeat peers (at 5 percent significance level). There was only one exception: The frequency of doctor visits in spring 2009 and fall 2009 was different for the two groups. Therefore, the results based on the repeat respondents, presented in Table 1.5, can be generalized to nonrepeat survey participants. The conclusions from the estimation of Equation (2) are valid for the entire cohort (more than 100 people each period) and not only the subgroup of repeat respondents.

Now we are in a position to answer the third question of our study, whether there is a link between health and happiness during crises. The answer is a resounding yes. All health domains were critical for happiness at some point in time for our survey participants. As the crisis unfolded, there was a special dynamic between health domains and the immediate deterioration and partial recovery of happiness. Emotional problems were the first responses to crisis; later, the buffer effect of good social relationships played a bigger role. Physical health deterioration was gradual, but it had a significant medium-term effect on loss of happiness.

Variations of Our Model

We tested the robustness of our model by three different methodologies: Creating a sociodemographic benchmark model of happiness; adding all four health domain indexes to the sociodemographic model; and alternatively, without sociodemographic data, just adding only one health domain index at a time to explain happiness and change in happiness. The results establish that our model of Equations (1) and (2) is fairly robust.

It is customary to relate happiness to sociodemographic characteristics. Thus, we also estimated a series of models, using sociodemographic variables as exogenous and happiness as an endogenous variable. Our socioeconomic model fit, measured by pseudo-R2, is comparable to other, similar models in the literature (Diener et al. 1999; DeNeve and Cooper 1998). Therefore, we found the quality and consistency of our data reassured.

We also tested the combination model; that is, we added our four health domain indices as exogenous variables in addition to the sociodemographic variables, and maintained happiness as an endogenous variable. The pseudo-R2 increased three to six times. This clearly indicated that including our health domain indices can significantly improve the predictive power of the happiness equation.

Further, we evaluated the relationship among the four health domains and their impacts on happiness. Thus, we ran the Probit models of Equations (1) and (2) with all possible combinations of the four health domain indices as exogenous variables, adding one index at a time—the total combination of 440 reduced models. The results show that adding a new health domain won't affect the significance level of the already-included health domain(s) for 88 percent (Equation (1)) and 84 percent (Equation (2)) of the time. Since this impact is limited, it's reasonable to consider the four health domains to be independent.

As the four health domain indices' impact on happiness varied across the time periods, as shown in Tables 1.4 and 1.5, and they are largely independent, we concluded that the most representative generalized model of happiness across all time periods is the full model, with all four health domains included, as we proposed in Equation (1).

FINANCIAL CRISIS AS A MAJOR INTERNATIONAL TRAUMATIC EVENT

Our study clearly shows that financial crisis is detrimental to happiness in the short and medium term. In fact, 75 percent of our repeat respondents experienced loss of happiness during the fall of 2008 relative to the precrisis time of spring 2008. The average level of happiness declined by 32.1 percent among all survey participants from spring 2008 to fall 2008 (see Figure 1.2). How significant are these values?

How Much Happiness Was Lost in the Financial Crisis?

Graham (2009) documented that in a one-year period, during the economic crises in Russia (1998) and Argentina (2002), average happiness declined by 8.7 percent and 10.7 percent, respectively. The comparable annual value

TABLE 1.6 Comparison of Loss of Happiness of Hurricane Katrina Survivors with the Impact of the Global Financial Crisis

Post-Katrina Surveys[*]				Our survey	
[1] Percent as satisfied with overall quality of life as before Katrina	57%	[2] The same level of current life satisfaction as in the year before the hurricane	48%	Percent as happy in spring 2009 as in spring 2008	52%
[1] Percent less satisfied now than before Katrina with overall quality of life	39%	[2] Decreased level of current life satisfaction relative to the year before the hurricane	43%	Percent less happy in spring 2009 than spring 2008	37%

[*]Questions of pre-Katrina status asked retrospectively
[1]One year after Hurricane Katrina (Kaiser 2007)
[2]Five to eight months after Hurricane Katrina (Kessler 2006)

from our survey shows the decline of happiness between spring 2008 and spring 2009 is 11.8 percent, close to the happiness losses due to the Russian and Argentinean economic crises. In our survey, between spring 2008 and fall 2008, the semiannual happiness drop was actually 32.1 percent; that is almost three times the annual value of 11.8 percent. In fact, according to Gallup, December 11, 2008, was the unhappiest day of the year in the United States (Askitas and Zimmermann 2011). Therefore, it is very likely that our data actually understates the loss of happiness due to crisis, since we did not conduct quarterly surveys—which reminds us of the significance of higher-frequency data collection.

Second, in Table 1.6, we compare the lost happiness due to the 2008 financial crisis with that of direct survivors of Hurricane Katrina, one of the worst natural disasters of the United States.

How Much Did Health Deteriorate?

We found that, during the fall of 2008, worry, feeling shocked, and being afraid dominated the emotional structure of our respondents. These emotions can be linked to conditions of facing immediate and concrete existential threat, overwhelming danger, harm, and loss (Roseman 2001). A possible way to appreciate the magnitude of the immediate impact of the

TABLE 1.7 Comparison of the Immediate Emotional Health Impact of the 9/11 Terrorist Attack on Population not Living in the Vicinity of the Attack, within Half a Year, with the Emotional Health State of Fall 2008 of Our Survey Participants

9/11 Surveys[*]		Our Survey Results of Fall 2008	
Frequently[**] irritable	9%	Frequently[**] get angry	11%
Frequently or on average worried	30%	Frequently or on average worried	76%
Frequently or on average depressed	71%	Frequently or on average lost in deep thought	64%
Frequently or on average sad, sorry, apologetic	n/a	Frequently or on average grief-stricken	27%
Frequently or on average astonished, nervous, jittery	n/a	Frequently or on average feel shocked	55%
Frequently or on average have fear	44%	Frequently or on average have fear	55%
Poor or fair quality of sleep	33%	Poor or fair sleeping quality	61%
Trouble concentrating	49%	Poor or fair concentration	50%

[*]Snyder and Park (2002)

[**]"On average and frequently" means that on a scale of one to four, respondents selected three to four (bad and worst) conditions to describe their experience.

financial crisis on emotional health in September 2008 is to compare it with the emotional health status of the general U.S. public's response to the 9/11 terrorist attack, through Table 1.7.

In the two very different events, the 9/11 terrorist attack and the financial crisis as it was experienced in September 2008, the percentages of people who often or very often felt angry/irritated, depressed, or fearful are comparable. Both surveys document a similar increase in problems with concentration. Even more striking, about twice as many people were worried and had problems with sleeping due to the financial crisis than after the terrorist attack.

Physical health was also affected by the crisis. Table 1.8 compares Hurricane Katrina survivors and our survey participants' self-reported physical health status.

In summary, we can conclude that the current financial crisis can be called a major international traumatic event, since its impact on human health and happiness is comparable to the impact of the terrorist attack of 9/11 and one of the worst natural disasters of recent U.S. history, Hurricane Katrina. Financial crisis, therefore, should attract similar attention and efforts from societies that they make to avoid other large-scale traumas, like terrorist attacks and direct exposure of its citizens to major natural disasters.

TABLE 1.8 Comparison of Deterioration of Self-Reported Physical Health of Hurricane Katrina Survivors with the Impact of the Global Financial Crisis

Post-Katrina Surveys[*]				Our survey	
[1] Percent reported decline in physical health since Katrina	19%	[2] Percent reported that physical health deteriorated since Katrina	30%	Percent reported worse physical health in spring 2009 than in fall 2008	35%

[*]Questions of pre-Katrina status asked retrospectively
[1]One year after Hurricane Katrina (Kaiser 2007)
[2]Five to eight months after Hurricane Katrina (Kessler 2006)

CAN WE JUST WAIT FOR THE NEXT FINANCIAL CRISIS?

By collecting longitudinal survey results of MBA students and current working professionals who are our former graduate students in finance, we set out to determine whether the financial crisis has had a measurable effect on broadly defined health and happiness. We presented empirical evidence and theoretical foundations to support a very significant loss of happiness that is due to the financial crisis in a highly educated international group. Happiness is lost because of emotional and physical health deterioration resulting from the crisis. The short-term happiness and physical health losses are similar in magnitude to Hurricane Katrina survivors' experiences, and the emotional health impact of the financial crisis is comparable to the effect of the terrorist attack of 9/11 in the United States. Therefore, we should treat the financial crisis as a major international traumatic event.

A key finding of the study is the documentation of a propagation mechanism: Namely, the effect of the financial crisis on people's broadly defined health changes over time. A decline in emotional health is instantaneous when the crisis breaks out, resulting in an immediate loss of happiness. When the negative impact of the original shock of a financial crisis on emotional health begins to fade, the crisis has already damaged physical health. At this stage, a vicious cycle of deteriorating physical health and deteriorating happiness might begin.

The question of the most effective government intervention arises: Should government focus on crisis management or crisis prevention? The difference is that if a government waits until the crisis breaks out, and attempts to manage the crisis once it has already happened, emotional health and happiness are already lost. Could a defensive strategy that aims to prevent mass losses of happiness become a new approach to financial market regulation? This is an important question, especially in light of the standards and expectations Aristotle raised. One of the key messages from the current research is that physical health and emotional health are critical to happiness, even more in times of crisis. To what extent do the current social and business environment and culture in general promote people's emotional, physical, social relationship, and economic health? These questions deserve to be seriously studied.

The next chapter develops a model and estimation of macroeconomic factors, including the outbreak of the 2008 Great Recession, on suicide rate for 27 Organization for Economic Cooperation and Development (OECD) countries as well as Latvia, Lithuania, and Slovenia. The rest of the book provides practical recommendations that can serve as guidelines to prevent stock market crises. Although the following chapters address stock markets, the recommendations have the potential to be utilized in any financial market. The measures we propose for quantifiable, adjustable, real-time oversight and regulatory variables are practical and can be implemented by any securities regulating agency. The goal of the recommendations is to improve the fairness and transparency of the financial markets, thereby perfecting the market equilibrium, protecting investors, and stabilizing the market. The ultimate goal is to prevent crises so that people's happiness and health can be protected and improved.

NOTES

1. This chapter was presented at the Western Economic Association International 86th Annual Conference, June 29–July 3, 2011, San Diego, California.
2. "Pyramid schemes . . . promise consumers or investors large profits based primarily on recruiting others to join their program, not based on profits from any real investment or real sale of goods to the public" (Valentine 1998).

CHAPTER 2

Profound Unhappiness in the International Recession

The Case of Suicide in Industrialized Countries

M. Harvey Brenner

A mong economists, a "new" literature has been developing emphasizing the role of human happiness in connection with economic well-being. Since the days of Adam Smith, John Stuart Mill, and the utilitarians, writing in the Scottish and French enlightenments, and their emphasis on science and technology as the basis for human welfare, economic growth has been viewed by economists as the foundation of material well-being and therefore of human happiness. As a consequence, the fundamental assumption of economic policy worldwide is to promote economic growth as the objective of human endeavors, thus theoretically leading to increased human happiness. In recent times, the assumption of implicit linkage between economic growth and human happiness has been questioned by some economists, psychologists, and sociologists.

A central problem in the empirical testing of whether economic growth increases happiness lies in the measurement of happiness itself. A second problem exists in the meaning of *happiness*. Does happiness imply a simple pleasure orientation (i.e., relative to *pain* in the utilitarian framework), as summarized in the philosophy of hedonism? Or does it really pertain to *well-being*? In the latter case, life satisfaction or *capacity*—derived from the Greek concept of *eudaemonia* and the *quality of life* literature—is ultimately to be preferred. This paper takes the position that since life satisfaction is notoriously difficult to measure, but is theoretically opposite to psychological depression, an appropriate negative measure of human happiness as well-being would be profound psychological unhappiness or mental depression. A traditional measure in the psychological and psychiatric literature of the presence in a society of such depression is the suicide rate. This chapter therefore utilizes the suicide rate among industrialized countries to examine the question of whether material economic improvement is an adequate inverse predictor of profound unhappiness in societies.

The suicide rate, like other sensitive mental health indicators, has been shown to inversely reflect business cycles from at least the mid-nineteenth century to relatively recent times (Brenner 1973; Brenner 1976; Brenner 1984; Andreeva, Ermakov, and Brenner 2008). A major test question before us relates to the largest recession since the 1930s, namely, the 2008 international recession and whether it has contributed to the suicide rate. In this test, we examine 27 Organization for Economic Cooperation and Development (OECD) countries, as well as the new Baltic States and Slovenia in terms of the influence of changes in productivity, labor force participation, and self-employment. It should be kept in mind that this empirical test is especially sensitive because suicide increases are known to respond almost immediately to gross domestic product (GDP) declines and unemployment increases, whereas mortality in general, and cardiovascular mortality in particular, tends to show its strongest recessional response two to three years after economic decline and lags for at least another decade (Brenner 1979; Brenner 2005).

In the present test, we must also take note that, apart from material and overall economic well-being, two other prominent theoretical views need to be considered in the case of suicide. The first is that there are traditions in certain societies of relatively extreme responses to shame, loss of honor, and stigma that are linked to especially high suicide rates. This is especially well known in countries such as Japan and Korea. Second, there is the sociological tradition attributable to Durkheim (2006), which looks upon suicide as largely due to *anomie,* or transformation of societal norms and institutions.

In developing a predictive model for suicide rates in industrialized countries we therefore concentrate on GDP per hour worked, employment, culturally influenced high suicide traditions (such as in Japan and Korea), and societies having undergone extensive economic transformation (in addition to the international recession), such as Estonia, Latvia, and Lithuania. In this problem, we focus not on total GDP per capita as it would affect the entire society, but rather on the productivity of the working population. Loss of employment among industrialized countries, in this study, is not confined to the unemployment rate but includes also persons who have left the labor force entirely as a result of inability to become reemployed; this population is measured as the *inactive population.* (Another technical expression for the inactive population would be the mathematical inverse of the labor force to population ratio.) Finally, we are as concerned about job growth, innovation, entrepreneurship, and investment in the future as we are with productivity and labor force participation. The primary indicator of these latter four phenomena is the rate of self-employment (as a proportion of the labor force). In our predictive model of suicide rates, we use these three economic indicators of material well-being, as well as dummy variables representing high cultural orientation to suicide (referring to Japan and Korea), and high economic transformation (referring to Estonia, Latvia, and Lithuania).

BACKGROUND

Policy makers worldwide uniformly look to economic growth as a primary national goal on the grounds that this is the basis of the standard of living. National GDP per capita, in turn, furnishes individual income, and thus becomes the basis of consumption and, theoretically, of pleasure in human life. This idea of pleasure, as reflected in economic thinking, originates with the utilitarian view of hedonistic sensuality (Bentham 1996); this utilitarianism speaks to the issue of ordinary usefulness and results in the short-term satisfaction of sensual pleasure. Such a view is originally attributed to the Epicureans of ancient Greece.

But does this view apply to deeper pleasures and sorrows as expressed, for example, by John Stuart Mill (1998), and does it take into account a future orientation with a view toward the longer-term consequences of human action? The eudaemonistic view of happiness typically expressed in Aristotle's writings would rather stress the achievement of success in the most important areas of life—including work, child rearing, and civic participation—and emphasizes autonomous self-directed behavior based on human reasoning. The question, then, is to what degree modern economic policy considerations focus largely on the issue of consumption and sensual pleasures as compared to production and the achievement of the central goals in life that are supported by culture.

A second problem lies in the contemporary measurement of happiness, which usually is taken as a response to a single question. The difficulty here is that such measures do not consider the depth of human emotion, but rather focus on a standard impression of people's short-term contentment with immediately preceding events. What is missing is the sense of deeper emotion that deals with behavior that is recognizable in general human experience and results from either deep appreciation of the joys of life or despondency over its disappointments. The research literature has had little involvement with the notion of relatively high levels of human joy, but, on the other hand, has devoted centuries of thought and scientific measurement, as well as clinical observation and treatment, to the issue of mental depression. The issue before us is whether standard forms of economic policy are related to the deeper concerns of human emotion that are well understood in the psychological and psychiatric literature, and whether they can predict such emotions.

The central empirical question we wish to explore is whether many of the ordinary elements of economic policy can provide us measures of evaluative success, if we rely on well-known but richly described and measured concepts such as depression. But which elements of economic policy are most pertinent to experiences of contentment or profound disappointment such as depression?

If we take the standard utilitarian approach, it will simply be relatively short-term hedonistic pleasures and we can apply the concepts of Benthamite utilitarianism and focus on the issue of consumption, which is largely a function of personal income. If, on the other hand, we focus on the more profound Aristotelian view of human performance, functioning, achievement, and rational self-direction, our focus will be on production rather than consumption. We will be interested in people's capacity to produce, that is, their productivity, to be employed, and to form new enterprises that will be the engines of growth of the economy, and thus provide both new employment and new industrial development.

TWO CONCEPTS OF HAPPINESS

In economic thinking, the concept of happiness has its origins in utilitarian theory, starting with Bentham, who expressed happiness in terms of the net sum of pleasures over pains in what he referred to as a *felicific calculus*. Thus, Bentham follows in the ethical tradition of classical Greek hedonism in which pleasure is taken as the greatest good that should be striven for and is, in fact, actually the goal of life. John Stuart Mill, also elaborating on the tradition of utilitarianism, however, distinguishes sharply between the quality of different pleasures (high versus low) and argues that it is basically the higher pleasures, involving reason and esthetics, that are the pleasures which should constitute the meaning of human happiness. Mill also makes clear, moreover, that in his conception it is not possible to measure pleasure itself or the net of pleasures minus pains.

Adam Smith, one of the fathers of modern economics, in his *A Theory of Moral Sentiments* (2009), regards happiness as those pleasant sentiments that conform to behavior, which is consistent with universal morality and the basic feelings of identity and sympathy that people have for one another. The special emphasis, consistent with Hutcheson (2002) and the Stoics, is to disallow harm to persons and to promote the common good of people in general along the lines of utilitarianism. Adam Smith strongly holds these philosophical positions, despite not being identified as a member of the utilitarian movement, and despite his argument in *An Inquiry into the Nature and Causes of the Wealth of Nations* (2008) that it is the greed of individuals that paradoxically—via the invisible hand—promotes economic well-being for the general population.

The Benthamite utilitarian perspective, which bases happiness on various degrees of pleasure and displeasure, is very distinctive from the eudaemonistic concept of happiness associated with Aristotle, which is more clearly understood in English as success—or achieving things worth doing. This includes achievement of the most important goals in life, including work, rearing of children, and processes such as the acquisition of knowledge and maintenance of friendship and, for other Aristotelians, the exercise of human reason. Interestingly, the exercise of reason is also absolutely intrinsic to the discipline of economics, which, at least in the micro discipline, is based on the concept of rational man.

Continuing in the eudaemonistic tradition, in the modern period, Martha Nussbaum and Amartya Sen refer to happiness as the basic component of quality of life. In this conception, capabilities of persons concerns their being and doing. Capabilities therefore involve being nourished, healthy, educated, and functioning at a level where persons can exercise genuine choice over the type of life they wish to live. This point of view conflicts not only with the Benthamite emphasis on pleasures and pains but also with the classical emphasis in economics on happiness as entailing the expression of choice of some consumer goods and services over others. The Nussbaum-Sen approach emphasizes equality and dignity in the self-determination of the content of individual functioning; this entails the choice of how and what to perform as against the type and extent of consumption. It should be pointed out, of course, that the classical Benthamite—and largely hedonistic—view that consumption provides the final pleasures, and work, or performance, is a means to the end of consumption is firmly denied in the framework of Aristotle, and of Nussbaum and Sen.

The distinction between happiness, as expressing pleasure, on the one hand, and happiness as expressing the ability and actuality of functioning must be further distinguished by the orientation, in both of these types of happiness toward the future as distinct from the present. In the Aristotelian view, which is the more common among modern philosophers, happiness is much more likely to be viewed from the standpoint of the long term, while pleasure is seen to be rather more short-term and identified with specific events and sensations. In the eudaemonistic view as stated in Aristotle's *Nicomachean Ethics* (Aristotle 2011) we find the statement "Call no man happy until he is dead." (Of course, it is understood that no person can be said to be happy after he is dead.) This phrase is obviously intended to emphasize the very long-term concept of the notion of happiness as describing a life well lived.

But from this long-term perspective, how shall we gauge the functional happiness of an individual in midlife? The solution must involve the current status of the individual's capability (or capacity) of functioning as well as his or her actual functioning, but, in addition, it must also include the probable future of the person's functioning. What is involved here is the attitude of the subject toward the future—namely, the degree of optimism or pessimism in visualizing the accomplishment of the most important goals in life. This, of course, involves a forecast of various scenarios of the future.

Is this future orientation, with intrinsic linkage to the present reality, an alien notion to traditional economic thinking? That future orientation is highly consistent with economic thinking is spelled out in the basic concept of economic man or rational man. Rationality requires the vision of a goal and the means to achieve that goal. Rational action requires that multiple projections of future end states be imagined as well as the various methods by which these end states can be achieved. Rational thinking, then, involves a choice of future-oriented ends and means. Thus, it can be said that the individual rational person lives mentally, to a large extent, in the future. This kind of thinking is quite familiar to economists where the tradition of expectations is dominant in commonsense theory. It is impossible to envision choice without taking into account what that choice is to bring. Thus, consumer confidence, wage, and inflation expectations and theories of investment are all consequent upon visions of the future. The powerful new formulations, indeed, of rational expectation theory are an expression of the idea that government policies can be nullified by consumers and investors who anticipate the consequences of those policies and thwart them.

The concept of potential in economics and philosophy also expresses the combination of current being and likely future existence in the same thought. Thus, we have such concepts as potential output of the economy (or potential gross national product), potential entrant of a new firm (in the theory of markets), and human capital (with its potential for productive activity). We conclude that the combination of actual and potential circumstances is a standard element of economic thinking from the standpoint of consumers, investors, producers, and policy makers. Indeed, rationality from both the commonsense and economic standpoints is not possible in the absence of a joint concept combining present and future states of mind.

The concept of potential is essential to Nussbaum and Sen's understanding of happiness (in the eudaemonistic sense), in which case capability, or capacity, is understood to be a crucial factor in quality of life. In the philosophical sense, in which Nussbaum and Sen write, potentiality is a latent ability, disposition, propensity, or power to achieve a certain outcome—or any broad class of outcomes. Thus, health, resources, and freedom, for example, are necessary to the potential for achievement or capability. But potentiality is, of course, not achievement itself—simply the likelihood of achievement given certain attributes of the person. It therefore requires a combination of potentiality and specific situations that make goal achievement a reality.

The objective approach to welfare or well-being identifies a set of resources, which are attributes or possessions of the individual. These resources are understood as having the potential, when optimally used, to effect desirable outcomes, specifically the achievement of life goals. However, the achievement of those goals depends not only on the capabilities or capacities that are inherent or developed attributes of the person, but on the ultimate ability of the person to take advantage of those capabilities such as to produce the desired achievements. This will clearly depend on many other factors in the environment—especially the economic environment of markets and government decisions. In other words, the potentials inherent in capability and capacity must ultimately be linked to the realistic probability of actual achievement.

A PSYCHOLOGICAL VIEWPOINT

Theoretical papers in psychology have recently tended to be far more supportive of the well-being, as compared to the pleasure/emotive, concept of happiness. Diener and Seligman formulate well-being so as to include pleasure, engagement, and meaning, with the idea that life satisfaction may reflect all of these (Seligman 2002). Pleasantness in life is characterized by positive moods, emotions, and pleasures. Positive and negative emotions and moods provide ongoing feedback about whether things are going well or badly. Moods and emotions can change rapidly because they reflect current evaluations of events. Pleasant emotions signify that events and situations are desirable, and unpleasant emotions signify that they are undesirable (Ortony, Clore, and Collins 1988). Engagement involves absorption and focused attention on what one is doing (boredom is the opposite of engagement; indicates the absence of interest and disagreeableness). Meaning, on the other hand, refers to the sense of belonging and the desire for achievement on behalf of a group.

The concept of *need* in psychology refers to something, or some state of affairs, which, if present, would improve the well-being of an organism. In this sense, a need may be something basic and biological (food) or it may involve social and personal factors that derive from complex forms of learning (achievement, prestige). In general, psychologists will tend to use qualifying phrases to delineate their particular sense of the term *need*. Among the more common concepts of psychological concepts of need is the *need-drive-incentive model*. This is a model of motivation that assumes the basic physiological needs are produced by states of deprivation, that such needs produce drives that are the true instigators of action, and that the action is directed toward the incentive components of the goal state.

Possibly the best known of the psychological needs is that of the *need for achievement,* as characterized by McClelland, Atkinson, Clark, and Lowell (1976), indicating the desire to compete with a standard of excellence. The *need for affiliation,* on the other hand, is Henry Murray's (2004) term for the need to be with other people, to socialize, form friendships, cooperate, and so on. The need for affiliation overlaps with that of the *need for intimacy,* which involves the need for close, warm, and intimate relationships. Finally, the *need for cognition* is a personality variable that reflects the extent to which an individual enjoys effortful cognitive activities, craves information, and likes to analyze complex situations. Perhaps most familiar to nonpsychologists—especially to management specialists and behavioral economists—is the hierarchy of needs as described by Maslow (1970). According to Maslow's theory, all human motives can be viewed as components of a hierarchical needs system. The seven main divisions in Maslow's system are: (1) physiological needs: food, water, and so on; (2) safety needs: freedom from threat, security, and so on; (3) belongingness and love needs: affiliation, acceptance, and so on; (4) esteem needs: achievement, prestige, status, and so on; (5) cognitive needs: knowledge, understanding, curiosity, and so on; (6) esthetic needs: order, beauty, structure, art, and so on; (7) need for self-actualization: self-fulfillment, realization of potential. Maslow conceptualized the hierarchy as invariant and argued that the lower the need, the more dominant it will become if unfulfilled. This hierarchical view of motivation is disputed, however.

The psychological literature generally treats the issue of needs as the crucial component of the general subject of motivation. Psychologists have tended to treat the issue of well-being in terms of work commitment and commitment to other persons (Diener and Seligman 2002, 2004), needs satisfaction (McClelland, H. Murray), and self-realization (Maslow). The common thread among these conceptions of happiness as well-being is the notion of achievement of the most important things in life including work, family, friendships, and choices of socioeconomic career.

UNHAPPINESS, HOPELESSNESS, AND DEPRESSION

Up to now we have been discussing the meaning of *happiness* from the standpoint either of pleasure or of achievement and functioning. Measures of happiness based on interviews, in the psychological and, more recently, the economic literature, have tended to focus on happiness as a short-term emotion largely reflecting the Benthamite, utilitarian, pleasure/pain-based point of view. These measures of happiness are intended to describe the range of ordinary, largely positive, feelings in a population. This type of measurement has failed to deal, however, with the more profound aspects of either melancholy or euphoria. In this chapter we examine the question of whether the more profound negative emotion—depression—is also correlated with the economic situation of populations as the more general, pleasure-based aspects of happiness have tended to be.

We thus require concepts and measures of psychological depression. The topic of depression is classical in psychiatry and psychology. It is among the top five leading causes of disability and disease burden throughout the world. Across the lifespan, stressful life events that involve threat, loss, humiliation, or defeat influence the onset and course of depression. However, not all people who encounter a stressful life experience succumb to its depressive effect. Diathesis-stress theories of depression predict that individuals' sensitivity to stressful events depends on their genetic makeup. Behavioral genetics research supports this prediction, documenting that the risk of depression after a stressful event is elevated among people who are at high genetic risk and diminished among those of low genetic risk (Caspi, Sugden, Moffitt, Taylor, et al. 2003). This research points to the fact that, as is probably true with virtually all illnesses, both physiological and psychological, vulnerability to illnesses involves some genetic component. It is therefore appropriate, in this analysis, to concentrate on the environmental—that is, psychosocial—elements. This approach is not different from the one routinely taken in the analyses of happiness that one finds in the economic literature. In fact, traditional research findings in this area are that happiness, as measured by the usual interview question, as well as *life satisfaction,* shows a considerable degree of genetic influence (Johnson and Krueger 2006).

Among the more widespread theories of psychological depression is the formulation citing hopelessness as the major predictive psychosocial element identified with depression (Metalsky, et al. 1993; Abramson, et al. 1989). At the same time, hopelessness has been identified as the principal psychosocial predictor of suicide (Beck 1963; Beck, et al. 1976; Beck, et al. 1990; Petrie and Chamberlain 1983).

More particularly, depression has been found to be the most common clinical syndrome preceding suicidal behavior in studies of both attempters and completed suicides (Barraclough, et al. 1974; Silver, et al. 1971). Hopelessness has been proposed by Beck (1963, 1967) as the variable linking depression to suicidal behavior. A close relationship has been found between hopelessness (defined as negative expectations about the future) and suicidal intent in a variety of clinical samples (Emery, et al. 1981; Minkoff, et al. 1973; Weissman, et al. 1979; Wetzel, et al. 1980). The Suicidal Intent Scale (Beck, Schuyler, and Herman 1974) measures the strength of suicidal desire behind the patient's suicidal behavior. The correlation between suicidal intent and depression has been consistently accounted for by hopelessness. With hopelessness controlled for, the correlation between depression and suicidal intent drops to nonsignificant levels. Petrie and Chamberlain (1983) found that hopelessness and depression show the same relationship to reported suicidal behavior and ideation as they do to suicidal intent.

HYPOTHESIS: HAPPINESS AS ACCOMPLISHMENT PREDICTS HAPPINESS AS PLEASURE

Two specific hypotheses are tested in this chapter. The first is that *wellbeing*—or the objective component of happiness, specifying life achievements and self-determination—predicts the emotional or subjective component of happiness as exemplified by expressions of affect such as pleasure and satisfaction (especially life satisfaction). In this study, the objective measures of well being include three standard macroeconomic indicators: productivity, the labor force participation rate, and the rate of self-employment as a proportion of total employment. The measure of expressed emotion (in this case, profound negative emotion) is depression or hopelessness as indicated by the national suicide rate.

The second hypothesis is that the relationship between objective wellbeing and standard measures of happiness as an emotional measure is also found when rather extreme measures of negative effect, such as suicide, become the outcome variable. There is a long history of examining the impact of the business cycle on suicide. This literature has displayed remarkable consistency when examined over historical time in relation to changes in GDP and the unemployment rate. GDP upturns typically predict declines in the suicide rate, while any increase in the unemployment rate—regardless of whether unemployment is associated with recession—virtually always results in suicide rate increases. This has been observed, with time-series analysis, in the United States and several European countries, where, typically, during the same year as GDP declines or unemployment increases, an increase in the suicide rate is observed. Other analyses have shown that there is a second wave of increase of suicide two years following the onset of recession. In the present study, we take a cross-sectional perspective, examining the differential suicide rate among 27 industrialized countries that belong to the OECD in addition to two Baltic states (Lithuania and Latvia) and Slovenia. These are among the wealthiest and most highly developed countries. The prediction is that the suicide rate will be higher in countries where productivity rates are lower, labor force participation rates are lower, and self-employment as a proportion of the labor force is low.

The Macro-economic Predictors

The rate of productivity, as measured by the national GDP divided by hours worked, or GDP per hour, is our first measure of objective well-being. This variable connotes work achievement, as well as the human resources, or human capital, required for that level of (worker) achievement. Human capital involves the investment in workers' formal education and training as well as on-the-job experience and skill development. Of course, workers' productivity depends not only on their long- and short-term training, but also on the technological quality of the equipment they use and the quality and entrepreneurial ability of management. Thus, productivity involves the capability of workers based on the technological sophistication they use and is embedded in them (in addition to their health, management quality, etc.). To bring workers' capability, or their potential productivity, to the point of actual productivity involves demand for their product, which bears on capacity utilization. An important feature of productivity is that it contains the idea that a product (or service) has been produced—thus involving a level of achievement. At the same time, productivity also assumes a notion of continuous and therefore future achievement. Therefore, it is future oriented, but that future is based on a currently ongoing process.

The second predictor is labor force participation. This variable is used rather than unemployment, (at first blush) the more common and, possibly, more acute indication of employment loss, because we are concerned not only with the immediate loss of employment but also with the longer term inability to find work, resulting in the much more profound loss of working ability through a movement out of the labor force. As a result, in the labor force participation rate, we have both the employment status of the individual and the potential—in this case, negative—for return to the labor force in the short or medium term. The labor force participation rate also combines the notion of the capability or potential of individuals to perform work within the economy, which is modified greatly by demand factors that will be decisive in whether or not employment takes place.

The third economic predictor is the national rate of self-employment as a proportion of employment. In other words, it is an indicator of the extent to which employment consists of single proprietor and heavily entre-preneurial firms. From one point of view, such single-person firms can be seen to generate the highest volume of new jobs. Thus, they are indispens-able as sources of new growth and renewal of the economy after recessions, in regionally declining areas, and structural changes in which technology may well improve (thus initiating higher productivity) but producing job losses. A primary source of reemployment depends on the generation of new industries and new local agglomerations of diverse small firms in con-stellations of urban areas (O'Flaherty 2005). For our purposes, other important properties of self-employment include the emphasis on entrepre-neurship, which involves investment toward a vision of the future, as well as autonomy of the individual proprietor. Interestingly, self-employment in multiple firms also requires firm integration in the surrounding community with extensive social ties. These social ties may depend on the relations to consumers or on relations among the small firms themselves. Indeed, it is well known that the linkages among highly innovative small firms have been much the source of technological development in the late twentieth and early twenty-first centuries. Taken together, the concepts embedded in self-employment include economic growth, employment maximization, in-vestment, self-determination, capability, and achievement.

In the model used in this chapter, we also consider two well-developed theoretical positions that are traditional for the understanding of suicide rates. One position is that in identifiable traditional societies we tend to find extreme reactions to shame, damage to honor, and stigma for which it is appropriate to terminate one's own life through suicide. Most famous in Western literature is perhaps Japan, but Korea is also identified with this tendency. In addition, we have the well-known explanation of differential suicide rates among countries that has been expressed by Durkheim. In this formulation, anomie or loss of traditional social norms is theorized to de-stroy meaningfulness in values and social relations as a result of rapid social change. Such acute social changes are found particularly when societies undergo disruptions to their political and ideological systems and have been marked in the economic transformations of the European communist countries to market economies in the 1990s. In our sample, examples are Estonia, Latvia, and Lithuania.

ANALYSIS

For the year 2008, the principal year of the international recession, a prediction equation is developed in which the outcome variable is the age-adjusted suicide rate for 27 OECD countries, as well as two Baltic states (Lithuania and Latvia) and Slovenia. As indicated above, predictors are productivity, as measured by GDP per hour worked; male inactivity rate (or the proportion of males not participating in the labor force aged 15 to 64 years old); and male self-employed workers as a proportion of total male employment. Categorical (i.e., dummy) predictors represent Asian countries (Japan and Korea) as well as, separately, two Baltic states (Latvia and Lithuania).

As can be seen in Table 2.1 and Figure 2.1, all predictive models are statistically significant. According to the beta coefficients, which, because they are standardized, allow comparison of the effect size of the relationships, the predictors representing the male inactivity rate and male self-employment are the most powerful. In this model these employment-based

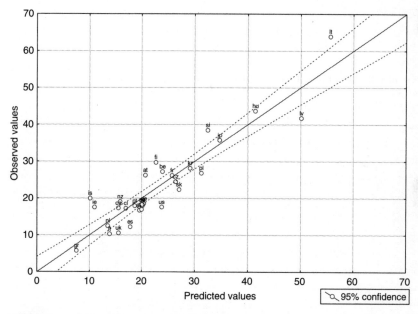

FIGURE 2.1 Regression Summaries for Male Age-Adjusted Suicide Mortality Rate (ASDR per 100,000), 27 OECD Countries (Without Chile, Luxembourg, Mexico, and Turkey) + 2 Baltic States (Lithuania and Latvia) + Slovenia. Year 2008 Only. Predicted versus Observed Values.

TABLE 2.1 Regression Summaries for Male Age-Adjusted Suicide Mortality Rate (ASDR per 100,000) 27 OECD Countries (Without Switzerland, Luxembourg, Mexico, and Turkey) + 2 Baltic States (Lithuania and Latvia) + Slovenia. Year 2008 Only.

$R = .92268673$ $R^2 = .85135081$ Adjusted $R^2 = .82038223$
$F(5,24) = 27.491$ $p < .00000$ Std. Error of estimate: 5.0622

N = 30	Beta	Std. Error of Beta	B	Std. Error of B	t(24)	p-level
Intercept			30.711	8.431	3.642	0.001
GDP per hour worked (US dollars, constant prices, constant Purchasing Power Parity (PPP) base year 1990)	−0.319	0.104	−0.479	0.157	−3.049	0.005
Male self-employed workers as a percentage of total male employment	−0.532	0.095	−0.987	0.177	−5.554	0.000
Male inactivity rate (percentage of male population aged 15 to 64 years old)	0.398	0.088	0.981	0.218	4.500	0.000
Dummy for Asian countries (Korea and Japan =1, other = 0)	0.298	0.080	14.062	3.781	3.719	0.001
Dummy for Baltic states (Lithuania and Latvia =1, other = 0)	0.359	0.093	16.917	4.417	3.829	0.000

Source of data: World Health Organization and International Labor Organization

variables are designated for males because, first, it is assumed that the primary influence of employment on the social status of the family is through male employment and, second, the research indicates that male actual suicide responds more sensitively to stress, whereas, attempted suicide for women shows a considerably sharper response rate to environmental sources. The three economic variables possess the correct sign: productivity is inverse to the suicide rate, employment inactivity is positively related to suicide, while self-employment is, again, inversely related to the suicide rate. The categorical variable for Japan and Korea is positively related to suicide, as is the variable for the transitional economies of Latvia and Lithuania. All in all, this model accounts for 82 percent (adjusted R squared) of the total variation in the suicide rates of males in the 27 highly industrialized countries.

Most important, this model deals only with the year 2008, the principal year of the international recession. It is therefore clear that this recession, at least in its early phase, acting through production and employment-based factors, has the most substantial influence on the suicide rate during 2008.

In order to further validate the robustness of the three main economic variables in accounting for variation in the suicide rate among industrialized countries, a second approach was taken. In this approach, a pooled cross-sectional design was used in order to observe whether the years including 2000 to 2008 would show similar relationships. Table 2.2 indicates that this is essentially true. All three production- and employment-related variables show strong statistical significance in relation to the total (i.e., combined male and female) suicide rate. In this analysis, again, Japan and Korea show a heightened sensitivity to increased suicide, independent of the effects of the economic variables. However, unlike the results of the first analysis, the transition economies did not show an elevated suicide rate during the entire period of 2000 to 2008. Rather, during 2000 to 2008 it is actually the German-speaking countries (Germany, Austria, and Switzerland) of the OECD that tended to show unusually high suicide rates, beyond what would be predicted by the principal economic variables.

CONCLUSIONS

The results, which can be seen graphically in cross-sectional multiple regression analyses, show that the three economic variables and two cultural factors account for more than 82 percent of the variance in male suicide rates. There is no significant decline in the importance of the economic variables during the early part of the international recession, as seen during the year 2008. This means that the strength of the economic variables remains

TABLE 2.2 Pooled Regression for Suicide Mortality Rate, Organization for Economic Co-operation and Development (OECD) + 2 European Union Countries, Years 2000 to 2008 Random-Effects Generalized Least Squares (GLS) Regression

Number of observations = 261
R-sq: within = 0.0572
  between = 0.6216
  overall = 0.5970
Random effects u_i ~ Gaussian
Wald chi2(6) = 47.55

Number of groups = 29
Observations per group: minimum = 9
  average = 9
  maximum = 9

corr(u_i, X) = 0 (assumed)

Prob > chi2 = 0.0000

Nonstandardized coefficients

Variable	Coef.	Std. Err.	z	P>z	[95% Conf. Interval]	
GDP per hour worked (constant 1990 US dollars at Purchasing Power Parity (PPP))	−0.172	0.055	−3.110	0.002	−0.281	−0.064
Labor force participation rate in male population aged15 to 64 years old	−0.279	0.091	−3.050	0.002	−0.458	−0.100
Total self-employed workers as percentage of total employment	−0.420	0.077	−5.430	0.000	−0.572	−0.269
Dummy (East Asia = 1, other = 0)	7.095	2.881	2.460	0.014	1.448	12.742
Dummy (countries with population under 1 million = 1, over = 0)	−1.502	4.066	−0.370	0.712	−9.472	6.468
Dummy (German-speaking countries = 1, other = 0)	4.979	2.427	2.050	0.040	0.221	9.737
Intercept	45.476	7.569	6.010	0.000	30.642	60.311

sigma_u 3.7971 sigma_e 1.2142 rho .9072 (fraction of variance due to u_i)

Elasticities after extracting regression

y = Linear prediction (predict) = 13.6032

Variable	Coef.	Std. Err.	z	P>z	[95% Conf. Interval]		X
GDP per hour worked (constant 1990 US dollars at Purchasing Power Parity (PPP)	−0.307	0.100	−3.060	0.002	−0.504	−0.111	24.257
Labor force participation rate in male population aged 15 to 64 years old	−1.627	0.540	−3.010	0.003	−2.685	−0.569	79.405
Total self-employed workers as percentage of total employment	−0.478	0.092	−5.220	0.000	−0.658	−0.299	15.483
Dummy (East Asia = 1, other = 0)	0.036	0.015	2.440	0.015	0.007	0.065	0.069
Dummy (countries with population under 1 million = 1, over = 0)	−0.004	0.010	−0.370	0.712	−0.024	0.016	0.034
Dummy (German-speaking countries = 1, other = 0)	0.038	0.019	2.040	0.041	0.001	0.074	0.103

similar to that of the period prior to the Great Recession; but productivity decline, employment decline, and self-employment have retained their strength in influencing the suicide rate.

This study confirms the fact that the economic situation of industrialized countries is the primary determinant of their suicide rates, and that the impact of economic decline on suicide can be observed during the year in which recession begins—even in the 2008 Great Recession. These results provide evidence of the opposite side of the coin of the direct link between economic welfare and happiness, as seen in the first chapter of this volume. In the present chapter, we observe that profound *unhappiness*, as measured by suicide, is directly linked to *loss of economic welfare*. We can therefore conclude that economic policy does indeed influence happiness—even if that policy emphasizes work and achievement and the outcome is a reduction of profound unhappiness, as conceptualized by mental depression and measured by suicide.

It is plausible to utilize a conception of happiness, or human welfare, as an indicator of the worthwhile output of economic policy. This is confirmed by a number of studies that use the answer to a one-sentence question on happiness or life satisfaction as their principal measure. At the same time, it is useful to concentrate on aspects of human emotion that people normally identify as having great importance—such as the preservation of life. In this respect, suicide has traditionally been one of those elements of human behavior that characterizes melancholy, despondency, hopelessness, and nihilism. In utilizing suicide as an indicator of profound unhappiness, one would expect to observe that the deepest recession since the Great Depression of the 1930s should bring about extraordinarily deep emotional reactions on the part of the general population. We now observe this phenomenon in the situation of suicide reacting sharply to declines in employment, productivity, and investment in a vision of the future.

Imperfect Competition and Antitrust Regulations in the Stock Markets

CHAPTER 3

Preventing Stock Market Crises (I)

Regulating Shareholding Concentration

Xin Yan

Lawrence R. Klein

Viktoria Dalko

Ferenc Gyurcsány

Michael H. Wang[1]

Are current secondary stock markets perfectly competitive? We present a unique hand-collected database from securities regulatory agencies that demonstrates stock price manipulation is a frequent and widespread event in the secondary market. Although countries that follow U.S. stock market regulation prohibit market manipulation by law, our findings show that market manipulation remains widespread and frequent in all the stock exchanges in our sample, including the United States, China, India, Japan, and Hong Kong. In-depth analysis of the manipulative objective of each stage of the popular Accumulation-Lift-Distribution scheme leads to the finding of monopolistic pricing in the stock market, similar to predatory pricing in the goods market. Therefore, we conclude that monopoly power is frequently exercised in the stock markets investigated, and this market failure needs to be corrected through additional oversight, monitoring, and regulation. In the spirit of antitrust in the stock market, we recommend three quantifiable and adjustable measures to securities regulators that aim at effectively preventing stock market crises triggered by large shareholding concentration.

IS PERFECT COMPETITION POSSIBLE
IN THE STOCK MARKET?

Is perfect competition possible? Yes, it is possible. Our series of analysis and regulatory proposals in this book makes perfect competition possible in the stock market if quantity monopoly and information monopoly[2] are well regulated. Our series is aimed not only for perfect competition per se, but for a more equitable and transparent perfect competition. This would lead to reduction of the severity and frequency of stock market crises, and tame their adverse impact, especially on small investors. Therefore, the set of regulatory proposals put forth in this book would promote more stable and predictable economic growth.

To build perfect competition with fairness and transparency in the stock market, we present a series of research findings based on financial economics. It is the first systematic study presenting frequent violations of perfect competition and providing a detailed view of the sources, mechanisms, and risks of the existing monopolistic practices and the generation and utilization of information monopoly in the secondary market. The immediate goal of the series is to propose quantifiable, adjustable, and cost-effective rules for daily regulatory operations in stock markets to protect investors, prevent crises, and promote stability. In the long term, these proposals seek to provide building blocks for a better global financial architecture that can prevent world-shaking crises.

After reviewing historical examples and contemporary cases of prosecution and litigation that occurred in stock markets of both developed and developing economies, we demonstrate that market manipulation was, and still is, chronic, frequent, and occasionally rampant. Reviewing the theoretical literature confirms our empirical findings that manipulators can profit without any other advantage than their large wealth. The theoretical literature also inspires antitrust action against monopolistic market manipulation. Among a number of manipulation strategies, we choose the Accumulation-Lift-Distribution (ALD) scheme for detailed analysis based on historical and current evidence. In principle, accumulation refers to the stage when the manipulator purchases a large number of shares of the particular stock, lift means the conscious effort by the manipulator to inflate the share price and induce other investors to buy substantial amounts of shares so that the price is pushed up further, and once the desired stock price is achieved, distribution follows, that is, the stage when the manipulator sells all or part of his accumulated shares to unsuspecting investors.

Critical areas of each stage of the ALD scheme have been identified as targets for regulatory measures to be recommended. These measures are intended to be effective, efficient, and feasible enough to be implemented by any stock market, compared to the existing law-centered approach. Furthermore, these measures are quantifiable, adjustable, and cost-effective so that regulators can conveniently incorporate them into daily regulatory operations.

Large and dominant concentration remains the foundation for nearly all large-scale manipulation schemes aimed at achieving substantial and often illegal profits. Therefore, large concentration is selected as the first regulatory target.

CONCENTRATION, MANIPULATION, AND MONOPOLY

Trading is directional; so is volume. We explicitly denote buy volume and sell volume; that is, we differentiate buyer-initiated trade volume and seller-initiated trade volume. Trading speed is the average measure of how fast trading volume is executed. It is defined as the executed volume over the time of order execution. It is also directional. Buying speed means the trading speed of buyer-initiated trading volume. Selling speed is trading speed of seller-initiated trading volume.

Concentration refers to the holding of shares of a particular stock by an investor at a given moment. Normally concentration implies accumulated buy volumes. It is necessary to differentiate concentration from market power. Concentration is simply a large position. Market power is broader. It includes not only a large position, but also superior information or a high reputation (Pirrong 1996). In this paper, we choose to focus on concentration, that is, having no other attachment to a simple large position. Short selling leads to a kind of "negative" concentration. Concentration can be normalized against the number of outstanding shares for a longer-run perspective. Concentration may, however, for short-term considerations, be normalized against the average turnover of a past period, such as the moving average three-month turnover.

For our purposes, we focus on manipulation that utilizes large-scale concentration to induce actively the desired trading, in both direction and speed, by other investors, which may lead to illegal or unfair trading, even single-stock crashes or marketwide crises. Generally speaking, large concentration is neither a sufficient nor a necessary condition to initiate manipulation. However, manipulation with large concentration may carry more systemic importance when considering the prevention of stock market crises. Thus, we choose to focus on this type of manipulation in this chapter. We will relax the need for large concentration when analyzing other manipulation strategies in later chapters. Manipulation is operated within a shorter timeframe than the time length it would take for the same concentration to make the same profit with no manipulative action of the same stock. Manipulation has two essential components: large concentration and inducement of high trading speed in an aggregate sense. Each investor's trading speed may or may not be high. But the total volume of all investors traded during a given time period leads to high aggregate trading speed. In the current chapter and the next chapter, we focus only on those manipulations that have both components present, either simultaneously or at different phases of the manipulation scheme.

In principle, building a large and dominant concentration is about changing the demand and supply relationship, or control over supply of shares in particular. In this sense, the manipulator becomes a monopolist and, later on, profitable supplier of shares. Inducing high trading speed can actually create substantial demand in a relatively short time period. Inducement can be trade based or information based or a combination of the two. Here, we focus only on those that have large wealth and information asymmetry in favor of the manipulator.

Large concentration itself is not sufficient for manipulation. Thus, large concentration does not necessarily lead to manipulation. For instance, if an investor buys and holds a large number of shares for a long time and then sells them at the market price, he may make a large profit, but the process does not qualify as manipulation since no artificial inducement of high trading speed is involved. However, a manipulation scheme aimed for substantial profit must include large concentration. Typical manipulations include ALD and bear raid schemes. The ALD involves a large concentration of purchased shares. Bear raids start with quick and heavy selling. So both concentration of sell volume and fast selling speed are used simultaneously by the manipulator. This scheme, therefore, starts with a large concentration of borrowed shares.

A monopolistic buyer can lower the price, and a monopolistic seller can raise the price to increase his profit in the goods market (Pindyck and Rubinfeld 2001). In the stock market, can monopolistic pricing be achieved simply with a large concentration of shares? Not yet. A monopolistic high selling price is not automatically obtained, in a relatively short time horizon, by simply having a large concentration of the shares in the stock market. Rather, the monopolist needs to try to induce other investors to execute high-speed trades so that the share prices are pushed up substantially in a rather short time duration. Then the manipulator can meet his expected price of closing his position, often within a planned time period. This is the key difference between achieving a monopoly in stock markets versus achieving the same end in goods markets.

Pure monopoly is rare in the goods market (Pindyck and Rubinfeld 2001). However, it can overtake a single stock at any time in the secondary market, but this is usually a temporary monopoly, the duration of which remains flexible. This sort of pure monopoly can transpire in simply a few days or last for more than a year (Clark, et al. 1934; Mei, Wu, and Zhou 2004; Aggarwal and Wu 2006; litigation cases in Tables 3.1 through 3.4), but oftentimes months or weeks are sufficient to achieve the manipulator's goals. The key, however, is not how long the monopoly lasts but rather utilizing a temporary monopolistic supply position and inducing large demand in a short period of time to realize substantial, often illegal, profit from the manipulation.

Monopolies in goods markets are rather exposed as the monopolist exercises the power. However, creating a monopoly in the stock market can be well hidden because such trades are conducted with less than effective and constant surveillance, nor are there preventive mechanisms to ensure interruption and deterrence. It is much easier and faster to build and exercise monopolistic power in stock markets than in the goods markets because controlling the supply of shares in the stock market is much easier and less time-consuming than controlling the supply of products in the goods market (Easterbrook 1986). Conversely, it is also easier and faster to discontinue one's monopolistic behavior once the targeted profit is achieved or the manipulator's large position is detected by other investors or by regulators. It does not involve most elements that monopoly in the goods market relies on, such as leadership and management, advanced technology, a healthy and skilled workforce, access to capital, constant production and marketing, and, often, numerous years to reach monopoly status. What a monopoly in the stock market needs is simply large wealth at its disposal, one motivated investor, and a limited skill set for manipulation. The manipulator can be located in any venue that is connected to his trading account. Thus, secrecy can be assured. The manipulator does not require much education. Even a college degree is optional (Schwager 1992). Given the cited conveniences, it should not be surprising that *monopolistic manipulation in the stock market is frequent and hard to detect under current regulation,* in addition to the legal difficulties recognized by some researchers.[3]

In summary, manipulation in the stock market is an exercise of monopoly power. The two terms are equivalent and will be used interchangeably throughout the remainder of our discussions in this chapter.

CAN STOCK MARKETS STILL BE MANIPULATED?

Historically, especially prior to the regulatory framework implemented by the Securities Act (SA) (1933), Securities Exchange Act (SEA) (1934), Commodity Exchange Act (CEA) (1936), and Glass-Steagall Act (1934), manipulation had been pervasive, chronic, and occasionally so rampant as to lead to frequent crises in financial markets (Pirrong 1995), including that of the United States.

Between 1868 and 1921, in the U.S. futures markets, 121 manipulation cases were detected in grains and meats by the Chicago Board of Trade and 28 in cotton. The shocking frequency of manipulation propelled the passage of the first regulation of the commodity futures market in 1922 (Grain Futures Act) (Pirrong 1996). Since 1922, regulatory acts, particularly the CEA (1936), have not eliminated manipulation in the futures market. Several serious and notorious manipulation incidents were recorded in 1977 (the Hunt soybean squeeze), 1979 and 1980 (Hunt cornering of the silver market), 1989 (the Ferruzzi soybean manipulation), 1991 (Salomon Brothers cornering of Treasury notes), and 1995 to 1996 (Sumitomo's manipulation of copper) (Pirrong 1996). Easterbrook (1986) argues that controlling the supply in the futures market is even simpler than in the goods market. In other words, the futures market is more likely to be manipulated by monopolists than the goods market.

In foreign exchange markets, Corsetti, Pesenti, and Roubini (2001) noted that high concentration was observed in speculative trading against the Malaysian ringgit in 1997, the Hong Kong dollar in 1998, and the Australian dollar in 1998. They concluded that highly leveraged institutions may establish large and concentrated positions in small- and medium-sized markets and materially influence market dynamics. The Financial Stability Forum (FSF) (2000) believed there is sufficient evidence to suggest that attempted manipulation can and does occur in foreign exchange markets and should be a serious source of concern for policy makers. In short, foreign exchange markets can also be manipulated.

Based on the Amsterdam Stock Exchange, de la Vega (1688) provided one of the earliest documents of stock pools,[4] which were used to manipulate stock prices.

A series of congressional investigations, that is, the Hughs, Pujo, and Pecora investigations (White 1909; Sheldon 1975; Pecora 1939), searched for the causality of the financial panics of 1907, 1913, and 1929, respectively. The Pecora investigation (1939) directly led to the Securities Act (SA) (1933) and the Securities Exchange Act (SEA) (1934) and establishment of the Securities and Exchange Commission (SEC), while the earlier two investigations did not entail in any legislature. But each did uncover major forms of market manipulation such as bull pools, bear raids, wash sales, and matched orders[5] (Thel 1990).

The U.S. stock markets enjoyed more stable development after the implementation of the SA (1933) and the SEA (1934). Since, according to Allen and Gale (1992), the legislature is disclosure-oriented, action-based manipulation is virtually eliminated and insider information–based manipulation is also greatly curbed. But how did this affect market manipulation based on trade and public information?

In 1688, de la Vega described a number of market manipulation tactics resorted to by some of the largest individual or pooled large investor groups in the virtually unregulated Amsterdam stock exchange of the seventeenth century. Even though regulatory frameworks, technological innovations, and societal changes have rendered today's worldwide stock markets very different from the earlier Amsterdam stock exchange, the very fundamental nature of investors' interest in profit maximization has not changed during the past 400 years. If anything, trading strategies have evolved to circumvent regulatory rules. The Great Crash of 1929 led to the modern regulatory framework of the SA (1933) and the SEA (1934) for the U.S. stock exchanges. After their enactment, most other markets in the world followed the lead of the United States (Allen and Herring 2001). Since then, stock markets in developed countries have had more stable growth and fewer panics, most likely because of the correlation between income and implementation of these regulatory principles (Carvajal and Elliot 2007). Other markets operating outside of the United States, such as Brazil and Hong Kong, have experienced far more severe volatility measured by the frequency of the substantial market index drops during the last three decades.[6] Table 3.1 illustrates this point by presenting the number of stock market index declines of more than 5 percent in Brazil, Hong Kong, and the United States between 1987 and 2008.

A large drop in a stock market index for several consecutive days might indicate the presence of manipulation, if the general market news cannot explain such a decline. Still up for question is whether or not some large investors continue to manipulate the United States and other markets to achieve substantial gains by generating extreme price volatilities, and, occasionally, causing—even if unintentionally—a market index collapse.

Manipulation Is Frequent in U.S. Markets

How have U.S. stock markets fared in the last three decades? According to Aggarwal and Wu (2006), of the 142 manipulation cases brought by the SEC between 1990 and 2001, about half included some form of trade-based market manipulation. Mei, Wu, and Zhou (2004) presented empirical evidence from the SEC prosecution of 159 pump-and-dump manipulation cases between 1980 and 2002. Following the previous empirical research, we created a hand-collected database from the SEC litigation documents. This database contains 394 enforcement actions, resulting in 252 civil actions and 142 administrative proceedings released from October 1, 1999,

TABLE 3.1 Number of Stock Market Cycles with Significant Losses per Year, in Brazil (BSVP), Hong Kong (HSI), and the United States (DJI) (1987 to 2008)

Year	BSVP	HSI	DJI
1987	23	5	5
1988	13	2	1
1989	16	3	1
1990	22	3	2
1991	23	2	0
1992	28	3	0
1993	9	3	0
1994	16	11	1
1995	19	3	0
1996	5	1	0
1997	12	11	1
1998	17	20	4
1999	7	4	1
2000	12	11	4
2001	15	11	3
2002	14	5	7
2003	3	1	0
2004	8	2	0
2005	6	1	0
2006	8	0	0
2007	7	6	1
2008	25	20	10
Total (> 5%)	308	128	41
Total (> 10%)	91	29	6

to September 30, 2009 (see Chapter 8 for details). For the purpose of demonstration, we present in this chapter 25 litigation cases chosen from *Select SEC and Market Data Fiscal 2008* by the SEC (SEC 2009). All manipulations occurred from 2001 to 2008. The 10(b)-5 rule based on the SEA (1934) was violated among other violations cited in each case under litigation. Out of the 25 sample cases, 21 included issuing false and misleading press releases, that is, and, as such, should be categorized as information-based market manipulation. Five cases involve trade-based manipulation, showing such manipulation tactics as matched orders or marking the close.[7] The 25 cases are listed in Table 3.2, with the five shaded rows indicating the listed cases involved in trade-based manipulation.

TABLE 3.2 Twenty-five SEC Litigation Cases in Market Manipulation (2001 to 2008)

Litigation Release Number	Manipulator(s)	Target Stock(s)	Manipulation Period	Manipulation Tactics Include:
LR-20341	Zev Saltsman and Menachem Eitan	Xybernaut and Ramp	06/2001–12/2004	multiple nominee accounts, false statements, and wash sales
LR-20430	Anatoly Russ	AGG	08/23/2006–09/19/2006	matched orders
LR-20456	Dean A. Esposito and other brokers	SCL Ventures and Weida Communications	01/2004–05/2004	marking the close
LR-20616	Edgar E. Chapman	FCBG	01/2005–08/2005	matched orders and fake trading
LR-20712	Bruce Grossman and Jonathan Curshen	IBOT	06/2008–08/2008	matched orders
LR-20412	Rhea Laws and 4D Seismic, Inc.	4D Seismic	04/2006–11/2006	collusion and issuing false press releases
LR-20442	Daryn P. Fleming and Mathew C. Bruce	International Broadcasting	10/28/2005–01/13/2006	issuing false press releases
LR-20451	Strategic Management & Opportunity Corp., et al.	SMPP	02/2004–08/2004	issuing a series of materially false and misleading press releases
LR-20466	Mario A. Pino	BCIT	05/02/2005–07/13/2005	issuing false press releases
LR-20496	Ryan M. Reynolds, et al.	Beverage Creations	12/17/2007–03/10/2008	pump-and-dump scheme, promotional mailers, and spam e-mail
LR-20499	Robert M. Esposito, et al.	Anscott Industries	04/2003–07/2003	disseminating false and misleading newsletters and spam fax
LR-20519	CMKM Diamonds, Inc.	CMKM	01/2003–06/2005	false press releases through Internet chat boards
LR-20530	SMSI, et al.	SMSI	01/2006–08/2006	issuing several false and misleading press releases
LR-20537	Paul S. Berliner	ADS	11/29/2007	drafting and disseminating a false rumor against ADS
LR-20555	Robert F. Gruder and Stinger Systems, Inc.	Stinger Systems	10/2004–03/2005	fraudulent material misrepresentations

(continued)

TABLE 3.2 (*Continued*)

Litigation Release Number	Manipulator(s)	Target Stock(s)	Manipulation Period	Manipulation Tactics Include:
LR-20620	GMC Holding Corp. and Richard Brace	GMC Holding	06/2005–03/2006	issuing false press releases
LR-20644	Mobile Ready Entertainment Corp. et al.	Mobile Ready	01/2007–07/2007	issuance of false and misleading press releases
LR-20645	Homeland Safety International, Inc. et al.	HSII (originally Sniffex)	10/2004–04/01/2006	collusion, a pump-and-dump scheme, and issuance of false press releases
LR-20648	U.S. Sustainable Energy Corp., et al.	USSE	10/2006–02/2007	issuing false press releases
LR-20675	Dmitriy Butko	numerous stocks	10/19/2006–11/30/2006	pump-and-dump scheme
LR-20684	Francisco Abellan, et al.	GHLT	10/2005–06/2006	issuing false press releases in a pump-and-dump scheme
LR-20733	William Todd Peever and Phillip James Curtis	IHI, later merged in-SHEP	01/2002–06/2003	multiple nominee accounts and mass mailing of deceptive newsletters
LR-20745	Matthew A. Sarad, et al.	Telomolecular	06/2006–09/01/2007	issuing false press releases
LR-20750	Stephen Michael Strauss	Chilmark	11/01/2006–12/11/2006	issuing false press releases
LR-20762	Rodedawg International Industries and Luis E. Pallais	RWGI	late 2005–early 2007	issuing false press releases

Manipulation Is Occasionally Rampant Worldwide

How did other stock exchanges perform during the same time period?

Influential and crisis-causing market manipulations were cited, to the knowledge of the authors, in Latin America, Europe, Asia, and Australia. The notorious manipulator Naji Robert Nahas triggered disastrous stock market crashes in both the Rio de Janeiro and the Sao Paulo stock exchanges on June 9, 1989. Within 10 trading days, the indices of both markets dropped 67 percent and 61 percent (local currency), respectively (Brooke 1989a; Carvajal and Elliot 2009). As part of his manipulation strategy, Nahas bought stock options and then forced the markets up by heavily buying and selling shares in trades that were actually between himself and his partners. Local stockbrokers estimated that, in the first half of 1989, half of the activity on the Rio exchange was created by Nahas and his associates. Nahas was indicted by the Brazilian government two months later (Brooke 1989b).

Another stock market crisis, caused by Delta Securities, affected the Athens Stock Exchange on November 6, 1996. The difficulty came from a failed clearing of Delta's Greek Dollars (GRD) 2.5 billion position. The crisis not only required passage by the Greek government of an emergency legislative act for settlement, it also triggered the largest investigation in Greek history of exchange members and their practices. A large-scale stock manipulation scheme was discovered. The basic practice used by the manipulation scheme was matched orders. Delta Securities was a strategic manager of the manipulation scheme. Nineteen individuals were found to be involved in severe price manipulation practices, to have abused confidential information, and to have conducted artificial transactions. They were fined for a total of GRD 2 billion ([U.S. Dollars] USD 7.3 million) (IOSCO 2000).

On March 1, 2001, Ketan Parekh, the so-called Bombay Bull, defaulted on a nearly 30 million Indian Rupees position on the Calcutta Stock Exchange, which caused the exchange to suffer a massive payments crisis that affected share prices across India. Following the default, Calcutta Stock Exchange officials had to draw over 500 million Indian Rupees from a special fund to cover losses; since then, the exchange has been fighting to survive (Bhaumik 2002). During the eight trading days between March 1, 2001, and March 13, 2001, the indices of the top three stock exchanges of India, that is, National, Bombay, and Calcutta stock exchanges, dropped 17 percent, 17 percent, and 14 percent, respectively (GFD 2009). After the comprehensive investigation by the Securities and Exchange Board of India (SEBI), Ketan Parekh and 17 other entities were indicted in 2007. Ketan Parekh was found to be the key person involved across the board in all dimensions of the stock market scam, which first surfaced in March 2001. He was also the mastermind behind large-scale market manipulation of nine stocks before the crash in the three major stock markets. The manipulative practices included self-deals (i.e., wash sales), cross-deals (i.e., matched orders), and market corners during the period from October 1999 to March 2001 (SEBI 2007).

Other internationally known market manipulation cases include Nomura Securities' dual-market manipulation in the Australian stock and futures markets in 1996. Two Nomura manipulators had planned to discount 10 percent to 20 percent from the closing prices of more than 300 stocks on the Australian Securities Exchange on March 28, 1996. The strategy had the potential to trigger a marketwide crisis, but failed to be implemented by local brokers (SFA 2000). Another well-known case took place in Hong Kong in 1998. It was called *double play* because both the stock and currency markets were being manipulated simultaneously by unknown speculators. Their activities almost caused a crisis, which was averted just in time by intervention of the Hong Kong Monetary Authority (Tsang 1998; Corsetti, Pesenti, and Roubini 2001). The more recent schemes include Jerome Kerviel's fictitious trading in futures and cash of stock indices in European stock markets that led the French bank Societé Générale to lose $7 billion in January 2008. At the time, the amount was the largest single loss any bank had then suffered (Clark and Jolly 2008). Winterflood, a market maker on the London Stock Exchange, was found by the U.K.'s Financial Services Authority (FSA) to be playing a pivotal role in an illegal share ramping scheme in June 2008 and indicted the next year (FSA 2009). The offices of the German automaker Porsche were raided by federal prosecutors on August 20, 2009, probing the firm's alleged market manipulation of Volkswagen shares. The allegation was made by BaFin, the German financial regulator, to the prosecutor's office after investigating Porsche's attempt to gain control of Volkswagen (Kirchfeld and Czuczka 2009).

Each of the cases cited showed rampant market manipulations that had the potential to or actually resulted in stock market crashes or exchange settlement difficulties during the past three decades. How frequent and chronic are stock market manipulations in global markets in recent years?

Manipulation Is Chronic and Frequent in Global Stock Markets

Lang (2004) presented a detailed analysis of how institutions manipulated in concert the Hong Kong stock market in 2003. Khwaja and Mian (2005) found compelling evidence for a specific pump-and-dump manipulation scheme in the Karachi Stock Exchange. To study this further, we selected litigation or prosecution by five securities regulatory bodies in both developed and developing economies. In addition to the earlier-referenced litigation cases brought by the U.S. SEC, there were 12 cases listed by the China Securities Regulatory Commission (CSRC) that occurred between 2000 and 2006 (CSRC 2009); 13 cases from 1999 through 2007 prosecuted by the Hong Kong Securities and Futures Commission (HKSFC) (HKSFC 2009); 25 cases filed for prosecution by the Japan Securities and Exchange Surveillance Commission (JSESC) between July 1998 and June 2008 (JSESC 2009); and 29 convicted or settled cases launched by the Securities and Exchange Board of India (SEBI) that span from 1999 through 2005 (SEBI 2009). These cases are selected as evidence of recent episodes of market manipulation in both developed and emerging markets. These cases, except for JSESC cases, are listed in the following tables and their selection criteria described here.

The 12 CSRC cases occurred between March 21, 2000, and July 20, 2006. Each case contains single or repeated manipulation schemes for multiple years, ranging from more than one year to more than five years. A large concentration (from 32.07 percent to 81.33 percent of tradable shares) and wash sales or matched orders were resorted to in each of these cases. The 12 cases all involve violation of Section 77 (formerly Section 71) of the Securities Act (2005), for the Prohibition of Securities Market Manipulation. At present, all of these cases have been closed and the manipulators disciplined, including being banned from stock market entry for time spans ranging from one year to life (CSRC 2009). The 12 CSRC cases are listed in Table 3.3 by ascending order in concentration.

We selected 13 prosecuted market manipulation cases that occurred between December 30, 1999, and May 17, 2007, at the Hong Kong Stock Exchange. Market manipulation is explicitly written in the title or text of each case. Nine cases involve marking the close. Five cases feature matched orders and/or wash sales. One includes fake trading.[8] The selection is made from the enforcement news issued by the Hong Kong Securities and Futures Commission (HKSFC 2009). The 13 HKSFC cases are listed in Table 3.4 by ascending order of maximum price change during manipulation.

All 28 SEBI cases were selected from the orders listed in 2009 press releases (SEBI 2009). These cases actually occurred, however, from 1999 through 2005. At the least, Regulation 4 (1995/2003), Prohibition against Market Manipulation, was violated in each case. Nearly all the cases (28) include matched orders and/or wash sales. Two cases involved the

TABLE 3.3 Twelve CSRC Prosecution Cases in Market Manipulation (2000—2006)

Manipulator(s)/Target Stock(s)	Manipulation Duration	Investment*	Concentration of Tradable Shares (%)	Self-dealing Days (%)	Maximum of Vs/Vt (%)**	Days with Trades (%)	Number of Accounts
Hantang Securities/ Tongfeng Electronics	09/20/2001— 09/03/2004	RMB 0.26 BLN	32.07%	64.58%	61.81%	64.58%	1,645
Hantang Securities/ Baihua Village	01/10/2003— 09/03/2004	RMB 0.17 BLN	34.81%	64.72%	80.04%	64.72%	2,495
Xingan Securities/ Sanjing Pharmaceutical	08/26/2002— 12/30/2005	43 MLN shares	44.21%	47.71%	not available	82.90%	1,766
Hantang Securities/ Feida Environmental	07/22/2002— 09/03/2004	RMB 0.4 BLN	59.26%	65.00%	75.60%	65.00%	4,294
Northern Securities/ Taishan Oil	03/21/2000— 12/30/2005	RMB 8.3 BLN	61.35%	52.70%	85.17%	86.70%	8,817
Hantang Securities/ Nanfang Shareholding	01/14/2002— 09/03/2004	RMB 0.57 BLN	63.11%	64.50%	79.92%	64.50%	1,696
Hantang Securities/ Langchao Software	06/27/2002— 09/03/2004	RMB 0.77 BLN	74.05%	79.70%	79.18%	80.64%	1,872
Hantang Securities/ China Software	09/20/2001— 09/03/2004	RMB 0.60 BLN	76.63%	59.82%	80.23%	59.82%	4,554
Hantang Securities/ Hengda Real Estate	09/26/2000— 09/02/2004	RMB 0.7 BLN	79.48%	52.48%	95.79%	52.84%	2,296
Xianghe Holding, et al./ Sanmu Group	11/05/2001— 01/31/2005	RMB 4.4 BLN	80.00%	85.60%	98.80%	97.80%	3,879
Southwest Securities/ Zheda Wangxin	02/08/2001— 09/20/2004	RMB 3.3 BLN	80.68%	30.60%	60.00%	62.12%	1,783
Cui Junshan/ Jinde Fazhan	12/04/2000— 07/20/2006	RMB 2.1 BLN	81.33%	64.58%	99.59%	97.71%	3,917

*Investment is either in renminbi (RMB) or in number of shares

**Vs is self-dealing volume and Vt total trading volume

TABLE 3.4 Thirteen HKSFC Prosecution Cases in Market Manipulation (1999 to 2007)

Manipulator(s)/ Target Stock(s)	Manipulation Period	Manipulation Tactics	Maximum Price Change During Manipulation
Wong Wei Yin Peter/ SiS	05/18 and 20 and 06/09 and 15/2004	marking the close	10%
Wong Chi Kit/ Yeebo	02/12/2001– 03/09/2001	marking the close	14%
Chaw Chi Wai Ivan/ VST	05/05/2005– 08/26/2005	marking the close	14%
Cheung Wan Chiu/ Innovis	02/08, 14, and 16/2005	marking the close	16%
Chow Lung On/Tern	05/10/2002	matched orders	28%
Wong On Ching/ Victory	09/2000	matched orders for marking the close	30%
{X}*/Tradeeasy	10/18/2002	marking the close	30%
Wang Fang/Fujian	12/30/1999	marking the close	37%
{X}/MUI	01/09/2003– 05/21/2003	marking the close	60%
Chan Chin Yuen, et al./ASH	08/01/2005– 09/05/2005	matched orders	78%
Leung Kam Lai, William/5 stocks	11/11/2005– 03/21/2006	marking the close	80%
Stephen Lee Sing Wai/ Essex	02/14/2003– 03/31/2003	matched orders	120%
Yeung Fong Shiu/a derivative warrant of ICBC	05/17/2007	fake trading and wash sale	300%

*{X} means the name of the manipulator was not disclosed to the public.

manipulation tactic of advancing the bid. They are listed in Table 3.5 by ascending order of price change due to manipulation.

Prosecution Rate of Market Manipulation Is Low

From July 1, 1998, to June 30, 2008, based on investors' complaints, the JSESC sought to prosecute 25 cases that had been investigated for market manipulation. Those cases were found in violation of Article 159, the

TABLE 3.5 Twenty-eight SEBI Prosecution Cases in Market Manipulation (1999 to 2005)

Manipulator(s)/Target Stock(s)	Manipulation Period	Manipulation Tactics	Daily Volume (%)	Total Price Change (%)
Murari Lal Goenka/CIL	06/24/2005–11/7/2005	wash sales and matched orders	29%	5%
Porecha Global Securities Pvt. Ltd. and Shri Arun Porecha/MTL	10/23/2000–11/10/2000	matched orders	99.89%	15%
Tropical Securities & Investments Private Ltd./DCM	03/14/2001–04/24/2001	wash sale	23.95%	21%
Shri Vasant H. Bissa/SLIL	01/02/2002–09/13/2002	wash sales and matched orders	51.60%	70%
Shri Vipul Bhagwandas Shah/GFL	07/31/2000–11/27/2000	matched orders and collusion	19.63%	89%
12 related entities/DFL	04/01/2001–06/28/2001	matched orders and collusion	50%	96%
P. Suryakant Shares and Stock Brokers Pvt. Ltd./OMML	04/08/2002–07/09/2002	matched orders	not available	135%
ASK Holdings Pvt. Ltd./GIL	12/19/2002–01/17/2003	wash sale and collusion to unload large quantity	27.72%	195%
Chandrahas R Kulkarni/HTL	11/16/1999–03/31/2000	circular trading*	90%	196%
Shri Minoo Pestonji/APL	08/02/2000–08/31/2000	wash sales and advancing the bid	not available	197%
Shyam Lal Sultania/NIL	04/25/2005–11/08/2005	matched orders	12.53%	238%
Ravi Vishnu Securities Ltd./AOIL	11/06/2000–12/29/2000	matched orders and advancing the bid	55%	316%
Shri Mahendra A. Shah/SCL	10/01/1999–01/04/2000	creating artificial volume and price rise	19%	448%

Company/Broker	Date Range	Manipulation Type		
M. Bhiwaniwala & Co./Bacchhat	03/01/2004–3/31/2004	matched orders	35%	562%
Pivotal Stoxare Ltd./OTPL	11/01/1999–02/09/2000	collusion in price lifting to unload large quantity	25.46%	565%
Shri Tushar Jhaveri/EIL	06/26/2000–09/05/2000	wash sales	41%	635%
Mukesh Dokania & Co./ACCL	07/02/2001–10/15/2001	wash sales	50%	678%
Purshottam Lal Kejdiwal/BIL	06/09/2005–09/16/2005	wash sales	1.30%	702%
Ahilya Commercial Pvt. Ltd./SLPL	04/21/2005–09/16/2005	wash sales and matched orders	13.38%	880%
Shyamlal Sultania/SPL	03/17/2005–07/14/2005	matched orders	12.55%	1,067%
A. V. Shares & Stock Broking Private Ltd., et al./GCML	06/17/2005–09/20/2005	matched orders	90.97%	1,108%
EXV Finvest Pvt. Ltd. and two directors/MHL	01/01/2001–08/31/2001	matched orders	80%	1,130%
S. Jhunjhunwala & Co./TCL	01/01/2004–08/03/2004	wash sales and matched orders	28%	1,270%
12 related entities/DFL	04/10/2002–08/31/2002	matched orders and collusion	75%	1,345%
Sanchit Financial and Management Services Ltd/EIL	11/24/1999–02/11/2000	matched orders	not available	2,400%
G. R. Industries & Finance Ltd. and partners/GRIFL	09/07/2004–02/28/2005	matched orders	83%	8,410%
Dinesh Kumar Lodha/RFSL	02/16/2004–02/28/2005	matched orders	54.60%	11,438%
Dhanlaxmi Cotex Ltd./SIL	07/02/2001–01/02/2002	circular trading in price pegging**	> 21%	n/a

*Circular trading is equivalent to matched orders. We have, however, noted from a few SEBI cases that circular trading can also occur among more than two colluding parties.

**Several brokers from Dhanlaxmi Cotex Ltd. conducted circular trading for price pegging. This manipulation tactic is not for profit making but for floating share prices for the public company to issue a large number of shares. It is called price pegging.

Prohibition of Market Manipulative Acts, of the Financial Instruments and Exchange Act (2007). They are all listed in the JSESC Annual Reports (JSESC 2009). No case reveals the name(s) of the manipulator(s), and, given the lack of consistency in data presented in all the cases, we cannot construct a meaningful table out of them. Rather, the reader is referred to Table 3.6, which shows the ratio of prosecuted cases to complaints in market manipulation.

Out of 11,514 public tips stating market manipulation, which were mainly trade based, only 25 were found through investigation and filed for prosecution during the 10-year span from July 1, 1998, to June 30, 2008. That is a mere 0.2 percent. And the rate of conviction can be even lower. One can develop a sense of how poor effectiveness and low efficiency regarding securities legislation and enforcement procedures can be. This is mainly because many nonrampant daily manipulations are difficult to detect and even harder to prosecute if pursued through legal procedural channels.

The German securities regulator is said to be toothless. And the country's weak rules lead to few market manipulation convictions. For instance, 1,300 tips in 2008 ended up with 11 cases convicted, or a conviction rate of 0.8 percent (ANE 2009). There were 6,000 complaints in the year 2000 about manipulation in Canadian stock markets. How many of them were investigated, the convicted manipulator Marino Specogna questioned (Specogna 2003).

TABLE 3.6 Ratio of JSESC Cases Filed for Prosecution to Total Complaints Citing Market Manipulation (1998 to 2008)

Business Year*	Market Manipulation Complaints	Cases Filed for Prosecution	Ratio of Prosecution Cases to Complaints
1998	51	1	2%
1999	162	3	2%
2000	317	4	1%
2001	601	5	1%
2002	759	0	0%
2003	680	2	0.3%
2004	1,435	2	0.1%
2005	2,705	1	0.03%
2006	2,678	3	0.1%
2007	2,126	4	0.2%
Total	11,514	25	0.2%

*Business year begins on July 1 and ends on June 30 of the following year.

In emerging stock markets, Goyal (2005) points out that it takes up to two years to settle a SEBI case in India, and the conviction rate is poor. In 2001 to 2002, 21 out of 111 cases were completed; the completion rate was 19 percent. The conviction rate is likely lower. Nageswaran and Krithivasan (2004) argue that only 16 convictions were handed down out of a total of 775 litigation cases in Malaysia in 2002. The conviction rate based on litigation is only 2 percent. Those low conviction rates from the regulatory agencies of both developed and emerging economies obviously justify nonlegal measures for daily regulatory operations.

Other indicators such as how many years does it take to progress from complaint to conviction, what is the cost to cover all legal procedures, and how many human resources are involved in each case can be further calculated to measure the effectiveness and efficiency of the legal approach. We leave this work for future research.

The previously cited empirical findings, which only detail instances reported, investigated, and prosecuted, reveal that manipulation remains a chronic, frequent, and occasionally rampant issue facing stock markets in the twenty-first century. McGoun (2008) also argues that markets are indeed inherently manipulable. Chris Cook, former director of the International Petroleum Exchange in London, observes from the oil futures market that, "The market is the manipulation" (Cook 2009). The far-reaching implications of these cases underscore the convicted Canadian stock market manipulator's confession that manipulation of untold numbers of stocks occurs every day (Specogna 2003).

One fact, however, does remain clear: Every stock market can be manipulated under the current regulatory framework. How does the theoretical literature justify the existence of stock manipulation?

THEORETICAL LITERATURE ON MARKET MANIPULATION

Hart (1977) models a general stock market with one monopolist and numerous price-taking traders. In a Walrasian equilibrium framework, Hart (1977) derives general conditions for the existence of profitable speculation in a dynamically unstable equilibrium, and, in some cases, in a dynamically stable equilibrium. He concludes that under fairly general conditions, the manipulator can profit at the expense of small traders simply by engaging in speculative activities.

Kyle (1985) modeled one monopolist and numerous nonmonopolists in one stock market. The monopolist has insider information while market makers cannot always distinguish if a trade has been placed by a monopolist or noise traders. By assuming a linear relationship between return and volume, Kyle (1985) proves that the monopolist can maximize profits in speculative trading by exploiting his monopoly power in continuous auction equilibrium.

Jarrow (1992) states explicitly that the goal of his paper is to prevent market manipulation. Large wealth is a sufficient condition for a manipulator to make a profit by trading only. With large wealth, the manipulator can realize a profit even without an informational advantage. Here, the most important characteristic of the manipulator is that gain can sometimes be achieved without risk.

In practice, this characteristic of a manipulator is extremely important. Several early historical findings supported Jarrow's point. In the seventeenth century, de la Vega (1688) recorded that a manipulator is a rational individual who avoids risk; moreover, a manipulator of stocks will not start trading before his calculations assure him that he will profit. In the first half of the twentieth century, Mathias (1936) found that a pool manager not only specifies the stock to be manipulated, but also plans the duration and scope of the operations.

Allen and Gale (1992) study conditions when manipulation is profitable. They find, again, that a manipulator can make a profit by buying and selling a large volume of shares. The finding operates under the assumption that small traders cannot distinguish between an informed large trader and a manipulator who has large wealth but no insider information. Indeed, the crucial condition giving the manipulator an advantage rests in his having large wealth at his disposal. Allen and Gale (1992) also categorize three kinds of market manipulation: action based, information based, and trade based. They point out that trade-based manipulation is difficult to detect and thus has not been effectively regulated. In reality, of course, a manipulation scheme can either be trade based or combine trade-based and information-based manipulative tricks (see Tables 3.2 through 3.5).

Cherian and Jarrow (1995) assert that trade-based manipulation is an exercise of market power. The authors' justification of this claim to market power is based on two different grounds. One is Walrasian, meaning that large buys increase the aggregate demand, and therefore increase price (the opposite of a large sell). The other reason underlying their claim is expressed in a market-microstructure explanation, in an information-effect model. That is, if a market maker cannot distinguish between a speculator and an informed trader because of the large volume, he will raise the price when a speculator buys and lower the price when a speculator sells. The manipulator's large wealth and ability to remain unknown give him both a trade and an information advantage in the manipulation scheme.

The research mentioned earlier makes different theoretical assumptions but arrives at the same conclusion: Manipulation schemes based on large trades only are theoretically profitable. Large wealth is explicitly or implicitly understood to be the main precondition for manipulation. Secrecy is also important. The next question is how to utilize large wealth and secrecy to ensure a manipulation scheme yields a large profit? In other words, what is the key in the manipulation strategy after a large concentration of shareholding is built up? Avery (1998a, 1998b) answers the question to a certain extent. According to Avery (1998b), the manipulator's success depends on whether he can induce herding, which would ensure that many other traders' buy volumes follow each other in a relatively short time period. Another important insight that Avery (1998a, 1998b) has provided is that a manipulator can trade multiple times while other investors trade only once. However, Avery (1998a, 1998b) does not explain how the manipulator induces other buy volumes to follow.

This question will be fully discussed in the next chapter. Here we only note that the essence is that large buy quantities are necessary to push up the price to a sufficient height within a short time. To put it another way, high buying speed lifts prices. Herding of small investors can be induced as a part of these events, but it is a consequence and not a reason. Literature on herding has not shed much light on this research, because its analysis starts after herding is activated; very little emphasis has been placed on trying to understand how herding is generated by manipulation. Hirshleifer and Teoh (2009) conclude, after reviewing references listed on 18 pages on herding, that the source of thought contagion has not yet been explored to any appreciable extent in the literature on herding. In brief, a complete manipulation strategy is mainly composed of two phases: Build a large concentration and induce a high trading speed. Early empirical literature, such as Montgomery (1933) and Clark, et al. (1934), supported this point. Numerous enforcement orders displayed in Tables 3.2 through 3.5 show it.

In addition, Fishman and Hagerty (1995), John and Narayanan (1997), and Huddart et al. (2001) point out that manipulative trading may occur due to the presence of mandatory disclosure laws. Historical and contemporary cases show that manipulation can occur with or without a disclosure requirement of listing companies. So a disclosure requirement does not provide a sufficient or a necessary condition that could limit or eliminate manipulation. Chakraborty and Yilmaz (2004) argue that manipulation is possible at any equilibrium by the informed speculator who can trade repeatedly, under the conditions that the horizon is long enough and every individual investor is uncertain about the existence of an insider. However, the time horizon depends on the manipulator's strategy. It can be longer than a year, and it can be as short as two days (for example, Aggarwal and Wu 2006; Mei, Wu, and Zhou 2004).

Starting with Hart (1977) and Kyle (1985), throughout the literature, the manipulator has always been portrayed as an explicit or implicit monopolist. As described by Cherian and Jarrow (1995), his power to affect market prices can come from the two sources, already cited: large wealth and identity secrecy. Schwartz (2001) observes that the tendency of the order flow to concentrate in major stock market centers raises fears of monopolistic power. In the same volume of Schwartz (2001), the then Acting Commissioner of the Securities and Exchange Commission, Laura S. Unger, questioned whether antitrust policy should be enacted for the U.S. equity markets. Allen and Herring (2001) note that banking regulation includes antitrust laws to prevent banking crises. Given that global stock market crises occurred frequently, why is it that antitrust laws have not been implemented in the stock market?

The theoretical literature has provided answers to such fundamental questions as can manipulation occur based on large trades only?, how does the stock price get lifted up by the manipulator?, what does the manipulator do during the distribution stage?, and how does the stock price behave after he finishes selling his shares and there is no more support for the artificial price? And what are the effects of the manipulation stages on investor protection, on market stability, and, even, on the potential leading to a crisis? These critical questions have not been answered by the theoretical literature.

Therefore, we abstract the concept of antitrust regulation from the theoretical research. To find sufficient evidence for us to transform the concept into a principle of regulatory proposals, we rely mainly on empirical data. The prosecution cases from both the empirical literature and our collected database not only enable us to understand critical areas informing a complete manipulation scheme, but also reveal the true purpose of each individual stage in the scheme where the manipulator has seemingly conflicting objectives.

WE CHOOSE THE ACCUMULATION-LIFT-DISTRIBUTION SCHEME TO STUDY

It is essential to understand in detail how a manipulator builds a large and dominant concentration, and induces large buy quantities so that, subsequently, effective regulations can be proposed. Therefore, we follow the entire cycle of one manipulation scheme rather than conducting a conventional longitudinal or cross-sectional analysis. Cross-sectional analysis provides information about the prices (and sometimes the trading volume) of multiple stocks at a given moment, and longitudinal study tracks the price (and sometimes the volume) history of one particular stock. Both are stock price centered. Neither focuses on the trader. Nor can either uncover the true purpose behind each trade, let alone a complete trading strategy.

As a contribution to regulatory efforts, this paper selects one well-known manipulation strategy. It belongs to long manipulation; that is, the manipulator profits from owning the shares (as opposed to short manipulation, when profit is obtained by first selling a security short). The scheme is characterized by three stages, a trilogy of *accumulation, lift, and distribution*. These categories were first used by Lang (2004) and were also described by Montgomery (1933) and Mathias (1936), based on the experience of the New York Stock Exchange. It is denoted as the ALD scheme throughout the remainder of this chapter.[9]

We choose the ALD scheme to study because long manipulation enjoys the most popularity among manipulation schemes (Pirrong 1996). Aggarwal and Wu (2006) found that 84.5 percent of 142 SEC litigation releases from 1990 to 2001 focused on long manipulation. However, the most compelling reason is that in our database, the 103 prosecution cases presented in this chapter, we found 101 of the cases (98 percent) were either an ALD scheme or a general long manipulation scheme.

Before the SA (1933) and the SEA (1934) were passed, Montgomery (1933) vividly describes the proliferation of bull pool manipulation schemes. He stated that one needs to understand the manipulation methods used by the pools or other forms of organized speculation to have a complete picture of the market conditions. He pointed out that the ALD scheme is a typical pool method and many aspects of the methods employed tend to be nearly universal. According to his description of the ALD scheme's progressive steps, the first demands that the manipulator must have, or have access to, large wealth to dispose of at will. Then, during the accumulation stage, two important issues arise: the protection of the process from other buyers by using the shake-out tactic, and sufficient number of shares to be absorbed from the outstanding shares so that the supply of shares in the hands of other investors is reduced to the degree that the next step can be executed. Once the accumulation stage is completed, the manipulator has a number of tactics to raise the share price. This happens because the supply of shares in the hands of other traders has been greatly reduced, and therefore the price impact of the buy volume is relatively large. During this stage, the crucial point is to induce high buy volumes within a short time period. This is usually accomplished via induced herding: A large number of small investors follow up with buy orders. The manipulator's objective at this stage is to purchase as few shares as possible while striking to achieve a higher price level. Once the desired price level is reached, or if there is a serious decline in the price, the manipulator will start to distribute, that is, to sell his holdings to a large number of small investors and occasionally large investors.

Mathias (1936) presents the most detailed to-the-point description of an ALD scheme that reflects the previously styled scenario. That is, during both the accumulation and the distribution stages, the manipulator tries to trade in small quantities so as not to generate too large a price impact. The lift stage is the time to mark up stock prices; it is during this time that he will try everything possible to pump stock prices. Once the lift stage's objective—increased prices—meets or exceeds expectations, the manipulator needs to distribute his large quantity of shares carefully. Sometimes he will even strategically buy a few shares while selling a large amount, to make the price change look like it is climbing a little during the dropping trend to avoid the suspicion of other investors or regulators.

Another important observation Mathias (1936) has made suggests that since the ALD scheme is a form of manipulation that depends on a large concentration of shareholding and high buying speed of shares within a relatively short time, it can cause dramatic distortion of the targeted share price within a very short time span. This type of manipulation can greatly change the ecology of a stock price's time series. If one uses a buy-and-hold order (for the same number of shares and sells at the same price level that would accrue without manipulation but rather from the stock's natural development) as a comparison, the artificiality of the ALD scheme greatly shortens the time within which the same profit can be achieved. The consequence of such a scheme for the stock market is that such a short-term and artificially created form of intense volatility generates the systemic risk, the vulnerability of all the investors in the stock, or the entire market that may lead to panic selling or stock market crises. Allen, Litov, and Mei (2006) make the same observation on the 10 successful stock market corners before 1934.

MANIPULATIVE OBJECTIVE OF EACH STAGE OF THE ALD SCHEME

A successful ALD scheme demands the manipulator have access to a relatively large amount of wealth. The objective of the accumulation stage is to turn large wealth into a large number of shares at a reasonably low price while reducing the uncertainty in trading costs due to other investors' following. The essence of this stage is to control the supply of shares or, put differently, to build up a dominant concentration of shares in preparation for the next stage of manipulation. To achieve this objective without interruption or delay, the manipulator needs to deter other serious buyers. For ultimate profit maximization, the manipulator wants the price impact of each buy order to be minimal, so as to ensure that the total transaction cost at this stage remains low. As for the basis of the ALD scheme, the underlying characteristic during this stage is to manipulate the share supply.

When the accumulation has been completed, the supply of the shares that could be in the hands of other traders has been greatly reduced. Therefore, at the lift stage the price impact of buy volume is effectively increased. The stock becomes very attractive for small investors because of its fast and continuously rising prices (Bernheim and Schneider 1935). At this point, the value of the stock can increase rapidly and positively impress investors who want to trade on what seems to be a quickly rising stock.

As can be seen from all the recent regulatory cases drawn from both the SEC and other regulatory agencies that are presented in our database, the manipulator always engages in some form of deceptive activity to pump up the stock price by a substantial percentage within a short period of time. The manipulation can be simply trade based, such as wash sales, matched orders, and fake trades; it can be information based, such as issuing false and misleading press releases and spreading rumors on Internet bulletin boards; or any combination of these devices. The essence is to create high demand in as short a period of time as possible. Therefore, it is at this stage that the manipulator can achieve the large price impact his tactics seek. Even though he may pretend to be busy with executed (wash sales or matched orders) or nonexecuted (fake trading) transactions, his intention is to increase his shareholding by as little as possible at this stage. Eventually other market participants decide to enter the market with the supposed heightened demand, and thus small investors or, at times, even large investors can be induced to buy. These activities will result in large price increases, all transpiring over a very short time period. From the regulatory cases listed earlier in this chapter, herding of small buy volumes is very likely generated by the manipulator's seemingly high turnover. In essence, this stage targets manipulation of demand within a collapsed time frame. In other words, the scheme manipulates buying speed.

Regarding price impact of buy volumes, the manipulator has opposing objectives during the accumulation and lift stages. He wants to minimize buyers' price impact during accumulation. But he wants to maximize buyers' price impact during the lift phase. Viewed from the vantage point of manipulative emphasis, accumulation is trading volume manipulation, or manipulation of supply; lift is manipulation of demand in a short time period, or of buying speed. Because one stock may be at the accumulation stage of a manipulation scheme when another stock is at the lift stage of another manipulation scheme, the observable price impacts for the two stocks will be significantly different. This is one reason why cross-sectional data analysis cannot effectively reveal manipulation. Therefore, one has to follow the complete cycle of the ALD scheme to understand seemingly conflicting objectives and seemingly inconsistent price behaviors.

After the accumulation and lift stages have been executed, the remaining stage, distribution, is invoked to obtain the ultimate realized profit. Once the price level has met or surpassed the price target, the manipulator starts the distribution process. The objective at this stage is that his sell volumes have minimal price impact, which explains why he wishes to remain anonymous throughout the process. Therefore, he sells in sliced volumes in a gradual fashion. Sometimes, he buys some shares to avoid other investors' suspicion. But the real purpose is to sell. The manipulator can proceed in this fashion when he does not have to rush to close his position.

But it is just at this stage that the manipulator faces more risk than at any other stage in turning his unrealized gain into realized profit. His major concern is loss of secrecy, which would be immediately followed with uncertainty and increasing transaction costs. Several situations can trigger this. One is that serious selling by other investors occurs before or during the distribution process. The other is if a large short-selling volume would enter the manipulated stock before or during the distribution stage. Naturally, the ALD long manipulators can be subject to attack by short sellers who try to profit by detecting large positions built by the former. There were several well-known historical cases of cornering short sellers analyzed recently by Allen, Litov, and Mei (2006). The third scenario is a major unexpected event that prompts panic selling, such as the onset of a war, a natural disaster, or an epidemic. If any of these unexpected scenarios should occur, the manipulator's best decision, based on profit maximization (more accurately, loss minimization), is to sell all of his holdings as soon as possible to avoid any uncertainty that could accrue due to time delays. Thus, a manipulator can turn sharply from a slow to an extremely fast selling speed.

The manipulator's losses can become systemic risk of the market. The manipulator's response to risk can lead to several possible consequences. The best-case, most orderly scenario would arise if he does not panic and sells as planned via slow distributions, which is very unlikely. A second, less-orderly scenario would arise if he suddenly sells his accumulated shares. This will, in turn, generate a large price drop in the stock in a short period of time, but other stocks in the market are not affected. The worst-case scenario arises when a sudden large sale of stocks causes marketwide panic selling, which can develop into a single stock crash or even a marketwide crisis. Empirical literature shows that the share price collapses after the completion of the distribution process by the manipulator (Aggarwal and Wu 2006; Mei, Wu, and Zhou 2004; Allen, Litov, and Mei 2006), which is confirmed by the former manipulator (Specogna 2003). The consequences of the price collapse of a manipulated stock have similarity to a quick dump of a large position by the manipulator. The market suffers no matter if the manipulator's distribution is smooth or rushed by uncertainty.

The above analyses have revealed that concentration building and buying speed manipulation mark the two key elements in the ALD scheme. However, each is used in a separate stage of an ALD scheme. The scheme at the distribution stage is prone to generating systemic risk, extreme price drops, or even a marketwide crisis. To achieve the regulatory principles stated earlier, one needs to prevent both large concentrations and fast trading speeds.

ARE MONOPOLISTIC PRACTICES INVOLVED IN THE ALD SCHEME?

In the previous section, we have analyzed the manipulator's objective at each stage of the ALD scheme. In the current section, we will try to understand what is underlying the scheme, particularly at the accumulation and lift stages. In other words, the question we ask is: Are monopolistic practices involved in the ALD scheme?

Predatory pricing is a typical monopolistic practice in the goods market (Motta 2004). The monopolist has a large market share. To gain control over supply, he lowers prices substantially to drive all other competitors out. Consumers will benefit during this process, which may not last very long. However, once most other competitors are forced out by extremely low prices, the monopolist controls all or the majority of the goods supply. Then he can set much higher prices, which will be to the detriment of the welfare of consumers. The essence is for the monopolist to gain absolute control over supply, so that he can set monopolistic prices later (Motta 2004).

In the stock market, no consumers exist. All investors are *de facto* competitors for trading profits. When an ALD manipulator, an investor with large wealth to dispose of, starts to accumulate large quantities of shares at relatively low price levels, his objective is to gain control over share supply for later distribution at an inflated price. During the accumulation process, he expects low cost and no competition from other buyers. Although he tries to keep the price impact of his purchase as low as possible, he cannot prevent other investors from buying the same stock, either randomly or out of rational calculation. And he cannot foresee how many buy volumes will arrive because his accumulation pushes up share prices, even though at a slow pace. To make his accumulation successfully completed at low costs, he decides to shake out other buyers of the same stock. That is, he sells some accumulated shares to drive down share prices. Other buyers will be scared to see a sudden and deep drop of the share price, which is expected to continue climbing. They will have to sell all the shareholding just bought recently to avoid further loss. Once all other buyers have exited from the stock, the manipulator stops the shakeout process and resumes accumulation till his target is reached. The shakeout is similar to the drive-out used by a monopolist in the predatory pricing process in the goods market. The shared essence in both scenarios is to gain clean and absolute control over supply so that later distribution at a higher price is possible.

Large concentration of shareholding does not automatically lead to high-rising share prices. The manipulator with a large concentration cannot fix share prices as a monopolist in the goods market does. He has to do price lifting, through either executed and/or unexecuted trades, or through issuing touting information through mass media, to induce substantial buy volumes in a short time period. Since we focus on trade-based manipulation in this chapter, only price lifting through fictitious trades, fake trades, or other trade-based tactics is to be discussed. The accumulation and lift stages together complete predatory pricing in the stock market. Detailed analysis of several major tactics widely used in trade-based price lifting are presented in Chapter 4.

In sum, a monopolistic practice, shake out, is used in the stock market to build a large concentration of shareholding at the accumulation stage. Different than a monopolist in the goods market, the monopolistic investor in the stock market has to do price lifting through either trade-based manipulation or information-based manipulation or other types of manipulation. Both accumulation and lift stages together complete "predatory pricing" in the stock market. Now the monopolistic investor has gained absolute control of share supply and induced large buy volumes in a short time period, which is followed by inflated share prices. He has established a monopolistic position so that he can distribute his shareholding at the lifted price.

ANTITRUST AGAINST ALD MANIPULATION

Monopolistic pricing exists in the ALD manipulation. Carrying forward the antitrust spirit abstracted from the theoretical literature, we analyze and target antitrust measures for each stage of the ALD manipulation scheme.

The manipulator desires to convert large wealth to large concentration of shares. Hence, the maximum number of accumulated shares by a financial investor can be a regulatory target. The pace of accumulation during a given time period can be another important target.

There are two main methods of lift. One is trade based, which divides into two types. The first type of trade-based manipulation depends on creating false and relatively high daily turnover through executed trades (e.g., wash sales or matched orders) or unexecuted orders (e.g., fake trading). Both come with large orders even though no new shares are added to the manipulator's previous position of accumulation. The second type of trade-based manipulation is to advance bidding prices. Therefore, the daily volume of either executed or unexecuted orders, in absolute terms, by the manipulator can be a candidate for regulation.

The other type of lifting is information based. Touting the stock that the manipulator has already accumulated is its key feature. The print and electronic media as well as other telecommunication platforms have provided easy conduits for manipulation. Information-based manipulation has to be effectively regulated, and measures will be proposed in Chapter 8.

At the distribution stage, other traders' selling speed presents a threat to the manipulator's gain; subsequently, it can threaten the stability of the manipulated stock and possibly that of the entire stock market. It can also serve as a regulatory target for the purpose of investor protection, market stability, and, to some extent, crisis prevention. The next chapter on regulating price lifting will address this issue.

Behind each ALD scheme, the manipulator strives to obtain the power of monopolistic pricing, similar to the monopolistic behavior, predatory pricing, in the goods market. Evidence shows that a firm's profit is strongly and positively associated with its market share in the goods market (Viscusi, et al. 1995). We have demonstrated in this chapter that theoretical and empirical research as well as enforcement cases have firmly established that large investors have the ability to obtain monopolistic power as well as illegal and/or unfair profit through large concentration of shares. Antitrust legislature was initiated for the U.S. goods market in 1890.[10] We need to draft and enact antitrust regulations to prevent stock market manipulation as well.

To carry out antitrust regulations against ALD manipulators, four areas can be targeted based on the analysis presented in this section. They are large concentration of shareholdings, trade-based price lifting, touting stocks on media platforms, and fast selling speed. We target only those manipulation schemes that involve large concentrations of shares in this chapter.

EXISTING APPROACH AND OUR PROPOSAL TO REGULATE MARKET MANIPULATION

Stock market manipulation is chronic, frequent, and occasionally rampant. How does the existing regulation deal with manipulation? What are its strengths and weaknesses? How effective are the regulatory procedures already in place? These questions need to be answered before detailing our proposals.

The legal framework underpinned by the SA (1933) and SEA (1934) has presented guidelines on regulating market manipulation. The current approach by enforcement agencies focuses on the manipulator. Since the conditions governing whether a manipulator can be convicted are very strict, manipulation as a crime is virtually unprosecutable under current legislature (Fishel and Ross 1991; Markham 1991; Kyle and Viswanathan 2008). This can be seen in the very few instances in which someone accused of stock market manipulation is actually convicted relative to the number of investor complaints registered each year with international stock markets. Table 3.6 shows, partially, low effectiveness and efficiency in enforcement outcomes in JSESC investigations. The legal approach is necessary when rampant manipulation brings about serious financial and societal consequences. In these instances, manipulation is prosecuted as a criminal case and only legal resolution is considered appropriate.

Market manipulation is a daily phenomenon affecting stocks and related derivatives traded at any stock market. Most daily manipulations are not rampant. Rather, many manipulation schemes cause a certain degree of price volatility but do not result in marketwide panic or crises. Targeting the manipulators behind those schemes through the legal framework is financially costly and time consuming. Often, cases go on for years before being resolved. The probability of winning a case against a manipulator remains low in the end (Markham 1991). It is not surprising that Fishel and Ross (1991) question whether the legal approach is the most expeditious avenue to prosecute cases that did not result in untold damage. In brief, the existing approach, being *ex post* and time consuming, cannot effectively fulfill, efficiently and at a low cost, the daily tasks of investor protection, crisis prevention, and promotion of market stability.

Therefore, for chronic and frequent but not rampant acts of manipulation, the regulatory measures proposed in this chapter are limited to being quantifiable, adjustable, inexpensive, and workable at a day-to-day operational level. The existing legal prosecution approach should remain, but most likely the frequency of resorting to legal enforcement will be markedly reduced, if our recommendations are implemented. With both regulatory and legal measures, the goal of investor protection, crisis prevention, and market stability will come closer to becoming a reality.

REGULATORY PROPOSAL: A GENERIC RECOMMENDATION

Since each stock market has its own unique regulatory emphasis and cultural characteristics, we will only provide a set of examples as a generic recommendation. These suggestions reflect the principles inherent in anti-trust law but also take into consideration the need to address both long and short time horizons. The specific proposals for a particular stock market need, however, are to be determined after careful analysis of the trading data generated by the market.

The ALD manipulation schemes can take days, weeks, or months, sometimes more than a year to complete. Therefore, time lengths have to be considered in designing regulatory measures. Different limits on shareholdings should be set for different time lengths.

- *Measure one:* Throughout the lifetime of a stock, a financial investor cannot, at any time, hold or borrow more than X percent of the outstanding shares of any stock.
- *Measure two:* During any calendar year, an investor is allowed to increase or decrease his holding in a stock a maximum of Y percent of the outstanding shares.
- *Measure three:* During each trading day, any investor's total orders, executed or unexecuted, added in absolute values, are not allowed to exceed Z percent of the average daily volume of the previous month.

The actual percentages X, Y, and Z are to be determined by interested regulators based on their priorities. These proposals have multiple effects. First, they prevent dominance. Second, they substantially prevent, if not eliminate, wash sales (self-dealing), matched orders (cross-dealing), and fake trading. Third, they curb short-term manipulation tricks such as marking the close. They also prevent large-scale short selling.

To prevent circumvention, three more measures have to be in place. One is that large positions near the proposed limits must be monitored for future changes. Another is that collusion needs to be effectively prevented. The third is that multiple accounts set up by one investor for one stock have to be well curbed. More in-depth analysis and measure construction will be given in the next chapter on regulating price lifting.

BENEFITS OF REGULATING CONCENTRATION

Monopolistic concentration lies at the foundation of ALD schemes and many other long or short manipulations. Limiting concentration to a sufficiently small amount makes it impossible for any investor singlehandedly to affect the stock's liquidity substantially. In addition, regulation over concentration of shareholdings would provide several other immediate benefits to the market.

- Perfect competition, with all of its desirable features, can become a reality in the secondary markets. No investor, individual, or institution is too large to set the price artificially, based on his position, or disrupt the normal mechanisms of the market. Therefore, antitrust regulation would actually be able to increase its effect more broadly than before.[11]
- In addition to perfect competition, stock trading becomes more equitable and transparent for every investor. This is the most fundamental protection of investors, particularly small investors. It is one of the key measures needed to prevent stock market crises.
- Limiting concentration to a small percentage of outstanding shares renders the lift stage uncertain though not completely irrelevant. This is because liquidity is well guarded from manipulation. Thus, one source of artificially created price volatility can be eliminated. The stability of the stock market in this aspect would be vastly improved.
- Limiting concentration makes the distribution stage different from the scenario of a large and dominant concentration. No investor can profit substantially from other investors' painful losses. That is, no investor has absolute advantage over other investors. Even if panic strikes one or numerous investors, due to the small positions now taken, the aggregate impact on a drop in prices would be substantially limited. Therefore, in this regard, crisis prevention and stability maintenance would be fundamentally improved. Unintentionally coordinated marketwide selling is beyond concentration regulation. In this rare scenario, even though every volume would be small, simultaneous selling by a large number of small investors can create major damage to the market as well as large investors. Therefore, Chapter 9 will address this issue with careful analysis and propose effective regulation.
- Heavy selling pressure due to large concentrations of sell shares would be basically eliminated. Together with regulation of price lifting and price depressing, which will be fully explored in the next chapter, bear raids would not be possible.
- Profitable long-term investments would be extensively protected and the encouragement of long-term investing carried out. The safety of nearly all investors and most listing companies would be vastly improved. The ecology of the stock market would also become more natural and sustainable for both capital raising and honest investment.
- To regulators, the most important consideration is that quantifiable, adjustable, and inexpensive measures are effected that enable daily operation with certainty. Particularly, such measures are meant to avoid expensive legal battles that can continue for years without resolution. It is our aim to increase regulatory effectiveness and efficiency.

■ A host of other socioeconomic benefits could accrue. For instance, peace of mind of stock investors can be made sustainable. Economic data in the areas related to the stock market are less volatile and more honest. Therefore, economic growth in this regard becomes more predictable from both a short-term and a long-term perspective. In other words, a more scientific stock market for all participants and the society is within sight.

CONCLUDING REMARKS AND FUTURE RESEARCH

Regulating large concentrations of shareholdings, in addition to other regulatory measures to be proposed, will afford investors a more perfect competition that strives for fairness and transparency. It will significantly improve protection of investors, particularly small investors, in addition to existing disclosure-oriented regulations. It will greatly enhance stock market stability by reducing artificial price volatility and maintenance of constant liquidity. It will bolster investors' confidence and prevent marketwide crises by reducing the price impact of each position.

Regulating concentration can be considered a key element of the antitrust measures that aid the stock market's drive to prevent monopolistic manipulation. It would be the first important constructive step to building perfect competition by ensuring increased fairness and transparency.

The next chapter presents unified analysis of varieties of trade-based tactics aimed for price lifting. The regulatory measures proposed in the two chapters complete our recommendations for regulating trade-based manipulation.

As follow-up research, one can analyze other financial markets, such as futures markets, employing the methodologies developed in this chapter. Another possible extension is to study whether the current proposals can be utilized as building blocks to be added to the future global financial architecture.

We asked in this chapter if financial markets in general, and stock markets in particular, can be manipulated. We also presented some evidence of futures market manipulation. There are theoretical models that show that in equilibrium, futures market manipulation can be profitable. These models were Kyle (1984) and Vila (1986) for futures markets with physical delivery, and Kumar and Seppi (1992) for futures markets with cash settlement at delivery. The book by Pirrong (1996) combines both empirical and theoretical work on the possibility and actual strategies of futures market manipulation with physical delivery. Hence, we do have indications that market manipulation in futures markets still exists.

The mechanism of manipulation they describe is similar to the ALD scheme we presented in this chapter and has the following characteristics at each stage:

- Accumulation: In futures markets, the trader is required to post a good-faith deposit, a fraction of the value of the security. That is, accumulation is much cheaper. If the contract is settled by physical delivery of the product, accumulation also happens through the purchase and storage of the underlying commodity. This might be a reason why several famous and rampant futures market manipulation cases are corners.
- Lift: The methods described by Kumar and Seppi (1992) and others are trade-based manipulation in the underlying spot market, to profit on a futures market long manipulation scheme. It is a cross-market lift. We discuss lifting techniques of trade-based manipulation in Chapter 4, and techniques of information-based manipulation in Chapters 5 through 8.
- Distribution: For futures, the distribution is guaranteed. There is no real risk for the manipulator that he cannot exit his position. The reason is that when the futures contract was created, a counterparty, which is usually the exchange itself, agreed to settle the contract on the delivery date.

Overall, we can conclude that manipulation in futures markets exists, and high concentration is one of the key requirements of those manipulations that can generate systemic risk. Therefore, the recommendations on limiting accumulation in the stock market we propose here can be applied as a significant step toward preventing market manipulation in the futures market.

NOTES

1. This chapter was presented at the Asian Finance Association 2011 International Conference: "Frontiers in Finance: Asia-Pacific and Beyond," Macau, China, July 10–13, 2011.
2. Quantity monopoly means large and dominant concentration of shares in a publicly traded company. It is mainly addressed in Chapters 3 and 4. Information monopoly is potentially price-moving information that receives substantial publicity and credibility. It is fully analyzed in Chapter 8, but the concept is introduced in Chapter 6 and partially developed in Chapter 7.
3. Some of the literature finds that it is difficult to prosecute manipulation in financial markets (Fishel and Ross 1991; Markham 1991; Kyle and Viswanathan 2008). However, we seek to propose preventive measures at the operational level and avoid legal involvement.

4. In stock pools or bull pools, "a number of traders pooled their resources to boom a particular stock. They appointed a pool manager." The pool manager manipulates the stock using trade-based or information-based techniques (Galbraith 1979).

5. Wash sales are "[i]mproper transactions in which there is no genuine change in actual ownership of the security or derivative contract" (IOSCO 2000). What we call matched orders are called improper matched orders by IOSCO: "[t]ransactions where both buy and sell orders are entered at the same time, with the same price and quantity by different but colluding parties" (IOSCO 2000). See IOSCO (2000) for the definition of different types of manipulative methods, as defined by the International Organization of Securities Commissions (IOSCO).

6. We define a stock market cycle with significant losses as one with consecutive trading days with at least a 5 percent total loss—that is, every day of the cycle the market index lost value, and it totaled at least 5 percent. The loss is calculated as the difference between the closing price of the last day and the closing price prior to the first day, divided by the latter. We count the number of cycles with at least 5 percent and at least 10 percent losses. Market manipulation usually results in a severe drop in the stock price once the manipulation is over. Therefore, the frequency and severity of the consecutive day's losses might provide an indication of the existence and frequency of severe market manipulation.

7. According to IOSCO (2000), marking the close means "[b]uying or selling securities . . . at the close of the market in an effort to alter the closing price of the security. . . . "

8. IOSCO (2000) definition of advancing the bid is "[i]ncreasing the bid for a security or derivative to increase its price." Fake trading involves placing an order for a limited time period that is reported on a public display facility to give the impression of activity or price movement in a security but canceling the order before execution.

9. As discussed earlier, both large concentration of shareholding and inducement of high trading speed are involved in a manipulation scheme. The term *pump-and-dump* may be vivid, but it does not connote the importance of high concentration. Therefore, we prefer to use the term *the ALD scheme* throughout.

10. The first antitrust legal framework in the world emerged in the United States in the post–Civil War era, initiated by the Sherman Act of 1890. Section 1 of the act prohibits mergers that would tend to create a monopoly or undue market dominance. It also prohibits price-fixing arrangements. Section 2 applies to firms that already dominate their market, and provides the right and the ways to reduce the monopoly power of the firm, usually by slicing up some part of the company, or demanding divestiture. With the addition of the Clayton Act and the Federal Trade Commission Acts, both passed in 1914, these three laws comprised the substantive framework for U.S. antitrust policy (Viscusi, et al. 1995). The Hart-Scott-Rodino Act of 1976 completes the basic arsenal of antitrust statutes.

11. There is a manipulation tactic, advancing the bid, which is seen in several prosecution cases released by HKSFC and SEBI (see Tables 3.4 through 3.5). It means "increasing the bid for a security or derivative to increase its price" (IOSCO 2000). It is not based on absolute trade size. This tactic is an important destructive force in perfect competition. How to resist this tactic effectively will be treated in the next chapter on regulation of price lifting.

CHAPTER 4

Preventing Stock Market Crises (II)

Regulating Trade-Based Price Lifting

Xin Yan

Lawrence R. Klein

Viktoria Dalko

Ferenc Gyurcsány

Michael H. Wang[1]

Inducing numerous trading volumes to follow in a short time period is the objective of the manipulator at the lift stage of the Accumulation-Lift-Distribution (ALD) scheme. Generating large price impact is the natural tactic to carry out the objective. However, after distribution of large quantities of accumulated shares, if no other large buy volumes enter trading in the stock, the share price will collapse; this may result in substantial losses for numerous investors and has the potential to lead to a stock market crisis. Large price impact can also be generated by heavy short selling or simply releasing large sell positions. Therefore, large price impact has to be regulated to protect investors, prevent crises, and maintain a stable stock market. This chapter, as a continuation of Chapter 3, focuses on price lifting in the ALD manipulation scheme and other related scenarios. For the purpose of surveillance and regulatory proposals, selected cases out of 103 prosecution cases from five regulatory agencies in both developed and developing economies are closely examined. The anatomy of trading activities of an investor during one trading day reveals nine variables that provide areas for surveillance and regulatory measures. The unified and practical approach based on the nine variables may be considered as solid candidates for proposal for securities regulators in their search for quantifiable, adjustable, and inexpensive measures to improve daily monitoring and regulatory operations.

HOW IS LARGE PRICE IMPACT BY OTHER INVESTORS INDUCED?

Recall that in the ALD manipulation scheme, two key elements are present. One focuses on building a large and dominant concentration of shares. The other induces numerous buy volumes in a relatively short time period, or a high buying speed. The latter can be more pervasive because a large share concentration is not always necessary to induce fast price lifting in other forms of long manipulation rather than in an ALD scheme. So how does a manipulator induce high buying speeds?

Generating large price impact is the natural tactic. For that purpose, a manipulator can choose from several options. The common option is trading large volumes. The literature provides abundant research on the price impact of trading volumes. Therefore, we start by reviewing research results pertinent to this aspect.[2]

EMPIRICAL RESEARCH ON VOLUME-BASED PRICE IMPACT

Since the literature on price impact by trading volume is abundant and data quality and processing have been improved greatly during the last 40 years, the literature review will be divided into two parts using Karpoff (1987) as the watershed study.

Kraus and Stoll (1972) find that block trades of 10,000 shares or more by institutions do affect market prices, with the average permanent price change estimated at around 1 percent. Their regression results clearly demonstrate that institutions' large-size trades affect daily price changes. This was perhaps the first empirical study to clearly establish that large volumes indeed affect equity prices. Holthausen, Leftwich, and Mayers (1987) also find a positive correlation between percentage price changes and trading volume increases for block trading.

Karpoff (1987) reviewed both the empirical and the theoretical literature, up to December 1986, to analyze the relationship between the trading volume (V) and the corresponding price change (dP), as well as its absolute value ($|dP|$). For stock markets, Karpoff's summary is that both $|dP| - V$ and $dP-V$ have positive correlation. This relationship exists in high-frequency (transaction level), daily, and even weekly observations. Therefore, a positive correlation is found to be almost universal.

Black Monday, October 19, 1987, drew additional research attention to institutional trades. The main reason may be the Brady Report (1988), since it finds that surprisingly few institutional traders triggered the precipitous price drop. This handful of institutions sold a historically high volume of shares in one day. The report concludes that a few traders moved a relatively illiquid market with large trades.

Lam, Li, and Wong (1990) analyzed the relationship between the variance of daily closing prices and the trading volume of the 49 constituent stocks of the Hang Seng Index between 1984 and 1988. An interesting finding in their work is that five stocks and the Hang Seng Index's variance showed a convex relationship with volume in 1987 while in all other years the relationship was concave. History recounts that on Black Thursday of October 24, 1987, the Hang Seng Index dropped 45 percent (Zheng and Huang 2006). Hasbrouck (1991) finds that the price impact of a trade is a positive and concave function of the trading volume. His data derives from the New York Stock Exchange (NYSE) and the American Stock Exchange (AMEX) as well as consolidated regional exchanges recorded for more than 62 trading days in the first quarter of 1989.

Gallant, Rossi, and Tauchen (1992) have studied the daily closing value of the S&P 500 Index and the daily share volume traded on the NYSE from 1928 through 1987. Adjusted for calendar and trend effects, they find that the daily trading volume is positively and nonlinearly related to the magnitude of the daily price change. Hausman, Lo, and MacKinlay (1992) examine more than 100 stocks traded on the NYSE between January 4, 1988, and December 30, 1988, to estimate the conditional distribution of trade-to-trade price changes. The contribution of the paper is that it allows for and demonstrates path dependence of price changes: that previous order flow—price and volume—as well as time between trades does affect the price impact of the next trade. In addition, the graphs of the six sample companies illustrate that more liquid stocks have a smaller price impact from the same magnitude of trade.

Chan and Lakonishok (1993) find that institutional purchases result in a principal-weighted permanent price impact of 0.34 percent. The magnitude cited is smaller than that indicated in previous research because the authors do not distinguish between small and large trades, while the former concentrate on block trades only. Chan and Lakonishok (1995) investigate the price impact associated with trade packages. They find a rather sizeable average price change from the opening on the package's first day to the close on the last day at nearly 1 percent for buys, and -0.35 percent for sells. Wang (1994) concludes decisively that trading volume is always positively correlated with absolute price changes, whenever the market consists of informational and noninformational investors.

Keim and Madhavan (1996) examine unique data of only prenegotiated trades of a single institutional trader that trades in non-large-capitalization stocks. The database covers 5,625 block trades traded in the upstairs market during the period from 1985 to 1992. They find that price impact is positively and significantly correlated with trade size. The magnitude of the price impact exceeds that in most of the previous studies, since the investment fund examined traded smaller market capitalization, therefore less liquid, stocks. Their model predicts that the temporary price impact or liquidity effect of block trades is a concave function of order size.

Zhang (1999) belongs to the burgeoning literature of econophysics and he employs the concept of entropy to study the same relationship. He presents an argument for a square-root relationship between price changes and excess demand in stock markets. Plerou, et al. (2002) is a classic econophysics paper, measuring the impact of excess demand (and excess supply) on price changes in transaction-level data. Excess demand (supply) is defined here as the net buyer-initiated (seller-initiated) trade above the seller-initiated (buyer-initiated) trade at the given price. For the 116 most traded stocks in 1994 and 1995, Plerou, et al. find that the market impact function is concave and claim that the concave functional form is universal, whether the time interval for netting out demand and supply ranges from 15 minutes to one day. But the question remains of whether the concave form becomes convex, at least for certain stocks, during a crisis, which Lam, Li, and Wong (1990) noted in the Hong Kong Stock Market during 1987.

Chiyachantana et al. (2004) investigate the price impact of institutional trades in bullish (January 1997 to March 1998) and bearish (January 2001 to September 2001) stock markets of 37 countries. Several conclusions are drawn. One is that the larger the order relative to average volume, the higher the price impact. The other is that buy orders have higher price impact than sell orders of the same size in bullish markets, while sell orders have higher price impact than buy orders in bearish markets. The overall price impact for all international trades achieved by Chiyachantana et al. (2004) is 0.45 percent for 1997 to 1998 and 0.37 percent for 2001. Comparatively, Perold and Sirri (1998) had an estimate of 0.99 percent for price impact based on data from 1987 to 1991. Domowitz, et al. (2001) report 0.25 percent price impact for 1996 to 1998.

Gabaix, et al. (2006) provide ample empirical evidence of a square root relationship between a large trading volume and its price impact. Their data cover very large institutions trading huge quantities. The model they have developed is based on the observed power law distribution of fund size, return, and volume. Because their finding that large price fluctuations are caused by large institutions' frequent trading with sizeable orders even in the absence of information, they suggest this phenomenon has the potential to lead to extreme price fluctuations, and, as such, to extreme events such as Black Monday. Alexander and Peterson (2007) also use an increasing concave relationship between volume and stock price change, which was first documented by Lam, Li, and Wong (1990) and Hashbrouck (1991).

In summary, sizeable evidence demonstrates positive correlation between trading volumes and price changes for the past 40 years. Particularly since 1987, as research has focused more on large institutions, the literature has accepted a positive relationship between volume and price change as a very robust, general relationship. In addition, concave price impact functions have been found by numerous authors during the past two decades. Convex functions have also been reported by several researchers. In other words, the literature of volume-based price impact has solidly established that large volumes do move share prices nontrivially. Its repeated findings strongly support the theoretical literature in that manipulation with large volumes only is empirically possible.

For this chapter, we note that most studies reviewed with quantitative outcomes have arrived at average price impact of buy volumes around 1 percent. Does this agree with the results derived from the prosecution cases we collect?

THE SEBI PROSECUTION CASES

Out of the 103 prosecution cases drawn from five regulatory agencies in Chapter 3, nearly all of SEBI's (Securities and Exchange Board of India) cases explicitly list price and volume data due to manipulation (Table 3.5). The average daily price impact in terms of the share price increase due to manipulation is thus calculated based on the manipulation period and price data. Figure 4.1 exhibits distribution of the average daily price impact estimates of the 28 cases in Table 3.5. Figure 4.2 groups the average daily price impact under five categories, that is, 0 to 5 percent, 5 to 10 percent, 10 to 15 percent, 15 to 20 percent, and above 20 percent.

Out of 28 SEBI cases, six have average daily price impact estimates smaller than 2 percent. They represent only 20.7 percent of the cases. Even though the estimates of the daily price impact include other investors' contributions, these percentages still provide an understanding that there is some degree of correlation between the estimates and the previous results obtained in the literature. At the same time, there are many estimates above 2 percent (79.3 percent) or even above 20 percent (14.29 percent). This

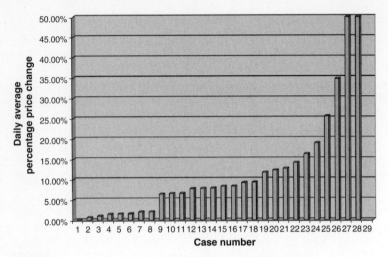

FIGURE 4.1   Average Daily Price Impact in the Target Stock

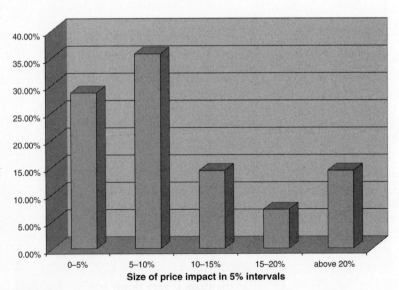

FIGURE 4.2   Distribution of the Daily Average Price Impact Estimates

outstanding abnormality warrants closer investigation. One particularly interesting question arises: What are the essential variables behind the tactics used by the manipulators to achieve very large price impact?

THE MANIPULATION TACTICS USED IN PRICE LIFTING

In the lift stage of an ALD scheme, all manipulation tactics are directed toward marking up share prices in a relatively short time period. The manipulator can induce large buy quantities within short time durations so share prices are pushed up mainly by other investors. The manipulator can also create and sustain regularly and significantly rising prices. The purpose is to render a fast-rising stock very attractive so that the manipulator can quietly distribute his holdings when sufficient buy volumes of other investors flow in at the inflated price level.

During the lift stage of an ALD scheme or general price lifting, several manipulation tactics are evident among the 103 prosecution cases listed in Chapter 3. They fall into two main types, trade-based or information-based (Allen and Gale 1992). Trade-based manipulation tactics represent fictitious trading that includes wash sale (self-dealing) and matched orders (cross-dealing), advancing the bid, marking the close, and fake trading. Information-based tactics are treated in Chapter 8. Trade-based tactics are often carried out with collusion or multiple nominee accounts. In the following, we will select dozens of typical cases from the 103 cases studied according to the trade-based manipulation tactics, that is, fictitious trading (wash sale and matched orders), advancing the bid, marking the close, and fake trading. Six more China Securities Regulatory Commission (CSRC) cases are added regarding fake trading, which makes the total cases studied 109 in this chapter. Several cases studied involved more than one type of manipulation tactic.

Fictitious Trading

Fictitious trading includes both wash sale and matched orders, with the former being self-dealing. The latter, matched orders, is cross-dealing and requires collusion or multiple nominee accounts. Whether self-dealing or cross-dealing, the essence is the same in that almost simultaneous trading of two opposite orders of the same quantity and at the same price is used in either type. In this sense, we do not specifically distinguish between wash sale and matched orders. Rather, we rely on figures drawn from fictitious trading in general.

Fictitious trading involves several variables. Two orders are placed almost simultaneously except when the stock is very thinly traded. The trading directions of the two orders are always opposite. The numbers of shares in the two orders are precisely or nearly equal. Most likely, advancing the bid is also included even though exceptions may exist. This is a crucial element that is often ignored by regulators. Without advancing the bid, how can share prices be lifted by a tangible 20 percent with only two fictitious trades of 200 shares each (see Table 4.4)? Since the bid of the buy order is equal to the ask of the sell order, it warrants instant execution. Depending on how heavy daily turnover is in the stock, both single and multiple fictitious trades are probable. The key is to effectively raise share prices within short time periods while not even one or a negligible number of costly shares are added to the already accumulated, less expensive shares. In other words, net ownership in the traded stock has no meaningful change.

Fictitious trading has most often been used by numerous manipulators in the selected CSRC and SEBI cases. In the Hong Kong Securities and Futures Commission (HKSFC) and Japan Securities and Exchange Surveillance Commission (JSESC) cases, fictitious trading has also been frequently seen. Surprisingly, very few instances have been found in Securities and Exchange Commission (SEC) cases. Table 4.1 lists seven CSRC cases with available data detailing fictitious trading.

The seven CSRC cases in Table 4.1 show a large concentration of shareholdings, high trading frequency, and numerous nominee accounts pursuing fictitious trading. However, time intervals between matched fictitious trades are not available for any listed case. Daily price increase information is not available either. The lack of these data prevents us from further investigating these trades. However, the rampant usage of fictitious trading is evident. Next we list six SEBI fictitious trading cases individually that presented price lifting data due to manipulation.

In the following, we highlight the key fictitious trading features by presenting selected details of the six SEBI cases that are listed in Table 3.5 in Chapter 3. The time intervals between matched fictitious trades are examined first. The tactic, advancing the bid, frequently used in fictitious trading, derives from the price lifting patterns seen in the two selected SEBI cases. Fictitious trading is also found in price pegging. One case in particular presents many interesting details.

Time Intervals between Matched Orders Are Negligibly Short

- Case 1. Order against M/s. Porecha Global Securities Pvt. Ltd. and Shri Arun Porecha (WTM/PS/IVD/ID-3/03/Sept/09) (released on September 18, 2009)

  Large matched orders were observed between Arun Porecha (AP) and Porecha Global Securities Pvt. Ltd. (PGSPL) as well as between Jayant

TABLE 4.1 Seven CSRC Fictitious Trading Cases

Manipulator(s)/Target Stock(s)	Manipulation Duration	Investment	Concentration of Tradable Shares (%)	Self-dealing Trading Days (% of total)	Maximum of Vs/Vt (%)	Days with Trades (% of total)	Number of Accounts
Hantang Securities/ Hengda Real Estate	09/26/2000– 09/02/2004	RMB 0.7 BLN	79.48%	52.48%	95.79%	52.84%	2,296
Hantang Securities/ Nanfang Shareholding	01/14/2002– 09/03/2004	RMB 0.57 BLN	63.11%	64.50%	79.92%	64.50%	1,696
Cui Junshan/Jinde Fazhan	12/04/2000– 07/20/2006	RMB 2.1 BLN	81.33%	64.58%	99.59%	97.71%	3,917
Hantang Securities/ Baihua Village	01/10/2003– 09/03/2004	RMB 0.17 BLN	34.81%	64.72%	80.04%	64.72%	2,495
Hantang Securities/ Feida Environmental	07/22/2002– 09/03/2004	RMB 0.4 BLN	59.26%	65.00%	75.60%	65.00%	4,294
Hantang Securities/ Langchao Software	06/27/2002– 09/03/2004	RMB 0.77 BLN	74.05%	79.70%	79.18%	80.64%	1,872
Xianghe Holding, et al./ Sanmu Group	11/05/2001– 01/31/2005	RMB 4.4 BLN	80.00%	85.60%	98.80%	97.80%	3,879

TABLE 4.2 Time Intervals of Fictitious Trades between PGSPL and AP as Well as JAK

Date	Time	Member	Buy/Sell	Order Size	Share Price
10/23/2000	14:03:33	PGSPL	Sell	100,000	Rs. 96
10/23/2000	14:03:33	PGSPL	Buy	100,000	Rs. 96
10/24/2000	12:40:47	AP	Buy	100,000	Rs. 96
10/24/2000	12:40:47	PGSPL	Sell	100,500	Rs. 96
10/25/2000	13:21:30	PGSPL	Sell	100,000	Rs. 96
10/25/2000	13:21:31	JAK	Buy	100,000	Rs. 96
10/27/2000	11:57:59	PGSPL	Sell	200,000	Rs. 100
10/27/2000	11:58:01	JAK	Buy	200,000	Rs. 100
10/30/2000	12:12:24	JAK	Buy	100,000	Rs. 100
10/30/2000	12:12:24	PGSPL	Sell	100,200	Rs. 100
10/31/2000	13:30:31	PGSPL	Sell	100,000	Rs. 100
10/31/2000	13:30:33	JAK	Buy	100,000	Rs. 100
11/01/2000	15:18:10	JAK	Buy	100,000	Rs. 98.85
11/01/2000	15:18:12	PGSPL	Sell	100,000	Rs. 98.85
11/02/2000	12:22:30	PGSPL	Sell	100,000	Rs. 100
11/02/2000	12:22:31	JAK	Buy	100,000	Rs. 100
11/03/2000	14:30:55	JAK	Buy	100,000	Rs. 105
11/03/2000	14:30:57	PGSPL	Sell	102,500	Rs. 105
11/06/2000	11:28:10	AP	Buy	100,500	Rs. 107
11/06/2000	11:28:11	PGSPL	Sell	100,500	Rs. 107
11/07/2000	11:27:20	AP	Buy	100,000	Rs. 115
11/07/2000	11:27:20	PGSPL	Sell	100,000	Rs. 115
11/08/2000	14:36:41	JAK	Buy	100,000	Rs. 115
11/08/2000	14:36:41	PGSPL	Sell	100,000	Rs. 115
11/09/2000	12:34:41	JAK	Buy	100,000	Rs. 114.95
11/09/2000	12:34:42	PGSPL	Sell	100,000	Rs. 114.95
11/10/2000	12:49:32	PGSPL	Sell	100,000	Rs. 111
11/10/2000	12:49:34	JAK	Buy	100,000	Rs. 114.90
11/10/2000	12:52:39	PGSPL	Sell	99,900	Rs. 114.90
11/10/2000	12:52:40	JAK	Buy	99,900	Rs. 114.90
11/10/2000	12:53:46	PGSPL	Buy	99,900	Rs. 111
11/10/2000	12:53:47	JAK	Sell	99,900	Rs. 111

Amerchand Kalidas (JAK) and PGSPL. Table 4.2 shows the details. Special attention should be paid to the time intervals between matched orders.

For all of the 16 pairs of matched orders, the time intervals fall between 0 and 2 seconds. In seven sell-and-buy pairs, the order sizes are equal. In nine buy-and-sell pairs, six order pairs have equal sizes, while the other three have marginally larger sell orders than buy orders. Regarding the transaction prices of the 16 pairs, 15 pairs have equal prices. In one scenario, the buying price is 3.5 percent higher than the selling price, with the buy order being entered 2 seconds later than the sell order.

This prosecution case shows four aspects of fictitious trading. It always contains one buy order and one sell order. There is one pair where both the buyer and the seller are the same trader. The other 15 pairs are matched orders between two colluding brokers. The time interval between the two orders in any pair is negligibly short. It never exceeds 2 seconds. The quantities of the two orders, depending on which order is placed ahead of the other, are basically equal. The prices quoted and the actual execution prices are, in general, equal between the two orders in the 16 pairs.

- Case 2. Order against M/s. Sanchit Financial and Management Services Ltd. (WTM/TCN/160/ID3/JAN/09) (released on January 22, 2009)

This case is comprised of equal order sizes and executed quantities in matched orders but with more diverse time intervals, ranging from 3 seconds to 44 seconds. These varying time intervals are still negligible since the stock is thinly traded. The two colluding parties are SFML and NAM (see Table 4.3).

TABLE 4.3   Time Intervals of Fictitious Trades between SFML and NAM

Date	Time	Member	Buy/Sell	Order Size[*]	Time Interval
01/07/2000	14:50:10	NAM	Buy	500	
01/07/2000	14:50:23	SFML	Sell	500	13 sec
01/07/2000	14:50:49	NAM	Buy	500	
01/07/2000	14:51:03	SFML	Sell	500	14 sec
01/07/2000	14:51:34	NAM	Buy	500	
01/07/2000	14:51:48	SFML	Sell	500	14 sec
01/07/2000	14:52:02	NAM	Buy	300	
01/07/2000	14:52:09	SFML	Sell	300	7 sec
01/07/2000	14:57:46	NAM	Buy	1,000	
01/07/2000	14:57:49	SFML	Sell	1,000	3 sec
01/07/2000	14:58:36	NAM	Buy	800	
01/07/2000	14:58:47	SFML	Sell	800	11 sec
01/07/2000	15:15:46	SFML	Buy	2,000	
01/07/2000	15:15:49	NAM	Sell	2,000	3 sec
01/07/2000	15:16:51	SFML	Buy	1,600	
01/07/2000	15:17:11	NAM	Sell	1,600	20 sec
01/17/2000	13:44:46	NAM	Sell	900	
01/17/2000	13:45:30	SFML	Buy	900	44 sec
01/18/2000	11:32:36	NAM	Sell	1,500	
01/18/2000	11:32:54	NAM	Buy	1,500	18 sec

[*]All orders were executed in full as placed.

This case confirms the four aspects of fictitious trading discussed in Case 1. There is one self-dealing occasion made by NAM. The other trades consist of matched orders between the two colluding parties, SFML and NAM. The time intervals between the matched orders are generally negligible. They vary from 3 seconds to 44 seconds, with the majority being below 14 seconds. The share quantities of the two orders are exactly equal, regardless of whether a buy order is placed ahead of a sell order. The only missing link is that the prices of the matching orders are not provided by the court order. However, the prosecutor indicated that the quotes remain the same for the matched orders on all fictitious trading occasions.

Advancing the Bid Is Involved in Fictitious Trading

* Case 3. Order against M/s. Purshottam Lal Kejdiwal (WTM/KMA/ERO/ IVD/121/08/2009) (released on August 21, 2009)

The prosecuted broker, Purshottam Lal Kejdiwal (PLK), was manipulating the stock BIL by trading exclusively matched orders with another broker, Badri Prasad & Sons (BP), during the investigation period from June 9 to September 16, 2005. Table 4.4 lists selected transaction data.

This table clearly shows the price lifting path taken through the execution of matched orders with the advancing-the-bid tactic being embedded. However, as in many other court orders examined, the prosecutor did not point out the importance of advancing the bid in generating price increases. There were no other investors in the stock except the two colluding manipulators. With orders ranging between 200 shares and 1,000 shares, the share price was pushed up at a daily average of 19.7 percent for a total of 498 percent within just eight trading days. The only explanation for these

TABLE 4.4   Fictitious Trades with Advancing the Bid by PLK and BP in BIL

Date	Previous Closing Price (Rs.)	Opening Price (Rs.)	Exchange Volume	Broker Volume	Price Increase
08/31/2005	2.35	2.85	1,000	500	21.30%
09/01/2005	2.85	3.4	1,000	500	19.30%
09/02/2005	3.4	4.05	1,000	500	19.10%
09/09/2005	5.75	6.85	600	300	19.10%
09/12/2005	6.85	8.2	2,000	1,000	19.70%
09/13/2005	8.2	9.8	1,000	500	19.50%
09/14/2005	9.8	11.75	400	200	19.90%
09/15/2005	11.75	14.05	460	230	19.60%

dramatic and consecutive price increases is the higher bid of each order over the previous closing price, which is also the last traded price. This is a solid example of fast price increases due to fictitious trading with large bid advances in a thinly traded stock.

- Case 4. Order against M/s. S. Jhunjhunwala & Co. (WTM/KMA/ERO/ IVD/166/11/2009) (released on November 20, 2009)

The quote from the court order reads, "The order log would show that the Broker had placed orders on both the buy and the sell side for the same quantity and price (though price was higher than the previous days' price)." This clearly shows using the advancing-the-bid tactic in fictitious trading conducted by S. Jhunjhunwala & Co. (SJ) and his colluding partner in consecutively lifting up daily prices in the stock (TCL) (see Table 4.5).

Details further add to the evidence presented in the paragraph quoted from the court order. First, advancing the bid existed, particularly when there were only 100 shares in the daily volume in the stock, while the share prices increased by the amounts from 4.6 percent to 4.8 percent. Second, it is certain that advancing the bid was applied by the manipulator and his colluding partner on each of the eight consecutive trading days, since there are no other investors. Third, because of the precisely matched orders on each of the fictitious trading occasions, the manipulator incurred no trading cost other than the commissions but effectively lifted up the share prices by a daily average of 4.7 percent and in total 44.3 percent in eight consecutive trading days.

TABLE 4.5   Advancing the Bid in Fictitious Trading by SJ and Partner in TCL

Date	Previous Closing Price (Rs.)	Opening Price (Rs.)	Exchange Volume	Broker Volume*	Price Increase
04/21/2004	74.5	77.9	100	50 (CD)	4.60%
04/22/2004	77.9	81.55	100	50 (CD)	4.70%
04/23/2004	81.55	85.1	24,000	24,000 (SD)	4.40%
04/26/2004	85.1	89.2	8,000	8,000 (SD)	4.80%
04/27/2004	89.2	93.45	8,000	8,000 (SD)	4.80%
04/28/2004	93.45	97.9	100	50 (CD)	4.80%
04/29/2004	97.9	102.6	5,000	5,000 (SD)	4.80%
04/30/2004	102.6	107.5	100	50 (CD)	4.80%

*CD means cross-dealing, or matched orders, and SD self-dealing or wash sale.

- Case 5. Orders against M/s. Mukesh Dokania & Co. (WTM/TCN/ERO/ 98/JAN/2009) (released on January 19, 2009)

The manipulator is Mukesh Dokania (MD). The issuing company is Ashika Credit Capital Ltd. (ACL). The manipulator bought 947,700 shares, which is 50 percent of the total buy volume from July 12 to October 15, 2001. He sold 947,700 shares, which is also 50 percent of the total sell volume. Table 4.6 lists the trading data during the investigation period from July 12 to October 15, 2001.[3]

TABLE 4.6 Mixed Fictitious Trading with Nonmanipulative Trading by MD in ACCL

Date	Buy Quantity	Buy Rate (Rs)	Sell Quantity	Sell Rate (Rs)	Price Increase (Rs)	Price Increase (%)
07/12/2001	90,000	5.5	90,000	5.5	0	0
07/13/2001	90,000	5.5	90,000	5.5	0	0
07/16/2001	6,000	8.1	6,000	8.1	2.6	47.30%
07/17/2001	100	10.1	0	0	2	24.70%
07/18/2001	100	10.4	0	0	0.3	3.00%
07/19/2001	101,000	9.6	100,000	9.6	−0.8	−7.70%
07/20/2001	140,000	9.6	140,000	9.6	0	0
07/24/2001	0	0	100	12	2.4	25.00%
07/25/2001	55,000	12.5	55,000	12.5	0.5	4.20%
07/26/2001	0	0	200	13.7	1.2	9.60%
07/27/2001	300	14.3	0	0	0.6	4.40%
07/30/2001	150	15.8	150	15.2	1.5*	10.50%
07/31/2001	0	0	200	16.6	0.6*	3.80%
08/01/2001	0	0	50	17.5	0.9	5.40%
08/02/2001	100	18.5	0	0	1	5.70%
08/09/2001	102,000	20.3	102,000	20.3	1.8	9.70%
08/13/2001	50	24	0	0	3.7	18.20%
08/14/2001	91,500	25.2	91,500	25.2	1.2	5.00%
08/21/2001	50	32.7	0	0	7.5	29.80%
08/24/2001	0	0	500	37.7	5	15.30%
08/27/2001	75,600	38.4	75,600	38.4	0.7	1.90%
09/03/2001	50,000	39.9	49,750	39.9	1.5	3.90%
10/08/2001	8,000	39	8,000	39	−0.9	−2.20%
10/12/2001	40,000	43.7	40,000	43.7	4.7	12.10%
10/15/2001	100,000	42.8	100,000	42.8	−0.9	−2.10%
Total	949,950		949,050		37.3	678%

This is an actual trading log including both manipulative and non manipulative trades. The price lifting path is not particularly consistent or uniform. But the eventual price increase of 678 percent in three months remains tremendous. This stock may not be thinly traded because the manipulator's buy volume of nearly one million shares is only 50 percent of the total buy volume.

Fictitious Trading Can Be Used for Price Pegging

- Case 6. Order against M/s. Dhanlaxmi Cotex Ltd. in the matter of M/s. Soundcraft Industries Ltd. (WTM/TCN/100/IVD3/Jan/09) (released on January 20, 2009)

To maintain the price level so that reissuing preferred shares (SIL) by Dhanlaxmi Cotex Ltd. would be successful, a number of brokers at the Bombay Stock Exchange (BSE) including Kolar Sharex Pvt. Ltd. (KSPL), AMS Stock Management Pvt. Ltd. (AMS), Churiwala Securities Pvt. Ltd. (CSPL), M R Share Broking Pvt. Ltd. (MRSB), and Park Light Investment Pvt. Ltd. (PLIPL) indulged in circular trading at BSE in their attempt to create artificial volumes. Analysis of trades conducted by the prosecutor for selected dates during the period of investigation reveals the pattern of fictitious trading among the aforesaid BSE brokers. The uniqueness of this case is that three, four, and five brokers worked in concert to make circular fictitious trading, respectively. And the manipulation is not intended for profit but for the purpose of price pegging. Three scenarios are selected to demonstrate that three, four, and five brokers are colluding in fictitious trading in circular fashion. Arrows indicate the flow of sell orders from one broker to another. Simultaneously matching buy orders are not shown.

1. Three brokers colluded in fictitious trading on July 2, 2001
   KSPL: 1,000 shares → CSPL: 900 shares → PLIPL: 1,100 shares → KSPL
2. Four brokers were colluding in fictitious trading on July 2, 2001
   AMS: 2,700 shares → KSPL: 3,500 shares → MRSB: 1,300 shares → PLIPL: 1,450 shares → AMS
3. Five brokers were colluding in fictitious trading on July 30, 2001
   KSPL: 730 shares → PLIPL: 1,650 shares → MRSB → CSPL+ AMS+KSPL
   MRSB: 600 shares → CSPL: 800 shares → KSPL
   MSRB: 500 shares → AMS: 625 shares → KSPL
   MSRB: 445 shares → KSPL

In this case, serious advancing-the-bid tactics may not be included because the brokers' goal is to maintain the share price above a certain level. And orders are matched between any two brokers, since no broker intends to accumulate any shares. Trading in short time intervals remains a concern for brokers because they want to avoid as many transaction costs as possible. The main purpose of this sort of concerted fictitious trading is to create the appearance of many buy volumes entering into trading to induce other investors to buy the stock being manipulated.

In summary, fictitious trading involves more aspects than other known forms of long manipulation. Its effectiveness in price lifting and efficiency in reducing trading costs are outstanding among all the manipulation tactics studied in this chapter. Since fictitious trading relies on a multifaceted approach, one needs to understand these facets so corresponding regulatory measures can be proposed to monitor and prevent this form of stock price manipulation.

The first facet is advancing the bid. A large bid advance provides the key to achieving consecutive and dramatic price increases. Hence, focusing on regulating bid advances will yield one effective measure. Because the time interval between two matched orders in fictitious trading is always negligible, this presents another facet in fictitious trading governing the manipulation of liquid stocks. For manipulation of thinly traded stocks, the time interval, in theory, may not necessarily be very short. But since detection is far easier if a few investors are trading, surveillance may be sufficient to curb fictitious trading. In this scenario, a quick price increase due to a small number of orders being placed can automatically act as an effective basis for surveillance. The third facet may concern the equal or nearly equal quantities of matched orders in fictitious trading. This provides a solid basis for surveillance. If orders placed by one trader have been consistently matched nearly instantly, by his own or other investors' opposite orders, then surveillance can readily generate a warning flag for regulators. Either no or a negligible change in net ownership is another area where regulation can play a valuable role.

Marking the Close and Advancing the Bid

Marking the close is often combined with advancing the bid. The distinction is that the former refers to advancing the bid at the closing minutes only.[4] The uniqueness in marking the close is that it gives no time for the market maker or matching computer when placing large numbers of buy orders in a short time near the close. To ensure a higher opening price on the next trading day, the bid of each buy order has to be higher than the best bid in the stock. These orders will pile up and be rolled over to the next trading day. Thus, the opening price will be effectively higher by generating an accumulation of buy orders at distinctively higher bids. Then the manipulator can sell all or part of the shares accumulated earlier at inflated prices the morning of the next trading day. This practice often causes the share prices to drop not too long after their peak in the morning. This explains many of the scenarios where share prices are marked up in the closing minutes of the market and the next day's opening prices are higher than the previous closing prices. For the first few minutes, the prices continue to rise. Very soon though, the prices peak and a sharp drop in their value follows.

Since marking the close is a special type of the advancing-the-bid manipulation, we list prosecution cases involving both tactics in the same table. We choose seven marking-the-close cases that have explicitly or implicitly indicated the closing price inflation out of 13 HKSFC cases presented in Chapter 3. These are listed in Table 4.7.

There is one SEBI case that explicitly prosecutes advancing-the-bid manipulation. Trade-by-trade data are shown in Table 4.8.

Lessons Learned from the Cases Listed in Tables 4.7 and 4.8:

- The order sizes for either advancing the bid or marking the close are not large because the manipulator does not want to risk increased trading costs. The size can be as small as 100 shares, but buying even such a small number of shares consecutively can push up the share price dramatically, for instance, more than 37 percent (Case 1 in Table 4.7).
- The bid advances can be from 4 percent to 150 percent higher than the market price.
- Numerous consecutive small orders are seen near the close in Case 1.
- Marking the close is locked in during the closing minutes, while advancing the bid can be employed anytime during the trading day (Table 4.8).
- Both marking the close and advancing the bid aim to increase share prices by placing small orders.

Marking the close can be used for short-term manipulation (Cases 2, 5, and 7 in Table 4.7). Another purpose is to reduce the margin deposit (Case 3 in Table 4.7). Doing so can also be used to mark up the closing price for the sake of improved performance of mutual funds during year-ends (Case 1 in Table 4.7), quarter-ends, or month-ends (Carhart, et al. 2002; Hillion and Suominen 2004; Comerton-Forde and Putniņš 2009).

The interesting fact is that the general advancing-the-bid cases are very few among prosecution cases studied. This may be because manipulation by advancing the bid incurs only nontrivial trading costs. It is not as efficient as fictitious trading that includes advancing the bid.

TABLE 4.7 Seven HKSFC Cases Involving Marking the Close and Advancing the Bid

Manipulator(s)/ Target Stock(s)	Manipulation Period	Number of Orders (Total Number of Shares)	Bid Over Market Price	Price Increase	Purpose
Wang Fang/ Fujian	12/30/1999	13 consecutive buy orders at 100 shares (1,300 shares)	Not available	From previous closing price HK$0.140 to HK$0.192 (37%)	A higher year-end closing price
Not disclosed/ China Development	01/02/2002– 03/07/2002	20 buy orders at 100 shares (2,000 shares)	2%–23%	Not available	Sale on next trading days
Poon Lak To, Joseph/ Pioneer Global	03/15, 23, and 27/2001	20 buy orders at 100 shares (2,000 shares) at each close	9%–18%	Not available	Reducing margin deposit
Choi Kam Tui/ Climax	07/04/2001– 09/21/2001	20 buy orders at 100 shares (2,000 shares) at each close	4%–150%	Not available	Sale at higher prices
Not disclosed/ SEEC	On a few days from 02/ 2002– 03/2002	7 buy orders (2,000 to 4,000 shares)	6–8 spreads higher	Not available	Sale at higher prices next day
Not disclosed/ MUI	01/09/2003– 05/21/2003	20 buy orders at 100 shares (2,000 shares)	Higher than market price	Pushed up the closing prices by 8% to 60% higher than previous closing prices	Inducing other investors to buy the stock
Wong Wei Yin Peter/SiS	05/18 and 20 and 06/09 and 15/2004	Several buy orders at 100 shares	Higher than market price	Pushed up the closing prices by 8% to 10% higher than previous closing prices	Sale at higher prices next days

TABLE 4.8 Trading Costs Incurred in Advancing-the-Bid Manipulation

SEBI Case of Shri Minoo Pestonji Manipulating APL Stock

Manipulation Period	Number of Buy Shares	Bid/Last Traded Price (Rs.)	Advance (Rs.)	Price Increase (%)	Trading Loss (Rs.)
On 08/16/2000 at 13:34:57	3,000	2.3/1.85	0.45	24.30%	1,350
On 08/21/2000 at 10:15:38	100	3.4/2.95	0.45	15.20%	45
On 08/22/2000 at 10:05:42	500	4.0/3.2	0.8	25.00%	400
On 08/28/2000 at 10:06:21	200	4.75/4.2	0.55	13.10%	110
On 08/30/2000 at 13:11:03	500	5.45/4.85	0.6	12.40%	300

Fake Trading

Compared to the ALD scheme, a large concentration of shares may not be required in fake trading because the lift phase is carried out within a time frame as short as minutes. Price increases raised by fake trading are as humble as a single digit in percentage. Strictly speaking, illiquidity is not needed to induce following buyers. Fake trading cases listed in the six CSRC announcements show these considerations.

The essence of fake trading is that it uses repeated fake orders placed with each bid just a bit below or occasionally a bit above the best bid, but these placed buy orders are quickly canceled before execution. This is because only the top five bids next to the best bid are displayed by exchanges under the CSRC. The manipulator's objective is to create the appearance that multiple large buy orders have been entering the bidding process within a very short time period, for instance, within a couple of trading hours. The manipulator expects numerous buyers will follow his lead, so that the share prices will be raised in a limited increment, say 3 percent, within one or two trading days. Then the manipulator will distribute all or most of the shares bought before the first fake order, at a slightly inflated price. Even though the profit derived from successful execution of each manipulation scheme is limited, the time period needed to achieve such gains is extremely short. This scheme can be repeated numerous times in just a month or so after the initial scheme was carried out. The collective profits reaped from numerous repeated manipulations can be substantial. The previous analysis is long manipulation oriented. Fake trading can also resort to short manipulation. In such cases, the process works in a manner opposite to the tactics employed by a long fake-trading scheme. The six CSRC fake-trading cases hand-collected for this chapter are listed in Table 4.9.

What Lessons Do the Six Fake-Trading Cases Listed in Table 4.9 Teach?

- Fake orders prove to be large. This is understandable because large order placement is needed to create the false impression of large volumes entering the bidding process. Therefore, large wealth is needed to generate repeated fake orders. In the six CSRC cases, funds used range from RMB18 million ($2.6 million) to RMB400 million ($58.8 million).

- Fake trading is linked to fast trading in order to realize the manipulator's objective to induce high demand in a short period of time. The highest frequency recorded was 12 orders (3.3 million shares) traded in 27 minutes, or 0.44 orders per minute. Put simply, fake trading is characterized by a short manipulation time period. Fake trading can be completed within half an hour, since price inflation can be as low as 1.29 percent, as noted in case 1. The longest time period noted was a little bit over one trading day, cited in case 2, in which the share price rose 4.84 percent.

- Fake orders are designed to be seen by other investors in order to create the false appearance of a continuously increasing high demand for the stock. In the six cases, the top five bids and the bottom five asks were displayed momentarily. Not one case involved a bid of a fake order outside the displayed bids and asks.

- Fake trading aims to distribute early accumulated shares at slightly or largely inflated prices. In the six cases, price inflation varied from 1.29 percent over a span of just 16.5 minutes to 15.7 percent executed in less than one trading day.

- This scheme bears zero cost; thus, it is the least expensive among the studied forms of manipulation used to lift prices within a short period of time.

In summary, there are three elements that are found in a fake trading scheme. The first involves large orders. The second element is incomplete display. The third feature is high frequency in order placements. In other words, the time intervals between two consecutive orders need to be very short. These three elements suggest implications for the section regarding surveillance and regulatory proposals, to be discussed shortly.

TABLE 4.9 Six CSRC Fake Trading Cases

Manipulator/ Target Stock	Manipulation Period	Number of Fake Orders	Number of Fake Shares	Price Increase (RMB)	Price Increase %	Numbers of Shares Sold	Profit Over Time*
Mo Jianjun/South Express	02/16/2007, 11:11:13– 11:27:40	4 buy orders	3,068,000	6.12–6.22	1.63%	153,700	RMB 21,518 over 16.5 minutes
Lu Daojun/4-D Shareholdings**	01/23/2008, 9:39:24– 10:07:12	12 buy orders	3,300,000	9.29–9.74	4.84%	1,582,993	RMB.349,600 over one day
Zhang Jianxiong/ ST Raw Medicine	07/03/2008, 11:07:22– 7/4/2008, 9:24:53	7 buy orders	5,130,000	4.91–5.68	15.70%	1,800,000	RMB 1,342,008 over one day
Mo Jianjun/ Comprehensive Arts	03/09/2007, 10:50:54– 11:20:44	10 buy orders	5,210,000	15.62–15.83	1.42%	154,900	RMB 32,529 over 30 minutes
Mo Jianjun/China Tungsten	03/26/2007, 14:16:27– 14:54:51	11 buy orders	7,152,900	14.93–15.12	1.29%	243,400	RMB 43,812 over 38.4 minutes
Zhou Jianming/ Datong Coal	06/26/2006 morning	61 buy orders	40,090,000	10.22–10.59	3.62%***	4,331,579	RMB 606,420 over one day

*For cases 1 to 3 and 6, no buying price or time period was given for the shares sold. Therefore, the profit made and time consumed are estimates based on the lowest bid placed by the manipulator. Also for cases 1 to 3, only one round of fake trading has been selected from each case for demonstration.

**Two accounts were used.

***Estimate is based on the minimum and maximum bidding prices.

ANATOMY OF AN INVESTOR'S TRADES IN A STOCK DURING A TRADING DAY

The key findings of the current chapter are a set of observable and measurable variables. Any of the studied manipulation tactics targets one or more of the variables. Varieties in the tactics emerge when different variables are targeted individually and even multiple variables are manipulated at the same time. All of these seemingly unique manipulation tactics seek the same objective, that is, to achieve the desired price impact. Therefore, going one step further, we suggest a practical framework that we have derived from careful study of the statistical and individual characteristics of prosecuted market manipulation cases in the five economies that provide these data online. The variables we propose provide the space to maneuver for the manipulator, often standing out in one, two, or three of these variables simultaneously to induce more trades made by others, and for the manipulator to achieve his desired price. It is unlikely that any one manipulation tactic would be outstanding in every one of the variables. However, to our best knowledge, the prosecution cases do fit into the proposed framework. We use one trading day as the time horizon.

The framework is as follows:

- Total number of shares to be placed in each order, that is, order size.
- Total number of orders. This measures the frequency of order placement.
- Trading direction of orders. This affects the number of orders to be placed and the net ownership of the shares at the end of the day.
- The distance of the bid (ask) from the best bid (ask). This is the bid advance (ask depression). The advancing-the-bid manipulation tactic provides an excellent example of raising the bid advance to increase share prices.
- Time interval between two consecutive orders. A negligible time interval between two orders of equal quantities is used in fictitious trading.
- Timing, that is, when to place orders during the trading day. To place an order during the closing minutes of the trading day can result in tangible differences in the closing price. Marking the close shows the importance of timing in manipulation.
- Full execution, partial execution, or full cancellation. Voluntary cancellation of placed buy orders near the best bid (or best ask for sell orders) raises questions regarding the genuineness of the trades.
- More than one trading account. This is also a feature of fictitious trading.
- Collusion with one or more investors. This is critical in cross-dealing, which is one type of fictitious trading.

These nine variables occur under the investor's discretion when one examines trade-based manipulation tactics only.[5] However, there are many variables out of the manipulator's control. Market environment variables, such as news from and actions taken by the issuing company, business media reporting, the sudden entry or exit of large volumes, and regulation change, are beyond the investor's expectation. Occasionally, sudden and large national and international news events, such as the outbreak of war, epidemics, and natural disasters, can affect the entire market substantially. In this chapter, we limit our attention to the variables at an investor's full discretion for trade-based market manipulation. The following chapters will address other variables under or beyond an investor's control.

UNIFIED APPROACH TO SURVEILLANCE AND REGULATORY MEASURES

No matter how many varieties comprise trade-based manipulation tactics, each is about manipulating one or multiple variables of those listed above. A close examination of the studied prosecution cases reveals numerous lessons that can be converted into surveillance and regulatory measures. Therefore, surveillance and regulatory measures can be proposed based on the nine variables. The following eight proposals point to the areas to apply surveillance and regulatory measures. That is, they provide guidelines to stock market regulators. In some proposals, specific measures are given as examples.

1. Daily volume limit, proposed in Chapter 3, is one effective regulatory measure against all trade-based manipulation tactics. Volume-based price impact, particularly when intended for price lifting, can be limited in most known scenarios to the regulators' need. In addition, large positions need to be kept under surveillance. Their move has the potential to generate a high price impact or to induce a high price impact. The threshold of a large position depends on the quantity of the holding and the average daily turnover of the past month. In other words, the definition of a large position is a relative concept. Implementation is left for the regulators.
2. To effectively regulate price lifting by an unreasonably high bid (or a low ask aimed for price depressing), we propose an adjustable limit band. That is, it limits both bid and ask so that they will fall within a band.

At any trading moment, there are best bid and best ask in one stock. The midpoint is then calculated as the average of the two. The distance of the best bid from the midpoint is half of the width of the bid-ask spread. The distance of the bid proposed by an investor from the midpoint can be calculated prior to placement. The ratio of the latter divided by the former can be used as the foundation of our proposed limit. Expressed mathematically, let us denote D as the distance of any bid, b, from the midpoint, M, and W as the width of the bid-ask spread. Thus $D = \text{Abs } (b - M)$. The preset limit is L. Then,

$$D/(W/2) - 1 < L, \tag{1}$$

and the acceptable bid range can be expressed as

$$M - (W/2) \times (1 + L) < b < M + (W/2) \times (1 + L), \tag{2}$$

where $M + (W/2) \times (1 + L)$ is the maximum value of the allowable bid.

As a numerical example, let us consider that the best bid is \$9.99 and the best ask \$10.01. The midpoint is the average of the two, that is, $M = \$10$. Then $W = \$0.02$. If L is set as 1 percent, then $D < (\$0.02/2) \times (1+0.01) < \$0.0101$. So any bid cannot exceed the range from \$9.9799 to \$10.0201. If any bid smaller than the best bid is not going to cause a concern in price lifting or price depressing, only the right hand side of (2) has to be followed. The trading system needs to reject any bid that exceeds or equals the maximum.

For ask, the same range will be obtained. If any ask above the best ask is not a concern for price depressing or price lifting, then only the minimum value, $M - (W/2) \times (1 + L)$ needs to be observed in practice. That is, no ask is allowed to be smaller than or equal to the minimum. The trading system needs to reject any ask that is equal to or smaller than the minimum.

The regulator has the flexibility to adjust the value of L according to market conditions. If he needs a greater uptrend when he sees more buy volumes, then he may set L a bit higher. Fine-tuning L is an important part of daily regulatory activities.

3. We propose that the time interval between two consecutive orders by any investor cannot be less than 10 minutes at any given time during a trading day. Of course, this limit can be adjusted by regulators according to their need. This measure reduces the trading frequency in an intensified fashion. It decreases greatly the probability of fictitious trading or fake trading, especially in a frequently traded stock. It also weakens marking the close effectively together with a daily volume limit and another measure to be proposed shortly.

4. The next important variable to monitor and regulate is net ownership of shares at the end of the day. If B is denoted as the total buy volume

in the stock by an investor during the trading day, and S as the total sell volume (positive only), we can use the ratio of Abs $[(B - S)/(B + S)]$ as a measure of the relative net ownership. If a daily minimum N ($0 < N < 1$) allowed by regulation is given, then

$$\text{Abs}[(B - S)/(B + S)] > N. \qquad (3)$$

There are two scenarios to consider. One is if $B > S$. The other is if $B < S$. Let us look at the first scenario. Since $B - S > 0$, solving (3) for B, one gets

$$B > [(1 + N)/(1 - N)]S. \qquad (4)$$

By the same token, the second scenario yields

$$B < [(1 - N)/(1 + N)]S. \qquad (5)$$

A numerical example can be examined by setting N as 50 percent. For the total buy volume exceeding total sell volume, (4) gives $B > 3\,S$. Otherwise, (5) yields $B < S/3$, or $S > 3\,B$.

The daily minimum N cannot be too small; for instance, being close to 0, it will raise concerns regarding fictitious trading. N cannot be too large; for instance, being close to 1, because of the mathematical impossibility. Adjusting N between 0 and 1 is left for regulators.

5. Because of proposal number two discussed previously, advancing the bid and depressing the ask are effectively prevented. Marking the close is left with order size and timing. If only market orders are allowed during the final 30 minutes of the trading day, then the problem of an intended pile-up of buy limit orders near the close is eliminated. Subsequently, manipulative price lifting near the close is effectively curbed.

6. The sixth variable concerns the genuineness of trading. This tests whether cancellation of placed orders is too frequent or conducted for the purpose of display only. Displaying complete information would largely prevent fake trading.[6] Complete information means the entire cycle of an order from placement to execution or cancellation. A sufficiently long time interval between two consecutive canceled orders is another critical means to prevent fake trading. As an example, one hour can be set as the minimum interval between any two consecutive voluntarily canceled orders. The daily volume limit ensures the number of total canceled shares will be below a certain value. Combined, these three

measures will largely guarantee the genuineness of trading and prevent large-scale fake trading aimed at achieving share price manipulation.[7]

7. The seventh variable is multiple accounts. This invites surveillance before any regulatory measures. The true identity requirement of an investor, whether individual or institutional, to open a trading account may reduce but cannot eliminate the problem. Devising a penalty for lending one's identity or trading account to an investor for the latter's self-dealing is another effective deterrence. The third means strives to detect self-dealing in actual transactions with multiple accounts. Proposals one to four present effective measures to reduce fictitious trading to an acceptable frequency and scale if it cannot be completely eliminated. Therefore, both surveillance and regulation in multiple dimensions are needed to tackle the problem of multiple accounts.

8. The last variable in the approach is collusion. It also requires both surveillance and regulation. Collusion generally takes place between two or more large investors, sometimes including the issuing company and brokers. Since collusion can take place in numerous fashions, detection before trading is extremely difficult. However, surveillance of large limit orders can alert regulators. If each of one investor's three large limit orders—for example, more than 10,000 shares—is matched with the same price within a very short time interval, this investor can be marked as a candidate for collusion regulation. If matched orders come from the same investor more than twice, then this investor can be considered as a colluding partner. This three-and-two rule, based on the time frame of three consecutive trading days, can be applied to multiple colluding partners. This way, at least one manipulator out of the collusion can be detected. And a warning or a more serious administrative order can be issued to the manipulator. Hence, the effectiveness of the surveillance is measurable. On the regulation side, proposals one, two, three, and four are all applicable and effective.

Among the eight proposals comprising a unified approach, daily regulation of the total executed volume, the bid-ask spread size, the trading frequency, and the net ownership are the core measures to ensure that an investors' trading activity is not manipulative. Proposals five and six prevent orders that do not aim at genuine trades. The other two deal with more than one trading account. More surveillance is needed for the final two proposals. The eight proposals, acting independently or in combination, are effective, quantifiable, and adjustable. They are unified because they are derived by looking at the nine variables discussed in the previous section, rather than targeting one type of manipulation at a time. This approach gives a more complete picture and regulatory flexibility to securities regulators.

The anatomy of trading in a trading day serves the foundation for the eight proposals in the unified approach. The unified approach, the authors believe, will effectively detect, prevent, and curb manipulations aiming to induce a large number of buy volumes and to generate an extraordinary price impact. The cost generated by implementing the eight proposals will be limited compared to the ultimate goal of protection of investors, prevention of crises, and enhancement of market stability. Above all, regulating price impact is an important construct in building fair, transparent, and perfect competition in the stock market.

SELLING SPEED IN DISTRIBUTION AND SHORT SELLING

As concentration building and price lifting are well regulated, the picture is different when one looks at distribution of large positions or heavy short selling. Let us examine distribution first.

Distribution of large positions can be divided into two types. One type derives from the ALD manipulation scheme or other long manipulation strategies. The other type stems from nonmanipulative buy-and-hold investments. Since the ALD scheme has been closely studied and regulatory measures proposed for both the accumulation and lift stages, the selling speed of distribution is no longer a serious concern. Instead, monitoring distribution in general will be sufficient. Other long manipulation schemes include information-based ones, which will be fully addressed in Chapter 8. Still, a small portion of other long manipulation schemes may continue to exist. For instance, price pegging on its own is not necessarily a profit-seeking scheme. Early sections on the measures meant to substantially reduce price lifting manipulations can also be extended to cope with those schemes.

Distribution of large positions arising from nonmanipulative buy-and-hold investments, in general, will not cause share prices to collapse because demand for shares was not artificially manipulated to a low level. Supervising selling speed is normally sufficient. However, setting a selling speed limit becomes necessary when multiple distribution processes for the same stock begin to occur or an unreasonably high selling speed is forecasted or observed. For any given time horizon, the selling speed limit is actually the limit on the sell orders size. Slicing large orders in accordance with a preset limit may complete the implementation.

In a short-selling scenario, a daily concentration limit is one effective measure to prevent heavy selling pressure due to large sell volume. The limit band proposed earlier will substantially reduce the selling pressure due to an extraordinarily lower ask. These two measures, in addition to the trading frequency regulation, will be able to keep short selling in check.

CONCLUDING REMARKS

The nine variables of the trading activities of any trader provide a practical approach to improved surveillance and regulation of stock markets in order to fundamentally reduce the possibility of manipulation-induced stock market crises and improve market stability and investor protection. Adopting this approach will help to move the secondary market toward the ideals of fair and transparent perfect competition.

Each large investor needs to be monitored according to the nine variables proposed earlier. So surveillance should be extended to large positions and large orders. Coordinated small volumes need to be watched. A sudden spike or collapse in share prices needs to be monitored, too. All of these surveillance activities will enable the proposed regulatory measures to be more completely and effectively implemented.

Based on the selected prosecution cases, this chapter is mainly focused on price lifting by trade-based manipulation tactics. Hence, long manipulation, particularly the lift stage in the ALD scheme, is given more in-depth analysis. Selling and short selling, in a broad sense, are also analyzed. The general objective is to keep price impact—uptrend or downside—well monitored and regulated.

NOTES

1. This chapter was accepted for presentation at the 16th World Congress of the International Economic Association, Tsinghua University, Beijing, July 4–8, 2011.
2. The search for ultimate factors that shape large price impact is active. In addition to the literature of volume-based price impact, there is another main line of research, liquidity-based price impact (see for instance, Amihud 2002; Farmer, et al. 2004). However, defining liquidity is elusive (Amihud 2002). In this chapter, only the volume-based literature is reviewed as to compare with the empirical data contained in the prosecution cases collected in Chapter 3.
3. Our calculation based on the trading data shows that the buy volume by the manipulator is 949,950 shares and sell volume 949,050 shares, slightly different than the 947,700 shares quoted in the court order.
4. Depressing the ask is used if the manipulator's intention is short manipulation. Then marking the close will feature a large number of sell orders near the close, with the ask much lower than the best ask for the stock.

5. The investor can release potentially price-moving information publicly to manipulate the share price up or down. But this is information-based manipulation and will be fully analyzed in Chapter 8.
6. The alternative is displaying no order-placement information, but information of executed volumes instead.
7. Some regulators may prefer to limit the number of canceled orders per trading day. Then a quantitative measure can be made that requires each investor to have voluntary intraday cancellations up to three times, for example.

Preventing Stock Market Crises (III)

Regulating Earnings Manipulation

Xin Yan

Lawrence R. Klein

Viktoria Dalko

Ferenc Gyurcsány

Michael H. Wang[1]

Earnings manipulation is inconsistent with the concept of perfect competition that is fair and transparent in stock markets. Earnings manipulation has been pervasive and persistent in the United States for the past 50 years. Research turns increasingly to international evidence and cross-market comparison. Enron, WorldCom, Lehman Brothers, and a series of corporate financial scandals have repeatedly shown securities regulators and investors the destructive consequences of earnings manipulation. The Sarbanes-Oxley Act (SOX) responded quickly to curb accrual-based earnings manipulation. Real earnings manipulation increased substantially and persisted in the post-SOX era with intensity similar to that in the pre-SOX era. More fundamental than earnings manipulation per se, there are multiple causal factors that have not been carefully considered or thoroughly regulated. They include the marketing assistance and performance pressure exerted by securities analysts that prompt corporate managers to manipulate financial statements, given lax detection by auditors, off-target regulatory penalties, and incentives that encourage managers to manipulate earnings. This chapter, joining the effort to draft measures to regulate corporate insiders and security analysts, attempts to address the unfinished mission to eliminate this poor conduct.

Putting forth multiple proposals, the authors aim to provide securities regulators with effective, quantifiable, and adjustable measures to amend comprehensively the loopholes that have allowed earnings manipulation to damage investor protection and market stability as well as effect defenses to prevent stock market crises and global financial systemic risks.

HOW IMPORTANT IS EARNINGS INFORMATION TO INVESTORS?

In Chapter 4, nine variables were identified that are fully at the discretion of a trader in the stock market. There are, however, many other variables not under the trader's control. Most of these are associated with information, particularly the disclosed financial reports generated by public firms. The regulatory framework in the United States, consisting of the Securities Act (SA) of 1933 and Securities Exchange Act (SEA) of 1934, including later additions, largely focuses on disclosure requirements that a public firm must provide factual and complete information about its performance. However, the evolution of the regulatory changes triggered by corporate scandals and public and private litigation against public firms raised a question. How does a regulator such as the U.S. Securities and Exchange Commission (SEC) enforce the reliability, timeliness, and completeness of information disclosure? Is the enforcement sufficiently effective, together with other regulatory actions, to protect investors, maintain stock market stability, and prevent single-stock or marketwide panic?

A stock listed on the stock market is created and maintained by its issuing firm, which remains the guardian of its stock. Information disclosed about the issuer's performance is fundamental to the stock price. Once the stock is traded in the secondary market, however, several sources of information related to the stock influence the stock price. Analysts, particularly sell-side analysts, publish their recommendations and earnings estimates regularly before quarterly earnings are disclosed. Large investors, such as fund managers, frequently announce on TV or other media platforms their stock picks. Print and electronic media outlets, such as the *Wall Street Journal* and CNBC, tend to emphasize similar tones of the news about corporate and economic outlooks. What are the purposes behind these various pieces of information? Do they benefit or hinder investor protection, market stability, and crisis prevention?

From the vantage of issuer-generated information forward, one can track the information loop all the way to the investors' trading decisions. There is underwriter-generated information, sell-side-analyst-generated information, rating-agency-generated information, large-investor-generated information, media-generated information, regulator-generated information, and small-investor-generated information. The list is far from conclusive. The public audience awaiting this information is enormous, and the impact of these news pieces is profound, often with long-term consequences for stock prices, market sentiment, the investment culture, and other substantial societal factors. Therefore, the effects that this information generates need to be studied individually and examined systematically. The key is how these factors affect investor protection, market stability, and crisis prevention. Furthermore, their effects on competition among investors for profits need to be evaluated in depth.

From the complete information loop described previously, the disclosed financial statements and reports provided by the managers of a public firm are of primary importance. First, it is the original source and starting point of most other information pieces related to the stock generated afterward. Second, it is the type of information most trusted by the investors compared to other types of information (D'Avolio, Gildor, and Shleifer 2001). Third, regulatory frameworks and modifications made to them center on issuer-generated information (for example, the SA (1933), SEA (1934), Foreign Corrupt Practices Act (FCPA) of 1977, Private Securities Litigation Reform Act (PSLRA) of 1995, and SOX (2002)). After all these regulations are put in place, is the disclosed information reliable, complete, and timely?

Still, managers and other corporate executives remain in the position of generating insider information. Because of today's compensation structure, they are also investors with insider information.[2] Do the insiders place their trades according to the disclosed information or insider information that has not been announced to the general public?

Sell-side-analyst-generated information is of importance to investor protection, second only to issuer-generated information. It directly affects numerous investors' trading decisions, investor protection, and perfect and fair competition in the stock market. The Global Research Analyst Settlement in the United States in 2003 justifies the importance of this issue.

Investor-generated information is also of great importance to fairness, market stability, and crisis prevention in the secondary market. Although less researched traditionally, anecdotal information abounds and recent studies in the Internet domain are increasing.

Media-generated information, particularly around sudden unexpected news events, is also of significance to investor protection, market stability, and crisis prevention. The durable negative effect of crisis formation resulting from the overly optimistic cultivation of business media reporting of stock market activities cannot be underestimated.

Chapter 5 focuses on issuer-generated information, particularly earnings manipulation. Trading by corporate insiders will be dealt with in

Chapter 6. Chapter 7 will be dedicated to analysis of the sell-side analysts. General information-based manipulation, where the information can be generated by large or small investors, will be investigated in Chapter 8. In Chapter 9, media-generated information will be examined according to its impact on investors. Regulatory measures will be proposed in each chapter from the perspective of investor protection, market stability, and crisis prevention as well as the ultimate ideal of building perfect competition in the secondary market with fairness and transparency.

EARNINGS MANIPULATION IS PROBLEMATIC

The stock market is essentially a trust-based institution. Issuing firms raise capital from investors by providing earnings and other company-related information to the market. Regulators aim to ensure that the information provided by issuers is factual, complete, and timely. Investors provide capital to issuers in exchange for share ownership. The bond remains voluntary. Investors can choose to reduce or eliminate their ownership at any time. The decision to withdraw from share ownership can result from multiple reasons. When investor sentiment changes from trust to distrust, it frequently is in response to information provided by a public company.

The regulatory framework in the United States (mainly the SA (1933), SEA (1934), FCPA (1977), PSLRA (1995), and SOX (2002)) is chiefly disclosure oriented. Most other global securities regulations are based on the U.S. framework (Allen and Herring 2001). This highlights the significance of reliability and timeliness of financial reports provided by issuers.

However, earnings and other required information from issuers is not always reliable or timely. For numerous reasons, which will be analyzed in later sections, managers often manipulate earnings. Earnings manipulation existed half a century ago, and it still exists today (Jacobs 2010). The distorted information disclosure can thus mislead numerous investors, especially small investors. It directly hinders investor protection, which is the main goal of securities regulators in most nations. Such less-than-accurate disclosures can result in shocks to the market when earnings manipulation is uncovered. Immediately, intensive selling of the manipulated stock leads to a fast decline of the share price. It might even shake the stability of the stock market. Occasionally, earnings manipulation is so severe and protracted—in which case it is often labeled as accounting fraud by U.S. regulators—that it causes prolonged panic selling and eventual delisting of the share. This can inhibit the work of the corporation in raising capital in the future. It negatively influences corporate culture. It disgusts the general public, especially through heightened media reporting. It pressures lawmakers to come up with new legislation in a short time span. The Enron scandal provided a perfect example of these features and consequences of earnings manipulation for global stock market regulators (Healy and Palepu 2003).

Is earnings manipulation only a problem in the United States? Several recent studies present evidence that the problem occurs in many other nations, from developed markets to emerging markets (for instance, Leuz, Nanda, and Wysocki 2003; DeFond, Hung, and Trezevant 2007).

The terms *earnings management, earnings manipulation,* and *accounting fraud* are all widely used in the literature. While these three terms have differences in meaning, they share the same essence. That is, managers of listed firms distort earnings data to make more positive (occasionally negative) presentations to investors and other current or potential business partners. In this chapter, we do not distinguish earnings management from earnings manipulation. They all indicate some manipulative action veering between legitimacy and fraud. Basically, we use the definition suggested by Healy and Wahlen (1999) of earnings manipulation as occurring when "managers use judgment in financial reporting and in structuring transactions to alter financial reports either to mislead some stakeholders about the underlying economic performance of the company, or to influence contractual outcomes that depend on reported accounting numbers."

Due to our desire to provide regulatory proposals, we rely more on empirical studies, even though a few theoretical journal articles and news reports are also included. Most studies cited relate to earnings manipulation in the United States during the past five decades. A number of recent publications show international evidence along these lines. Since empirical research on earnings manipulation is overwhelming, we do not see the need to add new evidence of the existence of this phenomenon. Therefore, this chapter is mainly a review of empirical literature on earnings manipulation occurring through several avenues; particularly, we show how and why it is done by managers, how it relates to investor protection and market stability, how auditors behave after detecting earnings manipulation attempts, how it has evolved for the last 50 years, and why we need a comprehensive and thorough regulatory package to deal with it. Our analyses follow the literature's findings, with our focus on how these factors impact on investor protection, market stability, and crisis prevention. The regulatory suggestions are given as part of a serial effort in building a system that strives for perfect competition with fairness and transparency in the stock market.

Rigorous empirical research on earnings manipulation started with Healy (1985). Healy examined 94 public firms with bonus plans for managers in the period 1968 to 1980, and discovered earnings manipulation by managers to maximize their compensation. In detail, Healy found that managers manipulate earnings, up or down, by selecting accounting procedures and accruals, because there is a strong association between accruals and managers' income-reporting incentives under their bonus contracts. Since the mid-1980s, earnings manipulation literature has been a booming business, especially since the early 1990s, when executive compensation had a substantial equity-based portion (D'Avolio, Gildor, and Shleifer 2001; Cohen, Dey, and Lys 2008). We will start with a review of the literature that focuses on the nature of earnings manipulation.

HOW IS EARNINGS MANIPULATION DONE IN REALITY?

Two main lines divide the literature. One focuses on accrual-based earnings manipulation; the other on real earnings manipulation. We start with the former by examining major empirical research results.

Two seminal papers by Loughran and Ritter (1995) and Spiess and Affleck-Graves (1995) find that after the initial public offering (IPO) and seasoned equity offering (SEO), a large proportion of issuing firms significantly underperform the stock market for up to five years, compared to matching nonissuing firms. Brav and Gompers (1997) and Brav, Geczy, and Gompers (2000) replicate the findings by Loughran and Ritter (1995) for small firms' IPOs and SEOs. Their research firmly establishes the phenomenon of postoffer stock underperformance.

DuCharme (1994), Friedlan (1994), and Shivakumar (2000) find that earnings reported by firms making stock offers contain on average abnormally high levels of positive accruals around offer dates. Sloan (1996) documents that stocks with high accruals subsequently have underperforming returns. In other words, accruals are reliably, negatively related to future returns. DuCharme, Malatesta, and Sefcik (2001) show that abnormal accruals around IPOs are negatively related to postoffer returns. These studies repeatedly show that a clear association exists between abnormal accruals and postoffer stock underperformance. Furthermore, Xie (2001) reports that abnormal accruals are overpriced in general contexts, which is not limited to IPOs or SEOs.

What is the underlying mechanism of this association? Numerous publications have presented evidence of earnings manipulation being the undercurrent for this systematic postoffer stock underperformance (Friedlan 1994; Rangan 1998; Teoh, Welch, and Wong 1998a, 1998b; Degeorge, Patel, and Zeckhauser 1999; DuCharme, Malatesta, and Sefcik 2001; Chen, et al. 2006).

Friedlan (1994) documents evidence indicating that managers exercise accounting discretion in earnings manipulation prior to IPOs, based on a sample of 277 firms that went public in the United States between 1981 and 1984. Loughran and Ritter (1997) report postissue underperformance in the five years after 1,338 SEOs for 1979 to 1989. Their interpretation of the findings is that some issuing firms are intentionally, and successfully, misleading investors by engaging in earnings manipulation. Examining 1,265 firms from 1976 to 1989, Teoh, Welch, and Wong (1998a) find that managers tend to manipulate discretionary current accruals upward prior to the SEOs. However, lower postissue long-run abnormal stock returns and net income are also found when higher net income is reported by tuning up discretionary current accruals. They further point out that their finding is consistent with the argument that investors naively extrapolate preissue earnings without fully adjusting for the potential manipulation of reported earnings. Similarly, Rangan (1998), using a sample of 230 SEOs in the years 1987 to 1990, finds that earnings manipulation can reliably predict subsequent underperformance of stock returns. His research implies that issuing firms use earnings manipulation to temporarily mark up stock prices. Teoh, Welch, and Wong (1998b) document that IPO issuers with higher discretionary accruals have poorer stock return performance in the three years subsequent to going public. Based on statistical evidence, they conclude that the greater the earnings manipulation at the time of the offering, the larger the ultimate stock price correction that will occur. Degeorge, Patel, and Zeckhauser (1999) investigate the frequency of earnings manipulation in a sample of 100,000 quarterly earnings reports published by 5,387 firms from 1974 to 1996. The authors illustrate that executives have both the incentive and the ability to engage in earnings manipulation. DuCharme, Malatesta, and Sefcik (2004) show that abnormal accruals are highest for SEO firms that are subsequently sued and settlement amounts are also positively correlated with the levels of abnormal accruals for firms making offers from 1988 through 1997 in the sample of the firms analyzed. Chan, et al. (2006), based on U.K. data from 1971 to 1995, present convincing evidence to support the view that large positive accruals are a symptom of earnings manipulation. They interpret this as managers misleading investors into believing that future profitability will stay high.

Accruals-based earnings manipulation has the advantage that it incurs little operational cost for the issuing firm. However, this methodology is easier to detect. The Enron-Andersen scandal and a number of high-profile accounting frauds at the turn of the century revealed long-existing accruals' maneuvers to achieve a smooth earnings path. Passage of the Sarbanes-Oxley Act (2002) effectively deterred this type of earnings manipulation. But another type, real earnings manipulation, is more difficult to uncover, and has continued to persist during the post-SOX era (Cohen, Dey, and Lys 2008). Next, we examine papers on real earnings manipulation.

Based on a sample size of 823 class-action lawsuits from 1995 to 2004, Zang (2007) finds that, subsequent to the filing of the lawsuit, firms sued continued to manipulate earnings but varied their methods. That is, their levels of accrual-based earnings manipulation dropped abruptly, while their real manipulation levels increased significantly. Zang reasons the trade-off between the two types of manipulation is that accrual-based manipulation is costly primarily because of litigation risk, while the main costs of real manipulation are the economic consequences that can jeopardize the firm's competitive advantage. Cohen, Dey, and Lys (2008) examine the impact of the SOX passage on managerial choice between accrual-based earnings manipulation and real earnings manipulation. They document that firms that were heavily involved in accrual-based earnings manipulation in the pre-SOX period increased significantly their real earnings manipulation after the passage of SOX.

Although risking a greater economic cost, managers have more options in conducting real earnings manipulation. According to Zang (2007), some real manipulation focuses on managerial discretion concerning research and development (R&D) expenditures (Baber, Fairfield, and Haggard 1991; Dechow and Sloan 1991; Bushee 1998; Cheng 2004). Other types of real manipulation behavior that have been explored include stock repurchases (Hribar, Jenkins, and Johnson 2006), sales of profitable assets (Herrmann, Inoue, and Thomas 2003; Bartov 1993), sales price reductions (Jackson and Wilcox 2000), overproduction, managing advertising, and SG&A (Selling, General, and Administrative) expenditures (Gunny 2005; Roychowdhury 2006), derivative hedging (Barton 2001; Pincus and Rajgopal 2002), and debt-equity swaps (Hand 1989). Managers can use multiple tools to manage earnings simultaneously (Beatty, Chamberlain, and Magliolo 1995; Hunt, Moyer, and Shevlin 1996; Gaver and Paterson 1999; Barton 2001; Pincus and Rajgopal 2002)).

These findings along with the survey by Graham, Harvey, and Rajgopal (2005) verify that managers would rather take economic actions that could have negative long-term consequences to manage earnings. A surprising 78 percent of the responding chief executive officers (CEOs) in the Graham, Harvey, and Rajgopal (2005) survey admit to sacrificing long-term value creation to achieve a smooth earnings path.

To summarize, accrual-based and real earnings manipulation represent the two methods managers employ to manipulate disclosed financial statements. Accrual-based earnings manipulation is more convenient to conduct and less harmful to the firm, but it comes to light more easily. Real earnings manipulation wears multiple masks and is thus more difficult to detect.

However, it hurts the firm's competitiveness in a fundamental way. Earnings manipulation in either form misleads investors and can result in their trading losses, particularly for less-informed small investors.

EARNINGS MANIPULATION IS PERVASIVE

The famous speech by former SEC chairman Arthur Levitt in 1998 expressed his concern that too many corporate managers, auditors, and analysts were participating in an earnings manipulation game just to satisfy consensus earnings estimates and project a smooth and profitable earnings path. He pointed out that those managers of not only small firms but also big corporations tended to operate in the gray area between legitimacy and fraud to manipulate earnings (Levitt 1998). The belief that managers commonly engage in earnings manipulation is widely shared by academic researchers and business journalists (for instance, Bruns and Merchant 1996; Fox 1997; Loomis 1999; Dechow and Skinner 2000; Beneish and Vargus 2002; Karpoff, Lee, and Martin 2008; Kedia and Philippon 2009), who believe that managers of every corporation are doing it and view it as usual business operations (Graham, Harvey, and Rajgopal 2005).

What is investors' attitude toward the information made public by the issuing firm? Hand (1990) conducted tests and concluded that the stock market is composed of both unsophisticated investors, who fixate on earnings information, and sophisticated investors, who scrutinize issuer-reported information. The functional fixation hypothesis, that investors systematically fail to unravel earnings management, received empirical support in capital markets and in behavioral and experimental research (Sloan 1996). Sloan also confirms some analysts' experience that investors naively fixate on reported earnings. Investors, surveyed by the Public Relations Society of America Foundation, ranked the annual report, which contains audited earnings, as the most trusted financial information (D'Avolio, Gildor, and Shleifer 2001). Behavioral finance literature coined the term *investor credulity,* that is, investors do not adequately discount for earnings manipulation by the issuer (Daniel, Hilshleifer, and Teoh 2002) to explain this phenomenon. Not every investor is credulous, but the majority of small investors' naïve trust in earnings information leaves space for earnings manipulation by issuing firms (D'Avolio, Gildor, and Shleifer 2001; Shanthikumar 2009).[3]Cheng and Warfield (2005) find that corporate managers with stock-based compensation engage more frequently in earnings manipulation. This finding confirms Cheng and Warfield's view that the two preconditions behind the managers' incentive to manipulate earnings are:

(1) capital markets' investors rely on reported earnings to make their trading decisions and (2) managers can take advantage of increases in stock prices.

How do investors react to the earnings announcement? Early documentation of the association between accounting numbers and stock prices or returns was made by Ball and Brown (1968), Beaver (1968), and Rendleman, Jones, and Latanie (1982). According to Shanthikumar (2009), small investors buy shares at positive earnings announcements (Lee 1992; Bhattacharya 2001; Battalio and Mendenhall 2005; Hirshleifer and Teoh 2009). They buy more strongly when a firm has announced several positive surprises in a row than when a firm announces a single positive surprise. Shanthikumar (2009) further finds that the intensity of small traders' buying activity in response to positive-earnings-surprise strings is positively related to the length of the string. She points out that *earnings momentum* trading is the cause of the return patterns documented in Barth, Elliott, and Finn (1999), Kasznik and McNichols (2002), and Myers, Myers, and Skinner (2007). Investors' positive attitudes toward consecutive earnings surprises are transformed into actual rewards to managers. Barth, Elliott, and Finn (1999) find that, other things being equal, firms reporting continuous growth in annual earnings are priced at a premium to other firms, and that this premium increases with the length of the string.

Investors, particularly small investors, react enthusiastically to consecutive positive earnings above estimates. Managers greatly value their enthusiasm and strive to sustain it as long as possible, primarily through *smoothing* earnings (for instance, Ronen and Sadan 1981; Hand 1989; Levitt 1998; Barth, Elliott, and Finn 1999; Myers and Skinner 1999; Nelson, Elliott, and Tarpley 2002; Graham, Harvey, and Rajgopal 2005).

Two real-life cases aid in understanding managers who smooth earnings, even at great risk. Collingwood (2001) documents that Cisco reported EPS (Earnings Per Share) of 1 penny over estimates for 14 consecutive quarters between 1998 and 2001. Incidentally, Lucent had its own version of "14 consecutive quarters." Prior to the end of 1999 when its stock price peaked, Lucent's quarterly earnings had consistently met or beaten estimates. On January 6, 2000, Lucent made the first of a string of announcements that it had missed its quarterly estimates, and when it was revealed that it had used dubious accounting and sales practices to generate some of its earlier quarterly numbers, Lucent fell from grace. By October 2002, its stock price bottomed at 55 cents per share, and resulted in SEC litigation and an eventual merger with Alcatel (Loomis 2003; SEC 2004).

Cisco and Lucent are only two outstanding examples of managers paving a smooth earnings path. Myers and Skinner (1999) find that 399 firms reported 17 or more quarters of consecutive increases in quarterly EPS since 1987. Some of the 399 firms have reported consecutive increases in quarterly earnings for more than 10 years. This is clear evidence consistent with managers' preference for achieving smooth earnings paths (Levitt 1998; Nelson, Elliott, and Tarpley 2002; Graham, Harvey, and Rajgopal 2005).

Concisely speaking, investors value consistent earnings patterns. Managers respond with a string of smooth earnings surprises, even at legal risk and fundamental cost to the firm. Doing so forms a positive feedback loop of investor reaction to earnings manipulation and then back to investors. Soros (1998) refers to this phenomenon as *reflexivity*.

How do investors react if the reported earnings miss the estimates? DeAngelo, DeAngelo, and Skinner (1996) document that firms breaking a pattern of consistent earnings growth experience an average 14 percent negative abnormal stock return in the year the pattern is broken. Barth, Elliott, and Finn (1999) note that the premium of a string of earnings growth is reduced when the string disappears and is concurrent with economically and statistically significant stock price drops. Skinner and Sloan (2000) document that the stock price response to adverse earnings surprises is disproportionately large for growth stocks. In other words, when growth stocks report even small earnings disappointments relative to analysts' forecasts they suffer disproportionately large stock price declines. Shanthikumar (2009) finds that small traders sell strongly in response to negative earnings surprise, and more strongly if there is a string of such surprises. Recent studies report that executive propensity to manage earnings and to avoid negative earnings surprises has increased significantly over time (for example, Bartov, Givoly, and Hayn 2002; Lopez and Rees 2002; Matsumoto 2002; Brown and Caylor 2005).

The disproportionate *punishment* wielded by investors for negative earnings surprises heightens the need to report smooth and consistent earnings. Positive earnings reports result in more and continuous buying in the stock market, which in turn tends to lead to increasing stock prices. Managers benefit the most from high and rising share prices. Unless or until their firms go bankrupt, they have every incentive to continue providing optimistic information to investors. One of the obvious incentives is their increasingly stock-linked compensation, which rose from 25 percent of total compensation in 1992 to 45 percent in 1999 (D'Avolio, Gildor, and Shleifer 2001). Hall and Liebman (1998) document that the median exposure of CEO wealth to firm stock prices tripled between 1980 and 1994, and doubled again between 1994 and 2000.

Therefore, it is not surprising that managers are most focused on short-term stock performance. The increase in stock-based executive compensation makes managers keen to encourage climbing stock performance (Coffee 2003). Alan Greenspan (2002) testified that "the highly desirable spread of shareholding and options among business managers perversely created incentives to artificially inflate earnings to keep stock prices high and rising." Fuller and Jensen (2010) assert that "[a]s stock options became an increasing part of executive compensation, and managers who made great fortunes on options became the stuff of legends, the preservation or enhancement of short-term stock prices became a personal (and damaging) priority for many CEOs and CFOs." Several chief financial officers (CFOs) interviewed in Graham, Harvey, and Rajgopal (2005) confessed that every firm's executives treat earnings management as a usual business operation. This is supported by the conclusion made by Bruns and Merchant (1996) that "we have no doubt that short-term earnings are being manipulated in many, if not all, companies." Burgstahler and Dichev (1997) also find that earnings manipulation is a pervasive phenomenon that seeks to avoid lowered earnings and losses. Collingwood (2001) confirms this concern through an interview evidencing that earnings management pervades the U.S. financial system. Lev (2003) also points out the prevalence of earnings manipulation. Dechow and Skinner (2000) report that practitioners and regulators often see earnings manipulation as a pervasive problem that requires immediate remedial action.[4]

To summarize, public investors are enthusiastic about ever-increasing stock prices. Stock price benefits from consistent earnings growth, EPS growth, and positive earnings surprises. Reported earnings are critical to that achievement. Since a firm's earnings are subject to numerous unexpected factors, consistency in earnings is difficult to achieve and even more difficult to maintain. Given these considerations, earnings manipulation remains managers' preferred choice, even if achieved at considerable cost to the corporation. Based on stock options for managers and other incentives for the firm, and outside pressure from analysts' forecasts, as well as regulatory loopholes, managers make every effort to deliver earnings. This has contributed to the pervasiveness of earnings manipulation to such an extent that it is almost viewed by many as a natural development.

EARNINGS MANIPULATION IS PERSISTENT

In this section, we focus on three key events that occurred during the last three decades. They are firm restatements, SEC litigation, and class-action lawsuits arising from earnings manipulation. The association among the three is that voluntary restatement often triggers an SEC investigation that may lead to litigation. A class-action lawsuit would very likely follow the announcement of an SEC investigation (Coffee 1986; Karpoff, Lee, and Martin 2008; Choi, Nelson, and Pritchard 2009). We start with SEC enforcement.

Karpoff, Lee, and Martin (2008) examine the penalties imposed on the 585 firms targeted by SEC enforcement actions for financial misrepresentation from 1978 to 2002. They chose post-1977 SEC and Department of Justice (DOJ) litigation because the Foreign Corrupt Practices Act (FCPT) of 1977 removed the mission-impossible proof of *scienter* required by the SA (1933) and SEA (1934) and empowered the SEC to carry out enforcement action over earnings manipulation. Their work shows two interesting findings. One is that most enforcement actions are prompted by the firm disclosing potential problems, of which restatements are the most important leads. The number of enforcement actions equals 40.2 percent of the number of firms restating their financial statements when aggregating over all years. Another is that the evolution of SEC enforcement actions during this 25-year span goes from an average of 7.6 cases per year from 1978 to 1984, to 16.4 cases per year from 1985 to 1993, and to 38.6 cases per year from 1994 to 2002. The substantial jump in the number of enforcement actions from 16.4 to 38.6 per year may be explained by the enactment of the Private Securities Litigation Reform Act (PSLRA) of 1995. Choi, Nelson, and Pritchard (2008) find strong evidence that the PSRLA has discouraged securities fraud class actions that would likely have been deemed meritorious prior to the PSLRA. It implies reducing the deterrence effect by class-action lawsuits to financial frauds including earnings manipulation. Considering the difficulty of enforcement on earnings manipulation prior to the FCPT of 1977, the modest number of SEC litigation cases between 1960 and 1977 is still indicative of the persistence of earnings manipulation because not every case of earnings manipulation was detected and even a detected case might not have been enforceable because of inability to establish proof of intent. Palmrose (1987) studies 472 audit litigations for misrepresented financial information from 1960 to 1985. She finds that audit litigations were frequently concurrent with auditee litigations. This was particularly true for the 83 cases of business failures in which financial statements were manipulated. There was a general rise of accounting restatements in the 1992 to 2002 period (Coats 2007). Earnings manipulation also rose steadily from 1987 to 2001 (Cohen, Dey, and Lys 2008). The number of securities frauds alleged in significant class-action lawsuits rose dramatically from 1994 to 2004 (Dyck, Adair, and Zingales 2009).

Since the previous paragraphs present overwhelming evidence in public and private lawsuits demonstrating pervasiveness and persistence of earnings manipulation in the pre-SOX era, we now turn to the post-SOX era. The question is whether the phenomenon of earnings manipulation has been completely stopped by SOX or whether it survives with substantially mitigated extent, or whether it persists within similar trends.

With a sample size of 823 lawsuits initiated from 1995 to 2004, Zang (2007) investigated whether managers use real and accrual manipulation in managing earnings as substitutes. She finds that sued firms' accrual manipulation levels drop abruptly, while their real manipulation levels increase significantly. Cohen, Dey, and Lys (2008) examine the prevalence of both accrual-based and real earnings management activities in the pre-SOX period of 1987 through 2001 and the post-SOX period of 2002 through 2005, respectively. They document, in the pre-SOX period, increasing accrual-based earnings manipulation but declining real earnings manipulation. In the post-SOX period, however, accrual-based earnings manipulation declined significantly but real earnings manipulation increased significantly. Furthermore, the authors conclude that the overall frequency of earnings manipulation in the post-SOX period returned to the pre-SOX trend based on their sample of 8,157 firms and 87,217 firm-years from 1987 to 2005. These two findings confirm the survey by Graham, Harvey, and Rajgopal (2005) in that earnings manipulation is *sticky* in the post-SOX era because of the tendency of managers to substitute real economic actions in place of accounting discretion.

In brief, earnings manipulation has existed for a very long time. Literature of the past decades documents the phenomenon occurring for nearly half a century. Both economic conditions and legal changes have affected the amount of public and private litigation arising from earnings manipulation. However, even with the most severe legislation in SOX in enforcement, earnings manipulation still continues to the same extent, only in a different manner. This shows the persistence of earnings manipulation. This also shows that the regulations have not cut off all the sources of earnings manipulation.

AUDITORS FREQUENTLY FAIL TO STOP EARNINGS MANIPULATION

Earnings manipulation has been pervasive and persistent in the presence of a regulatory microscope for the past decades. Who should blow the whistle? The SA (1933) and SEA (1934) require financial reports of public companies to be audited, expecting the financial information to be reliable and complete. This is an essential measure for investor protection and maintenance of an orderly market. In other words, auditors are by law supposed to detect and prevent fraudulent financial statements including earnings manipulation (Coats 2007; Dyck, Morse, and Zingales 2009). Unfortunately, reality is not cooperative.

The most embarrassing and forewarning event for auditors was the Arthur Andersen collusion with Enron, which went on for years and led to the demise of this once-prestigious accounting firm (Healy and Palepu 2003; Brickley 2004). Other famous auditing firms have also been litigated against for collusion. In 2000, Ernst & Young settled for $335 million in a shareholder suit related to its work for Cendant Corporation, which had manipulated earnings for 12 consecutive years. In 2001, an SEC investigation revealed more than 8,000 violations at PricewaterhouseCoopers (Coates 2007). In 2004 and 2005, KPMG agreed to pay out nearly $700 million in fines and settlements related to criminal and civil actions (Reilly 2006). Occurrence of auditor collusion is not limited to the U.S. firms. According to Wang, Wong, and Xia (2008), recent major civil lawsuits against Chinese firms have involved KPMG in the Jinzhou Port scandal in 2001 and Deloitte & Touche in the Kelong Electric scandal in 2006. These are major news events revealed to the public through the media. What about numerous SEC litigations and class-action lawsuits against auditors in past decades?

Litigation against auditors due to their failure to prevent earnings manipulation and other managerial wrongdoing has existed for a long time. Palmrose (1988) lists 472 litigations against the largest auditors for audits performed from 1960 through 1985. Bonner, Palmrose, and Young (1998) document that out of 261 AAER (Accounting and Auditing Enforcement Release) companies with fraudulent financial statements, 98 (38 percent) accompanied auditor litigation from 1982 to 1995. Heninger (2001), using a sample of 67 client firms with alleged misstatements from 1969 to 1998, provides evidence that the probability of auditor litigation increases as clients report more income-increasing abnormal accruals in their earnings manipulation. Financial restatements provide important hints to the SEC for enforcement actions, which frequently involve auditors as defendants. According to Freund, Fuerman, and Shaw (2002), the probability of a non-routine circumstance restatement occurring in the lawsuits with auditor defendants is about 45 percent. Palmrose and Scholz (2004) found that out of 492 non-GAAP (Generally Accepted Accounting Principles) restatements announced from 1995 to 1999, the auditor litigations score 65 (13 percent). When counting the total number of litigations against 185 firms, the rate is higher at 35 percent.

Levitt (1998) emphasizes that auditors are public watchdogs, a belief shared by some researchers (for instance, Freund, Fuerman, and Shaw 2002). However, auditors that are paid by public companies for their services are never genuinely independent of their clients (Coffee 2006; Dyck, Morse, and Zingales 2009). When facing earnings manipulation attempts or other fraudulent accounting issues, auditors usually have three options. First, they may choose to collude with the firms they are supposed to audit independently. The Andersen-Enron and Andersen-WorldCom scandals are classic examples of what can happen when auditing firms overstep these ethical boundaries. Second, they may take no action. Nelson, Elliott, and Tarpley (2002) find, based on analysis of questionnaire data of 515 attempts in 1998, that auditors adjusted 44 percent of the attempted earnings manipulations. Their results indicate more generally that auditors are less likely to adjust earnings management attempted, while managers are more likely to attempt earnings management. Third, the best scenario is that auditors try to stop clients from pursuing illegal or unethical accounting procedures. If auditors do, they may bear an unduly high cost because no guarantee by regulators or others is given that they will not be fired by clients. Fuerman (2006) reveals that 50 percent of whistle-blowing auditors lose the firm account in the year the fraud is revealed, as indicated after examining 1,401 class-action litigation suits against auditees of Arthur Andersen and the Big 4 for the period 1996 to 2004. For the same period, Dyck, Morse, and Zingales (2009) find very weak evidence of auditors' incentives to blow the whistle (about 10 percent out of all who do), based on a sample of 216 corporate frauds consisting of U.S. firms against whom a securities class-action lawsuit has been filed. Understandably, auditors fear that they will lose business if they blow the whistle.

If earnings manipulation is persistent and pervasive, and if auditor independence is questionable, the direct consequence is that investor protection is poor with respect to the quality of earnings disclosure. So regulating earnings manipulation is an issue of improving investor protection. Recently, several researchers studied international experience of the link between investor protection and earnings manipulation. For instance, Leuz, Nanda, and Wysocki (2003) investigated investor protection versus earnings manipulation, based on financial accounting data from 1990 to 1999 for more than 8,000 firms from 31 countries including both developed and developing economies. Their results show that earnings manipulation is negatively related to outsider rights and legal enforcement. One question arises. Since auditor independence is not fully achieved in either jurisdiction, can investor protection be sufficiently improved with strong legal enforcement?

In short, empirical studies repeatedly indicate that auditors frequently failed to perform their duties in the past decades. Recent enactment of SOX is expected to improve the quality of corporate audits. The SOX drafters do see the need to remove conflicts of interest in auditors' interactions with firms they audit. However, auditors are still paid by their clients. Complete auditor independence has not been reached yet, even assuming that enforcing SOX would improve it significantly.

PROPOSALS TO EFFECTIVELY REGULATE EARNINGS MANIPULATION

From field surveys, litigation cases, and empirical research results, we can summarize the following key factors that work independently or jointly to maintain the pervasive and persistent problem of earnings manipulation.

■ *External pressure.* Analysts' quarterly estimates are the direct, frequent, and largest stressors to corporate executives. What is the role that analysts are playing? What are the net benefits of earnings estimates?

■ *Audit dysfunction.* Auditors are expected by law to play a regulatory role. Unfortunately, they are hired and paid by public firms. This is the fundamental reason why auditors frequently take no action after detecting earnings manipulation attempts.

■ *Limited regulatory effectiveness.* Regulations and enforcement are law-centered. Their effectiveness depends on successful detection, investigation, and collection of needed evidence. They are *ex post*. They are time and resource consuming. One of the regulatory limitations is that enforcement can target only a small number of cases with a higher probability of winning litigation. All these reduce the deterrence effect of regulation and enforcement. In other words, they encourage earnings manipulation.

■ *Personal incentives.* Corporate executives try to increase the cash value of their stock-based compensation and performance bonuses, as well as insider trading profits.

Since earnings manipulation is information manipulation, executives have absolute control of information generation. That is, they have monopolistic power over the information generation process. However, it is almost impossible to detect their intention behind earnings numbers and other corporate announcements. This poses challenges to designing financial tools for securities regulators. The following are our proposed measures aimed at providing more prudent and adjustable tools to securities regulators, so that they can regulate earnings manipulation more effectively jointly with other regulatory proposals we have made in Chapters 6 to 8, in addition to existing regulations.

■ *Measure one: Reducing external pressure.* Analysts' estimates are both marketing aids and stressors to corporate executives. We devote an entire chapter to analyzing the role sell-side analysts play in the information loop and investors' decision-making in Chapter 7. Chapter 7 also provides a set of financially prudent and quantifiable regulatory recommendations that are, besides other benefits, also expected to reduce the external pressure on management to manipulate earnings.

■ *Measure two: Improving auditing efficiency.* To make sure that auditors have complete independence and full capacity to perform their work in accordance with security regulations, we propose that: (1) auditors be paid solely by regulators; (2) public firms pay auditing fees to regulators but have no control on who the next auditor will be; (3) regulators appoint auditors and pay them accordingly; (4) auditors be involved in no business other than auditing; (5) their income needs be stable and predictable; and (6) as an option, auditors and auditing firms become not-for-profit entities, or even a part of the regulatory agency. In addition to scheduled audits, such as an annual audit, it is proposed that regulators have the authority to audit public firms randomly.

■ *Measure three: Enhancing effectiveness in enforcement.* Existing enforcement most likely results in a monetary settlement that includes penalties paid by the firm and some paid by executives. This measure, however, targets manipulating executives' least-sensitive area, and they apparently do not feel sufficiently deterred by the penalties incurred because these personal fines are often covered by insurance. Thus, in addition to existing monetary and criminal regulations, we propose some more prudent and adjustable tools for regulators. The most vulnerable areas of the manipulating executives and their firms are their reputations and capital-raising capacities. Hence, several exemplary measures are designed accordingly. One is to expose publicly and repeatedly the misdeed and manipulating parties in their communities for weeks. Regulators would also maintain records of these manipulations for as long as 10 years[5] as evidence for even more severe penalties if these violations are repeated in the future. The other is to require that the firm's credit rating be downgraded by one or more notches for a limited period such as one year. The downgrade will not be lifted after one year until the firm shows improvement.

■ *Measure four: Regulating trading by corporate executives.* In Chapter 6, we have proposed four adjustable and financially prudent measures to regulate effectively corporate executives' trading.

CONCLUDING REMARKS

Since the mid-twentieth century forward, particularly in the United States, earnings manipulation has led to problematic, pervasive, and persistent corporate misconduct toward market participants. Abundant empirical literature documents tens of thousands of detected cases of earnings manipulation. Enron, WorldCom, Lehman Brothers, and dozens of corporate scandals revealed at the turn of the century warned the global stock markets and corporate world. SOX and other regulatory moves have effectively curbed some avenues of earnings manipulation. However, the problem still finds new loopholes that persist to an extent similar to the pre-SOX era.

This chapter, together with related chapters on regulating security analysts and corporate insiders, is dedicated to identifying the key characteristics of the problem by drawing on the overwhelming evidence taken from public and private legal actions as well as market observations. The authors realize that earnings manipulation is not an isolated phenomenon. The practice of earnings manipulation has multiple causal factors, some pulling it from the front and others pushing it from behind. We focus on the main factors that directly and jointly cause misconduct. Then we propose regulatory measures based on the effects of those factors. The expectation is that the proposed measures, based on empirical regularity and past lessons, would give securities regulators a host of effective, quantifiable, and adjustable tools to regulate earnings manipulation along with extant regulations; and that these measures respond to contemporary demand and social justice. The effort is geared to improving investor protection, maintaining market stability, and preventing stock market crises. The ultimate goal is to contribute to perfecting competition with fairness and transparency in the global stock markets. And it is aimed at delivering a building block for future global financial architecture that guards scientific, health-promoting, and civilized economic development against systemic financial risk.

NOTES

1. This chapter was presented at the 9th NTU International Conference on Economics, Finance, and Accounting, Taipei, May 25–26, 2011.
2. Managers frequently face the strong temptation of making substantial trading profits at low cost from insider information such as earnings numbers. Some, if not all, of them may use their information about earnings overstatement to trade for their own benefit. From a trading point of view, those managers act as information-based manipulative traders (Beneish 1999).
3. Individual stock ownership increased from 35.6 percent in 1989 to 40.0 percent in 1992, and from 43.9 percent in 1995 to 51.8 percent in 1998 (Poterba 2001). Berkeley (2001) also reports nearly half of American homes owned equity in the stock markets in 1999.
4. Beneish (2001) doubts if earnings manipulation is pervasive because it is unobservable and managers' intentions behind earnings announcements are hard to detect. He suggests relying more on public and private lawsuits for insider

trading on inflated earnings for hard evidence of earnings manipulation. Recent research on insider trading connected with earnings manipulation shows promising findings (for instance, Summers and Sweeney 1998; Beneish 1999; Beneish and Vargus 2002; Bartov and Moharam 2004; Piotroski and Roulstone 2005; Bergstresser and Philippon 2006; Kedia and Philippon 2009).

5. A cancer patient is cured if no recurrence of the cancer in the 10 years after treatment is observed.

CHAPTER 6

Preventing Stock Market Crises (IV)

Regulating Trading by Corporate Insiders

Xin Yan

Lawrence R. Klein

Viktoria Dalko

Ferenc Gyurcsány

Michael H. Wang[1]

Corporate insiders may trade shares in their companies by utilizing their information advantage, such as access to manipulated earnings information. Once announced publicly by a credible disseminator with a large investor audience, this information advantage is attached to publicity and credibility. Subsequently, an information monopoly is formed. Trading strategies utilizing the publicized information advantage are therefore an exercise of monopolistic power. This type of trading by corporate insiders damages the fairness and integrity of the secondary market, and negatively impacts investor protection, market stability, and even crisis prevention. The existing insider trading regulations in the United States and many other nations are powerful, but their effectiveness is low when being enforced. This chapter proposes to add four new measures based on the financial reality that will provide securities regulators with controllable tools to implement. These tools pose a daily limit on trading volumes and share withholding percentage on corporate insiders. In addition, if the company's stock displays abnormal price behavior prior to the information release date, regulators have the right to postpone and investigate if there was any information leak in advance of public release. It is proposed that the CEO bear responsibility for such an event. These measures are quantifiable, are relatively easy to implement, and can be adjusted according to the regulatory priorities and local realities affecting securities regulators.

WHAT IS THE PURPOSE OF TRADING BY CORPORATE INSIDERS?

In the previous chapter on regulating earnings manipulation, we analyzed the information loop from its first creators—corporate executives—to market participants. In this chapter, we will address trading based on certain specific information, and its impact on perfect competition with fairness and transparency in the stock market.

According to the United States Securities and Exchange Commission (SEC), *insiders* are defined as managers, directors, and investors holding 10 percent or more of outstanding shares of public companies. *Insider trading* is also defined by the SEC as trading based on material and nonpublic information. Information is called *material* if, in case other investors were aware of it, it would likely influence their trading decisions.[2] *Nonpublic* means private or not known to the public. *Insider trading* is illegal in the United States. Because insider trading undermines investor confidence in the fairness and integrity of the securities markets, the SEC has treated the detection and prosecution of insider trading violations as one of its enforcement priorities (SEC 2010).

The focus of this chapter is different than that of the SEC. We consider members of the board of directors, top management, and large shareholders to be *corporate insiders*. *Trading by corporate insiders* includes both legal and illegal conduct. The illegal kind is the trading in a security based on material and nonpublic information.

As two SEC enforcers have pointed out: "Insider trading is an extraordinarily difficult crime to prove. The underlying act of buying or selling securities is, of course, perfectly legal activity. It is only what is *in the mind of the trader* that can make this legal activity a prohibited act of insider trading" (Newkirk and Robertson 1998) [emphasis added]. Indeed, how can one detect what is in an insider's mind to decide whether the trading is legal or not? Moreover, SEC regulations are basically law centered. That is, they are *ex post* because of the need for evidence, which has little preventive function except for certain deterrence effects when the penalty is expected to be relatively severe. Sometimes, trading by corporate insiders seems legal. However, the consequences of the trading can be detrimental to investor protection and market stability. Occasionally, it threatens systemic security. We construct the following two cases based on well-established empirical regularities.

> *First case: Sales by corporate insiders during a Seasoned Equity Offering (SEO).* In this example, 10 corporate insiders sell collectively 5 million shares (or 5 percent of the 100 million outstanding shares) of the company XYZ. Their insider information is their belief of the temporary overvaluation of the company stock, which could happen without any wrongdoing on their part. The company makes an announcement about the SEO one month prior to the offer date. The market reaction is positive. And the stock price runs up immediately after the announcement. The 10 corporate insiders sell their shares gradually during the one-month period and complete the sale of 5 million shares by the last trading day prior to the actual offer date. The stock price will climb for three more trading days following the SEO. Then it goes into the three-year-long underperformance with a cumulative return of −20 percent. (This stylized case is based on studies of Loughran and Ritter (1995); Spiess and Affleck-Graves (1995); and Kahle (2000).)

> *Second case: Sales by corporate insiders prior to voluntary financial restatement after 10 consecutive upward quarterly earnings surprises.* This example is a mimic of the Enron saga prior to its restatement in October 2001 (Amalgamated Bank et al. versus Kenneth L. Lay et al. 2001). All of the corporate insiders of the company XYZ participate in the sale scramble because the management team cannot find any meaningful way to sustain their consecutive upward earnings manipulation of 10 quarters. The total sale of 15 million shares, or 10 percent of the 150 million outstanding shares, starts two years prior to the restatement and is completed 35 trading days after the restatement. During the first year of the two-year period, the stock price increases from $75 to $90. Then it goes all the way down to $30 at the restatement. Within the 35 trading days following the restatement, the stock price continues to drop to less than $1. Bankruptcy filling is made immediately. The stock is eventually delisted.

The first case indicates that profit taking is the incentive of the participating corporate insiders. However, the second case shows that corporate insiders sell all their shareholdings to avoid expected loss. These two incentives have been found repeatedly by numerous researchers in the insider trading literature that we will review shortly.

It is important to clarify our terminology and subject of inquiry. Our subject is any and every trade made by corporate insiders. In some sense, our focus is narrower than insider trading, as defined and enforced by the SEC, since we consider exclusively corporate insiders and not anyone else who otherwise obtains insider information. On the other hand, our focus is broader than the SEC's scope of enforcement, as we include each and every trade by corporate insiders, and not only those *that proved* to have been done based on possession of material nonpublic information. To distinguish this key concept, we call the subject of this chapter *trading by corporate insiders* from now on. However, when we cite literature, we use the original terminology of insider trading when it is necessary.

Although the regulatory proposal to be made is for securities regulators of any economies, we base our literature review and analysis largely on the United States experience because most of the available literature on insider trading and related regulations is for the United States, where it is also believed that insider trading laws and enforcement are the toughest in the world (Du and Wei 2004; Bris 2005).

This chapter is, to a certain extent, an extension of our study on regulating earnings manipulation in Chapter 5. The reason we choose to focus on insider trading assisted by earnings manipulation follows. Trading by corporate insiders can potentially make use of the inflated stock prices due to one or multiple consecutive artificially inflated quarterly earnings reports (Richardson, Toeh, and Wysocki 2004). When corporate insiders foresee the unsustainable upward manipulation of earnings, they will sell some or all of their shareholdings to avoid expected loss, either before the break of a string of positive earnings surprises or before a voluntary or enforced financial restatement is announced (Ke, Huddart, and Petroni 2003; Kedia and Philippon 2009). Here we follow it with a full-scale analysis of the relationship between earnings manipulation and trading by corporate insiders, from the angle of investors competing for higher returns in the stock market. After the analysis we present the literature review on the incentives of earnings manipulations that enrich corporate insiders through trading. Before a close examination of insider trading research results, we briefly examine the controversial history regarding insider trading regulations in the United States. The recent literature on insider trading contains an important branch that focuses on earnings manipulation–assisted insider trading, which is of primary interest in this study. The empirical literature on the low effectiveness of insider trading regulations includes studies by researchers in economics and accounting and scholars in law, criminology, and other fields as well. To prepare for proposing financial measures to limit trading by corporate insiders, we elaborate on the information monopoly generated and maintained by corporate insiders. We propose the daily limit and share withholding percentage on trading by corporate insiders in an antitrust spirit. To prevent insider trading by other investors who may not be corporate insiders, we suggest two more measures. These measures are based on repeatedly observed abnormal price behavior prior to major corporate announcements.

We demonstrate the key feature of the first two measures with three simple examples. A discussion of all four of the measures is given, followed by the conclusion. In the following, we analyze the relationship between earnings manipulation and trading by corporate insiders.

THE RELATIONSHIP BETWEEN EARNINGS MANIPULATION AND TRADING BY CORPORATE INSIDERS

Earnings manipulation and trading by corporate insiders share the same purpose, namely, to increase the cash value of insiders' stock-based compensation and wealth. Earnings manipulation is only a means, not an end, while trading by a corporate insider is an end in itself, if we use realized wealth as the reference. Trading by an insider is potentially more profitable than trading by others, even without earnings manipulation, because of the information advantage of the insider. However, trading can be far more profitable if earnings are manipulated to meet insider desire.

Corporate executives are always insiders—since they are always in possession of potentially price-moving information that is known only by them, for example, how they plan to compile their next financial statement. And many of them are large investors, too. For rational investors it will be hard *not* to make use of insider information to their advantage to maximize their personal wealth. If insiders do not use their private knowledge to trade, and there are no other manipulations present, price should look as shown in Figure 6.1; if insiders trade according to the publicly announced news, price should look as shown in Figure 6.2.

Trading by corporate insiders benefits the doers but damages other investors' fair chances for profitable trades and an orderly market. Earnings manipulation affects a broader audience. It benefits the managers and other shareholders as well as the firm in the short term. However, the consequences it brings to the secondary market are serious. Empirical studies establish that manipulated earnings mislead investors and often result in long-term underperformance of the stock, loss to numerous investors, and a sharp drop in investor confidence in the stock. Once the manipulation is revealed, it tends to rattle the stock price or, at times, even the entire stock market. When earnings manipulation and trading by corporate insiders occur concurrently, the outcome is even more detrimental to investors who are not insiders, as well as

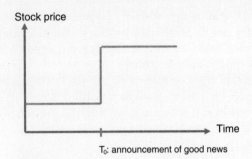

FIGURE 6.1   Price Behavior around Positive
News, in the Absence of Insider Trading and
Other Type of Manipulation

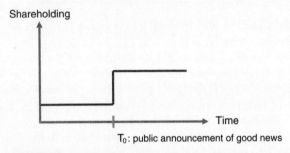

FIGURE 6.2   Shareholdings by Corporate Insiders, in
the Absence of Insider Trading and Other Type of
Manipulation

to the market. Enron provided an open-and-shut lesson for global stock markets and the corporate world (Healy and Palepu 2003). Trading by corporate insiders always implies utilization of an information advantage. Thus, insiders have one thing in common with information-based manipulators, which is information asymmetry that is to their advantage. Earnings manipulation is creating an information advantage for the manipulators by distorting facts. Therefore, if corporate executives do one after the other, they become information-based manipulators of share prices in the secondary market.

TRADING BY CORPORATE INSIDERS IS AN IMPORTANT DRIVE FOR EARNINGS MANIPULATION

Since we are focused more on achieving investor protection and market stability with fair competition, our vantage is from that of common market participants and regulators. Bearing the above analysis in mind, we have chosen to examine trading by corporate insiders that is concurrent with earnings manipulation, which is a special type of information-based manipulation of stock prices in the secondary market. Since earnings manipulation affects a larger pool of investors and may instigate more serious consequences to the stock market and to society, and normally occurs prior to insider trading, we begin with the main incentives for earnings manipulation.

The Main Incentives for Earnings Manipulation All Enrich Corporate Insiders

Corporate executives may have multiple incentives for earnings manipulation and those incentives may change at any time. These incentives may vary from one firm to another and be distinct from one executive to another. These incentives include meeting analysts' estimates, smoothing income paths, reaching targets set by compensation contracts or debt covenants, influencing stock prices by announcements of major corporate decisions, as well as any combinations of these incentives, according to the auditors surveyed by Nelson, Elliott, and Tarpley (2002). Some economists propose that a high and increasing stock price "makes it cheaper to pay employees with equity, to raise funds through share issues, and to make acquisitions. It also makes managers' stock options more valuable" (D'Avolio, Gildor, and Shleifer 2001). What do regulators say about these incentives? Dechow, Sloan, and Sweeney (1996) list 49 incentives in five categories behind earnings manipulation in the 39 AAER (Accounting and Auditing Enforcement Release) cases. They are Issue Securities (22, or 44 percent), Upwardly Trending EPS (11, or 22 percent), Earnings-based Bonuses (7, or 14 percent), Insider Trading (6, or 12 percent), and Other (3, or 6 percent). The first incentive can be utilized by corporate insiders in trading ahead of the announcement. The second incentive has direct benefits for stock-based compensation. The third incentive obviously directly benefits executive compensation. The fourth spurs extra effort to expand the cash value of stock-based compensation. Together, 94 percent of all the incentives directly or indirectly benefit corporate insiders. Only 6 percent of incentives are not known. Therefore, enforcement data shows that most incentives for earnings manipulation derive directly from corporate executives' desire to expand the value of their stock-based compensation. To reiterate, corporate executives are insiders. Their trades oftentimes are categorized as illegal insider trading because manipulative elements such as timing a trade relative to the announcement date and distorted disclosure information content are involved. As such, trading by corporate insiders is an important incentive for earnings manipulation.

Numerous investors take earnings information as the most important basis for their trading decisions (D'Avolio, Gildor, and Shleifer 2001; Shanthikumar 2009). Increasing stock prices automatically expands the cash value of managers' stock-based compensation and performance-related bonus plan. Therefore, expanding the cash value of stock-based compensation provides a strong incentive for corporate executives to manipulate earnings. Further, if corporate executives plan trades with a string of manipulated earnings, then huge profits are almost certain. Earnings manipulation is market misconduct. Insiders relying on it to increase their profits through insider trading engage in a dual form of misconduct. Since insider trading concurrent with earnings manipulation is the core interest, we now turn to the literature on insider trading. There is one controversial issue that needs to be clarified first.

Is Debate on Insider Trading Regulation Over?

When reading Bainbrighe (1999), who cites nearly 300 publications debating whether insider trading should be regulated or deregulated, an issue ignited by Manne (1966), we noted that most arguments are hypothetical and have little empirical support. Not one researcher considered that the quantity and speed of insider trading would make a substantial difference. For instance, an insider sale of 1,000 shares or 1 million shares of the same company with 50 million outstanding shares will have a huge difference in its price impact and affect public investors differently. The sale of 1,000 shares has barely any impact, but the sale of 1 million shares has a significant price impact and other consequences, if the insider sells those 1 million shares within one trading day. Without considering the quantity and speed, one can hardly assess the injury to the market and to scores of investors. Another issue not settled by the debaters is the need to separate trading from inside information advantage. We found these two aspects to be the key where real improvement can be made to reduce the damage caused by insider trading at a high trading speed and to separate trading from information advantage. In addition, it matters tremendously when insider sales intensify. This is particularly true when public companies are in financial distress.

The Enron saga and a series of eye-opening corporate scandals involving large quantities of insider trading at the turn of the century may have put a stop to the debate. The following quotation in a class-action lawsuit complaint describes how Enron insiders cashed in more than $1 billion by selling Enron stock assisted by ongoing earnings manipulation from at least 1998 to restatement in October 2001.

"Enron's consistently improving reported financial performance artificially inflated the price of the Company's stock to as high as $90.75 during the Class Period (from October 19, 1998, to November 27, 2001).

Meanwhile, Enron's top insiders sold 17.3 million shares of their Enron stock for proceeds of $1.1 billion" (Amalgamated Bank, et al. versus Kenneth L. Lay, et al. 2001).

The real story does not end at top insiders selling all of their shareholdings when they see no sustainable way to inflate Enron's earnings. Kenneth Lay, the chairman and CEO of Enron, openly asked Enron employees to buy Enron shares in late September 2001 (Sloan 2002). On October 29, 2001, Lay and the management locked down the firm's 401-K plan for two weeks, preventing employees from selling their Enron stock (Clardy 2003). Subsequently, thousands of Enron employees helplessly watched their retirement money vanish into pennies.

From the perspective of market participants, trading by corporate insiders is one form of trading strategy. It is based on information monopoly, which will be analyzed in the later text. Therefore, it is a manipulative trading strategy. It is like any other information-based or trade-based manipulation trading strategy, used either by institutional investors, individual investors, or corporate insiders. Market manipulation not only damages fair and transparent competition, it causes frequent mini-bubbles and single stock crashes. If an extremely large volume and extra-high trading speed are involved, market manipulation can trigger a marketwide panic or crisis. Thus, insider trading, like any other market manipulation strategy, needs to be effectively and prudently regulated. Even Manne (1970) acknowledged that manipulation is harmful. He further believed that if insider trading could not be effectively eliminated, then manipulation of stock prices would not cease.

In the post-SOX era with the addition of the recently passed Dodd-Frank Act, the question is not whether trading by corporate insiders should be regulated, but how it can be effectively and prudently regulated in global stock markets. Ma, Zhang, and Du (2009) survey studies by Chinese researchers on rampant insider trading in the 20-year-old stock markets in Shanghai and Shenzhen. They find that most Chinese researchers suggest that insider trading needs to be regulated.[3] This echoes Du and Wei (2004) that China and other emerging markets, which have more prevalent insider trading, do feature more volatile stock markets. International experience from 103 countries also speaks to more stringent insider trading laws and enforcement (Bhattacharya and Daouk 2002; Beny 2005; Bris 2005).

Literature on Insider Trading

Analyzing insider trades from a stratified random sample of 105 New York Stock Exchange (NYSE) companies from January 1950 to December 1960, Lorie and Niederhoffer (1968) document that insiders tend to buy more often than usual before large price increases and to sell more than usual before price decreases. Jaffe (1974) presents evidence that insiders do make abnormal returns and earn even more significant profits when they trade more intensively using a large sample of CRSP (Center for Research in Security Prices) data from 1961 to 1968. Finnerty (1976) obtains results that agree with Jaffe (1974) that insiders can outperform the market because insiders can foresee profitable trading opportunities with high certainty. Finnerty's data consist of 30,000 transactions from 1969 to 1972. Analyzing insiders' open market sales and purchases of 769 public firms from 1975 to 1981, Seyhun (1986, 1988) indicates that insiders can predict abnormal future stock price changes. He also differentiates the quality of inside information possessed by different insiders and points out that insiders can discern the differences in the value of their information and trade greater volumes of stock to exploit more valuable information. These empirical studies have established the existence of profitable insider trading in the U.S. markets.

By working on a sample of 68 companies listed on the American Stock Exchange throughout the three-year period from 1973 to 1975, Givoly and Palmon (1985) confirm previous findings that insiders make abnormal profits. Elliot, Morse, and Richardson (1984) examine insiders who trade around earnings announcements for the years 1975 to 1979. Their findings show weak association between the abnormal returns and the earnings announcement. This may imply that earnings information is leaked early and insider trading is rampant so the announcement effect is weak (Bhattacharya, et al. 2000). Karpoff and Lee (1991) find that an unusual number of insiders sell stock before common stock and convertible debt issues by using a sample of 179 primary security issues from 1975 to 1982. They conclude that some insiders intentionally trade before new issue announcements despite the expected legal and market penalties. Kahle (2000) documents that insiders intentionally sell at inflated stock prices when investigating insider trading patterns around issuance of convertible debt and seasoned equity from 1981 to 1992. These researchers focus on insider trading around announcements of large corporate events, which implies the value in inflating stock prices of such announcements to insiders.

Insider Trading Prior to the Announcement of a Takeover Deal

Announcement of a takeover tender offer is among large corporate events. Empirical research establishes that the target company's stock price starts increasing significantly several days or weeks prior to the announcement. In the meantime, the trading volume of the target firm's stock increases tremendously. Meulbroek (1992) analyzes 183 illegal insider trading episodes detected by the SEC from 1980 to 1989 to examine excess returns on the days of illegal insider trading. By looking into takeover cases and other major corporate news events, she finds that insider trading contributes significantly to the preannouncement price run-up, which confirms that insider trading is widespread. Meulbroek's finding is in line with earlier studies on 194 successful takeovers from 1975 to 1978, as investigated by Keown and Pinkerton (1981) and 172 successful cash tender offers from 1981 to 1985, analyzed by Jarrell and Poulsen (1989).

The public lawsuits in the two influential insider trading cases in the 1980s are very well documented and are presented in detail in the following. Cornell and Sirri (1992) use court data to analyze intraday insider trading prior to the announcement of acquisition of Campbell Taggart by Anheuser-Busch on August 3, 1982. They report that insider trading in Campbell Taggart caused a substantial price run-up of more than 20 percent before the tender offer announcement. Total insider purchase was 265,600 shares of stock, representing 29 percent of Campbell Taggart's volume from June 30 to August 2 and 1.8 percent of its total outstanding shares. Their findings are consistent with the findings of Meulbroek (1992). Chakravarty and McConnell (1997) investigate whether the share price run-up prior to the acquisition announcement of Carnation by Nestlé on September 4, 1984, was caused by trading by the convicted insider Ivan Boesky from June 6, 1984, to August 28, 1984. Between June 5, 1984, and August 31, 1984, Carnation's stock experienced a run-up of 26 percent. In the meanwhile, Ivan Boesky purchased 1.7 million shares of Carnation's stock, which constituted just under 5 percent of Carnation's outstanding shares, on the basis of insider information. They find that Boesky's purchases are positively and significantly correlated with daily and hourly changes in Carnation's stock price, but no correlation between prior price changes or prior non-Boesky trading volume and Boesky's purchases. They conclude that Boesky's trades caused the price run-up prior to the announcement.

How frequently do insiders trade, legally and illegally? Lakonishok and Lee (2001) show that for all the companies listed on the NYSE, Amex, and Nasdaq exchanges during the period 1975 to 1995, there were more than one million insider transactions per year. Jiang and Zaman (2007) mine the reported insider trading data from 1975 to 2000 and conclude that insiders are able to time the market, not due to contrarian trading strategy, but because they possess superior information about the future performance of the company.

Recent Literature on International Experience of Insider Trading

For 4,399 insider trading data from 196 companies listed on the London Stock Exchange between 1986 and 1994, Friederich et al. (2002) confirm an early finding that directors sell (buy) after an increase (decline) in prices. Using a sample of 119,179 news announcements made by U.K. companies and 8,086 insider trading events over the period 1999 to 2002, Korczak, Korczak, and Lasfer (2007) find that insider trading is more intense before bad than before good news announcements across all types of news-specific categories. In addition, insider trading before bad news announcements is concentrated more before news with high market impact, whereas insider trading before good news is related to less-price-sensitive news. Lower abnormal returns of trades by corporate insiders may be attributed to the two-month trading ban before an earnings announcement, the rule enforced since 1977 by the U.K. securities regulating agency. Linciano (2003) analyzes stock price behavior around announcements of 13 block sales and 16 takeovers in Italy in the period 1998 to 2000. He graphically presents significant price run-up about 10 trading days prior to the announcement dates.

After July 2002, German securities regulation has required disclosure of trading by corporate insiders with no delay. Using data from 3,079 insider transactions between July 2002 and April 2005, Dymke and Walter (2007) find corporate insiders in Germany exploit insider information while trading in their company's stock and realize substantial profits by doing so. Beltzer and Thessien (2007) report that insider trades are associated with significant abnormal returns, based on a sample of 2,051 insider trades initiated between July 2002 and June 2004. Using event-study methodology, they find insider trades that occur prior to an earnings announcement have a larger impact on prices.

Jaggi and Tsui (2007) report that managers of Hong Kong firms engage in upward earnings manipulation using positive discretionary accruals to maximize their private benefits on insider selling, by using a sample of insider trading transactions for the first quarter of the fiscal year that consists of 1,588 observations from 1995 through 1999. They document a positive association between upward earnings manipulation and insider selling after the fiscal year-end for Hong Kong firms. This positive association is especially evident before the 1997 Asian financial crisis. Chen, Wang, and Chen (2008) hand-collect 42 filed cases of insider trading and corresponding stock price information in Taiwan from April 10, 1993, to January 31, 2007. Their results show graphically that the cumulative abnormal return from 10 days to 1 day prior to the corporate announcement is 8.20 percent, which is significant. Zhang and Zhu (2003) utilize 1,078 announcements of merger and acquisition (M&A) and other large corporate events to test whether insider trading exists in China's stock markets. They find that not only does insider trading exist, but it is more rampant in China's securities markets than in the United States and the United Kingdom. Furthermore, because no short selling is allowed in China, insider trading takes place mainly prior to announcements of good news. Shi and Jiang (2004) document that the China Securities Regulatory Commission (CSRC) had litigated 11 insider trading cases up to April 2003. Most of the involved manipulators are corporate insiders. Insider information is based mainly on forthcoming M&A, SEO, and dividend announcements. Their conclusion is that insider trading raises the stock price levels and volatility. In general, insider trading worsens information asymmetry and market fairness, especially when a longer time horizon is considered.

Other emerging markets that have been studied regarding insider trading include Mexico by Bhattacharya, et al. (2000) and Indonesia, Malaysia, the Philippines, and Thailand by Hung and Trezevant (2003). Using a data set of corporate news announcements in Mexico from July 1994 through June 1997, Bhattacharya, et al. (2000) document that nothing much happens to a firm's stock price on an announcement date. They attribute the phenomenon of no market reaction to corporate news announcements to rampant insider trading prior to the announcements. Hung and Trezevant (2003) focus on public firms controlled by rich families in Southeast Asian countries. Using 1989 to 1996 data, a period before the Asian economic crisis, they identify 913 company-year observations of companies in Indonesia, Malaysia, the Philippines, and Thailand. Their results show that corporate insiders of Southeast Asian companies controlled by the richest families are especially aggressive in trading on their insider information of annual earnings before they are report to outsiders. What is the legal attitude toward insider trading in the region? Lopez (2000) states that no individual has ever been prosecuted, convicted, or jailed for insider trading in nearly 64 years of stock trading in Manila as of March 2000.

These studies, which cover insider trading transactions from 1950 to 2004, share three main findings. First, insider trading results in preannouncement abnormal returns. Second, insider trading is widespread worldwide. Third, corporate insiders buy before good news and sell before bad news announcements. The former trades correspond to profit making and the latter to loss avoidance incentives, respectively. Figures 6.3 and 6.4 summarize price behavior around positive news, in the presence of insider trading, as well as the corresponding asset holding by insiders.

These studies focus on insider trading by corporate executives without associating their abnormal returns with earnings manipulation, with one exception. The rise of stock-based executive compensation is a major reason behind the more recent spread of insider trading based on earnings manipulation. Even though no exact time is known when stock options became a substantial part of an executive's compensation package in the 1980s or earlier, researchers in the 1990s started investigating the link between insider trading and earnings manipulation against the background of

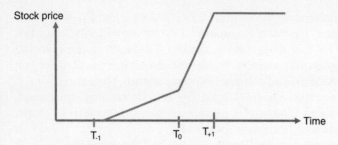

T_{-1} - T_0 : insiders accumulate shares based on private positive information
T_0 : public announcement of positive earnings surprise or other major good news
T_0 - T_{+1} : price run-up due to buy pressure
At T_{+1} : insiders keep their shares

FIGURE 6.3 Price Behavior around Positive News, in the Presence of Insider Trading

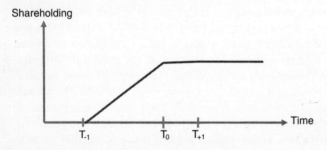

T_{-1} - T_0 : insiders accumulate shares based on private positive information
T_0 : public announcement of positive earnings surprise or other major good news
T_0 - T_{+1} : price run-up due to buy pressure
At T_{+1} : insiders keep their shares

FIGURE 6.4 Total Shareholding by Insiders

increasing stock-based compensation. Changes in compensation structure, analysts' roles, technology, regulation, and economic globalization in the last half century have all affected the truthfulness of earnings announcements and insider trading activities. We start with looking at how corporate executives' behavior changed due to increased stock-based compensation.

Evidence of More Trades by Corporate Insiders on Earnings Manipulation

Summers and Sweeney (1998) present evidence that insiders will engage in a high level of sales activity in their entity's stock in the presence of fraudulent financial reporting, based on a study of 51 firms for which an illegal act was reported by the *Wall Street Journal Index* from 1980 through 1987. From the sample of the 64 firms identified by using both SEC and media reporting in the period 1987 to 1993, Beneish (1999) documents that managers in sample firms are more likely to sell their holdings and exercise stock-appreciation rights at inflated prices in a period when earnings are overstated. Beneish and Vargus (2002) present evidence that the lower persistence of income-increasing accruals accompanied by abnormal insider selling is consistent with the notion that managers might manipulate earnings upward and then sell their own shares, based on a sample of 21,678 firm-years from 3,906 firms during the period from 1985 to 1996. Bartov and Moharam (2004) investigate the decision by senior executives of more than 1,200 listed firms to exercise a large number of stock option awards during the period from 1992 to 2001. Their findings suggest that senior executives used inside information to time abnormally large exercises of their stock options following inflated earnings through accruals manipulation so as to increase their cash payout. Kedia and Philippon (2009) use a sample of 539 firms that restated their earnings between January 1997 and June 2002 to argue that managers with larger stock and option holdings are more likely to engage in earnings manipulation because it boosts stock prices, thus permitting managers to make profitable trades. Their argument is evidenced by the fact that CEOs exercised a significantly higher fraction of their exercisable options during the misreported period. In addition, Kedia and Philippon (2009) show graphically that Enron's top executives sold a large number of shares during a string of upward earnings manipulations before announcing financial restatements in October 2001. Kedia and Philippon's results confirm the findings by Piotroski and Roulstone (2005), who utilize a sample of 25,893 firm-year observations from insider-trading data covering the period from 1992 to 1999 as well as the research of Bergstresser and Philippon (2006) on stock options exercised for the period 1993 to 2000.

In short, a large number of episodes of earnings manipulation carried out in concert with legal or illegal insider trading have shown positive links to stock-based compensation from 1980 to 2002.

It is undeniable that corporate insiders distribute a huge number of shares at lifted stock prices due to earnings manipulation (for example, Friedlan (1994); Rangan (1998); Teoh, Welch, and Wong (1998a, 1998b); Degeorge, Patel, and Zeckhauser (1999); DuCharme, Malatesta, and Sefcik (2001); Chan et al. (2006)). Corporations, after earnings manipulation before stock offering, endure lasting stock price underperformance (Loughran and Ritter 1995; Spiess and Affleck-Graves 1995; Kahle 2000). Equipped with upward earnings manipulation, corporate insiders prove to be superior information-based stock price manipulators in the secondary market. In summary, Figure 6.5 represents the price behavior around positive news, in

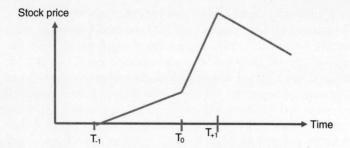

T$_{-1}$ - T$_0$: insiders accumulate shares based on private positive information
T$_0$: public announcement of positive earnings surprise due to earnings manipulation
T$_0$ - T$_{+1}$: price run-up due to buy pressure
At T$_{+1}$: insiders distribute their shares, which entails return reversal

FIGURE 6.5 Price Behavior around Positive News, in the Presence of Earnings Manipulation–based Insider Trading

the presence of earnings manipulation–based insider trading, and Figure 6.6 represents the corresponding shareholding by the manipulators.

Not only do corporate insiders who manipulate earnings become information-based manipulators, they are also monopolists due to absolute information advantage. This type of monopoly needs to be more fully studied. So far no regulatory framework has explicitly taken into account this fundamental mechanism.

To summarize, evidence shows that some corporate executives use insider information, including earnings manipulation, to make extraordinary trading gains at the expense of outside investors. Trading by corporate insiders involves an information monopoly, which will be analyzed later in

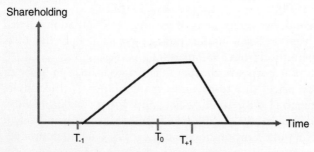

T$_{-1}$ - T$_0$: insiders accumulate based on private positive information
T$_0$: public announcement of positive earnings surprise due to earnings manipulation
T$_0$ - T$_{+1}$: price run-up due to buy pressure
At T$_{+1}$: insiders distribute their shares, which entails return reversal

FIGURE 6.6 Total Shareholding by Insiders, in the Presence of Earnings Manipulation–based Insider Trading

this chapter and more extensively in Chapter 8. Thus, it is information-based stock price manipulation. It is the form of manipulation most detrimental to fair competition in the stock market. To have perfect competition in the stock market, with fairness and transparency, this type of manipulation must be effectively regulated, while legal trading by corporate insiders is not too strongly restricted.

INSIDER TRADING WITH EARNINGS MANIPULATION IS NOT EFFECTIVELY REGULATED

Jaffe (1974) questions the effectiveness of the SEA (1934) on preventing insider trading by analyzing insider trades in five separate months during intervals from 1961 to 1968. He concluded that changes in regulation had no effect on insider trading because detection is difficult and punishment too light to serve as a deterrent. Using a sample of 179 primary security issues from 1975 to 1982, Karpoff and Lee (1991) find that an unusual number of insiders sell stock before common stock and convertible debt issues, which remained consistent with earlier empirical research results that insider trading occurs despite the prospect of legal and market penalties. In other words, all expected legal, firm, market, and personal costs added together are not high enough to prevent trading by corporate insiders completely before new issue announcements. Why? The following quotation of Stephen Bainbridge in the June 20, 2002, issue of the *Financial Times* may shed light on why corporate insiders risk legal and other consequences to engage in such misconduct (Xu 2008):

"Talking to folks in Silicon Valley, they say it (insider trading) is rampant. Despite increasingly severe penalties, people say 'I can make a million dollars and I have a million-in-one chance of getting caught.' They may be willing to take that risk."

And "even if detection were certain, one can imagine a situation where the monopoly profits were so high—in millions of pounds—that many would opt to break the law, grab the money, have plastic surgery and disappear" (*Financial Times* 1987).

Regarding insider trading statutes enacted in the 1980s,[4] Seyhun (1992) cites a number of reasons why they are not effective: No regulation of daily insider trading is available, enforcement resources are too few compared to insider trading activities, and the two legal requirements to prove illegal insider trading—legally material information and proof of fraud under criminal statutes—are too high a hurdle for regulators to clear before enforcement. Therefore, Seyhun concludes that insiders were able to trade profitably on economically important private information not covered by case law.

SEC Rule 10b5-1, enacted at the end of year 2000, may indicate that the SEC was trying to separate trading without insider information from trading with insider information by corporate insiders. But the SEC focuses on the information side and initiation phase of a trading plan, not the completion phase. And the SEC assumes that insiders can trade when not aware of future insider information. How is it possible that insiders are not aware of future information they are going to generate and disclose after they have submitted a trading plan? One can see that the SEC intends to protect the trading rights of corporate insiders when no insider information is involved. But the SEC does not consider the fact that corporate insiders are not just insider information takers, they are the insider information generators. And the SEC regulation considers only the time of the initiation of the trading plan, not its completion. More than that, the rule does not stop insiders from trading even when they obtain insider information after the initiation of their trading plan. This provides a safe harbor for those insiders who strategically initiate trades when no insider information is available, but close trades after the trader has insider information at hand. This is possible because the insider can manipulate both the timing and the content of the future information disclosure after the initiation of the trades (Jagolinzer 2009).

International Insider Trading Regulation

The previous studies all focus on U.S. insider trading regulations. What does the international experience suggest? Bris (2005) surveys insider trading laws and enforcement in a sample of 4,541 acquisitions conducted in 52 countries from January 1990 to December 1999. He finds that laws that proscribe insider trading fail to eliminate insider profits. In contrast, enforcement increases both the incidence and the profitability of insider trading associated with acquisitions. Increased insider trading profit can be more related to the simultaneous increasing weight of stock options for managers' compensation and booming stock markets in many countries, as well as the convenience and low commissions of online trading in the 1990s. However, the low effectiveness of insider trading laws and enforcement worldwide is obvious, a point that agrees with the evidence discovered by Bhattacharya and Daouk (2002).

Insiders' Timing of Trade to Avoid Legal Risk

Insiders have many regulation-adapting means to plan trades. For example, they shift from traditional insider trades that transact immediately prior to or following the earnings announcement date, to the current practice of holding shares for weeks, quarters, or even years before selling for profit upon consecutive upward earnings manipulation. Recent literature on insider trading sheds some empirical light on how insiders consider timing in their trades so that they can profit as usual, but without being detected by regulators.

Based on nearly 13,862 quarterly earnings announcements by 644 firms from 1984 to 1991, Garfinkel (1997) examines the effects of the Insider Trading and Securities Fraud Enforcement Act (ITSFEA) of 1988 on insider trading around the time of earnings announcements. He finds that increased regulatory toughness has affected the timing of insiders' trades around earnings announcements. However, the volume, frequency, and profits of insider trading were not investigated. The London Stock Exchange Model Code (1977) imposes a two-month close period, prior to company earnings announcements, in order to curb insider trading. Hillier and Marshall (2002) note that although the close period affects the timing of the trades by directors, it is unable to affect the performance or distribution of the trades. Directors consistently earn abnormal returns irrespective of the period in which they trade. Their data sample consists of 3,871 purchases and 3,521 sales spanning the period January 1, 1992, to December 31, 1996. Defining insiders as directors or officers, Ke, Huddart, and Petroni (2003) examine insider-trading patterns in advance of a break, following a string of quarterly earnings increases, and find that insider sales increase three to nine quarters before the earnings break. Their data sample contains 80,215 firm-quarters for 4,179 unique firms in the calendar years 1989 to 1997. The authors conclude that insiders initiate trades several quarters ahead of the break in order to avoid the appearance of trading on near-term material news about earnings, which is prohibited by regulations. In addition, there is little abnormal selling in the two quarters immediately prior to the break to distance themselves from established legal jeopardy. Matsumoto (2002) and Richardson, Teoh, and Wysocki (2004) document how managers manipulate earnings upward and guide analysts downward in the 1990s. Richardson, Teoh, and Wysocki (2004) further explore the regulatory change of the enactment of the ITSFEA of 1988 and the lifting of the short-swing rule for insiders in 1991, how insiders' trading behavior responded to this, and how the pattern of equity analysts' forecasts adapted to these changes. By using a sample of equity analysts' forecasts of annual earnings from 1983 to 1998, they found that in the post-1992 period analysts made optimistic forecasts at the start of the year and then walked down their estimates to a level the firm could beat by the end of the year. This finding corresponds to the allegations made by security regulators and the business press that firms play an earnings-guidance game to facilitate favorable insider trades after earnings announcements (for example, Cotter, Tuna, and Wysocki

(2006)). These instances illustrate the sophistication of corporate insiders in timing their trades by manipulating not only disclosed earnings, but also analysts' forecasts in adapting to regulatory changes. Piotroski and Roulstone (2005) utilize a sample of 25,893 firm-year observations from insider trading data available between 1992 and 1999 and find that the relation between insider trading and earnings performance shifted from current to future earnings news in order to avoid regulatory scrutiny under new legislation expanding the enforcement of insider trading laws.

Option Backdating

Option backdating, being unique to U.S. public companies, is a recent anti-fraud enforcement priority of the SEC. It is a new type of trading by corporate insiders. Thanks to the SEC regulation for executive compensation disclosure enacted in late 1992, data of stock option grants are available. Yermack (1997) uses a sample of 620 stock option awards to CEOs between 1992 and 1994 and finds that the stock returns during the 50 trading days after the option grant date outperform those of the market by more than 2 percent. In general, corporate executives choose the grant date before good news announcements or right after bad news announcements. Yermack concludes that the favorable timing of CEO stock option awards makes the awards look like a surrogate form of insider trading by CEOs. Aboody and Kasznik (2000) infer the dates of 4,426 stock option awards made between 1992 and 1996 to the CEOs of 1,264 firms. They document that a majority of option grant dates are scheduled that result in insignificant abnormal return before the awards. However, the subsequent 30 days see nearly 2 percent abnormal returns. Aboody and Kasznik (2000) have similar observations as Yermack that CEOs opportunistically manipulate the timing of their information disclosures so that their options are granted before announcements of good news and right after bad news. Lie (2005) focuses on the timing of awards for unscheduled option grant dates by comparing 1,668 unscheduled CEO stock option awards with 1,426 scheduled awards from 1992 through 2002. He finds a sharp V-shaped stock return pattern around the unscheduled award date. The average abnormal return during the 30 trading days leading up to the awards is -3 percent. After the unscheduled awards, there is a sharp reversal. The average abnormal return is 2 percent during the first 10 days afterward, and it is almost another 2 percent during the next 20 days. Lie (2005) explicitly suggests that backdating is evidenced in some unscheduled option awards, which is true particularly for awards between 1995 and 2002. Narayanan, Schipani, and Seyhun (2007) also report the V-shaped stock return pattern around the stock option grant date for 413 pre-SOX firm grant dates from January 1,

2000, through August 28, 2002. However, for 333 post-SOX 413 firm grant dates from August 29, 2002, through December 31, 2004, they observe almost monotonically upward-trending stock returns for the 90 trading days after the grant dates. They conclude that SOX has clearly reduced the practice of option backdating but has not fully eliminated it.[5]

Academic research detects this manipulative dealing by corporate insiders. A March 2006 issue of the *Wall Street Journal* ran an in-depth report on the six companies that played the option backdating game since the 1990s (Forelle and Bandler 2006). The SEC gathered full strength to regulate this type of trading- and disclosure-related manipulation in 2006 (SEC 2006).

Option granting most likely ends with stock trading. Option backdating is automatically linked to earnings manipulation in all the litigation cases we have studied. Hence, it falls within the scope of this chapter.

Insider Trading Prosecution Rate Is Too Low

What do scholars in law, criminology, and other noneconomic fields say about insider trading legislation in the United States and other nations? Tomasic (1991), in his influential book, *Casino Capitalism,* complained that he could not find any successful prosecution of insider trading in Australia's history of securities regulation at the time of his study. He expressed dissatisfaction with the ineffectiveness of the regulatory processes in Australia, noting that the number of insider trading prosecutions was very low, although a substantial number of alleged insider trading cases had been identified by the stock exchanges and the regulating agencies. This situation is not unique to Australia. Tomasic also found in both the United States and the United Kingdom that it is difficult to prove an insider trading case and that the courts are usually reluctant to regulate insider trading. Chapman and Denniss (2005) document that there were only six prosecutions for insider trading in Australia between 1990 and 2000. They point out that detection by the Australian regulatory agencies is both expensive and inaccurate. Even after a rare successful detection and completed investigation, achieving conviction presents further difficulties. McNally and Smith (2003) investigate the insider trading cases pursued by provincial securities commissions in Canada from 1980 to 2002. Their calculations show that on average less than one insider trading case a year has resulted in a conviction, although there are a large number of tips and facts citing insider trading offenses. McNally and Smith (2003) argue that the inefficacy of insider trading laws may reduce insiders' fear of prosecution and punishment. This insight is echoed by Cheng (2004), who studies regulatory statutes and enforcement actions as well as the prosecution rates in Canada and China. In the 19-year period from 1985 to 2003, the three provincial securities commissions in Ontario, British Columbia, and Alberta, Canada, conducted 23, 17, and 4 insider trading inquiries, respectively. Among 43 unique cases, 16 received convictions and two jail terms were imposed. Cheng (2004) concludes that neither Canada nor China has sufficient insider trading regulations to curb such pervasive misconduct. China had not made insider trading a regulatory priority until 2001, 10 years after the inception of its state securities markets. Both the provincial securities commissions and the Crown prosecutors are reluctant to take up insider trading cases in Canada. Lack of consistency in enforcement is shown by the infrequency with which insider trading cases are pursued in the two countries. Cheng believes that a primary challenge to enforcement comes from the fact that insider trading cases are too difficult to detect and prove in court. Szockyj (1993) conducted extensive research on the SEC and insider trading detection and regulatory procedures and concluded that the SEC "has achieved only limited success in its attempts to penetrate the secrecy inherent in insider trading."

These scholars in law, criminology, and other fields of social science are more interested in why the insider trading prosecution rate remains so low in several countries. The phenomenon shows that several key hurdles, such as proving materiality of information, set by insider trading laws are so difficult to overcome that they render the laws nearly unenforceable in reality. It shows the incompleteness of the law-only approach and that measures from other fields need to be included to ensure regulation is more effective and is capable of being made workable on a good scale.

In summary, illegal insider trading often happens after earnings manipulation. Both—illegal insider trading and earnings manipulation—are instances of financial misconduct. The legal approach will be effective only when all needed evidence is collected. This has proven to be rather difficult after the misconduct has been completed. We need to devise regulatory measures based on financial reality to reduce insider trading preemptively in addition to the *ex post* law-centered approach that currently exists.

INFORMATION MONOPOLY AND INFORMATION ASYMMETRY

Corporate insiders are the creators of potentially price-moving information. They have an absolute information advantage over public investors, who are information takers. Corporate insiders are different from the used car dealers in the classic paper by Akerlof (1970). The used car dealers are not creators of information about the quality of cars in their inventory. They are information takers, as are the car buyers. But time plays a key role in their decisions. The dealers know the information earlier than the buyers. There is an information asymmetry, and the dealers have an advantage. But they are not able to create information. They have only a time advantage over the buyers in utilizing their information asymmetry.

Corporate insiders are setters of information, because, unlike used car dealers, corporate insiders can create and change information. In other words, corporate insiders enjoy an information content advantage over public investors. They also access the information earlier than anyone else. Public investors are information takers. Therefore, corporate insiders have both a time advantage and a content advantage over public investors. In short, corporate insiders have an absolute information advantage over the uninformed investors. The advantage lies in the price-moving potential of the company's stock. Once the potentially price-moving information is publicly announced through a credible media outlet such as the *Wall Street Journal,* substantial publicity and credibility are attached to the information in addition to the issuer's utmost credibility. When the three elements, that is, potentially price-moving information, publicity, and credibility, are jointly disseminated to numerous investors, many of them will be convinced and trade according to the information. We may call this entity, composed of the three elements, an information monopoly. More complete analyses of information monopolies are seen in Chapter 8 when we focus on information-based manipulation.

From this analysis, we can say that corporate insiders possess an information monopoly, or monopolistic power from the information once it is publicly released, compared to outside investors. When corporate insiders trade on such information, they are information-based market manipulators. This monopolistic behavior needs to be regulated in the spirit of antitrust legislation.

PROPOSALS TO EFFECTIVELY REGULATE TRADING BY CORPORATE INSIDERS

Corporate insiders have an absolute information advantage, timing flexibility, and spatial secrecy when trading their company's shares. Once the potentially price-moving information is publicly announced through a credible mass media outlet, the information monopoly is formed. The information monopoly gives corporate insiders monopolistic power. One needs antitrust regulations to eliminate or substantially reduce the actual impact to trading gains of this information advantage. Trading itself may not be monopolistic. The information monopoly, when utilized in a trading strategy, transforms the latter into a manipulative one, thus leading to monopolistic trading gains. It is true that one can hardly detect or reduce the information advantage because of the awkward impossibility of detection of information about corporate insiders' minds (Newkirk and Robertson 1998). Trading, however, is needed to convert this information advantage into real wealth. Therefore, regulators can work toward a more equitable market on the trading side by reducing the capacity of the corporate insiders to turn the information monopoly into realized trading gains. Thus, we propose a regulatory solution by focusing on several aspects that are key to trading. One is trading volume. The other is trading speed, or number of trading days when the total volume traded is given.

Two Measures to Regulate Trading by Corporate Insiders

- *Measure one:* Our suggestion is to divide the total trading volume of any stock held by corporate insiders into numerous smaller trading volumes. Using a trading day as the unit, we propose to have a limit, say, 1 percent of the current shareholding, on the absolute value of the daily trading volume.

  Thus, the corporate insider may still have a full information advantage during any trading day. However, the insider cannot turn the advantage into the maximum trading gains that he or she desires after the announcement takes effect. This measure aims at regulating profit-seeking trades placed by corporate insiders. It has little effect when corporate insiders time one to five years in advance to plan sales of most or all of their shareholdings before serious loss or bankruptcy (Seyhun and Bradley 1997; Kedia and Philippon 2009). Hence, one needs another measure to deal with loss avoidance trades made by corporate insiders.

- *Measure two:* To hold corporate insiders accountable for the risk of their stock crashing, we propose to hold a substantial percentage, such as 50 percent of their total grants or investments, until one year after their tenure with the company is over. Then they can sell the remaining 50 percent of shares under the dynamic daily limit proposed in Chapter 3. We may call this the withholding rule.

Three Numerical Examples Can Illustrate the Mechanism of the Proposed Measures

- *First example: Sales by corporate insiders after earnings manipulation.* In this example, a corporate insider exercises his stock holding of 1 million shares (1 percent of 100 million outstanding shares). His information advantage is his knowledge of the current quarterly earnings with upward manipulation. He knows that the stock price will climb immediately after several consecutive upward-trending earnings announcements, and plans to sell all of his holdings right after the upcoming announcement. Assume that the stock price of the company climbs 8 percent on the announcement date after the news is released just before the stock market opens. Also, we assume that the market completely builds in the positive earnings surprise, in one trading day. The corporate insider completes the sales of 1 million shares by the end of the day.

When we closely examine the status of the information advantage before and after the announcement, we will see that the advantage starts from the moment when the manipulated financial statements are completed. And this advantage remains until the earnings announcement is available to all market participants. The announcement day sees the stock prices climb, which indicates the information advantage being transformed into trading gain at the end of the day. Afterward, the effect of the advantage disappears substantially or even completely, when no new buyers enter the market, based on the manipulated earnings disclosure. For demonstration purposes, we assume the complete disappearance of the effect after the announcement day in this example.

In this example, without our proposed measure, the insider makes full use of his information advantage. He will make an 8 percent return (or $80,000 in cash) in addition to the cumulative capital gains earned by holding the 1 million shares since the grant date. This is the scenario without our recommendation in place.

If we assume that our recommended regulatory measure is implemented, as a corporate insider he has a daily trading limit of 1 percent of his original total holding of 1 million shares, that is, a constant limit of 10,000 shares per day. That is, on every trading day, he can trade (sell, buy, or both) a maximum 10,000 shares.[6] Then he can make use of his information advantage for a maximum of 1 percent of his total shareholding on the day of the earnings announcement. If he chooses to sell all his shares, he will need 99 more trading days.

Assume he will obtain an information advantage again for the next quarterly earnings announcement at the rate of a further 8 percent return. He now has traded 2 percent of his total holdings with the effect of the information advantage and the other 98 percent without any such effect. Of course, he may choose other ways that he deems better to exercise the remaining 99 percent. But he cannot maintain the capacity of turning an information monopoly into predictable wealth on each of the remaining 99 trading days. Concisely speaking, he still has the information monopoly on any day. However, he cannot turn the advantage into trading gains for all but one or a small percentage of his total shareholding.

■ *Second example: Purchases and sales of the stock of an acquisition target company by a corporate insider.* Here, the insider is not trading his own company's shares, but the target—another public firm—that his company plans to acquire. Suppose he bought 200,000 shares in several days right after the acquisition decision was made but not announced, and he plans to sell all of them on the announcement date of the acquisition. Assume that the target stock price increases 15 percent at the end of the trading day when the takeover is announced. He would make a 15 percent return on 200,000 shares. This is the scenario if our proposed measure is not implemented.

Now we impose a constant 1 percent daily limit on an insider's sale of 200,000 shares. Since the daily limit becomes a flat 2,000 shares for the insider, he needs 100 trading days to complete the sale of 200,000 shares. Assume that the stock price increase due to the acquisition announcement lasts three whole trading days with a 15 percent, 7 percent, and 3 percent daily return, respectively, from the moment the public announcement is made. The announcement effect extends to three trading days, but on a declining scale. After the three trading days, he has no information advantage because the market has completely digested the takeover announcement. But he has 97 more trading days to complete the sale of his stock holdings. There is some chance that the stock price may increase during the 97 trading days. There is also some chance that the price may drop during the same period. He cannot control either. Thus, his probability of turning the information monopoly into trading gains for the holding of 200,000 shares has been greatly reduced without prohibiting him from trading. In brief, the corporate insider now carries downside risk in the takeover scenario. The insider may need to carefully balance out the expected gains and losses during the lengthy horizon after the announcement.

■ *Third example: Sales of total shareholding by a corporate insider to avoid loss due to expected bankruptcy filing.* Let us revisit the second case presented earlier, which echoes the Enron debacle. Suppose a CFO started selling his entire holding of 1 million shares about two years prior to an expected bankruptcy filing when the stock price stood at $75. He is careful to sell a small proportion at a time, say 10,000 shares. He is aware that all other corporate insiders are slowly selling their holdings, too. By half a year prior to the bankruptcy filing, he has sold his 1 million shares with a total profit of $70 million. Suppose the share price at that time is $40. Soon he resigns from the company. The stock price continues to decline to $30, when an earnings restatement is issued. It speeds up the drop of the share price from $30 to $0.95 in barely one month. Then bankruptcy is filed. And the stock is delisted.

This scenario could happen even with enforcement of the daily limit proposed in this chapter. Unfairness occurred when all of the corporate insiders slowly sold out their shareholdings while manipulating upward earnings and issuing other false and misleading information about the company's performance. Many retail investors were locked in for a long time before panic forced them to sell at severe losses. And those who sold at below $1 suffered near wipeout of all their investments. Unfairness is not the only problem. The trading by corporate insiders also contributed to the decline of their company's stock. They eventually speeded up the single-stock crash from $30 to pennies within just one month.

We now apply the 50 percent withholding rule toward the CFO's total grant of 1 million shares. He can sell only 50 percent of 1 million shares before his resignation, which is assumed to be $40 million in profit. His other half million shares will be virtually worthless one year after his resignation, since the company's stock has by now been delisted. Actually, with this heavy expected loss in mind, he may not dare to conduct accounting frauds as rampantly as in this example. The philosophy underlying this measure is to allow corporate insiders to face serious downside risk so that their personal interests would be more aligned with the interests of the corporation and everyone, including long-term shareholders. Compared to the clawback regulation contained in SOX, the proposed measure is preventive. The clawback regulation is still primarily an *ex post* measure even though it may have certain preemptive deterrence effect.

Regulating daily trading volume, in addition to the regulations proposed in Chapters 3 and 4, will limit and slow down, but not prohibit, trades by corporate insiders with insider information. Daily trading limits placed on corporate insider transactions with total shareholdings of more than 1,000 shares could be set, for instance, as the minimum of 1 percent of the current holding, a fixed number, and as a dynamic limit for every market participant, as proposed in Chapter 3. The constant daily limit is adjustable according to the priorities set by regulators. This leaves regulators ample flexibility in establishing these parameters.

Holding a substantial portion, say, 50 percent of the total shareholdings by corporate insiders, until one year after their tenures with the company are over will be preventive and avoid the legal difficulty in the reimbursement enforcement after the accounting fraud or other misconduct. Having this measure and the proposed daily trading limit as well as the clawback regulation in place, the efficiency of the profit-seeking and loss-avoiding trades by corporate insiders is expected to be greatly reduced. It is indirect but effective antitrust regulation of the corporate insiders' information advantage.

Corporate insiders are the *de facto* guardians of the company's stock. They live with the stock in any situation where the stock climbs strongly or declines sharply or remains flat. Is it fair to allow them to run away from the stock when they foresee severe risk in the company? The withholding of a substantial portion of their stock is a serious reminder that they are responsible from the beginning to the end of their insider positions with the company. The purpose of the measure is to discourage corporate insiders from focusing on short-term stock price gain and endangering the long-term prospects of their company.

With both profit-seeking- and loss-avoidance-oriented trading by corporate insiders in frequent check, the impacts of these two types of trading on market stability and fairness are greatly reduced. Equally important, the potential for systemic risk from trading by corporate insiders is extensively obviated.

Two Measures to Regulate Abnormal Price Behavior Prior to a Corporate Announcement

Not every trade based on potentially price-moving information is due to corporate insiders. But corporate insiders are the source of the insider information. How do regulators control the leak of insider information to other investors who obtain such information from corporate insiders? Existing insider trading laws have dealt with this issue. The approach is, in general, *ex post*. The enforcement effectiveness is greatly reduced because of difficulties in collecting all the necessary evidence. We propose two more preventive measures based on some of the patterns discussed previously: the pre-announcement price run-up for good news (and price decline before bad news). We recommend the following two additional measures to substantially reduce the monopolistic trading gains of temporary insiders and informed investors.

- *Measure three:* Any corporate announcement needs to be submitted to the regulating agency at least three days prior to the planned date of release. The regulating agency can call off or postpone sufficiently the public release of the proposed announcement and start investigation if the stock in question has displayed abnormal price behavior prior to the release date. Abnormal stock behavior can be defined as a significant price run-up prior to good news or a price decline prior to bad news. The numerical threshold value of significant price change can be established based on the past history of the stock, for example, 1 percent above the average daily return of the previous one month for a positive announcement (or 1 percent below for a negative announcement), contingent on no other major price-moving news events about the stock.[7]

The agency may hold for a while without taking any action. It may start to investigate the abnormal price run-up or decline and find the investors who possibly traded on insider information. An investigation for an abnormal price run-up, once publicly released, will likely cause the stock price to decline, which is contrary to the insider traders' expectation and, as such, it increases their downside risk. Hence, release of information from the investigation will improve deterrence. For pre-announcement price decline, public disclosure of an investigation may not be necessary. If the threshold is surpassed too frequently, say, three times a year by the same violator, a more severe measure is needed.

- *Measure four:* Breaking the abnormal price behavior threshold in measure three triggers the accountability of the issuer's CEO. The accountability pressures the CEO to self-regulate generation and release of any price-moving information. This is a more effective approach than putting all the burden on the regulating agency, since the CEO has full control over who can access the price-sensitive information. As a preventive measure, the CEO may be required to submit a list of insiders to the regulating agency of those participating in the preparation of any particular announcement.

DISCUSSION OF THE FOUR PROPOSED MEASURES

One may well ask why it is necessary to impose another daily limit on trades by corporate insiders since we have already proposed one for every investor in the market. The explanation is that the daily limit set forth in Chapter 3 is aimed at regulating trade-based manipulation that originates from large shareholding concentrations. The asymmetric information generated by the trade-based manipulator to his advantage is never disclosed, unless the manipulator is investigated. Public investors can only guess what causes the stock price to move up or down. Moreover, large and sudden price movements downward can cause panic selling because of the information's opaqueness. This type of manipulation has the potential to threaten the market's stability and to cause a marketwide crisis. But corporate insiders' trades pose more danger to fairness and transparency in addition to the market stability and security of their company's stock. The daily trading limit on corporate insiders is expected to substantially dilute their capacity to turn information monopoly into actual advantage in profit-seeking or loss-avoidance trades. It is not intended to eliminate such trades made by corporate insiders. It just forces more uncertainty and downside risk onto corporate insiders when they try to transform their information monopoly into unfair trading returns. And this limit targets more certain trading sides that can be fully controlled by regulators, rather than the uncertain and ever-changing information sides, which prove to be too hard to implement.

Would such a daily limit deprive corporate insiders of being able to trade legally? No. This limit is imposed only when corporate insiders trade their own company's stock and take over target company's shares. There is no such a limit if the corporate insiders trade other stocks, about which they have no inside information. An obvious benefit of applying the daily limit is that it encourages corporate insiders to concentrate on running their business because trading based on insider information is effectively curbed and one source of distraction is blocked.

The withholding measure is an amendment of the corporate insiders' responsibility to their own company's stock and that of outside investors who hold the stock. It actually encourages them to manage the company with a long-term priority and sustainable strategies rather than focusing on near-term stock performance. It targets the weak spot of corporate insiders if they have any manipulative plans. It does not hurt honest corporate insiders. Of course, successful implementation of this measure requires other players in the stock market to play fair, especially those who can move the market by releasing information and appearing on TV, on the Internet, or in print media. Chapters 7 and 8 aim at regulating information-based manipulation assisted by sell-side analysts and conducted by some investors who can significantly move the stock prices using media platforms.

Measures three and four are expected to target insider trading by any investors. They can be corporate insiders, temporary insiders, or informed investors who somehow obtain insider information prior to the announcement date. The accountability measure, or measure four, is upstream prevention, and the threshold measure, or measure three, is downstream prevention. The effects from implementing both measures occur prior to a corporate announcement. These two measures are expected to greatly reduce insider trading prior to major corporate announcements such as takeover offers or publication of annual financial reports.

The four proposed measures do not conflict with extant insider trading laws. They just add effective, easy-to-implement, and inexpensive means for regulators to employ. They also give flexibility such as computerization to regulators, since they are quantifiable and adjustable. So regulators maintain full control over the measures, while legal enforcement all too often results in uncertainties, years of difficult investigative work, and numerous time-consuming legal battles. Additionally, the work that regulators have to consider is how to define corporate insiders and their total shareholding, which may vary across companies. This is especially the case during takeovers and is left for regulators, given their priorities and market characteristics.

CONCLUSION

From the literature on insider trading, we see that the century-long phenomenon has had detrimental effects on investor protection and on achieving fair and transparent perfect competition in the stock market. From the research on the low effectiveness of insider trading regulations worldwide, we recognize that four measures, based on financial reality, are needed in order to improve the enforcement effectiveness and efficiency of the existing law-centered regulations. They target trading by corporate insiders, other insiders, or informed investors on the insider information. The principle of the four measures is to curb the transformation of insider information, which becomes an information monopoly once publicly released through a credible media outlet, into unfair trading profits. These four measures are expected to extend the insider trading regulations to daily operations and enhance their effectiveness, efficiency, and completeness. The four measures are also expected to be easy to implement and easily adjustable by regulators, since they are quantifiable. They are supposed to be inexpensive, too.

With an antitrust spirit to regulate information monopolies, the four proposed measures are expected to improve investor protection, as well as promote fair and transparent competition for trading profits so that the stock market moves toward more perfect competition. The proposed measures are also expected to enhance market stability and prevent systemic risk, particularly when insiders hold a significant portion of outstanding shares.

NOTES

1. This chapter was presented at the 9th NTU International Conference on Economics, Finance, and Accounting, Taipei, May 25–26, 2011.
2. *Materiality* is a legal term in the United States. We will focus on the finance aspect of material information. To distinguish, we use the terminology *potentially price-moving information*.
3. The state regulating agency, China Securities Regulatory Commission (CSRC), ordered the first insider trading penalty just three years after the opening of the

stock exchanges in Shanghai and Shenzhen in 1991. Since 2008, the CSRC has heightened its enforcement on insider trading. By August 27, 2010, CSRC had formally investigated 31 insider trading cases in 2010 alone. It issued administrative orders for 7 cases and furthered 12 cases for criminal investigation to the Ministry of Public Security (Cai 2010).

4. Two insider trading acts were passed and enacted in the 1980s. The expected total legal and financial costs are much higher for violators. The Insider Trading Sanctions Act of 1984 (ITSA) raised criminal penalties, imposed jail sentences, and elevated penalties equal to three times the amount of insider profits. The Insider Trading and Securities Fraud Enforcement Act of 1988 (ITSFEA) held top management accountable for employees' illegal trading and raised criminal penalties (Seyhun 1992).

5. Effective on August 29, 2002, SOX requires that most grants be reported within two business days following the execution date of the transaction.

6. Normally this limit should be below the daily limit for any investor proposed in Chapter 3. Otherwise, the latter is applied.

7. Monitoring pre-event volume increase is another regulatory dimension. A quantitative threshold can be produced using the previous month's daily average as a benchmark.

CHAPTER 7

Preventing Stock Market Crises (V)

Regulating Information Manipulation by Sell-Side Analysts

Xin Yan

Lawrence R. Klein

Viktoria Dalko

Ferenc Gyurcsány

Michael H. Wang[1]

Sell-side analysts possess potentially price-moving information gained through equity research. Its importance can be magnified by the publicity effect of a credible media outlet. The price-moving potential, the publicity it gains, and the credibility of analysts' research and the disseminator define the value of sell-side-analyst-generated information. These are the three pillars of the information monopoly of sell-side analysts.

In the current chapter we present evidence that analyst-generated information has investment value, but mainly to informed investors by assisting them in their (often manipulative) trading strategies. It has marketing value to issuers. It misleads and could hurt uninformed investors. It also creates and frequently sets off mini-bubbles and long-term underperformance that are detrimental to investor protection, market stability, and even systemic security. In brief, sell-side analysts are often assistants or colluders in information-based manipulation. There are powerful measures targeting wrongdoing by sell-side analysts in extant securities regulations. Repeated regional and global financial crises indicate, however, that more research needs to be performed and effective remedies need to be provided targeting the trading around public release of analyst-generated information.

This chapter proposes six measures for securities regulators that may be implemented to complement current securities laws and rules. The first five together are meant to fairly regulate, through effective oversight, trading by the informed trader who utilizes analysts' information monopolies. They enable related trading information to be more transparent, and involved analysts and their firms to be more accountable. The last measure proposes public service in equity analysis of every stock to all investors. These measures are all oriented to make the stock market a more level and transparent playing field for all participants, so normal, even perfect competition for trading profits with fairness and transparency can be enhanced, investor protection improved, price volatility contained, and systemic risk reduced.

WHAT IS THE ACTUAL ROLE OF SELL-SIDE ANALYSTS?

In the information loop from the issuer to investors making trading decisions, analyst-generated information is important, second only to the issuer's annual reports and business newspaper articles in the eyes of individual investors (National Credibility Index 1999). Earnings information is most relied on for investors to buy or sell shares, according to issuer managers' experience (Graham, Harvey, and Rajgopal 2005). Sell-side analysts are considered experts in the stocks or sectors they follow. Their investment opinions are ranked number three by individual investors as more relied upon information for trading decisions (National Credibility Index 1999).

Ideally, the earnings numbers are factual and complete, and the estimates are objective and transparent to investors and regulators. However, the reality has repeatedly brought about press allegations, regulatory enforcement, and class-action lawsuits against managers of public corporations for earnings manipulation, and against equity analysts for upward-biased forecasts or recommendations. Chapter 5 presents extensive analysis of earnings manipulation and proposes regulatory measures, based on enforcement actions and private lawsuits in the past 50 years in the United States. This chapter focuses on analyst-generated information and its impact on investors (particularly uninformed small investors), and its value to issuers, investment banks, and brokerage firms in the global setting. To understand the characteristics of this type of information, we have to be clear on what similarities exist between analyst and issuer-generated information from the perspective of the impact on investors' trading decisions. These similarities determine what role analysts are actually playing in the stock market.

Since their earnings estimates, recommendations, and stock price forecasts are published, they seem to provide a public service to a large number of investors. But do they truly act as public servants? We will review evidence of certain analysts reporting first to their proprietary trading colleagues, and also providing their client institutions with research data before public release. They are also marketing favorites for investment bankers to attract underwriting business. They attend closed-door conferences with issuer executives. They sometimes privately scorn the stocks they give public buy ratings to as junk. They frequently appear on TV channels such as CNBC or are reported by newspapers such as the *Wall Street Journal* or *Shanghai Securities News* (Ellis 2009). So who are they? What is the actual role they are playing?

Generally, buy-side analysts do not publish their research results and have a sole responsibility to investors who are clients of their fund. They have only one master—their fund manager at the firm that may be a mutual fund, pension fund, or hedge fund. They do not serve other people (Reingold 2006). In contrast, sell-side analysts publish their research. They publish free stock recommendations for the investing public. Their earnings estimates, or earnings per share (EPS) estimates, are circulated by financial data service firms. They are employed by investment banks, brokerage houses, or research-only firms. The most influential ones are likely to be employed by investment banks. Because they are financially supported by the investment banking department, they seem to serve the investment banking business of the firm that has public firms among their clients. Since their recommendations can be used by any investor, they seem to provide public services, too. In other words, they have three masters (Fisch and Sale 2003). Are they serving all of them? Or do they appear to serve them all but not equally in real terms? Massive evidence prompts questions whether they are fairly serving public investors.

This chapter tries to identify whom the sell-side analysts are actually serving, and whom they seem to serve but actually mislead. What value do they have to their three masters? What underlies that value? We start with the well-established regularity in stock price behavior around release of analysts' recommendations published in business media. Then we gather replicating empirical data from the U.S. stock markets, other developed markets, and emerging markets. The regularity reveals the key point to this chapter: The potentially price-moving information, its publicity, and credibility form an analyst' information monopoly. It describes the fact that only those informed of analyst-generated monopolistic information before release can surely profit. The uninformed are constantly misled and often lose in stock trading following analysts' recommendations.

HOW IS THE VALUE OF SELL-SIDE ANALYSTS' WORK DEFINED?

Literature shows that dissemination of any analyst's recommendations and estimates produces short-term abnormal returns in accordance with the direction and magnitude of the forecast, recommendation revision, and target price set by the analyst (Lys and Sohn 1990; Abarbanell 1991; Womack 1996; Francis and Soffer 1997; Brav and Lehavy 2003; Asquith, Mikhail, and Au 2005; Mikhail, Walther, and Willis 2007). In other words, any analyst's publications can move stock prices, and thus they have price-moving power.

Actually, any information about stocks, either analyst recommendations or stock picking by renowned investors, media reporting, and even gossip (Kiymaz, 1999) or rumors (Chapter 8) about stocks, have price-moving potential to a certain extent. How much market reaction the price-moving potential causes depends mainly on the publicity effect of the information disseminator.[2] The following section selects studies on stock recommendations by certain research analysts, published in business media columns. We pay attention particularly to what pattern the recommended stock price behaves before and after the time of publication of the analysts' recommendation, revision, or estimate. We also try to find out who might profit from the announcement effect and who might lose. For simplicity of presentation, we pay exclusive attention to buy recommendations. We begin with such recommendations in the related U.S. stock markets.

The U.S. Markets

Starting with Lloyd-Davies and Canes (1978), several researchers have examined the effect on stock prices of the publication of analysts' recommendations in the *Wall Street Journal (WSJ)* column Heard on the Street (HOTS). Some studies are motivated by the well-publicized conviction of R. Foster Winans, who was the column writer for HOTS from 1982 to 1984 (Liu, Smith, and Syed 1990). They may have different interpretations in their results, but the results in different time periods share the same pattern, that is, price run-up prior to certain buy recommendations published in the column, followed, however, by price decline (often lasting) after the publication. Let us examine some examples in detail.

Lloyd-Davies and Canes (1978) worked with a sample of 597 buy recommendations and 188 sell recommendations published in HOTS between

1970 and 1971. They present data that the stock prices increase continuously two days prior to the publication date of a buy recommendation. After peaking on the publication day, the price immediately declines for a week or so. One of their conclusions is that analysts' recommendations do provide inside information and are not merely self-fulfilling prophecies. Liu, Smith, and Syed (1990) examined *WSJ*'s HOTS column from 1982 to 1985 and reported significant announcement date returns for buy recommendations. Consistent with other HOTS research, their findings repeat the pattern of a few days of price run-ups prior to the announcement date of buy recommendations, followed, however, by continuous sessions of price declines after the announcement. They attribute the abnormal volume increases prior to announcement to advance trading by insiders.

Beneish (1991) examines the market reactions to publication of analysts' recommendations in HOTS using the period 1978 to 1979 and reports results similar to those of Lloyd-Davies and Canes (1978). Beneish (1991) also presents evidence that merely a secondary dissemination on *Wall Street Transcript* cannot explain the strong market reactions to the analysts' information published in HOTS, which enjoys a much larger readership. Bauman, Datta, and Iskandar-Datta (1995) report that the short-term price behavior around publication of analysts' recommendations in HOTS is consistent with previous HOTS studies. Their data provide evidence that in a very volatile market in 1987, the pattern of price run-ups prior to HOTS publication and price declines in the postpublication week still held true. These studies investigated stock price behavior around the publication date of presumably already released analyst-generated information. Their results have established regularity. In other words, for buy recommendations, the regularity is that price run-ups begin a few days prior to the publication date, and then the stock price declines occur in the postpublication week. The peak may shift from the publication date to one or two days after the publication date in a few studies, but the regularity otherwise remains.

If the HOTS column generates such regularity in market reaction, do other columns in the *WSJ* or different print media share this capability? First, we survey several studies of the *WSJ*'s Dartboard column. Barber and Loeffler (1993) analyzed returns and volumes around the announcement of analysts' recommendations appearing in the monthly Dartboard column of the *WSJ* from October 1988 to October 1990. The 95 stocks selected by analysts experienced a 4.06 percent abnormal return over the two-day period consisting of the publication day and the subsequent day, and a −2.08 percent return from day 2 through day 25. Based on the 216 stocks picked by the analysts between January 1990 and November 1994, Liang (1999) also documented the reversion pattern in the Dartboard stock prices. The two-day announcement abnormal return of 3.52 percent starts to reverse from the third day through 15 days. Investors who followed the analysts' recommendations lost 3.8 percent on a risk-adjusted basis. Investors who followed the recommendations of returning first-place winners lost 5.08 percent on a risk-adjusted basis. Greene and Smart (1999) examined 199 stocks recommended by 100 analysts in the Dartboard column between October 1988 and December 1992. Like Barber and Loeffler (1993), they documented price run-ups before the publication day and price decline thereafter. They argued that the column generates uninformed trading from its readers. Most abnormal returns following the column's publication disappear within a few weeks. What drives abnormal volumes and abnormal returns is the reputation of the analyst recommending the stock. This reputation, or credibility, enhances the price-moving power when publicity is a factor.

Next we examine research on *Business Week*'s Inside Wall Street (IWS). Mathur and Waheed (1995) reported significant excess returns preceding the publication of 233 firms with positive recommendations in IWS from June 1981 to December 1989. Similar to the price pattern documented for HOTS stocks, the price run-ups prior to the publication day decline in the subsequent days. More outstanding than HOTS stocks, the abnormal gains begin to accumulate about two months before the publication date. One aspect of note is that only implicit recommendations are given in the column, which is different from the outright buy or sell ratings in HOTS. Sant and Zaman (1996) documented similar price behavior for 328 stocks recommended in the IWS column from January 1976 through December 1988. In line with Mathur and Waheed (1995), the negative returns of the recommended stocks add up to an average of 6.80 percent after six months. Again, one can infer that price movements in connection with publications are due to the publicity effect on top of the potentially price-moving information generated by the recommending analysts.

Non-U.S. Developed Markets

Since the 1990s, increasing numbers of researchers have examined international experiences of publicized analyst-generated information in financial media. We start with developed markets.

Wijimenga (1990) used three weekly sources of Dutch stock recommendations for the period January 1978 until December 1983. He found strong and significant market reactions in the week of publication but no significant long-term abnormal returns. He also noted a slight reversal during 2 to 26 weeks after the recommendations. The price behavior is similar to HOTS stocks, that is, quick and sharp price run-up before publication and lasting decline thereafter. Pieper, Schiereck, and Weber (1993) investigated buy recommendations of German stock published in the *Effekten-Spiegel* for the years 1990 and 1991. They concluded that abnormal returns could be realized only by buying the stock prior to the publication of the recommendation. With a different focus, Menendez (2005) analyzed buy and sell recommendations published in one of the most important Spanish business newspapers for the period 1997 to 1999. He reported positive and significant risk-adjusted returns on the days before the buy recommendation is made public. However, there is no significant reaction on the announcement day or on the following day.

Schuster (2003) surveyed major business media, print or electronic, publishing analysts' recommendations from the 1970s to 1990s in Germany, Holland, Turkey, the United Kingdom, and the United States. He reviewed more than 30 cases that displayed statistically significant excess returns at the time of the publication for stocks recommended explicitly or implicitly by analysts. He concluded that the publicity effect of the business media played an active role in inducing substantial sharp increases in trading volumes and influencing stock prices. The importance of the regularity is that abnormal gains begin to accumulate a long time or shortly before the publication date. With few exceptions, a price reversal sets in shortly thereafter, and excess returns in recommended stocks are at least partially given up within a week. Many stocks slip into lasting underperformance, earning significant negative returns. These empirical findings repeatedly demonstrate that uninformed investors who initiate purchases after publication cannot profit systematically within a week; instead, they will lose in the long run. Why? Timing accounts for the difference. The initial price run-up prior to publication is of no use to uninformed investors because they do not have the same opportunity as the informed to participate in it. However, those uninformed investors who follow the publicized recommendations participate in the decline of prices caused by the distribution by the informed.

Schuster (2003) summarizes that the process of price run-up generated by the publicized analysts' buy recommendations and the subsequent price reversal constitutes a permanent stable pattern. This pattern or regularity is firmly established in developed markets. Do the emerging markets display similar reactions to publicized analyst-generated information?

Emerging Markets

Yazici and Muradoglu (2002) investigated whether published investment advice is helpful to small investors in generating excess returns by examining the stock recommendations of the Investor Ali column in the weekly, popular economics magazine *Moneymatik* in Turkey. Their sample consisted of

206 buy recommendations on 89 distinct stocks by Investor Ali on every Sunday during the period December 5, 1993, to December 28, 1998. The results showed that stock prices were substantially affected by recommendations and at the same time uninformed small investors lost in general. Long-term performance of the recommended stocks was even poorer. However, the informed investors related to the investment adviser made cumulative abnormal returns of 5.39 percent over the one-week period from the five days before the publication to the event date. Their explanation was that informed investors receiving the information before the publication date place buy orders at that time. After the event date, those investors sell the already accumulated stocks at inflated prices and exploit the excess returns while uninformed small investors have no chance for sure profits.

In contrast to the large institutional constituency in the U.S. stock markets, trading by individual investors amounted to 79 percent of total trade in Taiwan in 2003 (Shen and Chih, 2009). Based upon a total of 1,072 company buy recommendations by analysts of brokerage firms covering the period June 1, 2000, through January 31, 2003, Lin and Kuo (2007) reported that statistically significant positive market reactions are found prior to and on the date of publication in a major business newspaper of recommendations to the stocks listed in the Taiwan Stock Exchange. However, the return performance results, subsequent to the publication dates, were found to be significantly negative. Shen and Chih (2009) found a similar stock price pattern based on the buy recommendations published by analysts of investment banks in Taiwan from January 2000 to December 2003.

Similar to Taiwan, trading directly by individual investors is dominant in mainland China's stock markets. According to the China Securities Regulatory Commission (CSRC), individual investors held more than 99.5 percent of the accounts in the A-share market by 2000 (Tan 2005). This percentage varied little toward the end of December 2004 when 97.23 percent accounts were held by individual investors on the Shanghai Stock Exchange (Li and Wang 2010). Lee and Liu (2008) documented 5,373 episodes of the surging and receding of stock prices around the recommendations in the Shanghai Stock Exchange from 2000 to 2005. This was based on a large sample of recommendations in the weekly column Stocks Recommended by The Most Analysts This Week in the *Shanghai Securities News* every Monday. The general pattern was that positive abnormal returns are recorded both the day before and on the date of the analysts' recommendations. After the peak on the announcement date, the stock prices decline sharply the next day and do not rebound thereafter. Less-liquid securities suffer even greater price fluctuations, that is, larger initial rises and larger subsequent falls. Lee and Liu (2008) suspected manipulation may be involved in these mini-bubbles regularly created and set off by financial

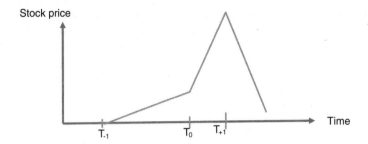

Stock price

Time

T.₁ - T₀ : insiders accumulate shares based on private information provided by the analyst
T₀ : public announcement of analyst "buy" recommendation
T₀ - T₊₁ : price run-up due to induced buy pressure
At T₊₁ : insiders distribute their shares, which entails return reversal

FIGURE 7.1   Price Behavior around Analyst Publicized Buy Recommendation

analysts. But who are the manipulators who buy before the buy recommendations and sell immediately on the announcement dates?

To summarize these studies in both developed economies and emerging markets, across the range of financial newspapers to business magazines in the last 40 years, evidence repetitively demonstrates the price patterns around publication of analysts' buy recommendations (see Figure 7.1). The patterns are significant price run-ups prior to the publicized buy recommendations and the subsequent price declines.

This confirms that analyst-generated information contains price-moving potential. But, in general, it does not benefit the uninformed. Only the insiders and the informed, who have access to the recommendation prior to publicity, can make profits. Next, we will pay particular attention to the difference that publicity makes.

The Publicity Effect on Market Reaction

What is the effect of publicity in causing a substantial market reaction after publication of secondhand information in a widely circulating business newspaper? Stice (1991) presented evidence that the method of disclosing and cost of acquiring earnings information make a significant difference. His results indicated significant market reactions to the *WSJ* earnings announcements, but not to the filing of 10-K and 10-Q reports with the Securities and Exchange Commission (SEC), although the filings are eight days earlier than the *WSJ* announcements. Regarding analyst-generated information, Han and Suk (1996) reported that the publication of the Research Reports column of *Barron's* significantly affected stock prices. For the positive recommendations, the market reaction on *Barron's* publication date was stronger than that on the analyst report issuance date 15 days earlier. The difference is a larger audience and the easier accessibility of *Barron's*. In other words, the credibility of *Barron's* in the eyes of investors is probably high. Evidently, the publicity effect by a credible publisher magnifies the price-moving potential of issuer- or analyst-generated information to the investing public.

The effect can be confirmed if comparisons with the original issuance of the information are made. Based on 1,460 recommendations published between January 1998 and December 2001, Schlumpf, Schmid, and Zimmermann (2008) investigated the impact that publicity in *Finanz und Wirtschaft,* Switzerland's major financial newspaper, had on dissemination of the same information released earlier by analysts to their firms' customers and asset-management departments. The uniqueness of Schlumpf, Schmid, and Zimmermann (2008) is that they analyzed how the first- and second-hand effects related to each other with respect to the size of the announcement effects as well as the persistence of the abnormal returns. Their results confirmed HOTS research with respect to price behavior around the publication date, albeit the announcement returns reported are in general smaller than those already reported. Again, it is the pronounced publicity by a credible newspaper that makes the difference.

These three observations clearly and repeatedly show that credible publicity empowers the price-moving potential of the recommendations. Now when the price-moving potential of analysts' recommendations goes hand in hand with the publicity of widely circulating media, who benefits and who incurs losses? This is a very critical question.

Uninformed Investors Are Often Misled or Hurt by Analysts' Recommendations

If certain analysts sometimes intend to induce retail investors to buy shares that their related institutional investors distribute, the consequence is the later losses by retail investors who follow those analysts. The losses are immediate and increasing when stock prices are falling. De Franco, Lu, and Vasvari (2007) provided solid evidence that some analysts strategically misled and harmed retail investors in order for related institutional investors to distribute large numbers of shares when stock prices were falling. This was documented during the dot-com meltdown, based on the alleged financial firms and their analysts in the Global Research Analyst Settlement (GRAS) of 2003. Shen and Chih (2009) and Lin and Kuo (2007) presented evidence from the Taiwan Stock Exchange that the proprietary trading divisions of 30 investment banks and 8 brokerage firms repeatedly traded against the stocks that their analysts recommended to the investing public through newspaper publications when the stock prices were falling in the period 2000 to 2003. Gasparino's (2002) *Wall Street Journal* article reports that brokers were "hyping stocks to win lucrative investment-banking work from corporate clients, and were misleading investors in the process." The alleged former "Queen of the Internet," analyst Mary Meeker, said after the Global Settlement of 2003, "People did lose money on the stocks I recommended" (Gasparino 2005).

From this research, the pattern of the significant price run-up prior to the publication of the analyst recommendations and its decline after the publication is repeatedly identified. But do any uninformed public investors profit from buy or even strong buy recommendations? Timing of trades makes a substantial difference. Analysts, like those corporate insiders analyzed in Chapter 6, are the generators of the recommendations before publication. Hence, they have an absolute information advantage in these recommendations. In other words, they are information setters.

It is probably hard to resist the temptation available to analysts and their firms and not to try to benefit, from time to time, from the information monopoly generated by their hard-earned research after publication. All investors, besides the analysts, are information takers. Thus, the timing of getting the information is key for profitable trades. Anybody who gets the information before publication is more likely to be able to make profitable trades. Those who do not get the information in advance are in a much worse position. Within a week after the publication day, the later they start buying, the more likely they are to lose. Exceptions are the short-sellers who begin short trades soon after the publication of the buy recommendations. But the majority of retail investors are not short-sellers. In some markets such as the Shanghai Stock Exchange, short selling is not allowed. Who can get the information before publication? They are analysts' colleagues, their employer's preferred clients, analysts' family members and friends, and other people who are in charge of uploading the potentially price-moving information for publication. If they trade, these people would make an almost sure profit. Uninformed before the publication of the recommendations are public investors who often naively follow the information. If these uninformed investors trade according to the recommendations, most of them cannot profit, but, instead, their chances of losing are high.

In summary, analysts' recommendations (buy) contain price-moving potential (price increase) that determines the direction of trading (buyer-initiated trade) for a larger group of uninformed investors. The recommendations can move the market in a significantly stronger way when published in a widely read newspaper such as the *WSJ* than if deposited in a less-accessed database. This shows that credible publicity makes a quantitative difference. Price-moving potential and credible publicity together construct the information monopoly, comprising the core value of sell-side analysts to insiders and the informed as well as issuers. However, the value turns into a disservice to most uninformed investors. In the following, we will find out why analysts do not fairly treat public interests but often mislead public investors and examine the empirical findings to understand the consequences of this disservice. After the examination, we will show how sell-side analysts can provide tremendous marketing power to issuers and special value to the manipulative trading strategies in their firm's proprietary trading arms when profit is made (or loss is avoided) out of conflicts of interest.

ANALYSTS CAN HARDLY ATTEND FAIRLY TO PUBLIC INTERESTS

Why do analysts not perform to the expectations of securities regulators and the investing public? We need to find out who pays them.

Analysts Are Not Financially Independent

What is the ultimate reason for financial firms to employ sell-side analysts? It is to generate business (Eccles and Crane, 1988). What is more treasured by these firms in their sell-side analysts' skills: Winning underwriting business or forecast accuracy? Inducing large and sustainable trading volumes or outperforming recommendations? Groysberg, Healy, and Maber (2008) worked with senior sell-side analysts' compensation data from one large investment bank from 1988 to 2005. They found that financial firms design analysts' compensation packages according to how much value analysts can create for their firms. For investment banks, the value lies in corporate finance fees. For brokerage houses, the value lies in trading commissions.

Groysberg, Healy, and Maber (2008) also found that total compensation is positively correlated with analysts' rankings by *Institutional Investor,* as voted by fund managers. Surprisingly, no evidence was found that analysts' compensation had a direct link with earnings forecast accuracy and stock recommendation performance. Michaely and Womack (2005) listed three factors that contribute the most to analysts' total compensation. They are the annual *Institutional Investor's* All-American Research Teams poll, investment banking fees generated, and stock transaction commissions induced by analysts' coverage. In addition, Michaely and Womack cited some estimates that investment banking departments cover more than half of the research department costs. Based on Unger (2001), sell-side analysts were assigned by investment banks or brokerage firms to attract and retain client issuers, and to generate trading volumes. Frequently, analysts own some shares of the stocks they cover. Fisch and Sale (2003) argued that analyst salaries reflect their perceived star quality, which has more to do with their skill at public relations than with objective research. Daniel Reingold, a former star analyst, sighs that Wall Street often rewarded the powerful and connected over the merely smart (Reingold 2006, p. 22). Gerry Rothstein, a former veteran analyst, answered his son's question of whether he should become a stock analyst, "Don't do it, unless you want to be a servant for investment banking" (Gasparino 2005, p. 10).

One can see that sell-side analysts are not financially independent. Rather, they are part of the profit-oriented business strategies such as attracting underwriting deals, maintaining lasting good relationships with institutional investors, and issuing price-lifting recommendations to induce huge buying volumes for their own firms to distribute shares. In the process, can they provide fair service to the public? Not really, as long as they are not paid primarily by retail investors but are supported through investment banking fees, brokerage commissions, and proprietary trading profits by issuers, investment banks, client institutions, and brokerage firms. They do not have fiduciary responsibilities to the investing public (Fisch 2007a). However, they are found to mislead or harm the investing public repeatedly while attending other interests. Practitioners verify such reality (Reingold 2006; Saumya, Sinha, and Jain 2006).

In short, out of the consideration that sell-side analysts have to attend to the interests related to their compensation, they can hardly treat the interests of a majority of public investors with sufficient attention, or they do not pay attention to them to begin with. This is the opposite of the expectation that analysts should serve as so-called public watchdogs (Hutton 2002). It does not appear that analysts' research is up to the "public good" that is referred to by Fisch and Sale (2003). It is not consistent with academic assumptions that analysts act as independent financial information intermediaries (for instance, Brooks and Wang 2004).

Individual Investors Systematically Lose in Stock Trading

In the academic publications on trading performance of individual investors, researchers have discovered quantitative evidence that individual investors lose systematically in the stock market. Odean (1999) randomly selected 10,000 trading accounts active in 1987 from a discount brokerage firm and examined all trades made in those accounts from January 1987 through December 1993. Taking out factors such as liquidity demands, tax-loss selling, portfolio rebalancing, or a move to lower-risk securities, these investors traded excessively in the sense that their returns are, on average, reduced through trading. Barber and Odean (2000) warned individual investors that trading is hazardous to their wealth after examining 66,465 households with accounts at a discount broker from 1991 to 1996. These individual investors, engaging in active trading, underperformed the broad market significantly. Barber and Odean (2000) showed graphically that the more frequently these investors traded, the lower the performance they achieved relative to the S&P 500 Index. These two studies are focused on individual investors in the U.S. markets. Similar or even worse trading performance of individual investors is reported from international stock markets such as those in Australia (Fong, Gallagher, and Lee 2009), Finland (Grinblatt and Keloharju 2000), and Taiwan (Barber, et al. 2009). We elaborate on these findings here in chronological order.

Grinblatt and Keloharju (2000) examined all trades on the Helsinki Stock Exchange from 1995 to 1996 and found that households statistically underperform relative to sophisticated foreign institutional investors. Barber et al. (2009) used data on all trades on the Taiwan Stock Exchange from 1995 to 1999 to show that individual investors have an annual performance penalty of 3.8 percent per year (2.2 percent of Taiwan's gross domestic product [GDP]) when trading against institutions. Fong, Gallagher, and Lee (2009) found that individual investors incur losses to institutional investors as a group, and that this is consistently the case from intraday trading, after going through the trading records on the Australian Stock Exchange over the 16-year period from 1990 to 2005.

The general lessons from these researchers' empirical findings are that individual investors systematically lose in stock trading, and the more they trade, the more they lose. With the earlier amassed evidence, one would wonder how uninformed investors have any chance to profit in the stock market in the presence of the joint manipulative power by analysts and other informed parties?

Going through Chapters 3 to 6, there is obviously trade-based manipulation in the secondary market. At each stage in the information loop from issuers to investors, there exists some form of manipulation. There is earnings manipulation by issuers, recommendation manipulation by sell-side analysts, and other types of information-based manipulation to be analyzed in Chapter 8. If all the information sources highly trusted by individual investors may involve manipulation or even fraud, is it possible that they will not lose systematically in trading stocks? The aforementioned research results echo a repenting analyst (Reingold 2006) that individual investors have no chance playing trading games on the uneven field of insider information flowing only among related institutional investors, issuers, and analysts. Some research, particularly in the field of behavioral finance (for example, Daniel, Hirshleifer, and Teoh 2002; Hirshleifer and Teoh 2009), attributes such a dismal reality to numerous individual investors' naïveté or credulous acting upon analyst-generated information and information from other sources. If there are no insider trading and manipulative trading strategies against them, would they still systematically incur trading losses?

ANALYST-GENERATED INFORMATION BENEFITS THE INFORMED

In the following sections, we will analyze how sell-side analysts serve the business interests of their employers, their client issuers, and institutional investors, but can hardly serve uninformed investors.

Analysts' Recommendations Are Inconsistent with Their Earnings Estimates

Bradshaw (2004) questions why analysts' recommendations are not consistent with their earnings estimates after examining 4,421 distinct firms for 46,209 firm-month observations over the years 1994 to 1998. Earlier research explained this puzzle as the analysts' incentive to "curry favor with management" (Francis and Philbrick 1993), or to enhance investment banking relationships (Lin and McNichols 1998), or to herd with other analysts (Graham 1999). Malmendier and Shanthikumar (2007) speculate whether analysts are really optimistic about the stocks they cover or are just publishing optimistic recommendations to induce retail investors to buy shares. Using 2,515 securities for 2,485 firms from February 1994 through December 2002, their findings show that analysts can speak in two tongues, targeting the more-sophisticated investors with the earnings forecasts and the less-sophisticated ones with the recommendations. The reason is that the less-sophisticated investors follow recommendations only, while the more-sophisticated ones follow forecasts but will discount recommendations. Their conclusion is that analysts may distort recommendations upward to trigger small-investor purchases, but may not distort forecasts that are more scrutinized by large institutional investors.

Mikhail, Walther, and Willis (2007) investigated small and large investors' trading responses to recommendation revisions by using 50,076 recommendation changes issued by 2,794 analysts covering 5,419 firms during 1993 to 1999. Mining transaction-level data, they found that small traders tend to react more to the mere occurrence of a recommendation, but do not properly consider analyst incentives when reacting to recommendations. Mikhail, Walther, and Willis provided additional evidence that small investors react in a more naïve way to analysts.

Analysts Have Been Overoptimistic for Decades

Bradshaw, Richardson, and Sloan (2006) documented analyst overoptimism for the period from 1975 to 2000 when examining their marketing role in corporate external financing. Goedhart, Raj, and Saxena (2010) found that analysts have been persistently overoptimistic for the past 25 years, with earnings growth estimates ranging from 10 to 12 percent a year, compared with actual earnings growth of 6 percent. On average, analysts' forecasts have been almost 100 percent too high. What is more, after the Global Settlement of 2003, the first three years since (2003 to 2006) witness that the estimates are more in line with actual earnings. Then analysts' estimates surpass actual earnings again in the following three years (2007 to 2009). Why are analysts' optimistic appearances necessary?

There is asymmetry in buy and sell recommendations relative to the trading volume generated. Positive initiation or revision of stock coverage opens up more opportunities to trade, especially inducing more new buyers. In contrast, negative coverage will be acted on by investors who already own the stock or who are willing to incur the additional costs of short selling (Cowen, Gyogoky, and Healy 2006).

Several empirical studies show the rationale behind many analysts' lasting optimism on the stocks they follow and the market in general. For example, McNichols and O'Brien (1997) argued that conflict of interest causes analysts to choose to cover firms for which they have more positive views. At least a portion of the observed overoptimism in recommendations is due to coverage selection, implying that conflict of interest and genuine overoptimism likely coexist. Michaely and Womack (1999) surveyed a sample of about 30 investment professionals on whether the optimism bias is intentional or based on conflicts of interest or other incentives. Most responses were consistent with the intentional or conflict of interest incentives. Using a large panel of information on the brokerage house employment and earnings forecast histories of roughly 12,000 analysts working for 600 brokerage houses between the years 1983 and 2000, Hong and Kubik (2003) found that these brokerage houses apparently rewarded optimistic analysts who promoted stocks. Considering the stock market mania in the 1990s, Hong and Kubik argued that investment bankers who underwrite a new issue to market want optimistic forecasts to place the shares at high prices. Stockbrokers want optimistic forecasts to get new buyers and thereby earn trading commissions, since not as many institutions or individuals are willing to short.

According to the testimony given by the then Acting Chair of the SEC, Laura Unger (2001), there are external pressures on analysts to remain optimistic about the stocks they cover. One is from institutional investors, such as mutual funds, that are clients of the analyst's firm. They may have a significant position in the stock covered by an analyst. An analyst may be inhibited from issuing a rating downgrade that would adversely affect the performance of an institutional client's portfolio. The most important career concern for an analyst is his Institutional Investor rating, which is based on the voting by fund managers. Another pressure is from issuers. The management of companies an analyst follows may pressure him to issue favorable reports and recommendations. Otherwise, an issuer may threaten to cut off an analyst's access to its management if the analyst issues a negative report on the company. Frequently, management calls up analysts and complains about ratings that are too low and tends to freeze out analysts who do not give positive recommendations (Francis, Hanna, and Philbrick 1997). Without earnings guidance from the issuer's management, the analyst's forecast accuracy loses foundation, and a string of less-accurate forecasts would cost him dearly in both career path and outside reputation. Internally, the investment banking department could pressure an analyst for favorable coverage of client issuers. Siconolfi (1992) tells a vivid story of how an investment banking colleague pressured an analyst with according compensation: "He wanted to know only whether she was 'going to help him get the deal done.'"

An analyst's compensation is substantially dependent on gaining and retaining underwriting deals, and he or she may have to compromise research objectivity for business interest. In a brokerage firm, an analyst's compensation is tied to the trading volume his research reports and recommendations can generate (Irvine 2001). The firm also desires to keep a good relationship with institutional investor clients. This would force the analyst to issue optimistic reports on the covered stocks. Oftentimes, an analyst holds shares of the stocks he follows (Schack 2001). For his self-interest, an analyst would have to remain optimistic about those stocks.

In brief, sell-side analysts' optimistic attitude may be a business rule across the entire financial industry. The basis is the investment banking and trading interests. The market environments during the mania in the 1990s and meltdown in 2000 and 2001 provided a magnifier to look closely at the actual reasons and purposes of analysts' optimism.

VALUE OF ANALYSTS' RECOMMENDATION AND FORECAST TO ISSUERS

With potentially price-moving information and credible publicity in hand, analysts' work has multifaceted value to issuers. First, their marketing power based on the price-moving potential can be utilized by issuers when conducting initial public offerings (IPOs) or seasoned equity offerings (SEOs). Second, they can walk down in earnings guidance games played by issuers. This multifaceted value to issuers can be seen from the insistence on reputation and a multitude of analysts by issuers when shopping for underwriters (Krigman, Shaw, and Womack 2001). According to the "selection bias" explanation, firms are likely to choose underwriters whose analysts are more optimistic about their prospects (McNichols and O'Brien 1997). Chen and Ritter (2000) reason that investment bankers sell not only underwriting service per se, but also favorite analyst coverage. We proceed with reviewing SEO, IPO and SEO long-term underperformance, and walk-downs.

Analysts Serve as Marketing Professionals for Issuers

Arthur Levitt, the former SEC chairman, claims, " . . . analysts' employers expect them to act more like promoters and marketers than unbiased and dispassionate analysts" (Levitt 2001; Jackson 2005). We will investigate how analysts can provide marketing services to their client issuers.

Earnings manipulation has been pervasive and persistent for the past 50 years in the United States, and more recently in other economies (Chapter 5). To demonstrate how sell-side analysts might assist issuers in earnings manipulation, we select an SEO process. Numerous researchers document how some managers manipulate earnings through accruals or real economic activities, so they expect to sell more SEO shares at inflated stock prices (Teoh, Welch, and Wong 1998; Rangan 1998; Gunny 2005; Zang 2007; Cohen, Dey, and Lys 2008). How do managers turn their offerings into ultimate success on their own terms? Two elements must be under managers' control before their attempts. One element is to prevent opposition from potential public watchdogs—auditors and sell-side analysts. The other element is to turn them into the issuer's marketing partners.

Since auditors are paid by the issuer, oftentimes they choose to be silent even when they are aware of an earnings manipulation attempt. Their signatures raise the credibility of the issuer's earnings and other financial information disclosed to the investing public. Sell-side analysts are not paid directly by the issuer. But their lucrative pay raises greatly depend on the underwriting business they can attract for their employer underwriter. On the other end, the issuer can threaten the underwriter by withdrawing from the underwriting business, which transforms into pressure from the underwriter to the analysts (Paltrow 1999; Siconolfi 1998; Hutton 2002). The issuer can also directly pressure the analysts by not providing them earnings information advantage (Francis, Hanna, and Philbrick 1997). Either willingly or unwillingly, some analysts compromise by distorting their actual research findings for optimistic coverage. For example, an investigation of Merrill Lynch by the New York State Attorney General prior to the Global Research Analyst Settlement (GRAS) revealed an analyst who publicly recommended certain securities for purchase, but privately described these same securities as junk. An analyst at Salomon Smith Barney who rated an issuer as a buy was discovered to have indicated to two colleagues that the company was a pig and should instead be rated "underperform" (Colombo 2007).

Next, we elaborate on how sell-side analysts can provide marketing services to the issuer. First, they cover the issuer's stock with favorable recommendations and rising target prices, which can induce huge buying volume and support the issuer's stock price. Second, they publish optimistic short-term and long-term earnings per share (EPS) growth forecasts that serve the issuer's lasting interests. This is because issuers' earnings information and sell-side analysts' ratings are the top information pieces for retail investors to make trading decisions (National Credibility Index 1999). Retail investors are likely to be convinced to buy the issuer's shares and push up the share prices, unaware of the issuer's earnings manipulation together with the sell-side analysts' touting recommendations (Bradshaw, Richardson, and Sloan 2003). Then the issuer successfully sells out the SEO shares at inflated prices. Some managers and other corporate insiders may also sell some of their stocks or options at inflated prices (Chapter 6). Involved analysts may make some profits from insider trading (Schack 2001). Obviously, the issuer is the biggest winner. The underwriter also benefits from the underwriting fees. Sell-side analysts get pay raises or bonuses because of their marketing contributions. Sometimes they make insider trading profits.

The Global Settlement of 2003 followed investigations into alleged conflicts of interest between investment banking and securities research at top Wall Street banks. Large-scale evidence uncovered by the investigations showed that the marketing strategies played by sell-side analysts are pervasive in the equity markets (for instance, Fisch and Sale 2003; Colombo 2007).

Evidence of Analysts' Marketing Service for Issuers' SEOs and IPOs

Lin and McNichols (1998) examined 2,400 SEOs in U.S. markets by domestic issuers for which there were 1,069 earnings forecasts and 769 recommendations by lead underwriter analysts during the period 1989 to 1994. They found that lead and counderwriter analysts' growth forecasts and recommendations were significantly more favorable than those issued by unaffiliated analysts. But current and subsequent year earnings forecasts issued by affiliated analysts both before and after seasoned equity offerings are generally not more favorable than those issued by unaffiliated analysts. For a sample of 63 IPOs recommended by underwriter analysts only, in the two-year span from January 1990 to December 1991, Michaely and Womack (1999) provided evidence that stock recommendations by affiliated analysts are more favorable but performed worse in the 30-month horizon. These two authors emphasize that buy recommendations of affiliated analysts after an IPO perform worse than those of unaffiliated analysts, both at the time of the recommendation and in the months that follow. They concluded that affiliated analysts' recommendations are intentionally upward-biased because of their interest in the issuer through the underwriting business. Dechow, Hutton, and Sloan (2000) directly linked the overoptimism in analysts' forecasts around equity offerings to the postoffering underperformance, using a sample of 1,179 firm-offerings made by 1,006 firms in the period 1981 to 1990. They found that sell-side analysts' long-term growth forecasts were systematically overly optimistic around equity offerings. They also documented that the postoffering underperformance was most pronounced for firms with the highest growth forecasts made by affiliated analysts. Affiliated or unaffiliated, analysts are generally upward-biased. We do not emphasize affiliation when addressing analysts' overoptimism.

After surveying the literature in analyst studies, Ritter (2003) advocated that more research is needed to study the marketing assistance that security analysts have provided to the issuers in corporate financing. To investigate comprehensively if sell-side analysts are involved in the marketing campaign for corporate financing, Bradshaw, Richardson, and Sloan (2006) used broad data sets with financial statements and returns data for 99,329 firm-year observations in debt and equity financing spanning 1971 to 2000. They also used analyst data in forecasting variables, including short-term EPS forecasts, long-term EPS growth forecasts, stock recommendations, and target prices from 1975 to 2000. Among several solid findings is a strong positive correlation between net external financing and overoptimism in analysts' forecasts. This relationship holds true for short-term EPS forecasts, long-term EPS growth forecasts, stock recommendations, and target prices. This evidence indicates strongly that analysts serve as the marketing professionals for issuers in the overpricing of security issuances.

Are related issuer's so-called successes and involved analysts' marketing victories good news to all investors? Maybe not. Next we analyze who does not benefit from the successes.

Analysts' Marketing Precipitates the Postoffering Underperformance

After an IPO or SEO and a quiet period, analysts start coverage of the newly offered or reoffered stock. Let us examine how a reality check fares for both the performance of the stock and the analysts' recommendations to the public investors.

With price-moving potential and credible publicity embedded in analyst-generated information and the prior empirical evidence, we may have better insight into the well-established phenomenon of the postoffering underperformance in IPOs and SEOs (Loughran and Ritter 1995; Spiess and Affleck-Graves 1995; Ritter and Welch, 2002). The long-term underperformance is similar to the postdistribution phase in the Accumulation-Lift-Distribution scheme (ALD) of trade-based market manipulation (Chapter 3). Because there are no large buy volumes to support the inflated prices after the offerings, the share prices will decline persistently even for years.

Marketing activities for the IPOs and SEOs by certain issuers such as road shows, and by related analysts such as overly optimistic target prices and recommendations, are comparable to the ALD manipulator's fictitious trading. This is because they share the same objective: to lift the share price for planned distribution (Chapter 4). However, these artificial efforts—some of them are even fraudulent—target only temporary price lifting, so issuers can offer IPO or SEO shares at inflated prices. Once planned shares are distributed to the market, issuers can hardly put in any substantial and genuine efforts to keep their share prices stabilized. The marketing power of underwriters' analysts can hardly last long, even though their favorable coverage and price forecasts are still in place. With no new large buy volumes entering the market, the share prices will naturally decline, even for a long time. In brief, affiliated analysts' marketing services to issuers seemingly help to inflate share prices, but de facto precipitate the subsequent decline in the new share price, even long-term postoffering underperformance. Numerous uninformed individual investors, some small fund managers, or other not-well-connected institutional investors can be trapped in this post-offering misery (Gasparino 2005; Reingold 2006). An extreme example is seen in the Enron scandal. On October 31, 2001, just two months before the company filed for bankruptcy, the mean analyst recommendation listed on First Call for Enron was 1.9 out of 5, where 1 is a strong buy and 5 is a strong sell (Healy and Palepu 2003). In other words, analysts' marketing power is limited because Enron's share price fell continuously from the end of 2000 to its bankruptcy filing in December 2001 in spite of overly optimistic recommendations.

Analysts' Walk-Down in the Full-Year Cycle of EPS Estimates

Hutton (2002) documented that most analysts provided beatable estimates for Enron for 16 quarters in a row since the first quarter in 1998 until its bankruptcy filing in December 2001. Cisco and Lucent both had their 14-quarters stories during the dot-com bubble (Chapter 5). Do analysts predict very accurately every quarter without insider information? Not necessarily. Issuers communicate with lead analysts to present earnings guidance shortly before each earnings announcement (Reingold 2006). The guidance makes some analysts seem to be accurate more frequently than others. It also enhances their careers and increases their reputations. In the end, their potentially price-moving information together with their reputation and publicity, and thus their marketing power, are increased. Maintaining a good relationship between analysts and issuers is beneficial for both parties.

How is walk-down played out in a full-year cycle of EPS estimates? Analysts start with an overly optimistic estimate for the first quarter, then walk down to the final quarter of the fiscal year so issuers can constantly meet or beat the EPS consensus out of all the analysts' estimates (Richardson, Teoh, and Wysocki 2004; Jensen 2005). One can see that "walk-down" of analysts' estimates in the full-year cycle is dependent on the earnings-guidance game initiated by issuers and joined by analysts (Levitt 1998; Cotter, Tuna, and Wysocki 2006). The purpose is to paint a rosy picture of the issuer's performance so its stock may keep holding investors and attract new buyers. Jensen (2005) uses the word *collusion* to describe the relation between sell-side analysts and their client issuers. In the process, uninformed investors are fooled in the double play.

Sell-side analysts do possess tremendous marketing power for issuers. This is particularly true during boom times. However, during the period of marketwide panic selling such as the dot-com crash, when stock prices were falling precipitously, their overoptimistic recommendations became evidence in public and private litigation of their manipulative disservice to the uninformed investing public (De Franco, Lu, and Vasvari 2007). In other words, analysts' marketing power for issuers lies in the price-moving potential, their reputation, the credibility of the disseminator, and the publicity of their touting opinions about issuers. Without the publicity, the marketing power is nonexistent. Buy-side analysts provide such examples.

VALUE OF ANALYSTS' WORK TO INVESTMENT BANKS AND BROKERAGE FIRMS

What is the value of the work of sell-side analysts to their employers, investment banks, and brokerage firms? In particular, what is their value to proprietary trading divisions?

Analysts' Collusive Role in Proprietary Trading Strategies

Investigating a sample of 50 firm-events covering the period March 1999 to July 2002 identified in the Global Settlement of 2003, De Franco, Lu, and Vasvari (2007) provided direct evidence on how analysts' misleading behavior, as part of the trading strategies by the GRAS firms, enriched institutional investors but harmed individual investors. These analysts of alleged top Wall Street firms compromised their private beliefs for business incentives and issued untruthful public reports. During the period, these GRAS firms' institutional holdings declined significantly. When they sold massive shares at the analysts' buy recommendations, a great number of individual investors were induced to buy. They were stuck in the falling market immediately. Shen and Chih (2009) found that analysts of investment banks in Taiwan provided the market with buy recommendations, while their proprietary trading divisions were selling the very same recommended stocks. These types of conflicts of interest gain profits for investment banks at the expense of numerous individual investors. Their data included 30 investment banks with proprietary trading divisions. The analysts of these banks issued recommendations in every Sunday's *Commercial Newspaper* and *Economic Newspaper,* respectively, from January 2000 to December 2003. The apparent conflicts of interest were part of manipulative trading strategies practiced by investment banks, whose proprietary trading divisions traded against the stocks recommended by their own analysts during marketwide price falling. Lin and Kuo (2007) documented similar conflicts of interest by analysts of eight brokerage firms in Taiwan from 2000 to 2003. Proimos (2005) documented an Australian case of a large investment bank selling heavily (about $17.5 million in proceeds) against its own analysts' buy recommendations on an Internet company in March and May 2000, when the dot-com crash was in its early phase.

Analysts Generate Trading Commissions for Brokerage Firms

In addition to their collusive role in the manipulative trading strategies used by brokerage firms, analysts' work has marketing value to their firms in generating trading volume, and thus commission revenue. By working with every trade of the largest 100 companies on the Toronto Stock Exchange for the period September 1, 1993, through August 31, 1994, Irvine (2001) found that analysts' coverage of a particular stock results in a significantly higher broker volume in that stock. On average, brokers increased their market share in covered stocks by 3.8 percent relative to uncovered stocks.

Trading incentives are important because every forecast or recommendation can potentially generate trade for the analyst's employer.

Using the same data set as in Irvine (2001), Irvine (2004) found further that analysts' buy and strong buy recommendations allowed their brokerage firms to capture significantly higher market shares in trading than did "hold," sell, or strong sell recommendations. The important implication, based on the finding, is that as long as stock research is paid for with trading commissions, the potential for upwardly biased recommendations remains. Jackson (2005) used detailed data on the trades generated by 23 institutional brokerage firms for all stocks in the Australian market for the period January 1992 to December 2002. He found optimistic analysts generated more trading volume for their brokerage firms. Also using Australian data, Aitken, Muthuswamy, and Wong (2001) reported that brokerage analysts' buy recommendations led to a higher market share in an event window around announcement, while sell recommendations did not. This finding contributes to the reasons brokerage analysts' recommendations are optimistic in general. Cowen, Groysberg, and Healy (2006) found that brokerage analysts release more optimistic opinions than other financial analysts, based on a large data set containing earnings forecasts, long-term earnings growth forecasts, and stock recommendations in U.S. markets during the period January 1996 to December 2002. The optimism exists in both boom times and downturns, which is explained as being tied with trading interests.

Analysts Tip Preferred Client Institutional Investors

Brokerage firms highly value their relationships with institutional clients. These relationships allow the firms to generate commission revenue and improve analysts' compensation (Irvine 2004). As analysts' research has price-moving potential, credibility, and publicity once released, the release will create profitable opportunities in a short run. Whoever obtains the monopolistic information prior to the release will make an almost certain trading gain. Based on this regularity established firmly in the stock market, some analysts prefer to provide tips about their reports to client institutional investors prior to their information release to the public.

Based on brokerage analysts' 9,065 buy and strong buy initiations from March 31, 1996, to December 31, 1997, and from March 31, 2000, to December 31, 2000, Irvine, Lipson, and Puckett (2007) investigated the trading behavior of institutional investors before the public release of these positive initial recommendations in the U.S. equity markets. They found statistically significant increases in the levels of institutional trading and net buying in the period beginning about five days before the public release.

Their results show the prerelease leakage of analysts' reports to client institutional investors.[3]

By focusing on brokerage analysts' recommendation revisions that were reversed in a relatively short period of time, Berglund, Farooq, and Westerholm (2007) sort through trading data on the Helsinki Stock Exchange over a 10-year period spanning from 1995 to 2004. In 139 out of 147 cases, they discovered there were some clients trading against the recommendations made by their brokerage analysts. In other words, Berglund, Farooq, and Westerholm showed that some of the recommendation changes issued by analysts may have been issued in order to facilitate trading by their brokerage firm's clients. Choi, Lee, and Jung (2009) tried to determine a direct link between information leakage and institutional trading by differentiating trading behaviors of clients from nonclients. By using a data set that contained upward revisions by brokerage analysts and matching daily transaction data for each stock traded on the Korea Exchange from 2001 to 2006, they found evidence in great detail that brokerage analysts routinely tip their client institutional investors before the public release of research reports.

Choi, Lee, and Jung (2009) also documented anecdotal evidence about information leakage. For example, the *Korea Times* reported in the article on September 2, 2007, that:

> *in the case of the 104 reports in which analysts raised recommendations, stocks rose 7.18 percent on average during the 10 days until the issuance of the reports, and recorded a 5.05 percent gain during the five days until the report publication. After printing of the reports, however, stocks rose only 0.38 percent in the first five days, and 1.92 percent in 10 days . . . It also means . . . that the buy recommendation reports may be leaked in advance.*

Analysts Inform Brokerage Colleagues

Using Nasdaq data based on analyst recommendations for Nasdaq-listed firms during the period from January 1, 1999, to July 31, 1999, Li and Heidle (2004) investigated whether brokerage firm analysts leak information, directly or indirectly, to the market makers of the same firm prior to release. They found that the changes in the recommending market makers' quoting behavior before recommendation revisions are statistically significant and are also economically meaningful. In addition to research information leakage to client institutions, Li and Heidle pointed out that analysts of a brokerage firm may leak their research information before release to the firm's proprietary trading teams and market makers who are firm insiders. Once the proprietary trading teams get tipped from their colleague analysts, the former can initiate trades with the information ahead of uninformed investors and exit by trading against the released information.

The worst scenario for uninformed investors is when analysts' recommend the stocks with buy ratings, which then experience continuous price falling, while the proprietary traders are selling heavily at the same time. That was a typical scenario during the dot-com crash (De Franco, Lu, and Vasvari 2007). Lin and Kuo (2007) used a total of 1,072 buy recommendations from June 1, 2000, through January 31, 2003, from eight brokerage firms published on every Sunday in *Economic Daily News,* a major financial newspaper in Taiwan. Examining the changes in selling volumes on the recommended stocks traded by the brokerage firms whose analysts published the recommendations, Lin and Kuo found that analysts recommended a majority of technology stocks that increasingly underperformed from June 2000 to January 2003. This is while the traders of the dealer department increased selling volumes on the recommended technology stocks. Unger (2001) reported from regulatory actions that analysts inform investment bankers of recommendation revisions. The *Wall Street Journal* reported that in 2004, an SEC fine of $10 million was levied over Bank of America's delay in submitting evidence that a senior executive traded on unreleased research reports by the firm's own analysts (Smith 2004).

Similar to corporate insiders, the brokerage firm insiders' incentive is loss avoidance when the price of a stock they own has substantially declined. However, uninformed investors are misled into this trap and experience immediate and increasing losses.

In sum, recent studies increasingly reveal the actual role sell-side analysts play in proprietary trading and other brokerage functions. One word that describes it accurately is *collusion.* In any scenario, analysts possess an information monopoly, in the form of publicized credible information of price-moving potential, to aid information-based manipulators or to provide insider information for others to execute manipulative trading strategies.

COMPARISON OF SELL-SIDE ANALYSTS AND CORPORATE INSIDERS

From the previously shown evidence that proprietary traders sell against colleague analysts' buy recommendations to avoid further losses, one important lesson can be extracted. Sometimes analysts' recommendations are not objective, but they still carry price-moving potential. This untruthful information has potentially detrimental consequences mainly to individual investors and some small fund managers or uninformed institutional investors (Gasparino 2005). What makes it so prevalent and powerful? Publicity effects. So separating publicity from the price-moving potential is of the essence in preventing the harm that can be caused by dishonest recommendations to the investing public, and eventually to the whole exchange and even the entire financial system. Before proceeding to regulatory measures over sell-side analysts' various misuse of their price-moving potential, we compare them with corporate insiders in terms of the types of information monopoly.

Both sell-side analysts and corporate insiders are generators of potentially price-moving information relative to other investors who are information takers. Hence, both information generators have information monopolies. According to the information loop from issuer-generated information to analyst-generated information and eventually to trading decisions, the former possess more price-moving potential than the latter (National Credibility Index 1999). After release and free dissemination, analyst-generated information gains publicity in addition to the reputation and credibility of the disseminators. Similarly after disclosure, in addition to the credibility, issuer-generated information gains publicity. Therefore, the information generated by both has price-moving potential, credibility, and publicity. In Chapter 6, we proposed four measures to regulate corporate insiders by targeting their trading that is prone to being based on insider information. Can we apply the same measures to the trading by the informed investors around public release of analysts' research? To answer this question, we need to examine the differences and similarities between analysts and corporate insiders, and between analyst-generated information and issuer-generated information.

The Differences Are Summarized as Follows:

- Analyst-generated information is voluntarily released and disseminated irregularly, while issuers are required by securities regulations to disclose regularly. An exception is that issuers occasionally disclose some price-moving information voluntarily, such as financial restatements.
- Analyst-generated information is intended to benefit the analyst's firm to begin with, while issuer-generated information is intended to benefit the corporation above all.
- Analysts have small or no shareholdings on the stocks they cover, while corporate insiders usually have large shareholdings of their company's stock.

When One Includes the Price Behavior around the Information Release, the Following Commonality Can Be Summarized

- There is price run-up long or shortly preceding announcement of the information, being either issuer generated or analyst generated.

■ The trading by the informed—corporate insiders or analysts' informed partners—shortly after the information release is always against the information and the induced trading.

Since two of the measures proposed in Chapter 6 would regulate corporate insiders' misbehavior by targeting their trading, apparently they can be applied to sell-side analysts by targeting their partners' trading. Sometimes, analysts have a small number of shares to trade against the publicly released information, albeit the shareholdings are trivial compared to their partners' in the stocks they cover.

LEGAL DIFFICULTY IN PROSECUTING WRONGDOING BY SELL-SIDE ANALYSTS

Analyst-generated information has price-moving potential; that is, it can affect investors' trading decisions significantly. Once it gets published by one or multiple credible media outlets, its price-moving potential together with its publicity and credibility form an information monopoly. It can prompt large numbers of investors to trade according to its face value. Once the information monopoly is utilized in a trading strategy, the latter becomes information-based manipulation. Repeated international evidence shows that proprietary trading teams of investment banks and brokerage firms collude with their colleague analysts in their manipulative trading strategies.

From all the empirical evidence presented in this chapter, it is clear that a part of the manipulative trading strategy is for analysts to disseminate recommendations to the investing public for free. The costly research generates large trading volume because of the credibility of the analysts and their firms as well as the media outlets that publish the recommendations that carry publicity effect. The information monopoly thus produced enables analysts to also serve as the marketing professionals for issuers. To be accurate, analysts provide information to assist the issuers' information-based manipulation strategies. The intent behind analysts' publications may be to gain profit or avoid loss for the analysts' firms, investment banks or brokerage houses, their client issuers and institutional investors, as well as other insiders. Subsequently, the strategy causes numerous uninformed individual investors to lose on trading.

This is particularly the case during marketwide collapses when analysts issue upward-biased recommendations or price targets for their firm to distribute masses of shares. It is hard to prove legally that analysts start with a *scienter* or bad intent, even though the later development of their business interest *de facto* hurts uninformed investors. Therefore, the securities regulations that require proof of scienter before conviction makes them hardly enforceable.[4] This may explain why public lawsuits against sell-side analysts are negligibly few. Regulatory additions that target the trading around public release of analyst-generated information are needed to enhance the effectiveness and efficiency of enforcement.

REGULATORY PROPOSALS

Since analyst-generated information has multifaceted value to analysts' firms, being either investment banks or brokerage houses, client issuers, and institutional investors, but can hardly be a fair service to uninformed investors, we propose the following measures to prevent manipulative trading around public release of sell-side-analyst-generated information.

- *Measure one:* At least 24 hours before public release, a sell-side analyst must disclose his and his firms'—as well as the client investors'—shareholdings in the target stock in the release to the regulating agency in confidence.
- *Measure two:* The regulating agency oversees his and his firm's trading activities in the target stock after this filing. Trading by the firm's clients in the target stock is monitored at the same time.
- *Measure three:* The regulating agency can call off or postpone for a sufficiently long period the public release of the analyst-generated information and start investigation if the stock in question has displayed abnormal price behavior prior to the release date. Abnormal stock behavior can be defined as a significant price run-up prior to a buy recommendation or a price decline prior to a sell recommendation. The numerical threshold value of *significant* price change can be established based on the past history of the stock, for example, 1 percent above (or below, for a decline) the average daily return of the previous one month.[5]
- *Measure four:* For each trading day on the day of and after the release, if trading against the released information, the analyst (or his firm or the client investors) can transact up to 1 percent of the absolute volume of his (or his firm's or the client investors', respectively) prerelease shareholding, or 3 percent of the previous month daily average volume (Chapter 3), whichever is smaller.
- *Measure five:* If he (or his firm or the client investors) are trading in the target stock according to his information release, then their daily transaction is subject to 5 percent of the previous month daily average volume only to prevent large trading speed (Chapter 3).

In addition to the five measures proposed here, we need one more measure to address the issue that some small stocks never get equity analyst coverage.

■ *Measure six:* The regulating agency can create its own research department. The researchers in the department are not sell-side or buy-side but public analysts.[6] They issue research reports covering all stocks by requiring that each and every issuer pay a fee.[7] To be objective, those reports should contain no recommendations or target prices. The department needs to publish the equity research through a credible media outlet. Furthermore, these analysts are also accountable if any significant price run-up or decline occurs prior to the publication. Alternatively for some regulatory agencies, equity analysis can also be contracted by the regulating agency to academic researchers if the agencies are unable to keep public analysts (Fisch 2010).

DISCUSSION OF THE REGULATORY PROPOSALS

We begin the discussion of these six measures in reverse order.

Discussion of the Six Measures

Measure six is to make analysts became more like true public watchdogs, as expected by existing securities regulations and the public. Their responsibility becomes to analyze publicly listed companies. They would provide in-depth analysis of each and every listing company's economic health for investors' reference, but not advice.[8] Hence, every listing company, large or small, would get basic coverage and exposure. The public analysts would also be accountable for any misconduct because they possess potentially price-moving information and credibility as well as publicity.

As of today, sell-side analysts (their firms and client investors) are similar to corporate insiders in that they all have the potential of making unfair trading profits based on their information monopoly. Therefore, measures one through five are, in principle, similar to the regulatory proposals targeting trading by corporate insiders (Chapter 6).

We have demonstrated that often the hidden purpose of publicizing a sell-side analyst's research is perhaps to tout or trash the target stock.[9] It can be part of a manipulative trading strategy. It can also be a marketing tool for the issuer. The more thorough regulation of sell-side analysts' activity would mean separating publicity from potentially price-moving information, that is, to prevent sell-side analysts from disseminating any stock-related information to the public, and to prevent them from talking about stocks in the media of any form. In this version, analysts could disseminate their research results to paid subscribers only. This regulatory proposal would have the merit of reducing stock price volatility. It would mitigate marketwide mania cultivated by sell-side analysts' long-term overoptimistic recommendations. Therefore, such a recommendation could be a key element in preventing stock market crises. In our opinion, this proposal might be implemented only by regulating agencies that weigh the consequences of financial crisis more seriously than any other issues.

Relevant Regulations in the Sarbanes-Oxley Act of 2002

The Sarbanes-Oxley Act targeted the conflicts of interest of the analysts involved in gaining and retaining investment-banking business from issuers. It requires analysts to reveal their conflicts of interest, regarding the stocks they discuss, in their reports or media presence. This is a very effective measure. This indicates that regulating sell-side analysts has become an important part of the evolution of equity markets.

China's Regulations of 2005

In 2005, the China Securities Regulatory Commission (CSRC) issued a new regulation. Brokerage houses and analysts are prohibited (1) from explicitly or implicitly assuring investors of any investment profits; (2) from colluding with affiliated entities to manipulate stock prices; (3) from providing relevant information to affiliated entities before making evaluations, predictions, or recommendations; and (4) from making any recommendations that are in the interest of affiliated entities at the expense of other investors (Lee and Liu 2008). These are all powerful and targeted regulations. This implies that establishing comprehensive regulations of equity analysts becomes the trend.

Dodd-Frank Act of 2010

The Dodd-Frank Act of 2010 requires separation of proprietary trading from investment banking. The separation may prevent one type of conflict of interest; that is, the bank serves as the underwriter or adviser to one stock's issuer and a large trader for or against the stock at the same time. This may mean that regulating sell-side analysts has multiple considerations.

Considering the importance and comprehensiveness in regulating sell-side analysts, our research is aimed at finding proposals to regulate the manipulative trading around public release of analyst-generated information. A set of recommendations made in this chapter is expected to provide a more preventive and practical solution that is easy to implement, in order to complement existing securities regulations so that they become more effective, efficient, and complete.

CONCLUDING REMARKS

Repeated and large-scale evidence from global stock markets in the last 40 years indicates that sell-side analysts possess an information monopoly in terms of price-moving potential, reputation, and publicity of their published research through credible media. The information monopoly can turn into great marketing power for issuers, attract underwriting business for investment banks, generate large trading volume and commission revenue for brokerage firms, as well as lift the price in information-based manipulation strategies initiated by proprietary trading departments. However, uninformed investors are not among the primary intended beneficiaries of the analysts' information monopoly. Rather, analyst-generated information misleads them and may result in systematic investment losses.

To improve investor protection, particularly for the uninformed investors, effective measures are proposed for securities regulators as additions to existing regulations. The essence of these proposals is to effectively prevent informed investors from completely utilizing analysts' information monopolies around public release of equity research in their manipulative trading strategies. They are expected to substantially reduce the degree of potential price volatility and prevent stock market crises caused by such manipulation based on an information monopoly. The final proposal is aimed to reinforce the public watchdog nature of analysts employed (or contracted) by the regulating agency.

Not only do the proposals target investor protection, they also have direct effects in reducing market volatility and preventing marketwide mania, which, based on the global financial history, often develops into panic. They have constructive effects for building more normal or even perfect competition in the stock market with fairness and transparency.

NOTES

1. This chapter was presented at the 6th Annual Seminar on Banking, Financial Stability, and Risk, Sao Paulo, August 11–12, 2011, hosted by the Banco Central do Brasil.

2. The credibility of the analyst, his firm, and the publisher is a given when we address the price-moving power of his publicized research. We will address in great detail the importance of credibility in Chapter 8. In this chapter, we mainly discuss the price-moving potential and publicity with a few instances that discuss credibility.

3. Although we focus on positive revisions by sell-side analysts, there are a few studies that show short selling increases prior to analysts' downgrade. Francis, Venkatachalam, and Zhang (2005) work on a sample of NYSE and Nasdaq stocks with monthly short positions during the period January 1992 to December 2000. They find that security analysts revise their earnings forecasts downward following the event month of unexpected short interest positions. Christophe, Ferri, and Hsieh (2010) show a sharp increase in short selling one to three days before analyst downgrade announcements, using daily short sales in Nasdaq stocks between 2000 and 2001. They attribute this predowngrade increase of short selling to tipping by the analysts prior to the downgrade announcements.

4. Fishel and Ross (1991) and Markham (1991) point out the difficulty of legally prosecuting market manipulators. Gasparino (2005, p. 311) records that "[a] federal judge, Milton Pollack, hurt investors even more by throwing out the research cases that have come his way, many of them involving Blodget's research, on the grounds that . . . he was 'utterly unconvinced' that Merrill was purposely attempting to mislead investors through Blodget's research."

5. Monitoring pre-event volume increase is another regulatory dimension. A quantitative threshold can be produced using previous month daily average as a benchmark.

6. Fisch (2007b) proposes to establish an SEC Analyst web site. It would maintain a central database of equity research. But collusion between an analyst and his proprietary trading colleagues cannot be prevented by disclosure requirement only. However, the capacity for the investing public to track sell-side analysts' historical performance would certainly be beneficial.

7. Choi and Fisch (2003) propose a voucher system for issuers to pay analysts, auditors, and other financial intermediaries. Once the funds are collected from issuers, then the objectivity of analysts' research reports is in question. Our proposal is for issuers to pay regulators. Then regulators sponsor analysts. This design solves the conflict of interest by avoiding direct financial transactions between issuers and analysts.

8. Some small stocks have never been followed by any analysts. Consequently, they become thinly traded. Chapter 8 will show that thinly traded stocks are more frequently manipulated. This adverse-selection problem can only be solved by creation of public analysts.

9. Perminov (2008, pp. 19 and 29) argues that information-based manipulation is preferred in the U.S. markets because mass media have gained enough power over investors to influence their trade decisions. In the meantime, biased analyst opinions have become common. He further argues that massive manipulations of analysts' upward-biased opinions may provoke stock market bubbles such as the dot-com bubble of the late 1990s.

CHAPTER 8

Preventing Stock Market Crises (VI)

Regulating Information-Based Manipulation

Xin Yan

Lawrence R. Klein

Viktoria Dalko

Ferenc Gyurcsány

Michael H. Wang[1]

What is the key to information-based manipulation? The manipulator possesses an information monopoly, exercises it in the trading strategy, and realizes unfair profit by trading against the publicly released information. The components of information monopolies are information with price-moving potential, its substantial publicity, and high credibility. With antitrust spirit in mind, we have recommended preventive measures targeting the inconsistency of the manipulator's trading with his publicly released information. The effectiveness of the measures lies in breaking the link between the manipulator's exercise of the information monopoly and his actual trading profit. These measures are quantifiable, adjustable, and easy to implement in daily regulatory operations. Compared to enforcement outcomes based on current disclosure-oriented securities laws, these measures are expected to be effective and efficient. They will benefit securities regulators in making related rules, in order to complement and perfect extant regulations. The reason to analyze empirical data and propose the measures in this chapter is to build perfect competition for trading profit in any stock market with fairness and transparency. The measures proposed have great potential to improve investor protection, enhance market stability, and prevent stock market crises.

ALL TYPES OF MARKET MANIPULATION COME DOWN TO PERCEPTION MANIPULATION

All stock-trading strategies come down to trading completion. A complete trading round-trip consists of two phases, the initiation phase and the closure phase. If the initiation phase is purchase, then its corresponding closure is sale. For simplicity of discussion, from now on we focus on investment strategies involving long position only. Short investment strategies are just in an opposite trading direction, but have a similar profiting mechanism.

A common investor usually relies on length of time for the share price to climb to a certain level for his closure to be made without extra effort. An investor who applies a long manipulative strategy tries to lift the share price artificially by inducing higher buying speed by others so he can close his trade with a substantial profit but a shortened time horizon. This profit is achieved either by his fictitious trading or by using an information advantage, which he has created or possesses. Thus far, we have fully examined trade-based manipulative trading strategies in Chapters 3 and 4. We have also analyzed how issuer-generated information and sell-side-analyst-generated information can be used by corporate insiders, temporary insiders, proprietary trading teams, brokerage houses, or institutional client investors to make substantial trading profits, in Chapters 5, 6, and 7. How do manipulators use mandatory or voluntary information disclosure or information distortion—such as false, misleading, or incomplete information dissemination—as a crucial link to gain illegal or legal but unfair profits? In Chapter 5, we listed the information loop from issuer-generated information, analyst-generated information, and so on, trickling down to the trading decision. Every type of information along the loop has price-impact potential. Put another way, it is potentially price moving. Therefore, a manipulative investor can attain unfair profit if he can either create information that is potentially price moving or use the advantage he gains by accessing the price-moving information ahead of the release of such information to the public.

In Chapters 3 and 4, trade-based manipulation was our focus for the suggested regulatory measures. Chapters 5, 6, and 7 discussed three particular and frequently encountered types of information manipulation or information-based manipulative trading. According to Allen and Gale (1992), a third type of market manipulation, action-based manipulation, completes the main types of market manipulation. The three types are categorized according to the manipulator's action.

However, market manipulation is not always successful, because a manipulative trading strategy involves both the manipulator and other investors. Only when other investors trust what they perceive, either from personal observation of stock price change, information disseminated by TV or newspaper, or message board posts on the Internet, will they trade according to the information they receive. In other words, for investors applying long position manipulation, only when numerous investors' perceptions are manipulated to their belief that the stock has a higher than originally perceived value will the trading strategy be successful. Hence, in the eyes of victim investors, the manipulator's trades, information dissemination, or real actions all contribute to the perception of actual or expected rising value of the particular stock price. In the context of the other investors involved, all types of stock manipulation become one: perception manipulation. This corresponds to Vanderwicken (1995) that "business has become a prominent player in the manipulation of perception." Since Chapters 3 and 4 fully treated trade-based manipulation, in this chapter we focus on the general features of information-based manipulation.

We begin with hand-collected market manipulation litigation data released publicly by the Securities and Exchange Commission (SEC) between October 1, 1999, and September 30, 2009. We analyze the cases from three aspects: Are major institutional investors involved in each litigation case? Are the manipulated stocks thinly traded issues? Is information-based manipulation included in the trading strategy?

Next, we will present an interpretation of the findings and discuss it.

ANATOMY OF SEC MARKET MANIPULATION LITIGATION CASES (1999 TO 2009)

We worked with four annual reports from the SEC for the fiscal years 2000 to 2003, that is, from October 1, 1999, to September 30, 2003, and six Select SEC and Market Data reports from fiscal year 2004 to fiscal year 2009 (SEC 2010). We obtained 10 tables from 10 fiscal years, that is, from October 1, 1999, to September 30, 2009, which list all enforcement actions under the SEC primary classification. Taking fiscal year 2009 as an example, the primary classification includes issuer reporting and disclosure, broker-dealer, investment advisers, securities offering cases, delinquent filings, insider trading cases, market manipulation cases, civil contempt, municipal offering, transfer agent, investment companies, and miscellaneous cases.

We focused on market manipulation cases because litigation cases under this category are the most relevant to this study.

For the 10 years from October 1, 1999, to September 30, 2009, there were 394 enforcement actions, resulting in 252 civil actions and 142 administrative proceedings. In addition to the 394 cases, there are four cases that do not qualify as stock market manipulation and are not included in our study. For these 394 cases, we ask the following three questions.

1. Are major institutional investors involved?[2]
2. Are the manipulated issues penny stocks or any other thinly traded stocks?
3. Is information-based manipulation included in the trading strategies?

Table 8.1 lists all the findings answering the three questions. Basically, there are 13 cases involving major institutional investors, or 3 percent of the total 394 cases. There are 316 cases (80 percent of the total cases) involving penny stocks or other thinly traded issues such as small-cap stocks. Two-thirds, that is, 67 percent, or 264 of the 394 cases involve information-based manipulative trading strategy.

The first percentage, the 13 cases involving major institutional investors out of the total of 394 cases, is surprising. Historically, institutional investors could be regarded as the key players to cause systemic risk and even an

TABLE 8.1 Anatomy of SEC Market Manipulation Litigation Cases (1999 to 2009)

Fiscal Year*	Number of Litigation Cases	Involvement of Institutional Investors	Information-based Market Manipulation	Thinly Traded Stocks
2000	48	0	33	38
2001	39	2	17	36
2002	40	0	28	33
2003	32	0	20	29
2004	39	0	27	27
2005	45	0	41	38
2006	27	1	22	23
2007	36	6	18	25
2008	50	3	30	39
2009	38	1	28	28
Total	394	13	264	316
Percentage	100%	3%	67%	80%

*The SEC fiscal year is from October 1 of the previous calendar year to September 30 of the current year.

occasional marketwide crash. Two basic facts support this argument. First, the total trading volumes used in their trading strategies are generally very large and have significant potential to shake one stock or a group of stocks, or, occasionally, even the entire stock market or global financial markets.[3] Second, they have large funds and the ability to borrow much more using high leverage (Soros 1995; Lewenstein 2000; Merced, Bajaj, and Sorkin 2008). A high leverage ratio, such as 30 to 1, enables institutions to trade much larger volume and empowers them to manipulate multiple markets simultaneously (FSF 2000). If they seldom appear in detected cases of market manipulation, how can the SEC foresee mounting systemic risk and prevent a stock market crisis?[4]

The finding that 80 percent of all the manipulated stocks are thinly traded issues such as penny stocks is consistent with recent empirical findings on SEC litigation data of the past 30 years. That is, for the 142 market manipulation cases from January 1990 to October 2001 reported in Aggarwal and Wu (2006), the percentage is 81 percent. For the 159 pump-and-dump cases selected by Mei, Wu, and Zhou (2004) between January 1980 and December 2002, it is 77 percent. This consistency suggests that most of the SEC's enforcement achievements in prosecuting market manipulators relate to penny stocks or other small-cap stocks, which bear high legal risk to manipulate and extremely few institutional investors deal with them. Aggarwal and Wu's (2006) caution that their results apply only to those manipulators who were detected bears important implications. It seems granted that the SEC targets, in both the pre-Enron and post-Enron eras, remain smaller stocks that major institutional investors generally do not deal with. Consequently, "SEC enforcement efforts, while significant, have tended to focus on weaker targets, suggesting that the big fish get away" (Cox and Thomas 2009).

No matter how rampant the manipulation of thinly traded stocks is, the outcome is mainly trading losses for numerous individual investors and a few small funds. However, it would hardly cause systemic risk to a stock exchange or a national financial system. It is easier for legal enforcement to prosecute manipulators of thinly traded stocks, but it does not have much meaningful impact on the prevention of systemic risk or crises. Together, these two percentages, 3 percent and 80 percent, may imply fundamentally why the SEC, and perhaps other global financial regulators, failed to foresee or prevent the 2000 to 2002 dot-com meltdown and the 2007 to 2009 global financial crisis, not to mention numerous stock market crises during the last 30 years.

The third percentage, that is, the 67 percent of 394 litigation cases related to information-based manipulation, provides the incentive for this chapter. Indeed, technology advancement opens up many new channels for information dissemination.[5] Internet message boards, e-mail campaigns, fax blast, and instant messaging, to name the most frequently encountered, are used for touting or suppressing stocks by manipulators. Traditional means, such as press releases, TV appearances, and postal newsletter mailings, are still widely used by information-based manipulators. General observations from the 394 litigation cases include the following platforms: analyst coverage, autodial equipment, e-mail, fax, instant messaging, Internet chat room, Internet message board, Internet radio broadcasting, investor conference presentation, investment newsletter (Internet, postal), investor correspondence, online interview, press, telephone, TV (interview, program), and web site (company, stock picking).

Who are the manipulators? They include the corporate executives, including president, chief executive officer (CEO), and chief financial officer (CFO), of manipulated stock issuers, stock promoters, telemarketers, securities analysts, TV commentators, registered broker-dealers, credible financial web site columnists, lawyers, operators of stock-picking web sites, writers of investment newsletters, information technology professionals, Wall Street traders, investor-relations professionals, and large shareholders.

No matter who the manipulators are and no matter what platform is used in information-based manipulation, in order to realize manipulative trading gains the manipulators have to close the positions they opened before information dissemination. There are three things to watch closely. The first is stock price behavior before dissemination of the potentially price-moving information. The second is the expectation of the price change after the information release, that is, rise or decline. The third is the trading direction of the information generator or his colluder relative to the expectation. That means that whether or not the manipulator trades against the expected price change due to his information dissemination becomes the key. The last one is especially important, and will be discussed later. Once we can find regularity in stock price behavior around the release of information, we are close to effective regulatory measures targeting information-based manipulation.

Recall Chapter 7, where we find repeated evidence in both developed and emerging markets of stock price behavior around the publication of sell-side analysts' positive recommendations or revisions. The price behavior is a significant run-up before the positive announcement and a sharp or slow subsequent price decline. This behavior has been documented for tens of thousands of observations in different parts of the world for the past 40 years. It is a pattern for sell-side analysts' positive recommendations. Does this pattern also exist in stock price behavior during information-based long manipulation schemes? If it does, what is the underlying mechanism?

INFORMATION-BASED MANIPULATION
SCHEMES IN PRACTICE

We start by examining stock price behavior during the short time window before, and immediately after, the release of positive information with price-moving potential. The information is disseminated for pump-and-dump trading schemes. For this purpose, we first study regulatory enforcement actions by the SEC and other regulators. Then we choose several well-documented phenomena on various information-circulation platforms. The platforms include TV, newspaper, instant messaging, and the Internet. Third, we proceed to examine, in more detail, online information-based manipulation. All of these efforts serve the same purpose of observing whether the price behavior had regularity before and after the release of positive (occasionally negative) information across different media platforms.

Securities Litigation Cases with
Information-Based Manipulation

Information-based manipulation mainly includes pump-and-dump and trash-and-cash schemes. According to the SEC, a pump-and-dump scheme is information-based manipulation (SEC 2010).[6] In this scheme, the manipulator purchases a number of shares of a target stock, and after the accumulation he touts the target stock by disseminating false, misleading, or even factual information to a large crowd of investors, expecting that they will follow his information and buy large quantities of shares in response, so the stock price will increase to the desired level. Then he sells all or part of his shareholding at the artificially inflated price. A trash-and-cash scheme works in the opposite direction to the pump-and-dump scheme. The manipulator sells short first. Then he downplays the stock by circulating negative information about its issuer, expecting other investors to sell the same stock in a rush, and the stock price will decline to his desired low. At the end of the scheme, he will buy back shares at a much cheaper price to cover his short position.

For simplicity of analysis and discussion, we focus on the pump-and-dump scheme, with a few exceptions in the rest of the chapter. We begin by reviewing the limited literature in this regard.

Aggarwal and Wu (2006) are among the first to have sorted out more than a hundred SEC litigation cases in market manipulation. About 56 percent of the 142 cases (January 1990 to October 2001) in their data set involve the spreading of rumors, which are surely information-based manipulation schemes. They show that stock prices rise throughout the manipulation period. Prices and liquidity are higher when the manipulator sells in hype-and-dump manipulation cases, relative to when the manipulator buys. After manipulation is over, the stock prices fall. The 159 cases selected by Mei, Wu, and Zhou (2004) are all pump-and-dump lawsuits spanning from January 1980 to December 2002. The general stock price pattern for the selected pump-and-dump cases is a large positive return of 97.6 percent over the period, from the date on which manipulation started to the date on which the maximum cumulative return was achieved during the manipulation period; a large negative return of 93.9 percent was recorded over the period ranging from the day after the date on which the maximum cumulative return of the manipulation period was recorded to the end date of the manipulation; a 56.2 percent decline was recorded over the six-month postmanipulation period.

Huang, Chen, and Cheng (2006) observe that market manipulation is a growing concern for many emerging stock markets, while empirical evidence in this regard is scarce. Huang, Chen, and Cheng (2006) hand-collected 53 manipulation cases prosecuted by the Taiwan Securities and Exchange Commission from January 1991 to December 2003. Among them, five cases, or 9 percent of the total, involved spreading of rumors, which is information-based manipulation; 48 cases, or 91 percent of all cases, were trade-based manipulation. The manipulated stocks tended to be small, and the manipulators were either insiders or large shareholders. The vast majority of the cases involved long manipulation. The prices of the manipulated stocks climbed continually during the manipulation period, and reached their peak at the end of the manipulation period. After the peak, they declined at a faster pace than when they climbed. For all 53 cases, the average cumulative abnormal return (ACARs) was just below 50 percent at the peak. The ACARs became negative during the postmanipulation period for every case.

The aforementioned three studies show, in general, a similar pattern for the target stock price during the manipulation period. The price increases during the long manipulation until the peak near or at the end of the manipulation period. Then it declines sharply or slowly in the postmanipulation period. However, all researchers discussed previously provide only average price changes for their samples and not individual cases. We cannot get a closer look at daily price behavior around the release of the stock-touting information for those information-based manipulation cases discussed in these papers. Therefore, next, we focus on individual stock price behavior from our own database around the day of information release by manipulators.

Table 8.2 lists five litigation complaints that contain price increases before the release of the touted information, and then the price declines to near or below the pretouting level.

Closer examination of the five cases enables us to compare the speeds of the price changes during and after the manipulation. Using the

TABLE 8.2　Price Increase before the Release of the Touting Information, and Price Declines after Manipulation

Litigation Release	Touting Period	Pretouting Price Run-up (%)	Price Drop Period after Manipulation	Posttouting Price Decline (%)
LR-19101	Mid-09/2004– mid-10/2004	1,700%	10/15/2004– 10/22/2004	4,400%
LR-20771 (Concorde)	One week in 08/2004	140%	08/12/2004– 02/2005	255%
LR-19655	09/01/1999– 06/29/2001	1,400%	09/25/2001 and soon	324%; 2,400%
LR-20939	12/19/2003– 01/2004	2,300%	06/15/2004	500%; 1,900%
LR-20684	05/15/2005– 06/19/2006	381%	06/19/2006– 08/2008	87,900%

premanipulation price and the peak as the two ends, we find that the stock price decline in the postmanipulation period was faster than its increase during the manipulation period in four of the five cases (LR-19101, LR-20771 (Concorde), LR-19655, LR-20684 (estimate)); it was slower in one case (LR-20939).

Rumors Can Move the Market Substantially with Media Reporting

In Chapter 7, we briefly mentioned that rumors about stocks can move the market. We elaborate on this issue in this chapter. The basic question is: What makes a rumor move stock prices?

According to Von Bommel (2003), rumors include honest, bluffing, and cheating types. Honest rumors, even though factual, can be utilized as part of manipulative trading schemes. The key is timing (Chapters 6 and 7), particularly when an announcement of the same information contained in the rumor follows shortly. No matter what type the rumor is, the objective remains the same: to induce investors to trade along the rumor so the rumor-monger can close the trade by betting against it for a profit.

Let Us Look into Two SEC Litigation Cases over Rumors

■ Emulex hoax (Litigation Release No. 17094, August 8, 2001)

　　　　Mark S. Jakob, 23, expecting a decline in the price of Emulex shares, wanted to make money by shorting 3,000 of these shares at an average price of $80 per share on August 17 and 18, 2000. By August 24, 2000, however, Emulex's price had risen to more than $113 per share, as a result of which Jakob had unrealized losses of more than $97,000. Jakob started a so-called e-mail hoax on August 24, 2000. By using an alias and purporting to act on Emulex's behalf, Jakob used a personal computer at El Camino Community College to send an e-mail message, instructing his former employer, *Internet Wire, Inc.*, to issue an attached press release. The press release appeared to come from Emulex and falsely stated that the SEC was investigating Emulex, that the company's CEO had resigned, and that the company was revising and lowering its earnings for the preceding quarter. The next day, on August 25, 2000, several news organizations published the press release. In a 16-minute period following the publication of the fake press release, 2.3 million shares of Emulex stock were traded and the price plummeted almost $61.00 or 58.63 percent, from $103.94 to $43.00, resulting in Emulex losing $2.2 billion in market capitalization. Following a trading halt by Nasdaq, Emulex resumed trading later that day, after the hoax was discovered, and the price rebounded to close at $105.75. On August 25, 2000, after the issuance of the false press release and just before trading was halted, Jakob covered his short position, realizing a profit of more than $54,000. Minutes later, Jakob purchased 3,500 shares, which he sold on August 28, 2000, at a profit of more than $186,000. Ultimately, Jakob turned a scary loss of $97,000 into a big profit of more than $241,000 from this hoax. Put differently, he made a return of 348.45 percent based on the loss of $97,000 before the hoax.

What Are the Lessons One Can Draw from This Hoax?

1. The Nasdaq may be systemically fragile and highly unstable.
2. *Internet Wire, Inc.*, released the hoax without questioning it.
3. The news organizations involved transmitted the hoax from *Internet Wire, Inc.*, as it was.
4. The media publication magnified the financially and socially destructive potency of the hoax, causing the falling stock price of Emulex and moving a large trading volume at an extremely high trading speed.
5. The hoax, even though completely baseless, had a price-moving effect, by addressing the issuing company in a believable way.[7]
6. Numerous Emulex investors reacted to the hoax the same way as panic-stricken depositors do in bank runs caused by baseless rumors.

■ Alliance Data Systems (ADS) case (Litigation Release No. 20537, April 24, 2008)

On November 29, 2007, Paul S. Berliner, a Wall Street trader formerly associated with the Schottenfeld Group, LLC, used Instant Messenger to spread a false rumor and caused a 17 percent decline in the share price of the rumored ADS stock within 30 minutes. At the same time he disseminated the rumor, Berliner sold 10,000 ADS shares short at prices ranging from $77.21 per share to $76.47 per share. He covered these short sales when the price of the ADS stock began to fall. Berliner made approximately $25,000 within 10 minutes from the time he sent out the rumor and shorted the ADS shares.

On November 29, 2007, approximately six months after Blackstone entered into an agreement to acquire ADS at $81.75 per share, Berliner drafted and disseminated a false rumor that ADS's board of directors was meeting to consider a revised proposal from Blackstone to acquire ADS at a significantly lower price of $70 per share. Berliner disseminated this false rumor through instant messages to 31 traders and other securities professionals. Within minutes, the false rumor spread rapidly across Wall Street. The media and certain subscriber-based news services quickly picked up the story and further disseminated it throughout the marketplace. As alleged by the SEC, heavy trading in ADS stock ensued, and within 30 minutes the false rumor had caused the price of ADS stock, which had been trading at approximately $77 per share, to plummet to an intraday low of $63.65 per share—a 17 percent decline in the share price. According to the SEC complaint, the false rumor had such a significant impact on trading in the securities of ADS that day that the New York Stock Exchange temporarily halted trading in the stock. Later in the day, ADS issued a press release announcing that the rumor was false and by the close of trading the price of ADS stock had recovered. On that day, 33,813,796 shares of ADS were traded—more than 20 times the previous day's trading volume of 1,561,923 shares.

The Lessons Learned from This Case Are the Following

1. The NYSE may be systemically vulnerable and unstable.
2. The news media published the rumor without questioning its basis.
3. Even Wall Street professionals believed in the rumor and passed it further around.
4. The rumor triggered extraordinarily heavy intraday volume, and the selling speed during the 30-minute session was high.
5. The rumor was not absolutely baseless but was exaggerated, which made it believable to institutional and individual investors alike, particularly because it was circulated by credible media outlets.

The two stories reveal that false rumors have an immediate and significant price impact when credible media transmit them. Little effort was involved in making up and spreading the false rumors. However, the NYSE and Nasdaq reacted to the rumors with heavy trading, accompanied by a rapid drop in price. Both hoaxes belong to a typical trash-and-cash scheme of information-based manipulation. While the ADS rumor was intended to make a quick profit, the Emulex hoax was motivated by a desire to avoid loss. Accidentally, they revealed how systemically vulnerable and highly unstable the Nasdaq and NYSE could be. Even though the hoaxers were later detected and convicted, the damage they caused to the Nasdaq and NYSE was surprisingly large. Do global regulators have measures in place to prevent similar incidents?

Investment Gurus Can Profit Significantly When Touting Stocks Publicly

According to the National Credibility Index (1999), investment gurus such as fund managers, famous individual investors, research analysts, and investment newsletter writers, or anyone who can make up believable investment stories, can move stock prices when they offer positive or negative opinions about certain stocks on media outlets that reach a large group of investors. In this section, we look at the price behavior around their media appearances.

Jim Cramer, Host of CNBC's *Mad Money* Show   The credibility of CNBC and the publicity of its *Mad Money* show hosted by Jim Cramer make his stock picks carry a certain market impact, even though his picks are based on other analysts' recommendations published earlier. *Mad Money* is claimed to be the most-watched show on CNBC, with an audience in excess of 380,000 potential investors each weeknight. Engelberg, Sasseville, and Williams (2006) worked with 246 initial recommendations given by Jim Cramer on *Mad Money* episodes between July 28, 2005, and October 14, 2005. Their results show that *Mad Money* viewers who decide to buy the recommended securities when the markets open the following day are losers in general. They also find stock price run-up and volume increase before Cramer's buy recommendations. Like the stocks recommended by analysts in the early *Wall Street Journal*'s Heard on the Street and *BusinessWeek*'s Inside Wall Street columns studied by several researchers (Chapter 7), the postrecommendation decline in share price is steep. In addition, Engelberg, Sasseville, and Williams (2006) also look into short positions in the post-show days and discover some short-selling trades then. Bolster, Trahan, and Venkateswaran (2010) examine the market impact of a larger sample of Jim Cramer's 1,538 buy recommendations and 693 sell recommendations made on CNBC's *Mad Money* show, spanning the period from July 28, 2005, through December 31, 2008. Their results suggest that Cramer's recommendations impact share prices of the companies that he mentions. The effects are short-lived and reverse immediately following the peak for buy recommendations, in line with the literature on secondhand recommendations by analysts (for instance, Liu, Smith, and Syed 1990). On average, there was significant price run-up about three days prior to the buy recommendations and a serious decline to below the beginning of the price run-up the day after the peak.

Thom Calandra, CBS MarketWatch Columnist The SEC litigation case LR-19028 is against Thom Calandra, a journalist and former chief commentator for the popular Internet web site CBS.MarketWatch.com, for secretly selling ahead of the public stocks he promoted in his prominent investment newsletter, *The Calandra Report* (*TCR*). The SEC allegation is that Calandra engaged in a practice known as scalping—buying shares of predominantly thinly traded, small-cap companies, writing highly favorable newsletter profiles recommending the companies to his subscribers, and then selling the majority of his shares when the increased demand he generated drove up the stock price. From March to December 2003, Calandra reaped more than $400,000 in profits by scalping 23 different stocks. We demonstrate how Calandra's scalping worked to his profitable trading by quoting the SEC complaint on Pacific Minerals, Inc.

"Pacific Minerals, Inc. is one example of a company in which Calandra illegally profited by trading on his *TCR* recommendations, using his 'Buy-Write-Sell' pattern to amass over $50,000 in profits from undisclosed trades in Pacific Minerals stock."

First, Calandra purchased a large block of shares in the company. Then, in mid-September 2003, Calandra wrote about Pacific Minerals in *TCR*. He recommended the stock to his readers on September 19 and again on September 22, when he predicted large gains.

Calandra cashed out of his investment in Pacific Minerals the very next day, on September 23, without disclosing to his readers that he intended to sell. Thus, Calandra in effect sold into the rise created by his rosy predictions, as demonstrated in Table 8.3.

In late October 2003, Calandra bought an even larger amount of stock in the company and orchestrated another rise in its share price (see Table 8.4).

In total, Calandra made nearly $53,000 in illegal profits (an 89 percent return) by scalping Pacific Minerals stock. A similar manipulation scheme was discovered by the United Kingdom's Department of Trade and Industry

TABLE 8.3   Calandra Illegally Profited by Trading on His *TCR* Recommendations, Using His Buy-Write-Sell Pattern

Buy	Write	Sell
9/16/2003: Calandra bought 6,000 shares of Pacific Minerals at $0.69 per share.	**9/19/2003:** Calandra wrote in *TCR* that Pacific Minerals will be a "certain beneficiar[y] of [owner Robert] Friedland's growing political and financial connections in China, Mongolia, and across Asia." **9/22/2003:** "The more immediate gains almost surely will be in Pacific Minerals, whose shares, even after rising sharply last week after [being mentioned in the September 19 *TCR*], are still worth less than $40 million Canadian . . . "	**9/23/2003:** Price of Pacific Minerals rose to $1.06 per share. Calandra sold all 6,000 shares.

TABLE 8.4   Calandra Repeatedly Illegally Profited by Trading on His *TCR* Recommendations, Using His Buy-Write-Sell Pattern

Buy	Write	Sell
10/22/2003: Calandra bought 25,000 shares of Pacific Minerals at $1.22 per share.	**10/28/2003:** Pacific Minerals, which "is only at the beginning of its meteoric stock rise," . . . "even after a considerable run-up this past week," . . . "is close to revealing stunning results."	**10/28/2003:** The price of Pacific Minerals rose to $1.95 per share. Calandra sold 7,000 shares.
10/23/2003: Calandra bought 10,000 shares of Pacific Minerals at $1.35 per share. **10/27/2003:** Calandra bought 7,000 shares of Pacific Minerals at $1.74 per share.	**10/29/2003:** "The floodgates are opening. . . . Shares of . . . Pacific Minerals are star performers."	**10/29/2003:** The price of Pacific Minerals rose to $2.68 per share. Calandra sold 30,000 shares. **10/31/2003:** The price of Pacific Minerals rose to $2.80 per share. Calandra sold 5,000 shares.

against a former *Daily Mirror* journalist, James Hipwell, in December 2005. Hipwell was later convicted of conducting buy-tip-sell market manipulation based on the newspaper's former City Slickers column (Tait 2005).

Wang Jianzhong, China's First Black Mouth In October 2008, Wang Jianzhong, a so-called *black mouth*—a licensed investment adviser who regularly issues stock recommendations to the public but secretly trades against them after issuance, which causes numerous investors to lose by following his advice—was barred for life from market entry by the China Securities Regulatory Commission. From January 1, 2007, to May 29, 2008, Beijing Shoufang, an investment advisory company, of which Wang was managing director, issued stock recommendations to the public through the company's web site, six major securities newspapers, and popular Internet gateways. Wang bought shares of the stocks recommended before their release and sold them soon after the release. He made 55 buy-write-sell trades and reaped RMB 125 million ($18.38 million) in quick profits. On one occasion, he gained RMB 20 million ($2.94 million). He was later tried for market manipulation in a Beijing district court (CSRC 2008; Sina 2009).

To sum up, pump-and-dump manipulation may be named differently when targeting a particular manipulator. But the underlying mechanisms in different pump-and-dump varieties remain the same. The manipulator buys shares of the target stock first, which often causes a significant increase in the target stock price. Then he releases the touting information about the target stock through credible media outlets. Numerous investors follow the released information, and the stock price inflates further. He then sells out or partially sells off as other investors rush in to buy the stock. Empirical research on information-based pump-and-dump manipulation is very limited, particularly when such questions are asked as who the manipulators are and what kind of media platforms they use in the scheme. While there is limited data to find institutional investors in SEC enforcement actions or other regulators' litigation cases, a line of research on such manipulation online is emerging. We turn our attention to the Internet.

INFORMATION-BASED MANIPULATION SCHEMES ON THE INTERNET

The rationale behind our attention to information-based manipulation schemes on the Internet is the following:

- Online and offline information-based manipulation schemes share the same underlying mechanism when viewed from the trading perspective.

- Empirical data from recent research on information-based manipulation online are increasing, while similar research on offline information-based manipulation is limited.
- The Internet is little regulated and SEC enforcement is inadequate compared to mushrooming online manipulation. Thus, information-based manipulation on the Internet is at a natural stage. That is, less sophistication is added to it. Therefore, it provides good opportunities for us to understand the key characteristics and underlying mechanism of such manipulation. In short, it provides a shortcut to uncover regulatory measures against general information-based manipulation.

There Are More Than One-and-a-Half Billion Internet Users Globally

According to the International Telecommunication Union, a United Nations agency for information and communication technology issues, 239,893,600 people out of the population of 310,232,863, or 77.3 percent, are Internet users in the United States (Internet World Stats 2010). For G-20 countries, including Argentina, Australia, Brazil, Canada, China, France, Germany, India, Indonesia, Italy, Japan, Mexico, Russia, Saudi Arabia, South Africa, South Korea, Turkey, the United Kingdom, the United States, and member countries of the European Union, 35.9 percent, or 1,576,277,616, of the population of 4,390,731,723 are Internet users (G-20 2009; Internet World Stats 2010). Online investing technologies can promote the belief that it is easy to become a successful investor given minimal time and effort (Looney, Valacich, and Todd 2006). As the number of Internet users is increasing, so is that of online investors. In the United States, more than 20 million accounts were active in 2001, and the number was expected to top 50 million in 2004 (Pettit and Jaroslovsky 2002). Assets in online brokerage accounts now exceed $1 trillion, clearly representing a substantial portion of America's wealth (Looney, Valacich, and Todd 2006).

Online Investors Lose More

Online investing is increasingly dominant in many Internet-savvy economies. Preliminary research shows that the convenience and low cost of trading online has dual effects. The negative side has not been well studied and nearly no regulations have been established for online investing. Barber and Odean (2002) compare the investment performance of 1,607 online investors in the United States from 1991 through 1996 to their performance before they switched to online trading. They outperformed the market by 2 percent annually before switching. After going online, they underperformed the market by 3 percent annually. Barber and Odean attribute the

performance decline to an increase in their trading activity and more speculative trading. Other researchers also find investors trade more frequently
online compared to other investors who do not trade online (Choi, Laibson,
and Metrick 2002; Konana and Balasubramanian 2005).

How do online investors perform in other markets in the world? Anderson (2007) investigates a sample containing 324,736 transactions conducted by 16,831 Swedish investors at an Internet discount brokerage firm
during the period May 1999 to March 2002. The online investors underperformed the market by about 8.5 percent per year on average, of which half
can be attributed to trading costs. Using a sample of more than 68,000
accounts and 9 million trades in stocks, bonds, options, and futures at the
largest online discount broker in the Netherlands from January 2000 to
March 2006, Bauer, Cosemans, and Eichholtz (2008) find that the average
individual investor who trades derivatives earns negative gross and net
alphas, while the gross alphas for nonderivative traders are close to zero.
Oh, Parwada, and Walte (2008) investigate trading performance of online
and nononline individual investors in Korea between January 2001 and December 2005. Their main finding is that online investors performed more
poorly, in general, compared to nononline investors.

Internet Message Boards

The Internet provides faster and more convenient delivery of financial information. This is the beneficial side for many individual investors who want
to make trading decisions themselves. However, it enables some investors,
individual and non-individual, to utilize unregulated cyberspace for manipulative trading strategies, most likely information-based manipulative
schemes. We do not intend to search for empirical findings that can predict
future returns. Rather, we are looking for pre-event abnormal returns that
can predict the content of all forms of Internet posting that may serve to
induce more new buy or sell volume according to the information. Although
there are mixed claims about whether Internet postings can predict stock
returns, one common pattern from almost all studies is that the stock price
begins to run up one or several days prior to the day on which the initiating
post talks positively about a stock. Then the stock price declines—sharply
or slowly—to the level before the initiating post. This pattern is essentially
the same as the price behavior around sell-side analysts' publicized positive
recommendations or upward revisions (Chapter 7). It is also similar to the
price behavior around information release in other offline touting activities
discussed earlier in this chapter.

By mining the time and date of every message posted for the 50 stocks
from Yahoo! message boards between January 1, 1998, and August 26,

1998, Wysocki (1999) pays particular attention to how short-sellers use Internet message boards to spread negative information or rumors about stocks on which they hold short positions. He detects a clear positive relation between short-sale activity and message-posting volume, which is consistent with the widespread anecdotal evidence that short-sellers are active participants on stock message boards. This finding is in line with the trash-and-cash scheme of information-based manipulation by the posting short-sellers. Only the platform for information manipulation is changed from newspaper or TV to an Internet message board with little regulation. Tumarkin and Whitelaw (2001) evaluate the relationship between the valuation of Internet service companies and investor opinions using a popular Internet forum, RagingBull.com, from April 17, 1999, to February 18, 2000. For strong positive recommendations, cumulative abnormal returns in the relevant five-day period before the event day are more than 3.5 percent, which is statistically significant. Stocks subject to strong positive changes in weighted opinion show the most significant increase in trading volume, but reverse to more normal levels approximately two days after the event day. This may imply that posters with strong positive recommendations engage in pump-and-dump trading using Internet posting as a tool to tout the stocks they have already held. Dewally (2003) examines the performance of stocks recommended on two newsgroup sites, namely, misc.invest.stocks and alt.invest.penny-stocks, for 798 (308) postings in the up (down) market from April 1, 1999, to April 30, 1999 (from February 1, 2001, to February 28, 2001). Positively recommended stocks experienced highly significant cumulative abnormal returns over the window Day −20 to Day −1 of 27.62 percent and 6.20 percent, respectively, in the up and down markets. However, the two-day cumulative abnormal returns after the posts were mostly insignificant. Dewally suspects that posters are touting a low-float stock after buying it cheap to generate significant price run-up prior to the posting, and selling the held shares at inflated prices, a typical pump-and-dump trading strategy.

Working with 45 stocks in the major indices with more than 1.5 million text messages from the Yahoo! Finance and Raging Bull message boards during the entire year 2000, Antweiler and Frank (2004) find that message board posts do not predict future returns, but a positive shock to message board posting predicts negative returns on the next day. The more significant finding is that bullishness of the posts follows trading volume increase, not the other way around. This is particularly true for the smaller-sized trades. They interpret this as part of market manipulation strategies. This finding agrees with Schuster (2003) that there is market before the information, not information before the market. Consistent with Tumarkin and Whitelaw (2001) and Antweiler and Frank (2004), Das, Martínez-Jerez, and Tufano (2005) suggest that people trade first and talk later, with returns preceding postings. The three researchers, using a small sample approach, carefully examine more than 170,000 messages posted about four stocks on The Motley Fool stock message board in the period July 1, 1998, through January 31, 1999. They find that there is a close relationship between sentiment levels, historical stock prices, and news, but fail to find predictive power of online postings forecasting returns.

Internet Chat Rooms

Online talk in Internet chat rooms, such as TheLion.com, affects stock prices, too. Sabherwal, Sarkar, and Zhang (2008) focus on 135 thinly traded microcap stocks that enter the real-time list of the 10 most discussed stocks 207 times on TheLion.com between July 18, 2005, and July 18, 2006. For positive recommendations, their event study shows that, on average, those stocks have a significant positive abnormal return of 3.81 percent on the day preceding the event and an abnormal return of 19.35 percent on the event day. The average trading volume on the event day is 7.06 million shares, which is much greater than the average daily trading volume over a three-month period of 1.08 million shares. However, the abnormal returns drop sharply after the event day. This pattern is susceptible to fast and substantial share distribution by the poster who initiated the discussion.

Since stock-related Internet posts can move the market, it is natural for manipulative trading strategies to be spread online. Leinweber and Madhavan (2001) believe that this is facilitated by the ability of the Internet manipulator to repeat or duplicate messages on multiple bulletin boards from his desktop or mobile phone. It takes mere seconds for newly created fake or partially factual messages to reach other participating investors. This is much faster than going through any other media platforms. The anonymity of the manipulator, which is so essential to a successful manipulative scheme, is a free gift because there are no identity regulations. Access to large numbers of potential investors is free or at low cost.

However, not every potential price-moving message can convince viewer-investors. Vilardo (2004) lists seven SEC litigation cases involving the Internet. They take various styles but share a common mechanism. That is, the manipulators try to convey their information through trusted news providers such as *Internet Wire,* or pretend to spread information from respected news agencies such as Bloomberg or issuers such as Lucent. In short, credibility of the information source is the key to those manipulators. We select four of the seven for more detailed exhibition.

In the PairGain case (LR-16266), the rumormonger tried to add credibility effect to his false but potentially price-moving information by pretending it came from Bloomberg news. The false information reached the market through a bogus web site designed to mimic a legitimate news source. The impact was a 30 percent rise in the stock price immediately after the rumormonger's touting post. Another SEC litigation case, LR-16451, tells that two manipulators sent numerous spam e-mail messages to fraudulently manipulate upward the stock price of 57 thinly traded companies after the duo bought their stocks. The two used the well-known acronym AOL and the misdirection hoax to increase credibility of their spam. The alleged perpetrator in the SEC litigation LR-16493 did self-dealing in creating multiple screen names and posting messages from instigation to action taking to induce other investor-viewers to sell Lucent shares. The purpose for the self-dealing, however, was to generate the atmosphere that the information source was Lucent, to gain ultimate credibility. Fortunately, the false rumor did not make much negative impact on Lucent's share prices. LR-18614 is about a trash-and-cash scheme. The alleged manipulator posted a fake Reuters news report on a stock message board dedicated to Sina Corporation. The false story announced that Goldman Sachs had initiated coverage of SINA with a "Market Underperform" rating. Within an hour of publication of the false story, the SINA stock price dropped by more than 3 percent. This manipulative trading strategy was information-based. Mimicking two prestigious information sources, Reuters and Goldman Sachs, was the key to the success of inducing a selling wave.

Spamming

Based on 111 Pink Sheets stocks and 7,606 relevant spam messages between November 2004 and February 2006, Böhme and Holz (2006) find a significantly positive abnormal return accompanies spam messages, but disappears within four days. They suggest that spammers act rationally and try to maximize their expected profit by lifting prices of thinly traded stocks via massive spam e-mailing. Their explanation of why spammers in their sample exclusively target penny stocks is that such stocks have low liquidity and little information coverage. Therefore, the mere mention of a particular stock may stimulate an investment decision and enables the spammers' pump-and-dump strategy to work with a high success rate. However, Böhme and Holz do not include the price and trading volume behavior prior to the spamming event; consequently, one cannot derive a picture of the whole possible cycle of the spamming pump-and-dump trading strategy.

Working with a sample of 307 Pink Sheets stocks touted by massive e-mail spamming between January 2004 and July 2005, Frieder and Zittrain (2008) find that these stocks experienced a significantly positive return on the day preceding such touting and during the day on which they were heavily touted. Trading volume also responded positively and significantly to heavy touting. However, returns in the days following the touting were significantly negative. Frieder and Zittrain suggest that the finding shows that spammers "buy low and spam high." In other words, spammers use touting to generate liquidity so they can dump their accumulated stocks more easily. Frieder and Zittrain (2008) also find that the disclosure mandate, installed by the SEC after 2000, actually provides a safe harbor for touters to send great numbers of spam e-mails. This may show that just disclosure does not effectively regulate market manipulation due to spamming. Based on 41,135 e-mails touting 785 firms from November 2004 to August 2007 from www.crummy.com, Hu, McInish, and Zeng (2009) find that pump-and-dump e-mail campaigns, both with disclosure and without, lead to a big decline in stock price from the peak spam day to the following days and in the long term.

Lease (2010) studies 81 stock-touting e-mails sent by promotion companies to potential investors from April 2009 through December 2009. There are 80 over-the-counter (OTC) Bulletin Board or Pink Sheets stocks in the sample. His result shows a significant (and in many cases, drastic) increase in prices and trading volumes on the day of, and few days following, the promotion. However, prices declined quickly below the prepromotional level only four trading days after the starting date of the promotion. Then prices continued to decline further in the next five months.

In summary, pervasive information-based manipulation has been constantly found online since the Internet was commercialized (Delort et al. 2009). The pattern of the stock price immediately around the initiating positive message or touting spam e-mails remains similar to that of other pump-and-dump schemes on various media platforms. It shows a significant price increase before and on the event date. The price peaks either on or after the event date and is followed by a sharp or slow price decline to below the pretouting level in a matter of days. Thousands of such schemes share the same underlying mechanism: inconsistency in the manipulator's trading accompanied by touting messages and induced trading.

Internet Information-Based Manipulation Has Been Poorly Curbed

How do securities regulators deal with online securities manipulation? As senior regulators from the SEC, Walker and Levine (2001) argue that the Internet has been littered with false and misleading investment information. The SEC brought 209 Internet-related enforcement actions between 1995 and 2000, with the majority since 1998. Market manipulation stands out as the most serious and extensive fraudulent behavior on the Internet. By summarizing several SEC litigation cases of Internet frauds including market manipulation and momentum trading, they find those frauds share the features of ease and cost-efficiency of Internet use, of relative anonymity of Internet users, and of substantial market impact of Internet communications. They consider abnormal stock price movement, particularly in advance of Internet communications, provides evidence of manipulative effect. However, proving a manipulative purpose, which is required in criminal conviction, is difficult. John Reed Stark is a former chief of the Office of Internet Enforcement. As an SEC regulator for 11 years, Stark (2001), reports that the SEC had brought more than 275 Internet-related securities fraud actions over more than four years since 1995. In June 1996, the SEC opened the Enforcement Complaint Center (ECC), an online mailbox through which investors could inform the agency electronically of possible violations of securities laws. The ECC generally receives between 300 and 400 investor complaints per day. Based on 200 trading days per year, a minimum of 60,000 complaints are made annually. This number shows a prevalence of Internet-related frauds in which market manipulation is the major component. SEC litigation actions total about 70 per year. So the rate of success from a complaint to a litigation action is 7 out of 6,000, or less than 0.117 percent! Smith (2006) compares the ASIC (Australian Securities and Investments Commission) to the SEC in the enforcement of Internet-related frauds. ASIC has used criminal action only, while the SEC has used a variety of administrative, civil, and criminal actions to punish numerous Internet-related violations of securities laws. Smith reports that there has been only one criminal prosecution for a pump-and-dump market manipulation in Australia. He concludes that the ASIC has not contended with sophisticated securities fraud faced by the SEC.

Just as Hittle (2001) admits, it is an almost insurmountable legal difficulty to curb Internet manipulation. He concludes that the SEC and other U.S. enforcement agencies face an uphill battle as they attempt to deter and detect perpetrators of Internet stock fraud to protect masses of online investors. This conclusion may apply to other international securities regulators—insofar as their securities laws require them to prove the alleged manipulator's intent to deceive and his information is material, without targeting his trading records.

We have observed that repeated evidence from recent research on Internet information-based manipulation shows that they share a common rationale with conventional information-based manipulation through offline media outlets. The rationale is the inconsistency in the manipulator's trading with his publicly released information and induced trading. This repeated finding leads to an in-depth analysis of the underlying mechanism of information-based manipulation in general, which will be presented in the following section.

ANALYSIS OF INFORMATION-BASED MANIPULATION

We analyze three aspects of information-based manipulation. First, what is the actual role of the manipulator relative to the induced investors? Second, what makes his manipulative strategy work? Third, what is the general characteristic of the trading action by the manipulator engaging in information-based manipulation? Each question is answered here.

The Manipulator's Exercise of Information Monopoly Induces Investors to Trade

Relative to induced investors, a successful manipulator possesses absolute advantage in the potentially price-moving information. The reason the advantage is absolute is that he generates the information. Thus, he is ahead of the induced investors in time to access the information. He has the sole power to change the content of the information anytime before public release. Therefore, he possesses monopolistic power over the induced investors in the potentially price-moving information when it gets substantial publicity through a credible mass media outlet. In short, he has an information monopoly within a certain period. That period starts from the generation of the information to public release of the information.

An information monopoly is an absolute advantage, in both timing and content, to its possessor over numerous nonpossessors. One who possesses an information monopoly may choose to trade to make an almost guaranteed profit; or he may choose to tip others to trade so he can gain a portion of the trading profit; or he may choose neither to trade nor to tip. In the last scenario, he does not make any profit from the information monopoly he possesses. The EntreMed story provides a vivid example that price-moving newspaper articles by journalists who do not trade on the reported stock can carry an information monopoly. But those journalists are not manipulators (Huberman and Regev 2001). Concisely speaking, an information monopoly is not equivalent to monopolistic trading or stock manipulation. Only when an information monopoly is used to increase the price or lower it in a trading strategy does the latter becomes monopolistic. That is, it becomes stock market manipulation. If the information monopoly is generated from trading only and disseminated by the stock exchange, which gives other investors the perception of a constantly rising stock price or an apparently increasing purchase volume, the trading strategy equipped with this kind of information monopoly is trade-based manipulation. If the information monopoly is generated from a false or misleading or even a factual press release that leaves other investors with the perception of an expected increase in stock price, the corresponding trading strategy becomes information-based manipulation. In general, exercising an information monopoly is the core of market manipulation. Without exercising an information monopoly, a trading strategy is hardly manipulative.

Information Monopoly Is the Product of Price-Moving Potential, Publicity, and Credibility

Suppose a stock in the manufacturing sector is the manipulator's target. What are the components that assemble the manipulator's information monopoly? The price-moving potential of the information (M) he generates, how much publicity it can get (P), and how credible the information source (C) is are the three multipliers that form information monopoly (IM). In short,

$$IM = M \times P \times C.$$

When M is zero, IM is zero because the information is irrelevant to the stock in question. For example, a news article about an NBA game in the *New York Times* does not have any impact on the target stock price, even though the amount of publicity and credibility that the newspaper carries is enormous. There is no information monopoly about the target stock. There is no entailed manipulation, either. In the following, we assume $M > 0$ for relevance to the chapter.

If a well-known investor possesses potentially price-moving information—not insider information—but reveals it to nobody, and he initiates trades along the information with minimal price impact and later closes them quietly without any fictitious trades, the trading round-trip has no information-based manipulation involved. In short, if $P = 0$, $IM = 0$, even though $M > 0$ and $C > 0$ (a well-known investor has high credibility to numerous investors).

If an anonymous investor posts a shocking stock message on the Yahoo! Finance message board, $M > 0$ and $P > 0$, two situations arise. The first situation is that no investor trades according to the information; then his manipulation attempt fails. The key lies in the fact that neither the poster nor the information source has any credibility. Generally, this kind of information will not result in an information monopoly for the poster. This happens to numerous Internet message board postings from unknown posters every day because every shareholder has a tendency to promote the stock he owns. In brief, because $C = 0$, $IM = 0$.

The second situation is that an investor or many investors follow the information to trade; then the manipulation partially or completely succeeds if the trade is made along the information prior to its dissemination and against it after the dissemination. The key in this situation is the credibility of the information. If the manipulator's message makes other investors believe the information comes from a credible source such as *Business Wire*, then they will be convinced instantly and trade accordingly. Litigation cases researched by Vilardo (2004) concerning Internet information-based manipulation show that credibility or pretended credibility is the success secret of the alleged manipulators. In this situation, $C > 0$; hence $IM > 0$.

One extreme scenario is when M is nearly zero. A false rumor about a stock can qualify as a zerolike piece of information. Since it is related to a stock toward which some investors are sensitive, the information content is a bit above zero. A credible news agency or media outlet publishes it as it is. It looks credible to some investors because of the credibility of the news agency or media outlet. They believe what they perceive and trade accordingly. Therefore, the potency of IM depends on how many investors the information can reach, or the publicity it can get (P), and how credible either the information generator is, or the information disseminator, or both (C). The Emulex hoax and ADS rumor elaborated earlier are vivid examples demonstrating that a widely spread false rumor from an unknown trader through multiple credible media outlets can still move the market drastically in a short time, or trigger a very high trading speed.

The potency of IM can be measured by the number of shares that are induced to be traded by the information. This is equivalent to how many investors' perceptions can be effectively manipulated. Since observation of the price behavior of a stock is the most convincing perception of many investors, direct manipulation of this perception without going though information generation and dissemination is another extreme. This happens when no publicity or media reporting is involved. No credibility is involved, either. A trade-based price-lifting scenario is a good example. When the manipulator is doing fictitious trading such as self-dealing, the manipulated stock price keeps increasing for a number of trading days in a row. This fact itself becomes important evolving information to many investors interested in the stock when it is disseminated by the stock exchange and picked up by many credible media outlets. The information monopoly thus produced covers the manipulator's intention to distribute the shares he has already accumulated when induced buy volumes are sufficiently large, while other investors can see only a stock with consecutively rising prices. Most of them perceive that the stock price will increase further without knowing when the increase will stop or even start to decline. Once they follow the rising stock to buy, the manipulator will soon trade against the following investors. In this scenario, no personal credibility is needed because what investors see is most convincing. In other words, ever-increasing stock prices provide all the components in IM. Therefore, $IM > 0$ in this scenario.

Many other scenarios occur within the domain bordered by the aforementioned extremes. That is, the information contains certain price-moving potential. Some publicity is achieved by the potential manipulator by going through a TV channel or a newspaper interview, or posting on several popular Internet stock message boards. The credibility of the media outlet or personal credibility or even pretended credibility, together with the price-moving potential and publicity, yields certain power of information monopoly.

Inconsistency in the Manipulator's Trading Completion with His Information

Exercising an information monopoly moves the market. When a trading strategy includes an information monopoly, it becomes a market manipulation scheme. A stock manipulator succeeds in executing his trading strategy because he possesses and exercises an information monopoly over the induced investors. And the three inseparable components forming the information monopoly are the price-moving potential of the information, the publicity of the information circulation, and the credibility of the information source. In this section, we try to uncover the universal characteristic in the behavior of the information-based manipulator.

The characteristic is inconsistency. To elaborate, it is the inconsistency in the manipulator's completion of trading with his information (Perminov 2008, p. 20). In the Emulex hoax, Jakob shorted the stock and then e-mailed *Internet Wire* so they would release the false information he made up. When numerous investors were induced by his rumor and sold a large number of shares in a rush, he bought back the Emulex shares to cover his short sales. Obviously, he closed his manipulation by trading against his information and the induced investors.

In a long trading strategy, the trader buys a stock before his media presence. The stock price increases, say, by 2 to 3 percent above the previous close without his purchase. Then the trader goes on TV or an Internet message board to tout the stock. He forecasts the stock price will rise a further 50 percent. Some investors are convinced. Why? Because they see the stock price rising. That is hard evidence. Nobody knows whether the trader can predict the future price, but the rising price in the immediate past supports him. In other words, his words carry some truth. If he is a well-known figure, such as an investment expert, a big-name investor, or some public figure (for example, a rap star; see Whitehouse (2011)), then his words seem even more credible. However, he never says when he will sell his shareholding after the price increases. That is the essence of his information monopoly. Meanwhile, he tells only the part of the truth that can induce other investors to follow him, but he hides the most important part of the truth—that he will trade against the induced investors soon. When he exercises his information monopoly against the induced investors, he will certainly gain at their loss in the near future when he sells all his shares at an inflated price, which is caused by the buy volumes of the induced investors. Perminov (2008, p. 7) states, "Speculators sell any stories to spread panic or enthusiasm. When the positive or negative trend has played out, they switch their attention to the opposite direction." This indicates when inconsistency starts in an information-based manipulative trading strategy.

The reason this type of inconsistency is universal across information-based manipulation schemes is that the long manipulator touts the target stock for the purpose of his distribution of the already-held shares at an inflated price. In thousands of observations in preceding sections, there is always a price run-up before the touting information release and a deep price decline back to prerelease level soon after the release. Thus, the inconsistency occurs in the short time window immediately following the release. The sale cannot be weeks after the release because of uncertainty during the prolonged postrelease time horizon. If a manipulator has owned the target stock for a long time, there may be no short-term price run-up preceding the release. He still sells against the touting information soon after its release. Therefore, the essence of the information-based manipulation strategy is the inconsistency of the manipulator's trading completion with his touting information and the induced trading.

Thus far, we have narrowed down the essence of a general information-based manipulation scheme. It is the inconsistency in the manipulator's trading completion against his released information and the induced trading. It is in the immediate short period after the information release. This can turn into an effective regulatory target.

REGULATORY RECOMMENDATIONS

As we have analyzed earlier in this chapter, the core of information-based manipulation is that the trader exercises an information monopoly. Regulatory proposals need to be designed to effectively break profitable but unfair trading from exercising an information monopoly. That is, they need to be in the antitrust spirit, whether an information monopoly exists for seconds or years.

Consistency Requirement Is the Regulatory Principle

For Anyone Who Is to Talk about One Stock—the Target Stock—on a Media Outlet Such as TV, Radio, Newspaper, or an Internet-Streamed Audio or Video Show, the Following Regulatory Measures Are Recommended

- *Measure one:* He has to disclose all the stocks he and his company are holding as well as a complete list of the company's clients holding the target stock to the regulatory agency at least 24 hours ahead of his media presence. The regulatory agency oversees his and his company's trading activities in the target stock from the time of his disclosure. The company's clients trading in the target stock need to be monitored, too.
- *Measure two:* If he or his company is trading against his public attitude toward the stock in his talk, he or his company is allowed to trade 1 percent of his or his company's shareholding in the stock daily. That is, for each trading day thereafter, he can transact 1 percent of the absolute volume of his prerelease shareholding or 3 percent of the previous month's daily average volume, whichever is smaller. The company is accountable if its clients are trading substantially against the information. The accountability threshold, which is defined by the regulatory agency, is based on the trading volume of clients against the information. If he or his company is trading according to his public attitude toward the target stock, then his daily transaction is only subject to 3 percent of the previous month's daily average volume, to prevent large trading speed (Chapter 3).[8]
- *Measure three:* The pre-event price increase or decrease and volume increase can be subject to quantitative thresholds. The regulating agency can call off or postpone his media presence sufficiently long if one of the thresholds is reached. The thresholds can be set up using the one-month daily average return before the event as a benchmark. A numerical example is 3 percent above the average, contingent on no other major price-moving news events about the stock.
- *Measure four:* If he or his company has no shareholding in the target stock, then he and his company are held accountable for issuing contradictory pieces of information about the same stock to the public and the company's clients. The accountability comes if the clients are trading against the information released to the public.

■ *Measure five:* A tracking system needs to be established to keep a history of those investors who have conducted serious or repeated information-based manipulation, in order to avoid or reduce the damage they may cause to the stock market and its participants.

Regulatory Considerations for Internet-Related Market Manipulation

■ *Measure six:* Web sites with 1,000 or more viewers must require any posters, including those who post in other individuals' blogs or bloggers who make stock picks, to submit identity data and disclose all of their shareholding positions 24 hours in advance. These data are to be shared with the securities regulatory agency.

■ *Measure seven:* All of the first five proposals apply. Adjustment may be necessary if a touted or trashed stock is a thinly traded issue or a large-cap.

■ *Measure eight:* Anyone who posts significant information (e.g., content of breaking news) or information about public companies, well-known figures (including public figures), organizations, brands, locations (e.g., the White House), events (e.g., September 11 terrorist attack), objects (e.g., museum exhibits), dates (e.g., national holidays), or other well-known things, is held accountable for the truthfulness of the information. Both the manager of the web site and regulators should verify the truthfulness of this information. They should take immediate enforcement actions to correct it if this information is not truthful.

Effectiveness of the Quantifiable and Adjustable Regulatory Recommendations

The effectiveness of the regulatory recommendations lies in their targeting the trading direction and quantity of the manipulator without the need to prove whether his intent is bad or his information is material or false. This target priority substantially increases the efficiency of enforcement. They are convenient because most of them are quantifiable. The predetermined percentage can be self-enforced by any investor, while the regulatory agency needs to oversee the outcome and ensure complete enforcement.

The numerical example used in the recommendations can be adjusted according to the market reality and regulatory priority of each stock market. The fundamental rationale of enforcing trading of the small percentage of the prerelease shareholding is to make it extremely difficult for the manipulators to control their unfair trading profit. This is how to alter the link between his exercising information monopoly and his actual unfair trading profit. He may create or obtain an information monopoly again in the future. However, he cannot easily profit substantially and unfairly by secretly creating and setting off mini-bubbles in the market; nor can he make easy unfair profit by exercising his information monopoly and generating price volatility. On the other side, the great uncertainty in the profitability of his information-based manipulation strategy will make him reconsider engaging in such manipulation.

For Internet information-based manipulation, anonymity is an additional obstacle to overcome. In other words, effective enforcement in cyberspace begins with transparency by knowing the identity and shareholding of the manipulator suspect. The rest will be similar to the five anti-inconsistency recommendations proposed previously. One more point to emphasize is that an effective regulation of the Internet web sites should be set up in a timely manner in a transparent, legal, and scientific way, so as to effectively regulate those web sites or blogs that issue and disseminate false information, rumors, defaming allegations, confusing half-truths, and other information that disturbs the community, spreads terrorism, instigates unrest, or frames a market crash.

The Proposals Are Complementary to the Current Regulations

We do not find many institutional investors in SEC market manipulation litigation cases released between October 1, 1999, and September 30, 2009. We did not have much luck in finding institutional investors engaging in information-based manipulation in public lawsuits from stock markets of other countries. One probable reason for such difficulty is the targeting priority by current securities regulations in the United States and other markets where the regulatory framework is based on the Securities Act of 1933 and Securities Exchange Act of 1934 passed during the Franklin D. Roosevelt Administration. The main targets are the intent of the alleged manipulator and the information he publicly disseminates, rather than his trading direction and quantity. This targeting priority often leads to no or partial enforcements, which likely consist of settlements, while the ratio of litigation to actual complaints is extremely low. In short, the enforcement effectiveness is very low.

What matters most in dealing with information-based manipulation is the manipulator's trading direction relative to his publicly disseminated information. What intent the manipulator has is hard to establish and it may be difficult to find out or proceed in a short time to preventive measures. If the information is investigated alone, one needs a relatively long time for detection and comparison with historical evidence, and even other efforts or social resources to find out if it is truthful, half truthful, or completely false. Our evidence from empirical data show that any stock-related information has price-moving potential. The crucial links are the credibility of the information in the eyes of recipient investors and the publicity it gets. The potentially price-moving information, its publicity, and perceived credibility jointly entail powerful price impact, or so-called information monopolistic power. Once the power is utilized in a trading strategy, the latter becomes manipulative. The evidence is obvious in the manipulator's inconsistency displayed by his trading against the released information to realize his profit. Therefore, our recommendations, based on the anti-inconsistency principle, complement the current regulatory measures with effective prevention as their primary function.

DISCUSSION OF INFORMATION MONOPOLY IN REALITY

Not only is inconsistency found repeatedly in information-based manipulative trading schemes, it is also behind earnings manipulation, corporate insiders' trading, and sell-side analysts' publicly released recommendations. It is an underlying mechanism for frontrunning, too. The following analysis will support this argument.

Corporate Insider Trading, Analyst Recommendations, and Frontrunning

When corporate executives manipulate their earnings and other issuer-generated information, they have an absolute information advantage over outside investors. That is, they have an advantage in both information content and release timing. Therefore, they possess an information monopoly once the information is publicly released. If they exercise the information monopoly in their trading, it becomes information-based manipulation. If they place purchase orders before an upward earnings announcement and sell orders soon after the announcement, this is well-studied corporate insider trading. In essence, it is short-run inconsistency. In contrast, there is long-run inconsistency. When corporate executives consecutively cook accounting books and announce estimate-beating earnings for years, their trades qualify as long-run inconsistency with their information content. Enron and Cendant provide two good examples in this regard (Chapters 5 and 6).

Information releases by research analysts entail multiple consequences. Their recommendations give them an information monopoly over uninformed investors. If those analysts trade against their recommendations, they engage in information-based manipulation. Oftentimes, the investment banks or brokerage firms that employ them have proprietary trading teams. When those teams trade against the analysts' recommendations, those analysts are colluders in the information-based manipulation schemes played by the proprietary trading teams. When sell-side analysts act as marketing pros for their issuer clients, then their role is assisting their clients' corporate insiders to engage in either short-run or long-run inconsistency in these insiders' trading strategies (Chapter 7).

In frontrunning scenarios, market makers or fund managers have discretion as to when and how to place their clients' large orders and their own small trades. That is, they have absolute advantage over their clients in both the initiating and the closing phases of a trade round-trip. In practice, they can initiate trades ahead of the clients' opening orders and close their trades ahead of closing the clients' positions. Therefore, frontrunning market makers and fund managers have information monopolies over their clients and certainly over other uninformed investors. When they engage in frontrunning games, they are exercising their monopolistic power. However, they do not need to release any information. Their manipulation is trade-based. For a market maker's frontrunning in 1998 in the Long Term Capital Management debacle, see Cai (2003).

Flash Crash and High-Frequency Trading

The flash crash in the NYSE on May 6, 2010, shook the U.S. stock markets and the SEC. It was the biggest one-day point decline (998.5 points) in the history of the Dow Jones Industrial Average (Easley, Lopez de Prado, and O'Hara 2010). The crash began at 2:42 P.M. With the Dow down more than 300 points for the day, the equity market began to fall rapidly, dropping more than 600 points in five minutes, for an almost 1,000-point loss for the day by 2:47 P.M. Twenty minutes later, at 3:07 P.M., the market regained a majority of the 600-point drop (Lauricella 2010). The plunge and rebound formed a sharp V-shape within minutes. It involved extra high selling and buying speed. As a result of this process, we may wonder what risk the flash crash generated to the NYSE? What caused this flash crash? Who lost dramatically? And who gained substantially?

The press and the academic literature (Creswell 2010; Hiltzik 2010; Lauricella 2010; Cardella, Hao, and Kalcheva 2010; Easley, O'Hara, and Yang 2011), as well as the regulators' investigations (SEC and CFTC joint report 2010), point to high-frequency trading (HFT) as the cause of the flash crash.[9] The literature analyzes the impact of the HFT in relation to the stock market from the perspectives of liquidity, efficiency, and quality. We provide another viewpoint from the angle of preventing systemic risk.

According to Gomber et al. (2011), trading very large quantities on aggregates within very short time periods is one primary characteristic of HFT. This refers to the high trading speed of either the buy or the sell transactions. Use of colocation is another key feature, because of the low latency requirement. The most critical, however, is showing coming orders by the exchange to a few subscribing institutional traders for 30 milliseconds or so before displaying them to the investing public (Duhigg 2009). These 30 milliseconds are precious. Because the execution time by modern computers goes down to microseconds, gaining a timing advantage of 30 milliseconds is more than sufficient for the traders engaged in HFT to make sure profits. The entire process is similar to frontrunning. However, the information monopoly is not generated by the traders, but instead is tipped by the exchange through subscriptions. Hence, it is more inclined toward insider trading by temporary insiders.

Who possesses the information monopoly? The exchange. In this special case, the information monopoly is naturally possessed by the exchange because it has full discretion over all coming orders in relation to how to display them. The exchange is privately owned. To seek a profit and competitive edge, it chooses to sell real-time data to a few subscribers and allows them to colocate their trading desks with the exchange site. This incurs a conflict of interest to the investing public.

The information monopoly is exercised by the exchange for a business interest. That is, the exchange discloses the order data to a few large institutional proprietary traders before all market participants are able to access it. This process is similar to leaking insider information to a few colluding partners with a more certain price-moving potential. Once the latter gains the monopolistic inside information, they utilize it in their trading strategies for profit seeking. Their trading strategies become an information-based manipulation. In brief, the exchange possesses the information monopoly and exercises it for the business interest. It is rent-seeking. The subscribing institutional investors utilize the information monopoly in their HFT strategies. Hence, they are information-based manipulators.

Since the HFT involves extra high trading speed, it poses a serious threat to stock market security. The rationale is the following. Today, HFT represents 40–73 percent of all trading volumes in the U.S. stock markets (Iati 2009; Creswell 2010; Hiltzik 2010). The high concentration of shareholding by a few large institutional investors should be of concern to securities regulators. In practice, if a large sell order is flashed to a few HFT investors before the market, they frontrun the order by placing their own sell orders. If many sell orders are placed within a very short time period, the manipulated stock price is pressed down substantially. Within seconds, the entire market becomes aware of the falling price. As a result, more sell orders flow in. They will be flashed repeatedly, which further triggers subsequent frontrunning sell orders by the HFT investors. The scenario becomes a vicious cycle. Consequently, the stock price falls continuously in a very fast fashion. The worst situation is when one or more of the HFT investors' algorithmic systems' risk parameters are reached, as then a crash is unavoidable without intervention (Dick 2010; Creswell 2010). The flash crash of May 6, 2010, is a warning sign to the SEC and all market participants.

After the crash, or regulatory intervention, buy orders may start to emerge. The HFT investors will frontrun again. The cycle reinforces the fact that more and more buy orders rush in for the manipulated stock and the price keeps going up. Therefore, rebounding can also be very fast. In general, HFT makes both the crash and the rebounding occur during very short time periods. The stock price will follow a sharp V-shape as time elapses. However, during the process, HFT investors profit extensively, while other, slower traders shoulder deep losses. Concisely speaking, HFT is a potential threat to the trading system; it generates extreme volatility and causes other investors to incur huge losses in a matter of minutes. Therefore, it is a systemic risk. The SEC is considering banning high-frequency trading (Cardella, Hao, and Kalcheva 2010).

In brief, market manipulation is essentially about generating or gaining an information monopoly and exercising it in trading strategies, regardless of various forms of schemes, legal or illegal.

CONCLUDING REMARKS

From both our hand-collected litigation data and empirical research of tens of thousands of observations, we repeatedly find a stock price pattern around positive information released during an information-based manipulative trading scheme. The pattern includes a postrelease price decline to below the prerelease level. Our analysis reveals that the inconsistency in the manipulator's trading completion with his publicly released information is the hidden mechanism of the price pattern. The reason the manipulator's information release can induce numerous investors is that he possesses an information monopoly and exercises it in his trading strategy. The potency of his information monopoly is composed of three elements. They are the price-moving potential of the information, the publicity it gets, and the credibility it has or pretends to have. When all three elements are in place, the perceptions of numerous investors can be manipulated to the extent that they trade according to the information immediately.

By targeting the manipulator's trading inconsistency in his publicly released information, we have suggested preventive measures for securities regulators. These measures are expected to be effective since they are quantifiable, adjustable, and easy to implement for daily operations. Because they are basically nonlegal proposals, they can be used together with current disclosure-oriented regulations. With recommended measures to prevent information-based manipulation and trade-based manipulation, we believe that implementation of these measures will contribute effectively and substantially to building perfect competition for trading profits in the stock market with fairness and transparency. They are expected to greatly enhance investor protection, market stability, and systemic security.

A PERSPECTIVE FOR FUTURE RESEARCH

Preventive actions can only follow the foreseen systemic risk. From Tulipmania of 1636 to the Great Crash of 1929, from the Asian financial crisis of 1997 to the global financial crisis of 2007 to 2009, it is hard to know how many historical stock market crises or other financial crises were foreseen by international securities regulators or other regulators. It is even harder to know how many of the influential market-rocking securities frauds were detected by local regulators prior to their breakout. But we do know several internationally notorious securities frauds were exposed because of their own implosion (Chapter 3).

On the other hand, empirical data show repeatedly that stock markets, either national exchanges such as the NYSE and Nasdaq, or OTC markets such as Pink Sheets, are very vulnerable to manipulation, particularly information-based manipulation. The Lebed case (SEC Release #33-7891) is very thought provoking. A 15-year-old high school boy was able to successfully make a profit of $800,000 from false touting information he posted repeatedly to major Internet message boards.[10] Institutional investors definitely can conduct information-based manipulation on a much larger scale because they have much more disposable wealth and more stock promotion resources such as research analysts. There are some institutional investors who have been caught in information-based market manipulation cases. One can reason from earlier analysis that they may engage in much more sophisticated manipulative trading strategies, which appear legal (Perminov 2008, p. 10). They profit quite systematically year after year until they are financially distressed by vast manipulative trading or unexpected market conditions. But regulators are not aware of the systemic risk they have generated long before the distress. Nor do regulators respond with any preventive action. The recent bankruptcy or near collapse of several Wall Street conglomerates such as Lehman Brothers, Bear Stearns, and Merrill Lynch is evidence of this reasoning.

An examination of SEC market manipulation litigation cases over the past decade shows serious problems, where some institutional investors were also involved in market manipulation. This may have revealed the tip of the iceberg of the regulatory priority of the agency. It may further reflect enforcement difficulties created and faced by the securities regulatory framework. To prevent future financial crises, securities regulators need to improve and enhance their capacity to forecast, prevent, and deal with crises; in particular, they need to emphasize research and empower their ability to foresee the risk-mounting trajectory of the financial system. Weather forecast becomes an important part of daily human activities. Securities and other regulators need risk forecast to monitor hot spots in the entire financial system, including stock markets in their daily operations. Monitoring stock trading by institutional investors is a crucial building block in this regard. Two of the most fundamental variables are the quantity and speed of large shareholdings in each stock market and interrelated markets. This will be addressed in our future work.

NOTES

1. This chapter was accepted for presentation at the 8th International Conference on Advances in Applied Financial Economics, June 30–July 2, 2011, Samos Island, Greece. Part of this chapter was presented at the 6th Annual Seminar on Banking, Financial Stability, and Risk, Sao Paulo, August 11–12, 2011, hosted by the Banco Central do Brasil.
2. Regional brokerage houses or self-proclaimed broker-dealers or stock promoters do not qualify as major institutional investors for our purposes.
3. Chapter 3 lists several stock market crises caused by large institutional investors. They are Naji Robert Nahas in Brazil (1989), Delta Securities in Greece (1996), and Ketan Parekh, the Bombay Bull, in India (2001). In addition, the near collapse of Long Term Capital Management in 1998 could have resulted in a multimarket financial crisis without the New York Federal Reserve's forceful intervention. The bankruptcy of Lehman Brothers on September 15, 2008, triggered the most severe global financial crisis since the Great Depression.
4. Perminov (2008, p. 11) reveals that large investors deny their participation in market manipulation. Even medium-sized fund managers don't like to discuss it. Furthermore: "But legal regulations in this field are too general and outdated. The total number of cases initiated by SEC does not compare to [the] real scale of this problem."
5. Perminov (2008, p. 19) argues that fictitious trading, or "painting the tape," is not widely used anymore in U.S. stock markets. Information-based manipulation is preferred because mass media have gained enough power over investors to influence their trade decisions. In the meantime, biased analysts' opinions have become common.

6. However, several researchers use "pump-and-dump" to describe either general market manipulation (for instance, Aggarwal and Wu 2006) or trade-based manipulation (IOSCO 2000; Khwaja and Mian 2005; He and Su 2009), in addition to information-based manipulation as defined by the SEC. In this paper, we focus on information-based manipulation. Thus, the pump phase in a complete pump-and-dump scheme features stock-touting information dissemination. In Chapter 3, we use the Accumulation-Lift-Distribution (ALD) triad to describe a trade-based manipulation scheme to emphasize the accumulation phase. The mere difference between the two is at the lift or pump phase. For trade-based manipulation, lift features such fictitious trading by the manipulator as self-dealing or cross-dealing. For information-based manipulation, pump is characterized by disseminating positive information about the target stock. The two share the same aim: to induce investors to buy the shares of the target stock so the manipulator can dump or sell a large chunk of shares. Here we do not concentrate on the accumulation phase. Because a large concentration of shareholdings is not required to initiate an information-based manipulation scheme, we prefer to use pump-and-dump to vividly describe the price-lifting phase as stock touting, instead of the ALD scheme.

7. If the hoax says that Emulex, a high-tech company, discovered a giant gold mine, it is not believable. But an SEC investigation, CEO resignation, and downward revision of quarterly earnings are all events familiar to investors. Therefore, they are believable without investigating the basis, and constitute the price moving effect, especially after credible media publish them.

8. These percentages are numerical examples for presenting convenience. Any regulating agency that is willing to implement the anti-inconsistency principle will have to define the percentages according to the agency's needs. To have a sufficient deterrent effect, the daily allowance cannot exceed 5 percent of the prerelease shareholding.

9. Some researchers do not believe that HFT was the trigger of the flash crash on May 6, 2010, but do recognize that it exacerbated market volatility (Kirilenko et al. 2010). Hasbrouck and Saar (2011) determined that HFT improves market quality, such as short-term volatility, concurring with Brogaard (2010).

10. Jonathan Lebed is not alone among his teenage peers. For instance, a 17-year-old high school boy, Cole A. Bartiromo, made a decent profit by doing Internet pump-and-dump manipulation in 2001 (LR-17540 and LR-17296).

CHAPTER 9

Preventing Stock Market Crises (VII)

Principles of Regulating News Reporting That Cultivates Long-Run Manias and Triggers Short-Run Panics

Xin Yan

Lawrence R. Klein

Viktoria Dalko

Ferenc Gyurcsány

Michael H. Wang[1]

A prolonged mania in the stock market will surely result in a marketwide crisis. To prevent a stock market crisis, it is necessary to curb such a mania. Because certain business news reporting can generate or cogenerate an information monopoly that can be and frequently has been utilized for market manipulation and other interests, and since media firms have financial and informational dependence on large corporations, some business news reporting is found to be upward-biased, particularly in economic boom times. The biased reporting frequentlies triggers short-run mini-bubbles and cultivates long-run mania in the stock market. A set of principles is proposed for securities regulators that are expected to effectively mitigate the generation of information monopolies and prevent such monopoly power.

Panic selling due to some sudden large news events needs to be regulated to protect investors of all categories and prevent marketwide collapse.

Both the breaking news reporting and the following panic selling will be regulatory targets in our proposed principles.

All eight principles we recommend are aimed for more objective, fair, and transparent business news and breaking news reporting, thus greatly enhancing investor protection and reducing the potential of a stock market crisis.

INFORMATION MONOPOLY AND CERTAIN BUSINESS NEWS REPORTING

Does some business news reporting generate or cogenerate an information monopoly? This is a crucial question to every investor and securities regulator. We start with scenarios where information monopolies are generated for manipulative trading.

Information Monopoly Utilized for Stock Trading

According to the National Credibility Index (1999), reporting on public companies enjoys high credibility among surveyed investors, second only to issuing companies' annual reports. The information loop starts from issuer-generated information, proceeds to media-generated information, then to sell-side-analyst-generated information, and so on, and ends at investors' trading decisions. We focused on one type of issuer-generated information, annually and quarterly announced earnings, in Chapter 5. There is considerable evidence from the past 50 years that repeatedly indicates that corporate information can and has been frequently manipulated by issuers' management. The underlying mechanism is that issuers possess an absolute information advantage relative to outside investors in both timing and content of the disclosed information. This type of absolute advantage has the potential to move the issuer's stock prices. Once it is announced through a media outlet such as the *Wall Street Journal,* substantial publicity and credibility are added to it. Thus, an information monopoly is formed, which can be utilized in trading strategies to make abnormal profits or avoid substantial losses. We demonstrated how the information monopoly is utilized by corporate insiders in their trading strategies by presenting empirical research findings from international stock markets in Chapter 6.

In Chapter 7, we found mounting evidence in both developed economies and emerging markets that sell-side analysts can and have manipulated their research releases for the last 40 years. This has the potential to move stock prices. Once published by credible mass media, it becomes an information monopoly that can be used for multiple purposes. It can be embedded in the profit-making or loss-avoidance trading strategy by the firm's proprietary trading arm and preferred client investors, it can be used as the marketing tool for client issuers, and it can be used for analysts' personal trading schemes.

We anatomized Securities and Exchange Commission (SEC) enforcement under the market manipulation category and examined more closely various information-based market manipulation schemes, particularly Internet-related, in Chapter 8. We have accumulated more evidence to demonstrate our preliminary understanding of the composition of the related information monopoly. In all the scenarios investigated, three features are included:

- Anyone—an institutional investor, individual investor, or noninvesting person—can create potentially price-moving information.
- An information monopoly is born when the potentially price-moving information is disseminated by a credible media outlet for substantial publicity.[2]
- The information monopoly thus produced can be utilized for profit making or loss avoidance in business practices, which include stock trading, marketing, or reputation building.

Information Content in Information Monopoly

In Chapters 5 to 8, our target is manipulative trading, as we are interested mostly in how an information monopoly is utilized for market manipulation. In this chapter, our focuses are how an information monopoly is utilized for general business interests and the effect of such utilization on the stock market. We are particularly concerned with whether utilization of an information monopoly is closely linked to abnormal price volatility and systemic risks that frequently lead to stock market crises.

Since our subject is business news reporting related to individual stocks and stock markets in general, we pay attention to its content and presentation, that is, who provides the content and how business news is presented. The reason we emphasize these two is that for a mass media outlet, such as the *Wall Street Journal, New York Times,* and CNBC, high publicity and credibility are attached to any news disseminated. If the news is related to any stock or stock exchange, it has a price-moving impact on the market. In other words, any news reporting related to a stock, a public company, or a stock market as a whole, published by a credible media outlet with a large circulation, can be considered an information monopoly.

From the vantage of formation of an information monopoly, business news reporting by a mass media outlet enjoys both publicity and credibility.

Comparatively, issuers lack publicity, although mandatory disclosure gives them limited publicity to professional investors (Stice 1991), and Internet information-based manipulators do not have sufficient credibility (Vilardo 2004; Chapter 8). Even sell-side analysts, after submitting their research to market data services, have to republish their recommendations in business media to gain more market reaction (Beneish 1991; Chapter 7). In short, they all need publicity and credibility to gain an information monopoly over the investing public. Business news reporting by a large media outlet can provide both at the same time.

Since publicity (P) and credibility (C) are given for a specific media outlet (at least for a period of time when there is no dramatic change in its audience or reputation), we now focus on the potentially price-moving information (M) contained only in business news. Since $P \times C$ is a constant, information monopoly, or IM, is proportional to M. It is expressed mathematically as:

$$IM = \text{const} \times M,$$

where const is a constant, const $= P \times C$. Our focus turns to information that carries price-moving potential. In quantitative terms, $|M| > 0$. To elaborate, M is positive for potentially price-inflating information, that is, $M > 0$; M is negative for potentially price-deflating information; that is, $M < 0$. For information unrelated to stocks or stock markets, one cannot say for certain that $M = 0$. For some seemingly irrelevant information such as in news that addresses politics, terrorism, public health, or natural disasters, if numerous investors' overall psychology is affected, they may choose to sell or buy instantly at the arrival of the information; hence, $M \neq 0$. The 9/11 terrorist attack triggered marketwide selling in panic. Although the news only had direct relevance to airline stocks and some tourism stocks, the overall psychology of the investing public was seriously affected (Drakos 2004). Thus, the information from the news reporting became very relevant to all stock markets in the U.S. and some other nations. The recent severe earthquake and its aftermath in Japan caused a marketwide sell-off in the Tokyo Stock Exchange.[3] In these two scenarios, $M < 0$. If a news event is not stock-related, nor is it large, and investors' overall psychology is not affected, $M = 0$. Thus, we address an information monopoly brought out by a single news event. Repeated reporting on the same event or concept related to stock markets will be discussed later in this chapter.

The research questions we address are: Does certain business news reporting affect stock prices? If yes, is it a causal factor in frequent mini-bubbles in the stock market? Does it contribute to formation of a mania in a long time horizon? We are particularly keen about the last question since a long-run mania will result in a crisis.

A PROLONGED MANIA IN STOCK BUYING LEADS TO A MARKETWIDE CRISIS

> *The history of speculative bubbles begins roughly with the advent of newspapers.*
>
> —Robert Shiller (2000, p. 71)

A stock market crisis usually is interpreted as a sudden and substantial drop in the stock market index at its onset. However, one often observes a mania, even a prolonged mania, at its formation. First, though, investors—and not *deus ex machina*—need to lift the general level of securities prices to an exceptionally high level.

Charles Mackay (1841), the author of an early, well-known European study on financial crises, pointed out that widespread mania preceded widespread crises in each of the three cases he studied. He drew his cases from France, England, and Holland—analyzing the Mississippi, the South Sea, and the tulip bubbles. The occurrence of the same type of crises is confirmed by Kindelberger (2000) and Shiller (2000), among others. Investors behave the same way, specifically buying securities when prices rise and selling when prices fall. De Long et al. (1990) labeled them "positive feedback investors."

A prolonged mania in the stock exchange is a sufficient condition for a marketwide crisis, but not a necessary one. The Roaring Twenties led to the Big Crash in October 1929; the 1990s' "irrational exuberance" ended with the dot-com meltdown. But multiple stock exchanges with 50 to 94 percent drops in 2008 were triggered or precipitated by Lehman Brothers' unexpected bankruptcy (Robertson 2008). Not all economies experienced lengthy preceding manias in the stock markets, but other financial markets saw soaring oil prices, overlending in housing markets, or excessive holding of mortgage-backed securities.

The following sections will reveal that when more and more, and eventually a very large number of, individual investors make the same decision, this kind of coordinated movement can result in excessive buying. Some large institutional investors follow the increasing optimistic market trend at a later stage. As this trend continues for a lengthy period of time, eventually individual and institutional investors incite a mania. Charles Mackay (1841) famously called this behavior the "extraordinary popular delusions and the madness of the crowds." A coordinated large number of buy volumes for the same stock during a short time period cumulatively has a high price impact on the stock. When the same behavior spreads to different stocks, the stock market index escalates dramatically. The focus of our study is to find out if and how mass media, and more specifically certain business news reporting, generates mini-bubbles in the short run and manias in the long run. The ultimate purpose is to propose principles to regulate business news reporting to prevent or substantially slow down formation of a mania, thus reducing the risk of a potential crisis, while not hindering freedom of the press.

SOME BUSINESS NEWS REPORTING IS CAPABLE OF MOVING STOCK PRICES IN THE SHORT RUN

From the earliest times, news has affected investors' behavior to varying extents. Much of the current literature analyzes whether investors' reactions are a rational or an emotional response to the news; thus far, no overall consensus has been reached. From the perspective of financial crisis prevention, we are confronted with somewhat different questions. We want to know if some business news reporting can move the market. We pay attention to both the information content in the business news and the reporting style.

Single News Events That Move Stock Prices

A single news event can be a single news report by one media outlet that is not echoed by other media outlets. It also can be one news story republished by multiple media outlets in a short time period without any follow-up. The following lists several single news events that caused substantial market reaction.

EntreMed Story Perhaps among the most extreme news events that show how much business reporting impacts price, the EntreMed saga of 1998 is worth close examination. Huberman and Regev (2001) report that a Sunday *New York Times* article on a potential development of new cancer-curing drugs caused EntreMed's stock price to rise from $12.063 at the Friday close, to open at $85 (605 percent jump) and close near $52 (331 percent rise) on Monday. It closed above $30 (149 percent increase) in the three following weeks. The reporting style and the publicity effect carried by *New York Times* front page articles contributed to the close attention paid by numerous investors, which turned into a permanent rise in share prices, although no new information was presented, as the potential breakthrough in cancer research already had been reported in the journal *Nature* and in various popular newspapers more than five months earlier. The reporting style[4] carried high price-moving potential for most investor-readers who were not familiar with cancer research. This may indicate that the broad publicity effect on top of a very credible newspaper can move stock prices substantially with some seeming price-moving potential. The seeming price-moving potential depends on the reporting style of the story that contains no new information content.

Emulex Hoax and ADS Rumor   Chapter 8 has detailed analysis of two typical scenarios, the Emulex hoax and the ADS rumor, where rumors produced a substantial price impact when published by credible mass media. One lesson learned is that none of the involved media outlets questioned the basis of the pretended press release by the issuing companies. They simply transmitted the stories as they were, without minding the consequences to the related stocks.

The EntreMed saga was a stand-alone news event by a single newspaper, while both the Emulex hoax and the ADS rumor involved multiple media outlets. All three scenarios ended with a substantial price impact. Although the EntreMed saga was based mainly on already reported information while the other two baseless rumors were pretended to be newly released by the issuing companies, the price impact caused in each of the three was largely due to the style of presentation, which seemed to carry price-moving potential, and the broad publicity effect and credibility of the media outlets. Thus, an information monopoly was created in all the three cases. It was utilized in the Emulex and ADS cases by the initiators in their trading strategies but perhaps not in the EntreMed saga. However, the dramatic market impact wins credibility for the *New York Times* once again and likely personal fame for the journalist who wrote the EntreMed article.

All three events show how vulnerable investors' trading psychology is. Not only retail investors but also professional traders can be motivated by inaccurate business news reporting. On the other hand, they also reveal how powerful business news reporting can be relative to investors. Simply put, in these three scenarios, business news reporting moves stock prices substantially.

More Evidence That Some Business News Reporting Moves the Market   According to Liu, Smith, and Syed (1990), R. Foster Winans, an author of the *Wall Street Journal*'s Heard on the Street (HOTS) column, was prosecuted by the SEC in 1984 for tipping four stockbrokers in manipulative trading based on price-moving information contained in the columns. The eventual conviction suggests that the HOTS column had a substantial impact on stock prices. Thom Calandra, former *CBS MarketWatch* columnist, utilized his information monopoly over reader-investors by engaging in the "buy-write-sell" manipulative scheme multiple times with substantial profit. Obviously, market reaction to his column was significant along his recommendations (Chapter 8; more details can be found in SEC Litigation Release No. 19028).

James Hipwell and Anil Bhoyrul were formerly financial journalists for the *Daily Mirror*'s City Slickers column in the 1990s. The column gave stock tips to its readers. The two were found guilty of stock market abuse by the U.K.'s securities authority in 2000. They were buying shares before these "investments" were recommended to readers in their daily column, and the two journalists sold out at a profit once the share price had risen (Murphy 2005; Tait 2005). Again, they were able to run the share-ramping schemes because of the substantial market impact of the City Slickers column.

Chapter 8 devotes a subsection to research on CNBC's *Mad Money* show. The objective there is to examine the price behavior prior to and immediately after the show. In this chapter, the emphasis is on the postshow reaction by investors through significant increase of trading volumes. We do not emphasize manipulative trading. *Mad Money* is claimed to be the most-watched show on CNBC, with an audience in excess of 380,000 potential investors each weeknight. Engelberg, Sasseville, and Williams (2006) worked with 246 initial recommendations given by Jim Cramer on *Mad Money* episodes between July 28 and October 14, 2005. In addition to the observation of volume increase and price run-up before Cramer's "buy" recommendations, they find that Cramer's impact on trading volume is long-lived. Turnover of the smallest firms relative to their sizes climbs to a range between 300 and 900 percent during the three trading days immediately following the recommendation. It then remains statistically significantly large for the next 13 trading days.

All the above cases share one commonality. The newspaper columns and TV show have delivered a substantial information monopoly to their followers. The involved journalists have the capacity to make use of the information monopoly conveniently for their own manipulative trading schemes, in addition to those of the information providers.

So far, we have presented individual scenarios in which an information monopoly can be perceived from prosecutions or research findings in the past 30 years. Studies on an aggregate level reveal more convincing facts.

Literature on Price Impact of Publication of Sell-Side Analysts' Recommendations

Chapter 7 documents dozens of studies on market reaction to sell-side analysts' thousands of "buy" recommendations published by mass media. The shared regularity of all the findings is prepublication price run-up for positive recommendations and volume increase, followed by a price reversal or slow decline for an extended time with a high turnover ratio. Price run-up prior to media publication implies that informed investors expect a substantial price impact from publication of analysts' recommendations. Hence, they buy a large number of shares to be recommended and cause pre-event price run-up and volume increase. The publication does induce enormous following volumes, which are observed in all the studies of media publication of analysts' recommendations. Particularly, they detect significantly higher trading volume around the publication day. The postpublication price reversal or slow decline is triggered mainly by distribution of a substantial amount of shares by the informed.

Beneish (1991) particularly points out that it is the publicity effect of the *Wall Street Journal* that makes the substantial difference in price impact, compared to the less known *Wall Street Transcript*. This agrees with Stice (1991) on earnings announcements. The recommendations can move the market in a significantly stronger way when published in a widely read newspaper such as the *Wall Street Journal* than if deposited in a less accessed database. It is the publicity effect of a credible media outlet that amplifies the price-moving potential of the analysts' recommendations. That is, potentially price-moving information provided by analysts, publicity, and the credibility of the media outlet together construct the information monopoly. When the information is disseminated to the investing public, substantial price impact is ensured. This information monopoly has been utilized by analysts' own firms, their preferred client investors, and other related investors to gain manipulative trading profit (Chapter 7).

Recent Literature on the Short-Run Price Impact of Business News Reporting

Mitchell and Mulherin (1994) try to find a link between daily number of headlines reported by *Dow Jones Headlines Tape* and market reaction, covering 2,011 business days from 1983 to 1990. They find a significant relationship between the number of news stories and aggregate measures of trading activity, such as trading volume and the absolute value of firm-specific returns. Gadarowski (2002) uses a firm-size-adjusted count of Dow Jones News Service stories to examine firm and portfolio returns using about 1,500 firms per year over the period from 1980 to 1995. He finds that high news counts predict lower subsequent returns, particularly for low book-to-market firms, over the next two years. He attributes this finding to behavioral pricing. Chan (2003) uses monthly returns to examine stock price patterns following headline news as compared to those without news for thousands of stocks between 1980 and 2000. He finds a larger drift in stock prices following public news and reversal after a stock price jumps without news coverage. In other words, follow-up news can help to maintain a transitory higher return for a longer time period.

Counting the number of words instead of the number of news stories, Tetlock (2007) measures quantitative interaction between media reporting and stock market movement. He shows that daily pessimistic contents in the *Wall Street Journal*'s Abreast of the Market column are associated with stock price falls and the reversal afterward of the Dow over the period from 1984 to 1999. Tetlock et al. (2008) examine whether the abovementioned interaction can be applied to individual S&P 500 firms from 1980 to 2004. They conclude that negative words in the media reporting forecast low firm earnings and stock prices with a delay. In other words, media reporting can convey "hard-to-quantify aspects" of firms' earnings and returns. One question remains: What happens to the trading activity and price behavior if the Abreast of the Market column is dominated by positive words?

The above studies all focus on the national media. We turn to local media to examine if any similarity exists. Engelberg and Parsons (2009) investigate if media effect has a causal impact on investors' trading decisions by examining local newspapers in 19 major U.S. cities that published earnings announcements by S&P 500 firms between the pre-Internet years from 1991 to 1996. They find that local press coverage increases the trading volume of local retail investors by nearly 50 percent. The local media–local trading effect is significant for both buying and selling activities. They interpret that, in their setting, media effects are real and substantial, and media coverage stimulates local trading activity. Gurun and Butler (2010) document that local media report more positively about local firms with advertising spending than nonlocal firms with no such expenditure, covering eight local newspapers, one national newspaper, and one national newswire in the years 2002–2006. Because stock market investors may rely on information from the media in making trading decisions, such positive bias, or hype, drives local individual investors to invest more in local firms. This is particularly true for firms held mainly by individual investors and firms with thinly traded stocks.

What does international experience tell us about the media effect on market reaction? Schmitz (2007) compares marketwide reactions and individual investors' reactions to business news reporting or broadcasts. He analyzes individual investors' transactions in stocks and warrants—reaction to 300,000 business news releases on German TV and in newspapers from 1998 to 2006. Schmitz concludes that the data support several key facts: After unusually high media news coverage of a firm for several days, the trading volume of the firm's stock far exceeds the prenews trading volume. In addition, there is a measurable price impact during the first day after the announcement. Also, good news generates an abnormal increase of 1.12 percent on average, and bad news decreases the stock price by 1.24 percent. His findings show immediate and short-run impacts of news reporting to related stocks.

As the Irish Minister for Finance, Lenihan (2010) argues that journalists, using emotional words, have a tendency to paint self-fulfilling pictures by undermining or promoting public confidence in the economy. Wisniewski and Lambe (2010) investigate the impact of press articles with the negative phrases "credit crunch," "financial crisis," and "bank failures" on financial stocks in the U.S., U.K., and Canada from the end of January 2005 to the end of May 2010. They graphically show that the intensification in pessimistic press coverage can lead to a fast and steep decline of stock prices of financial institutions. They further argue that journalists play an active role in creating a self-fulfilling kind of reality in addition to objectively describing economic reality. Aman (2010) recognizes that the role of the mass media in the stock market, particularly in non-U.S. economies, remains relatively unexplored in the finance literature. He uses non financial firms listed on the first section of the Tokyo Stock Exchange from April 2003 to March 2006 in his sample, a total of 2,921 firm-year observations. The media in his study include the Nikkei, the largest business newspaper in Japan, with daily circulation larger than the Wall Street Journal. He finds that not only the corporate behavior as the originating source of information, but also the diffusion process by media activity, may have a significant influence on the large drops of stock prices. His finding supports the notion that intensive media reports on a firm provoke extremely large reactions by investors to corporate news. In sum, the evidence in Aman (2010) as well as Wisniewski and Lambe (2010) clearly indicate that crash (large price drop) frequency increases with negative media coverage. If we understand these findings from "pump-and-dump" strategies that trade against business news reporting or "trash-and-cash" strategies that frontrun published negative news, then the information monopoly delivered by some business news reporting can be utilized in manipulative trading strategies.

Corporate information releases are a major source of business news reporting. Earnings announcements are regularly reported by business media. Unlike earnings quality, which is the focus in Chapter 5, media effect and corresponding market reaction interest us more in this chapter. Gaa (2008) sorts through 263,627 quarterly earnings announcement observations from 1984 to 2005, with a corresponding 68,102 potentially relevant *Wall Street Journal* articles during the same period of time. His findings include significant premia or high risk-adjusted returns for "neglected" stocks—typically small firms with low analyst coverage, low institutional ownership, and little trading activity. Fang and Peress (2008) have similar findings. Both results may have some positive implication for less manipulated stocks. Using 54,582 earnings announcements from 2,508 firms that were listed on NYSE and Nasdaq between January 1, 1993, and December 31, 2002,

Peress (2008) examines whether the postearnings announcement drift is caused by a lack of media coverage, which is used as a proxy for investors' inattention. He finds that announcements with more media coverage generate stronger price and trading volume reaction at the announcement and less subsequent drift. His results show preannouncement price run-up (decline) for positive (negative) earnings surprises. One may question which is the trigger for postannouncement drift—investors' inattention or insider trading or both?

Corporate managers not only provide earnings and other corporate information to preferred media outlets, they also manage media coverage. Ahern and Sosyura (2011) work with the 1,000 largest completed mergers of U.S. publicly traded firms announced between January 1, 2000, and December 31, 2008. For acquisitions that use the acquirer's stock as payment, they focus on media coverage during the private negotiation period and find fixed exchange ratio acquirers actively manage the media to temporarily increase their stock prices.

Corporate managers oftentimes use an advertising campaign to support both their products and their share prices. Fehle, Tsyplakov, and Zdorovtsov (2005) investigate stock price behavior and trading activity for firms employing TV commercials in 19 Super Bowl broadcasts over the period 1969–2001. They document significant positive abnormal returns for firms that are readily identifiable from the ad contents. Their results also show that small investors engage in significant abnormal net buying activity in shares of recognized Super Bowl advertisers. This finding is in line with Barber and Odean (2008), who found that individual investors are net buyers of attention-grabbing stocks.

Super Bowl broadcasts are rare but extreme events for advertisers. Do public firms display similar behavior to increase publicity of both their products and their stocks through advertising? Based on 5,751 firm-year observations over the period 1993–1999, Grullon, Kanatas, and Weston (2004) document that advertising expenditures are positively associated with the liquidity of common stock as evidenced by a lower bid-ask spread. Their results imply that a firm's advertising not only serves to inform potential consumers of the firm's products but also serves to increase the publicity of the firm's stock among investors. Hence, increasing advertising about a firm results in more individual investors as well as institutions purchasing its stock. Chemmanur and Yan (2008) find from IPO and SEO firms during the 1990s that those firms increase their product market advertising in their IPO year or SEO year relative to non-IPO and non-SEO years. Their findings are consistent with practitioners' experience that firms tend to increase their product market advertising prior to an IPO or SEO since it increases visibility of their issues in the financial market. Lou (2009) analyzes advertising expenditures of U.S. public firms for the period 1974–2006. His results show that an increase in advertising expenditures is accompanied by buying pressure from individual investors and higher contemporaneous stock returns, and is followed by lower subsequent returns. One explanation he gives is in line with the inattention literature that individual investors buy attention-grabbing stocks.

Clearly, relevant business news should and does move stock prices. There is general agreement among researchers that price and trading quantity are affected by the arrival of potentially price-moving information from public firms, equity analysts, or even unknown people. Mass media amplify the price impact by adding publicity and credibility to the price-moving potential. In summary, it is the information monopoly generated together by the information provider and reporting media outlet that underlies the substantial short-run market impact.

SOME BUSINESS NEWS REPORTING AFFECTS INDIVIDUAL INVESTORS IN THE LONG RUN

As we analyzed earlier, mass media have substantial power in terms of publicity and credibility. They can deliver an information monopoly through business news reporting if it carries potentially price-moving information. Basically, the information monopoly thus generated is proportional to the price-moving potential of the information contained in the business news. The question is: Does the potential move the market up or down in the long run before a serious stock market crisis? If the answer is yes, then how?

Business News Reporting Is Frequently Upward-Biased

For long-run impact of news reporting to the stock market, we examine how researchers from related fields, such as economics, finance, communication, journalism, and psychology, look at the issue and list key results from their empirical studies.

Andreassen (1987), based on a sample size of 54, tests whether media reports presented after a positive change in stock prices make an investor believe that the trend will continue. The result shows that media try to explain the past price rise by attributing it to the good business conditions of the issuer, and such explanatory reporting implies a forward-looking attitude. Based on studies about CNBC commentary on NYSE and Nasdaq market indices, Morris et al. (2007) find from experiment that media commentary, more dominant by agent metaphor, influences investors to take uptrends as meaningful signals of tomorrow's direction, while investors take downtrends when object metaphor is more frequently used by media commentators as nondiagnostic. Furthermore, they suggest that increased media commentary may be one of the many forces that contributed to overvaluation of most stocks in the 1990s, consistent with the argument by Shiller (2000). Stiglitz (2011) states that the media play a central role in moving the herd, or the media-following investors, toward a bubble in the years before the crisis. These studies show that related business journalists and editors have a tendency to put an upward spin in their reporting in economic boom times. Schiffrin (2011) documents, "[S]ome reporters I interviewed said their in-boxes were full of angry e-mails from readers who accused them of putting air in the bubble as the economy grew throughout the nineties and kicking the economy as it went down."

Vanderwicken (1995) concludes that the media have become players in the manipulation of perception. Regarding the stock market, he notices that when media are willing to report such news sources as rumors, they transform rumors into news, which affects viewer-investors' trading behavior. In other words, media reporting can change stock market reality based on rumors unless timely clarifying action is taken. He further alleges that newspapers reporting business news are just propaganda agents for corporations, which more likely promote their stocks. Schuster (2003) argues that news reporting by mass media is upward-biased and ignores risk, particularly during stock market boom times. Since the way mass media report creates and fosters coordination of the trading decisions of numerous investors, with no risk awareness, constant media hype can bring about a more and more unstable market movement as marketwide stock prices are continuously inflating. According to Bauder (2009), Abrams Research surveyed 100 top business and financial journalists in January 2009. They are from the *Wall Street Journal, New York Times, Fortune, Forbes,* CNBC, CNN, *Business Week, Portfolio, Silicon Alley Insider, Slate, Fast Company, MarketWatch, Financial Times* plus top financial bloggers. Sixty-two of them suggest that business and financial journalists were overly exuberant about the economy.

How did business media perform during the full cycle of the subprime crisis in the U.S.? By examining 730 articles from major U.S. business media, that is, the *Wall Street Journal, The New York Times,* the *Los Angeles Times,* the *Washington Post, Bloomberg News, Fortune, Business Week,* and *Forbes* and one U.K. finance newspaper, that is, *Financial Times,* between January 1, 2000, and June 30, 2007, Starkman (2009) argues that the business press fails to provide the public with fair warning of looming dangers during the years prior to the peak of the subprime market. He particularly points out that there were almost investigative stories about basic business practices of large lenders such as Countrywide and securitization providers such as Lehman Brothers. He alleges that corporate cultural influence over the business press is related to the existence of the latter. Adapting to corporate interests becomes the priority of the editor and owners of business media firms. Convincing consumers to buy their products and investors to purchase their stocks are two main components of corporate interests.

The repeated reporting on an overly optimistic theme may be able to sustain the mass media's business interests as long as possible in a boom time and frequently is practiced by business news reporting. Madrick (2001) finds that the term *New Economy* was not used very pervasively between 1985 and 1994. The year 1995 saw an increase in its appearance in print media (325 times), particularly in *Business Week*. Near the end of the 1990s, that is, 1998–2000, the growth became dramatic (1,048, 3,215, and 22,848 times, respectively). Its appearance in print media in 2000 was 7,000 percent more compared to 1995. Madrick attributes this growth to soaring stock prices and advertising expenditures by Internet companies in particular, because the value of ad pages bought to promote Internet services rose by 183 percent in 2000 over 1999, to nearly $280 million. To reader-investors, *New Economy* is a big but simple attention grabber. The media exploited their desire to hear only good news. Therefore, he concludes that media articles containing *New Economy* sounded exhortatory and promotional. Shiller (2000) has similar findings for various terms centering on *New Era* in the second half of the 1990s. He also finds such terms were used frequently during economic growth and stock market uptrend times of 1901, the 1920s, 1950s, and 1960s in addition to the 1990s. Lowenstein (2004) agues that business journalists had a tendency to endorse, rather than seriously challenge, the tenets of the New Economy in the 1990s.

Clark, Thrift, and Tickell (2004) suggest that mass media play a functional reinforcing role during a speculative bubble, especially during the 1990s.

Massive examples of business media and increasing stock prices being mutually reinforcing are shown in repeated reporting on CEOs of large corporations, star analysts, and savvy investors. It is well known that coverage of public firms is dominant in business news reporting. CEO coverage is one of the most representative. Meschke (2004) documents CEO interviews broadcast on CNBC between 1999 and 2001. These interviews do not contain new information. However, they lead to higher trading volume and a significant mean price increase of 1.65 percent on the interview date. His results may suggest that the financial news media are able to generate transitory buying pressure by catching the attention of enthusiastic investors. Based on two indices of media coverage and positive coverage of Fortune 500 CEOs for the period 1992–2002, Nguyen (2009) finds that the market impact of media coverage is significant. That is, firms with the highest level of CEO media coverage and positive coverage outperform those with the lowest levels by 8 and 7 percent per year, respectively. Who are these CEOs? Hamilton and Zeckhauser (2004) point out that publicity about a CEO may attract and maintain the attention of equity investors and product consumers. They search for the number of stories that contain CEOs' names in the *New York Times* for the years 1970 and 1999 and find that the total number is above 5,600, with a minimum of 116 and a maximum of 235. One can sense the intensity of the coverage of CEOs by the newspaper, although the paper is not limited to business news reporting. Also, they find the concentration is high around CEOs of large companies, such as GM, AT&T, and Chrysler in the early 1980s, when CEO coverage was at its peak. Altogether, 20 percent of CEOs have 80 percent of coverage, and CEOs of large-cap companies get more repeated coverage than those of medium to small companies. Clark, Thrift, and Tickell (2004) report that during a TV show, the host never questions how truthful the interviewees' stated opinions are. In other words, media outlets assist and amplify interviewees' propaganda on the stocks they promote (Kurtz 2000).

Securities analysts and their recommendations often are covered by the media. Gasparino (2005) counts that the *Wall Street Journal* mentioned the former star analyst Henry Blodget, of Merrill Lynch, nearly 100 times during the three years since his famous Amazon call (one-year target price of $400) in 1998. The *New York Times* cited him about 60 times and the *Washington Post* more than 50. In 1999 alone, Blodget appeared on TV nearly 80 times. Brown and Caylor (2005) attribute increased media coverage of analysts' earnings forecasts as one main causal factor of why investors reward firms for reporting quarterly earnings that meet or beat analysts' estimates and penalize firms for missing analysts' estimates since the mid-1990s. Bonner, Hugon, and Walther (2007) examine the effect of more media coverage of securities analysts on the market reaction to the analysts' earnings forecast revisions for the period 1997–1999. They count the number of appearances of an analyst's name associated with his employer in all media sources included in the Dow Jones Interactive database. It yields 75,807 references on media coverage for the analyst and year to the quarterly forecast revisions the analyst issued during that year. They find that media coverage is positively related to investor reaction to forecast revisions and that investors react more strongly to forecast revisions issued by analysts whose names are more familiar.

To summarize, business news reporting has frequently been upward-biased, especially during boom times. This is seen not only from who provides information in the reporting, but also from whom to report on or cover, as well as how the show is handled.

Individual Investors Are Affected More by Business News Reporting

Marketwide results of stock prices and trading quantities are derived from the trading activities of mainly two distinctive investor groups: institutional or professional large investors and individual, mainly amateur, small investors. Behind the marketwide reactions, we find telling differences in the behavior of these two groups.

How does business news reporting influence individual investors' trading decisions? The National Credibility Index (1999) shows that business stories are considered second only to issuer announcements in credibility to individual investors. Golding (2003) points out that individual investors' trading decisions are critically influenced by business news, unlike the decisions of institutional investors. By interviewing dozens of fund managers in "the city," London's Wall Street, Davies (2005) reports that professional investors are influenced only slightly by the media, but retail investors are strongly affected by stock-related news reporting. The abovementioned findings strongly support the belief that some business news significantly induces small individual investors to trade. As such, the related business news results in high observable trading speed. Given the logic of price impact function, this can generate a high price impact as long as there is sufficient similarity among the reactions of small individual investors.

Schmitz (2007), testing the Hong and Stein (1999) model, also finds that individual investors react to business news with a higher abnormal trading quantity than institutions, and small investors react with about a one-day delay after a news release, relative to institutional investors. Barber and Odean (2008) find that individual investors' and institutional investors' buying and selling behaviors differ markedly. Small investors are more likely to be net purchasers of stocks that are attention grabbers, in sharp contrast to institutional investors. Barber and Odean (2008) identify three ways a stock becomes an attention grabber: by previously achieved by high absolute returns, by high trading volume, and by high media coverage. Not surprisingly, these facts can be well utilized in manipulative trading strategies.

The relationship between media content and stock prices on an aggregate level has significant economic relevance. How is the relationship on an individual level? By surveying 479 college students in 2008, Brandes and Rost (2009) analyze the relationship between media guidance and individual tendency to buy stocks. Their key findings are that (1) media usage increases a person's propensity to buy stocks, (2) media guidance tends to affect stock purchasing decisions more than any other information resource, and (3) more media exposure increases reliance on media guidance in such decisions. These two findings explain in part why some business news columns tend to tout attention-grabbing stocks to attract new audience and keep current sub-scribers. Pervasive and frequent use of analysts' upward-biased recommenda-tions is one of the major sources of business news content (Chapter 7). Corporate earnings information is one of the topics most covered by business news reporting. However, as Chapters 5 and 6 document tens of thousands of observations by dozens of researchers, earnings have been manipulated upward most of the time and downward only occasionally. And corporate insiders always enjoy the insider information by frequently making unfair profit or avoiding substantial loss. In short, an information monopoly formu-lated together by issuer-generated or analyst-generated information and busi-ness news reporting underlies some manipulative trading.

How does some business news reporting induce individual investors to trade? Shiller's *Irrational Exuberance* (2000) dedicates an entire chapter to the role of media in bubbles. He proposes that the media have historically played an important role in all three phases: setting the stage, triggering a crash, and propagating the crisis. In Shiller's account, the media play a very important role in the positive feedback mechanism during the mania and the negative feedback mechanism during the panic. In other words, business news reporting has cultivating, triggering, and precipitating roles in induc-ing herding. There is more evidence regarding the role of the business media in generating a mania, not in one but in 23 emerging markets. Veldkamp (2006) finds that increased coverage of business news—media frenzies—re-sults in a surge in stock prices. In addition, this process is contagious, as it contributes to rises in other countries' stock markets.

In brief, some business news reporting substantially affects individual investors' decision making. Its impact on institutional investors is less signif-icant, particularly at early stages of a long-run mania. However, when mu-tually reinforcing mini-bubbles and upward-biased reporting are repeated for a long while, especially at the later stage of the mania, some medium to large institutional investors are increasingly influenced by the euphoric at-mosphere in the stock market. Substantial loss or closure of several large funds on Wall Street during the dot-com crash of 2000–2002 may have pro-vided evidence for this argument. One example is the long successful Quan-tum Fund's bet on the Internet company VeriSign that turned sour in 2000 (Lattman, 2010).

Individual Investors Herd

Now we have a broad picture showing that business news reporting is upward-biased most of the time during economic boom times. Individual investors are more affected by business news reporting. How do investors, particularly individual investors, behave in the stock market under media influence? We turn to behavioral finance, which documents investors' herding repeatedly in both developed and emerging stock markets. Our primary interest is in the link between business news reporting and individual investors' herding in the stock market.

Christie and Huang (1995) argue that herding is easier to detect during periods of market stress when studying return data from U.S. stock markets. Chang, Cheng, and Khorana (2000) propose different tests of herding and find supporting evidence of the existence of herding in the emerging stock markets of South Korea and Taiwan. Kim and Wei (1999) and Choe, Kho, and Stulz (1999) find herd behavior in the South Korean stock markets around the Asian Crisis in 1997. Bowe and Domuta (2004) document evidence of herding in the Jakarta Stock Exchange before, during, and after the 1997 Asian Crisis. Demirer, Gubo, and Kutan (2007) examine whether herding exists in a large number of international stock markets between March 1998 and April 2004. They find evidence of herding in Asian and Middle Eastern markets. Tan et al. (2008) show that investors of dual-listed Chinese A and B shares display significant herding behavior. Particularly, herding by A-share investors in the Shanghai market is stronger during periods of rising trends (1997–2003). One needs to notice that China's A-share markets were dominated by individual investors, similar to other emerging markets such as in Indonesia, Taiwan, and South Korea.

There also is recent evidence of herding in developed stock markets. Hwang and Salmon (2001) find statistically significant evidence of herding in the U.S. and U.K. equity markets before the Russian Crisis in 1998. Using data from the Italian Stock Exchange, Caparrelli, D'Arcangelis, and Cassuto (2004) have detected herding in extreme market conditions. Shapira and Venezia (2006) analyze the trading behavior of both professional and amateur investors in Israel between 1994 and 1998 and find amateur investors have a stronger tendency to herd than professional ones. Cajueiro and Tabak (2009) present evidence of herding behavior for a large set of stocks in the Tokyo stock market.

Some researchers explicitly focus on herding by individual investors. Feng and Seasholes (2004) and Tan (2005) provide more evidence of herding of individual investors in China. Kumar and Lee (2006) observe more than 1.85 million retail investor transactions in the U.S. markets from 1991 to 1996 and find return comovements for stocks that retail investors dominate.

The empirical studies use different criteria to detect herding in stock markets in international settings. Daily, weekly, and monthly data are used. Results are sometimes mixed when counting evidence of herding. One thing is for sure: Different techniques have provided evidence of herding in multiple markets, developed and emerging, under different market conditions. However, we are not clear from these empirical studies about what causes herding. What are the durations of herding? What are the consequences of herding? In sum, our expectations of finding links between business news reporting and individual investors' herding cannot be fulfilled from empirical herding literature at this moment. We expect more research to come in this regard.

Has any theoretical herding research shed light? Contemporary theoretical models of herding were pioneered by Banerjee (1992) and Bikhchandani, Hirshleifer, and Welch (1992), both viewing herding as a general social phenomenon. However, the role of media in herding is not mentioned in either paper. Avery and Zemsky (1998) examine herding in the financial markets. They try to explicitly model herding behavior among individual investors in the financial markets. Since they assume the price is efficiently set up, they do not examine media's role in herding, either.

The role of investors' sentiment behavioral bias has been the major focal point in the herding literature. Shleifer (2001) argues the fruitfulness of pursuing this line of study. Daniel, Hirshleifer, and Teoh (2002) review the majority of the literature on herding, without explicitly mentioning the link between investors' herding behavior and business news reporting. The main focus of the reviewed literature is on investors' sentiment stemming from a psychological weakness that they refer to as credulity.

A recent comprehensive review of the burgeoning herding literature, including herding of individual investors, is found in the *Handbook in Finance* chapter written by Hirshleifer and Teoh (2009). Regarding media's role in herding, very limited research is available, with the exception of Robert Shiller's work, which focused on popular ideas in financial markets. While celebrating the achievements of the 18-page list of references, they point out the lack of sufficient understanding of thought contagion.

Behavioral finance focuses more on individuals' psychological biases and interactions between individuals when making trading decisions. Mounting evidence discussed in earlier sections and in Chapters 5–8 show that individual investors frequently and substantially rely on business news reporting for their trading decisions. We suggest that the sources of thought contagion include business news, in addition to word-of-mouth communication and other factors such as market manipulation. We expect more literature to emerge in behavioral finance regarding triggers of individual investors' herding.

WHY IS BUSINESS NEWS REPORTING USUALLY UPWARD-BIASED?

Certain key business conditions of the media firms influence business journalists' work, discussed in particular by Bagdikian (2000), Chomsky and

Herman (2002), Davies (2008), Bennett (2005), Shoemaker and Reese (1996), and McChesney (2008). These scholars list four aspects that stand out. Who are the owners? Who are serving on the board of directors? What are the main revenue sources? What are the main sources of news, and which are most cost-effective?

Media Firms' Business Interests

Over the last 30 years, the media industry was consolidated into a few large conglomerates. In the early 1980s, it was estimated that just 46 companies in the world controlled most of the global business in daily newspapers, magazines, television, books, and movies. The number became 23 by 1990. In 2004, the multinational media companies that controlled most of America's daily newspapers, magazines, radio and television stations, book publishers, and movie companies stood at 5 (Glaberson 1995; Bagdikian 2000; Bagdikian and Emeritus 2004). Furthermore, it is common to have overlap between corporate board members in media firms and their corporate clients (Bagdikian 2000; Bagdikian and Emeritus 2004; Moore 2003).

Two-thirds of the average newspaper's revenue in the United States comes from corporate advertisements (Wells and Hakanen 1997). In particular, mass media often shape content according to the needs of their advertisers, to "deliver" the "right demographic" group, in the right frame of mind. Hence, media content adjusts to the needs of advertisers (Solomon 1997; Postman and Powers 1997). Glaberson (1995) reports, "It is now common for publishing executives to press journalists to cooperate with their newspaper's 'business side,' breaching separations that were said in the past to be essential for journalistic integrity." Starkman (2009) expresses similar concerns. Sometimes the advertisers' impact is extremely explicit. For example, Chrysler Corporation sent a letter to more than 50 magazines, demanding that they send Chrysler advance summaries of articles they were planning to publish, while implicitly requesting these magazines avoid articles on "political, social material and editorial that might be construed as provocative" (Baker 1997). Bagdikian (2000) has been sounding the alarm about the effect of mass advertising on the truthfulness of news.

What is the aim of advertising? What do advertising corporations seek from their general audience? Certainly, buying their products and services, and this aspect is seen everyday in newspapers, TV commercials, and Internet search pages. But public corporations need another type of financial support, to provide liquidity for their stocks and occasionally raise additional equity from their audiences (Grullon, Kanatas, and Weston 2004; Fehle, Tsyplakov, and Zdorovtsov 2005; Chemmanur and Yan 2008;

Lou 2009). Even if some corporation's product advertising is not very effective, it often still continues to spend aggressively on advertising. Corporate managers understand the importance of awareness and positive attitudes among the investing audience to support its stock price (Joshi and Hanssens 2004). From a certain aspect, the collaboration between related business journalists and advertising clients is similar to the collaboration between certain sell-side analysts and their investment banking clients. Financial journalists are not independent financially, just as sell-side analysts are not financially independent. Hence, related financial journalists have to contribute to the revenue generation of their media firm through biased news reporting for advertising clients. It is similar to some sell-side analysts' biased coverage of investment banking clients.

Pursuing cost minimization is critical to media firms' competitive edge today. Minimizing the cost to news sources is primary. There are three main news sources: media firms' own business journalists, news wire agencies, and public relations (PR) firms. Distribution of news from these three sources in the U.K. and in the U.S. reveals the priority of media firms. Quality of news from the sources reflects why upward bias is fundamental to them. Since news agencies simply transmit corporate press releases, we pay more attention to how business journalists report and how PR firms guide business news reporting.

Interests of Business Journalists, News Agencies, and Public Relations Firms

Let us start with media firms' own business journalists. In the U.K., 12 percent of news is original (Davies 2009, p. 95), coming from the journalists' own investigations. What is characteristic of business news written by journalists employed by the media firm?[5] Dyck and Zingales (2003) document a positive correlation, in both cross-sectional and time-series manners, between the way earnings announcements are reported in a press release and the way they are reported by the business media in both boom times (1998–1999) and down times (2001–2002). Their findings support the *quid pro quo* bias hypothesis; that is, journalists write upward-biased articles in exchange for sustainable access to private information from their sources. The main source of news for business journalists, employed by media companies, is top corporate executives, particularly the CEO. The CEO provides "guidance" to the journalists regarding some future or ongoing corporate events.[6] Such "guidance" determines the content of the news. Therefore, the relationship between the business journalists and the covered corporation's CEO is very similar to the relationship between the sell-side equity analysts and the covered company's CEO (Chapter 7). Thus, the codependence between journalists and their primary source of information results in a relationship that may also be called collusive (as Michael Jensen (2005) calls the relationship of sell-side analysts and the covered issuer).

In addition to the content, corporate management influences the timing of the publication of the news. Generally, company management demands the news to be published after trading hours, and preferably over the weekend. This way it allows sufficient time for the management to notify major corporate insiders about the news and the time of its publication in advance.[7] Since corporate management needs publicity in addition to their potentially price-moving information and credibility to form a complete information monopoly that can be used for manipulative trading profit, the demand is out of its business interest.

Relative to employing journalists, especially investigative journalists, much more cost-effective suppliers of news are available for the news media company. In the U.K., in the five most highly respected British daily newspapers, 80 percent of the news originates not from its own journalists, but from the other two, and significantly cheaper sources of news—news agencies and public relations (PR) companies (Davies 2009, pp. 92–96). As early as 1987, interviews with thousands of American business journalists (Hamilton and Kalt 1987) report that "business/economics reporters are twice as likely to rely on press releases, and spend less time (24 percent) than others (31 percent) doing research for their story." This reliance is even more pervasive today, which is confirmed by Dyck and Zingales (2003), Davies (2009), and Davies (2010).

Second is news agencies. In the U.S. and the U.K., there are few major wire agencies, such as the Press Association (PA), Associated Press (AP), Reuters, Dow Jones, and Knight Ridder. They publish any press release sent to them from public companies as it is. Moreover, they tend to recycle each other's news. In the U.K., 70 percent of news stories are partly or fully rewritten versions of wire agency copy (Davies 2009, p. 74).

Third is public relations (PR) firms. Even though there are numerous small PR companies, the largest 100 corporations hire a handful of large PR firms. In the U.K., 54 percent of news originates from PR companies (Davies 2009, pp. 87 and 180). In the U.S., it is estimated that 44 percent of news originated from PR companies between 1991– and 2004 (Sallot and Johnson 2006). Cameron, Sallot, and Curtin (1997) review earlier estimations, and find that 24 to 80 percent of news content in the U.S. was influenced by PR professionals.

Combining the "rules of the news factory" and the presence of PR firms, Davies (2009, p. 194) summarizes the main reasons for upward-biased news: "Certainly, PR produces plentiful distortion and significant falsehood, but the media themselves, operating as a news factory, as we have seen, first become structurally weakened to the point where they routinely betray their own function by passing on unchecked PR to their readers and viewers, and second, work with rules of production which are themselves a significant source of falsehood and distortion." Since PR firms have omnipresent influence on news about their client companies, we next try to understand the interaction between them and media companies and how they control business news reporting.

The Role of the PR Industry in Shaping Upward-Biased News

There are more PR agents in the United States who write the news than journalists (Chomsky and Herman 2002), and business news often is only a rewritten version of the corporations' own press releases (Solomon 1997). This is particularly true of business news reporting in the U.K. and U.S. (Tambini 2008; Starkman 2009). According to the Generally Accepted Practices of the PR industry (Swerling et al. 2010), PR firms are being hired to manage corporate communications/reputation in all large companies surveyed. In addition, in practice, PR companies' performance is being measured by a number of outcomes. Among them, the most important is influence on corporate reputation. The list also includes PR companies' influence on stock performance, at par with the importance of PR's contribution to the sales of the client (Swerling et al. 2010).

What Do Actually PR Companies Do? According to Davies (2009), PR Companies Generate the Following:

- Pseudo-events: At its simplest, it couples journalists with carefully selected information. Often the pseudo-event is disguised. Examples include press release and press conferences.
- Mass of pseudo-groups to facilitate grassroots activity on their behalf.
- Pseudo-experts, for example, think tanks that are funded by corporations with specific PR interest.
- Pseudo-evidence: Surveys, polls, and specifically commissioned research. Abusing evidence, selecting only the findings it wants to promote.
- Pseudo-quotes.
- Pseudo-leaks.
- Pseudo-wars.
- Celebrity reporting, riddled with fabrication.
- Fabrication of news on broadcast outlets: TV news stories appear as mainstream journalism produced by the TV station, but are prepackaged "Video News Release"

PR companies are also actively involved with the investigative work of the business journalists, besides sending them material to publish. Those smallest proportions of the news that are written originally by journalists employed by the media firm confront PR professionals in their job in a rather peculiar way. PR firms act as gatekeepers to many companies' CEOs and CFOs. In fact, if a journalist publishes news about the client company of a PR firm that the latter disapproves, the PR firm, in retaliation, would deny access by the same journalist to all other clients of the PR firm. Since leading PR firms are few, each large PR firm can have as many as 20 of the largest corporations among its clients; thus, it becomes prohibitively expensive for journalists to publish unfavorable news about a large firm.[8]

What is the consequence of the increasing involvement of PR companies in corporate communication to the stock market? Sallot and Johnson (2006) conclude: "Clearly (PR) practitioners set, frame and build considerable portions of the agenda for the news media and the public." That is to say, PR companies decide a "considerable portion" of what the public thinks about and how they think about it. Therefore, certain business journalists, when publishing unchecked news coming from PR companies, become de facto marketing agents themselves for the corporation that hired the PR firm. This situation is similar to that discussed in Chapter 7 where some sell-side analysts become marketing agents to the firm they cover. In the long run, continuous upward-biased news flows to the stock market from major channels of information dissemination. It cultivates euphoric optimism among investors and sets the stage for prolonged mania. This situation is a solid example of a continuously generating information monopoly that maintains beneficial market conditions and satisfies the business interests of the listed companies.

In summary, business news reporting is frequently upward-biased, especially during economic boom times. This is partly due to the "rules of the news factory," the strategies media companies adopt to increase profitability. An overwhelming proportion of news/events originate from PR firms, whose sole job is to create and maintain a positive public image for their clients. PR firms end up both setting the agenda and framing the agenda in the news media; thus, the news necessarily presents the client corporations in the best possible light. This may be one of the long-run causal factors of stock market mania which historically have led to crisis without exceptions.

We have collected evidence and structural reasons that the current regulatory system for media results in upward-biased business news, at least in the U.S. and the U.K. Media firms' commercial success does not depend on their service to the investing public, nor does it depend on the provision of objective, all-around, and truthful news about topics important to the stock market. There is no market mechanism that rewards objectivity or fairness. Neither is there any market mechanism that punishes biased and misleading business news. Therefore, to achieve objective and fair business news, new regulation would need to be considered in securities enforcement. Consequently, business news reporting would be in line with fair, transparent, and perfect competition for trading profit in the stock market and prolonged "irrational exuberance" would be avoided.

PROPOSED PRINCIPLES TO REGULATE RELEVANT BUSINESS JOURNALISTS AND MASS MEDIA[9]

An information monopoly over uninformed investors is composed of potentially price-moving information, its publicity, and credibility. The information can be generated by issuing managers, securities analysts, reputable investors, and other market participants. It also may be generated by some business journalists. Publicity to a large investor audience must be provided by mass media. Credibility may include several parts: the credibility of the information source, of the press, and of the eventual disseminator through business news reporting. The disseminator's credibility is of more importance because reporting implies that the information is sufficiently credible. At the least, mass media enable large-scale publicity, contributing their own credibility, and confirm the credibility of the information in addition to a separate information source that generates potentially price-moving information and carries certain credibility. At most, a mass media outlet can create potentially price-moving information alone. In combination with the publicity and credibility it already possesses, it has the capacity to generate an information monopoly all by itself.

Mass media often claim that they are not responsible for the opinions expressed by their invited personnel. However, they actually are generating the information monopoly together with the invitees. If that information monopoly is used in manipulative trading or seeking other profits, uninformed investors or other followers are likely to be manipulated to incur losses. So mass media in this scenario are indeed responsible.

In Chapters 5–8, we have proposed multiple measures to regulate anyone who uses media platforms to generate an information monopoly for his manipulative trading strategies. In this chapter, we see the need to make related business journalists accountable for generating or cogenerating information monopoly power that is utilized for manipulative profit making or loss avoidance (Tambini 2008). Related media firm executives also are accountable when a conflict of interest is found behind their subordinates' biased reporting. We propose the following principles to regulate related business journalists.

Principles to Regulate Related Business Journalists[10]

- *Principle one:* Anybody who publishes significant information (e.g., the content of breaking news) or information about public companies, well-known figures (including public figures), organizations, brands, locations (e.g., the White House), events (e.g., September 11 terrorist attack), objects (e.g., museum exhibits), dates (e.g., national holidays), or other well-known things, are held accountable for the truthfulness of the information. Both the media firm's management and regulators should verify the truthfulness of this information. They should take immediate enforcement actions to correct it if this information is not truthful. This principle aims for more objectivity in business news reporting.
- *Principle two:* For any stock-related news reporting, column articles, TV programs, or other forms of dissemination, if the regulatory agency observes prereporting of substantial and quantifiable price moving, the agency may sort out the trading data and investigate the journalists or commentators involved. They are accountable if manipulative trading is found. The agency may penalize them for any tipping or manipulative trading. It should treat the wrongdoing journalists or commentators the same as manipulative investors in this scenario. The principle aims for more fairness in business news reporting.
- *Principle three:* Repeated reporting on the same newly emerged term or sentence, such as *New Economy,* should serve as the criterion for investigation. A preventive measure is that the media outlet should provide forums to discuss the content, clarify the meaning and boundaries of the repeated term or sentence, and ensure different opinions are simultaneously expressed in an explicit way. The principle aims for more rational business news reporting in the long run.

Principles to Regulate Relevant Media Firms

There is no comprehensive regulation in place that actually supervises and enforces transparency and fairness in business news reporting. Some concerns we discussed above are addressed by the recently issued administrative order by the China Securities Regulatory Commission on print media (CSRC 2010).

In the Following, We Suggest Principles to Regulate Media Firms That Disseminate Business News Regarding Stocks and Stock Markets

- *Principle four:* This principle aims for transparency in business news reporting. Since some business news reporting can so effectively influence investor behavior, the regulatory agency should pay attention to conflicts of interest behind such reporting. Therefore, it is necessary to monitor and regulate a media organization's relationship with its advertisers and with its other main sources of revenue and financing. Disclosure of the business interests of media organizations in promoting certain firms and industries would enable business news audiences to take such ties into account when evaluating business news content. Disclosure alone will not be the end of effective regulation. It is a first step toward transparency.

- *Principle five:* Fairness cannot be achieved if news reporting is not factual. So evidence has to be sufficiently supportive of the reporting and references have to be presented if anyone in the audience wants to develop a more extensive understanding. The evidence and the references form the foundation to withstand future challenges, such as legal procedures. Clearly, there always is more than one type of consequence of a single event. Therefore, we recommend that media organizations provide both business information and analysis of such information at the same time. The analysis should include at least two different opinions, with equal weight, which evidently oppose each other.

- *Principle six:* The Securities and Exchange Act of 1934 generally prohibits public firms from disseminating false or misleading information, or failing to disclose materially relevant information. Why should the media organizations that disseminate corporate information and business news be exceptions to this rule? The surveillance and legal enforcement that apply to corporate managers should be expanded to include related media organization executives, to hold them accountable if their organization disseminates false or misleading or incomplete information, or fails to disclose relevant information.

So far in this chapter, our focus has been how business news reporting affects individual investors' trading behavior, particularly in long-term horizons. The primary concern is the upward bias in business news reporting during economic boom times. In the rest of this chapter, our subject turns to the impact of some breaking news on the investing public, particularly the downside impact that triggers immediate marketwide panic selling.

Panic is a key feature of any financial crisis. In the banking industry, bank runs are driven by the panic of depositors, who fear loss of their savings. In the stock market, panic drives investors to cash out their stock holdings immediately. Kindleberger (2000) and Reinhart and Rogoff (2009) have presented in detail the major panic-driven financial crises in all financial industries throughout the history of market economies.

Why should panic selling be a regulatory target? Panic selling results in immediate loss of numerous investors. It causes excessive stock price fluctuations. It may trigger or precipitate a stock market crisis. Thus, it has the potential to lead to a systemic risk.

EMPIRICAL RESEARCH ON THE IMPACT OF SOME BREAKING NEWS ON STOCK MARKETS

Breaking news events include large and sudden occurrences that are related to war, political developments, natural disasters, and epidemics.[11] In particular, historical records of the wartime performance of stock markets in Europe and the United States during the two world wars are of interest. Several recent unexpected incidents such as the September 11 terrorist attack in 2001 and the SARS (severe acute respiratory syndrome) epidemic in 2003 have also been selected to survey their affects on global stock markets' reactions.

Not All News Events Move the Market, but Some Do Cause Panic Selling

Whether the news media trigger stock market panic remains a key question for many researchers. Cutler, Poterba, and Summers (1989) found that several major market movements did not accompany any particular major news reportage, most notably Black Monday in 1987, as indicated by surveying the top 50 daily S&P Index movements between 1941 and 1987. Fair (2002) made a similar survey for trading days between 1987 and 1999. He identified 69 events that led to a one-to-five-minute S&P 500 futures price change greater than or equal to 0.75 percent in absolute value. Fair (2002) drew the same conclusion as Cutler, Poterba, and Summers (1989) that many major market movements occur without major relevant news events spearheading the market's volatility. This is not a puzzle for us, since trade-based manipulation generates price movement at any time without any other contingencies, such as information. In other words, dramatic price movements can happen either with or without being spurred by news (Chapters 3, 4, and 8).

Cutler, Poterba, and Summers (1989) and Fair (2002) do, however, recognize that several other stock market movements have been accompanied by breaking news stories. The findings supporting this assertion are substantial. In Cutler, Poterba, and Summers (1989), 49 major news events between 1941 and 1987 were listed in their Table 3. Seven news events moved the S&P Index by more than 3.21 percent in absolute terms. In other words, these in-tandem market movements qualify among the top 50 largest market movements, as illustrated in their Table 4. Those seven news events were "Eisenhower suffers heart attack (−6.62 percent)," "North Korea invades South Korea (−5.38 percent)," "Truman defeats Dewey (−4.61 percent)," "Japanese bomb Pearl Harbor (−4.37 percent)," "Orderly transfer of power to Johnson (3.98 percent)," "US declares war against Japan (−3.23 percent)," and "Soviet letter stresses peace (over Cuban missile crisis) (3.22 percent)."

Looking over the seven news events, the start of or end of a potential war is a major type. Political power shifts or maintenance of the U.S. presidency is another. In other words, sudden and large nonbusiness news events also move the stock market substantially.

All of the abovementioned papers focus on the U.S. stock market. Do other stock markets experience similar or different volatility when major news events occur? We start with a historical review of several European stock markets.

World War I (WWI)   In the twentieth century, the largest impact of political events on international stock markets was brought about by WWI. Several researchers on stock market history have expressed this conclusion. Bittlingmayer (1998) found that major political events related to WWI generated substantial volatility on the Berlin Stock Market. For instance, the start of WWI marked a net real decline of 43 percent of the German stock market between January and December 1914. The author argues that sudden political events clearly caused large stock market movements on the German as well as other major world stock markets. As such political events were frequent during the year, volatility became persistent.

Not only was substantial volatility experienced in major international stock markets during the outbreak of WWI, but emergency closures were enforced in dozens of stock exchanges also. The Paris, Berlin, London, and New York stock exchanges were closed by July 31, 1914. Stock exchanges in other cities such as Madrid, Toronto, and Rome, as well as in Johannesburg and Shanghai, plus stock exchanges in all South American cities, were closed by August 1, 1914 (Michie 2006).

Reopening dates varied for each stock exchange that was closed because of the war. The New York Stock Exchange did not fully reopen for four and half months, which became the longest shutdown in its history (NYSE 2009). The Paris stock exchange reopened in December 1914, the same month as the New York exchange. The London Stock Exchange remained closed until January 1915. So did Johannesburg. Amsterdam reopened in February 1915, while Berlin did not reopen until December 1917 (Michie 2006).

Political News Events Employing monthly data for the period 1985–1997 and a sample of 17 emerging markets, Bilson, Brailsford, and Hooper (2002) found that there is a significant relation between political risk and returns only in emerging markets, particularly in the Pacific Basin economies. The earlier observations by Diamonte, Liew, and Stevens (1996) resulted in the discovery that changes in political risk have a larger impact on returns in emerging markets than in developed markets, based on 24 emerging stock markets and 21 developed stock markets analyzed between January 1985 and June 1995. Since these findings are all based on monthly data, the immediate impact of political risk on stock market volatility, which remains the key interest in this chapter, is not available.

Kim and Mei (2001) examined the empirical return data from the Hong Kong Stock Exchange between May 22, 1989, and December 12, 1993. Out of 16 days with a change of 4.7 percent or larger in the Hang Seng index, 12 days seemed to respond to significant political news events that occurred in either Mainland China or Hong Kong. The authors concluded that political developments in Hong Kong have a significant impact on its stock market volatility.

Based on the above findings, political news events, especially domestically related ones, have significant impact on most emerging stock markets and a few developed markets as well. A single-day market index swing of over 20 percent has been recorded. This provides evidence of the need of regulatory measures over global stock markets when large, unexpected political events suddenly occur.

September 11 Terrorist Attack Chen and Siems (2004) documented the return of each of the 10 largest global stock markets on September 11, 2001, and on September 17, 2001, the first trading day after the four-day trading halt imposed by the NYSE and Nasdaq. Every stock market surveyed showed substantial index declines, ranging from −4.05 percent (Toronto) to −8.45 percent (Hong Kong). The NYSE had a −7.13 percent decline and Nasdaq −6.83 percent, both on September 17, after the four-day trading halt.

Carter and Simkins (2004) recorded the single-day point drop of the Dow Jones Industrial Average and the Nasdaq Composite Index on September 17, 2001. On that day, the Dow fell almost 684.81 points, its largest point drop ever. The Nasdaq declined by 115.83 points. Even though the drop was across-market, the airline sector was hit the hardest, experiencing a 53 percent one-day drop in U.S. airline stocks. Drakos (2004) detailed the percentage drop for each major U.S. airline stock. Continental Airlines' stock had a return of −68.16 percent, followed by Delta Airlines (−59.04 percent), United Airlines (−56.59 percent), American Airlines (−50.07 percent), and Southwest Airlines (−27.52 percent).

SARS   The outbreak of severe acute respiratory syndrome (SARS) in 2003 temporarily created panic among millions of people. Globally, SARS is believed to have infected around 8,000 people and killed 800 (Cooper and Coxe 2005). Several months after the short-lived shock subsided, the global economic data showed that this particular shock did not cause major economic damage. The Asian Development Bank estimated that the economic impact experienced because of the SARS outbreak totaled around $18 billion in East Asia, or approximately 0.6 percent of gross domestic product (Fan 2003). However, the fact that such a short-lived epidemic with a relatively small health impact could generate such widespread global panic and spawn such disproportionate economic impact remains a remarkable example of the economic damage such incidents can incur (Smith 2006). In particular, it triggered substantial losses in the stock markets of the affected areas, which had plummeted drastically. In fact, the decline was so precipitous, it deserves to be examined closely.

Chen, Jang, and Kim (2007) documented that the tourism industry in Taiwan, one of the SARS-hit areas in Asia, suffered seriously. Taiwanese hotel stocks experienced the highest share price decline (approximately 29 percent) within a month of the SARS outbreak. Seven publicly traded hotel companies suffered steep declines in both earnings and stock prices during the SARS outbreak.

One may ask why disproportionate impacts on both economic activities and the daily lives of millions were affected by such a minor epidemic that occurred in a short time period. Some researchers find that the way the media reported it may have contributed to the fears generated.

Smith (2006) attributed the most significant of all contributing factors and the disproportionate impact experienced to the perception, communication, and management of the risks presented by SARS. Keogh-Brown and Smith (2008) focused on the general consensus that the media coverage of the SARS outbreak was excessive, sometimes inaccurate, and sensationalist, and they further questioned the possible role of the media in exacerbating or dampening the impact of SARS upon economic activity. Rezza et al. (2004) argued that during outbreaks of infections, both the media and the public are often criticized for overreacting.

As a specific example, Wilson, Thomson, and Mansoor (2004) searched the *New Zealand Herald,* which has the largest daily circulation for a newspaper in the country, for a three-month period beginning with the World Health Organization's first global alert (March 13–June 11, 2003) and found 261 articles. Of the 261 articles, 48 percent had a headline with the word *SARS*. They found that while most of the content remained accurate according to public health standards, some comments veered toward the overly pessimistic. "Particular terms were used that could be considered alarming (e.g., using the word 'outbreak' in 38 percent of the articles and 'deadly' in 32 percent). Similarly, at least one of the following terms was used in 15 percent of the headlines: kill, killer, deadly, panic, and death (n = 38). Some examples of headline phrasing included the following: 'doctor dies of killer virus,' 'nature's terrorism strangles Hong Kong,' 'SARS deaths leap,' 'panicking crowds flee,' 'creeping panic over epidemic,' and 'SARS virus . . . mutating rapidly.'"

In summary, several patterns seem to emerge by reexamining evidence gleaned from different stock markets during different time periods of the past 100 years. First, major deleterious events, especially domestic ones, often rattle stock markets. Generally speaking, the impact of a large event on any stock market in the world depends on the event itself, on the relevance of the event to investors, on the size of the stock market, and on the regulatory framework overseeing the stock market. Second, it is difficult to gauge the extent to which investor reaction to a highly volatile stock market is imminent, especially when trying to calculate reaction to major events. Nor can one predict how long investors' reactions to such events will last. From historical records, an impact can generate substantial market index swings immediately upon the information's arrival at the stock market. A market index drop can be extremely volatile but brief, such as Black Monday, or volatile for days, weeks, or months, such as the volatility displayed during WWI (Bittlingmayer 1998; Michie 2006). Put simply, panic selling exists in both scenarios. Third, media reporting with emotional metaphor may precipitate panic in the general public and panic selling by numerous investors.

TRADING HALTS, CIRCUIT BREAKERS, AND PRICE LIMITS: EFFECTIVENESS AND LIMITATIONS

We now examine the roles of current regulatory mechanisms and explore how much impact they have on curbing panic selling.

Three Main Regulatory Mechanisms That Halt Trading

From history, we learn that the first type of regulatory mechanism is discretionary closure of the stock exchange, or a marketwide halt to trading. During WWI, prolonged market closures lasted for months and even years (Mitchie 2006).

Circuit breakers present another mechanism to halt trading. The difference between discretionary trading halts and those triggered via circuit breakers is one of activation initiated by preset limits. In other words, circuit breaker halts of trading are rule-based. This methodology was proposed by the Brady Report (1988) and implemented for the first time at the New York Stock Exchange in October 1988 (SEC 2009).

Price limits are the third type of mechanism that may reduce buying or selling speed on the aggregate and delay the total buying or selling quantity. Generally these limits are set for a specific stock. Normally there are limits established for both upside (ceiling limit) and downside (floor limit) transactions. Similar to circuit breakers, price limits are rule-based. Stock-specific trading halts can, however, also be discretionary.

The three mechanisms find commonality in their shared characteristic: setting in place a mechanism to temporarily halt trading. The variation comes from the trigger employed. If the trigger is based on preset rules and limits, the mechanism is a circuit breaker or price limits. If the trigger is activated by discretionary orders, its emphasis is on halting trading or initiating a market closure. The duration for which trading can be halted can be preset, as with a circuit breaker or price limits, or discretionary, as with trading halts or market closure. Taking the past 100 years and global stock markets into consideration, the duration for which trading can be halted has been minutes, hours, days, weeks, and months. The longest period was probably seen during WWI, when the Berlin Stock Market was closed for more than three years between 1914 and 1917 (Michie 2006). However, after WWII, no halt to trading in any country lasted longer than one year.

Regulatory Objective

Regulators claim that the intended goal in activating any of the three halt mechanisms is to gain time for market makers to match sell orders with buy orders (Kim and Yang 2004). This is true for certain markets like the NYSE, whose trading is based on specialists. But for many electronic markets, such as the Australian Stock Exchange or the Shanghai Stock Exchange, what does this objective target?

A look at the impact of September 11, 2001, on the NYSE after a four-day halt, compared to major markets around the world that did not halt trading, shows that the Dow dropped over 7 percent on September 17, 2001, in the same order as the index drops experienced by the LSE, FSE, and HKSE on September 11, 2001 (Carter and Simkins 2004; Chen and Siems 2004). This is one clear case showing that the four-day halt was not long enough to eliminate the risk of panic selling. One may ponder, if the halt had been lifted after President George W. Bush launched the war against terrorists in Afghanistan on October 7, 2001, how would the Dow have then behaved?

From the broader perspective of protecting investors and maintaining market stability, effecting halts to trading may delay the execution of trade by panic sellers or, if the duration of the halt is long enough, mitigate the desire to sell due to panic. This may contribute, partially, to protection of investors who plan to sell out of panic before the trading halt and to the stabilization of the stock market. Have these two objectives been realized? The following research results, especially those gleaned from empirical data, may contribute to such a reality check.

What Does Current Research Conclude?   Kim and Yang (2004) have achieved a comprehensive review of the literature regarding price limits, firm-specific trading halts, and cross-market circuit breakers. Except for insufficient research on the cross-market circuit breaker section, the general conclusion is not very encouraging regarding the three regulatory mechanisms being discussed.

Kim and Yang (2004) include empirical research on the effect of price limits from both developed and emerging stock markets, such as the Tokyo Stock Exchange, the Korean Stock Exchange, the Taiwan Stock Exchange, the Istanbul Stock Exchange, and the Athens Stock Exchange. Only one supporting paper by Lee and Kim (1995) shows that price limits decrease volatility using the daily stock price data drawn from the Korean Stock Exchange from 1980 to 1989. Six other papers, to varying degrees, show no supportive evidence or opposing findings. Chung (1991) examines the price limit system used by the Korean Stock Market and finds no evidence that restrictive price limits decrease the volatility of stock prices. Chen (1993) examines the effect of varying daily price limits on stock price volatility using Taiwan Stock Exchange data. By comparing stock price volatility across three different price limit regimes, Chen finds that price limits do not provide a cooling-off effect. Kim and Rhee (1997), based on daily stock price data of the Tokyo Stock Exchange from 1989 to 1992, find that price limits simply allow volatility to carry over to subsequent days rather than decrease volatility. Bildik and Gulay (2004) use a similar methodology to study the effectiveness of price limits employed by the Istanbul Stock Exchange and reach the same conclusion. Phylaktis, Kavussanos, and Manalis (1999) conclude that volatility did not increase or decrease after the adoption of price limits by the Athens Stock Exchange. Gan and Li (2001) find that price limits do not have any significant effects on the means or variances of stock returns. Kim and Yang (2004) summarize the empirical and theoretical research results (not cited in this chapter) and conclude that the existing studies seem to suggest that price limits are not effective in eliminating panic selling in stock markets.

There are only a few studies that examine the performance of market-wide circuit breakers, mostly because data are not available. For example, the NYSE circuit breaker has been triggered only once since its implementation in 1988. Clear conclusions cannot be drawn based upon such insufficient data and mixed empirical research findings.

Regarding the effect of halting trading for firm-specific or cross-market variations, the related researchers conclude that the empirical evidence concerning employing trading halts indicates that such stoppages do not reduce stock market volatility. This finding seems consistent across different markets and use of halting mechanisms. However, information transmission during trading halts promotes the price discovery process, which is included in the intended goal.

Our Analysis

What is the full cycle of panic selling following a large, sudden news event? By the full cycle, we mean the period during which the postevent stock market index rebounds to the level of the pre-event close. The cycle can take as little as one trading day. It may take weeks or months. After the September 11 terrorist attack, all the major stock markets in the world experienced a minimum 4 percent decline. However, the rebounding time period varied. The New York Stock Exchange took only six trading days for the Dow to bounce back to the preattack level. The Norway Stock Exchange took 107 days before the full cycle (Chen and Siems 2004). The similarity of all market indices' performances lies in the pattern of the cycles. If one uses three stages to describe a general cycle, it starts with a sharp and deep plummet in the market index. This is stage one. The next stage features bottom-out. The index may take a quick dip and start to rebound without looking back. It may take a double-dip before consistent rebounding. Once the bottom-out stage is over, the third stage sets in. It is either a quick rebound or a slow recovery.

Applying a trading halt will shift or reshape the full cycle. Lift of the applied trading halt before a solid good news event will not eliminate panic selling. It simply delays or shifts to the date of lifting the halt. However, if the lift is intended for after a solid good news event, panic selling may be reduced, even substantially. Soon rebound starts.

From Both Regulatory Consideration and Existing Research Results, We May Draw the Following Conclusions on Employing Cross-Market Trading Halts:

- Trading halts are necessary when facing a national or international disaster such as the onset of a war, a large-scale epidemic, or other serious natural or human disasters. This sort of halt is initiated to protect investors, both individual and institutional, and to prevent the collapse of the stock market. This is particularly true when a catastrophic event breaks out that shocks all investors.

- Current research results, though mixed, do not show a sufficient success rate for the current practices—the intended purpose has not been realized well. The main reason may be attributable to the short time allocated to the trading halt before a positive news event such as cease-fire in the case of war, or the ability to cure an epidemic or bring other risk factors under control.

- A trading halt is in any form an *ex post* approach to respond to an unexpected large news event or large price swings with or without major news. The best the current practice of instituting a trading halt can do is to delay extreme price movements but not eliminate them. At best, it can only delay the risk. But no tangible effect on the seriousness of the risk can be generated by such a short and temporary intervention. It needs to be improved. From analysis of the full cycle of panic selling following a large unexpected news event, we may find ways for improvement.

- There are emerging concerns over unexpected fast price swings due to increasingly dominant high-frequency trading. The flash crash of May 6, 2010, emphasized the necessity of effective preset intervention. Price limits reduce trading speed on the aggregate and decrease panic selling quantity over each related trading day. In particular, they contain intraday price volatility within the preset bracket.

REGULATORY PRINCIPLES IN CASE OF BREAKING NEWS

The following two principles are proposed to regulate both the stock market and news reporting when a breaking news event occurs. For consistency, they are numbered in sequence from the earlier six principles.

- *Principle seven:* From the analysis of a full cycle of panic selling due to a large unexpected news event, one can combine a trading halt and price limits to achieve a smoother cycle. Immediately after the breaking news, a marketwide trading halt needs to be applied. When the regulatory agency decides to lift the halt, it may put a price limit on each stock. If the price limit is not reached by a certain percentage of all stocks, it may be increased to a higher limit. Once a preset percentage of all stocks do not drop to the limit, the price limit can be completely removed.

- *Principle eight:* Media reporting needs to be objective and not emotion-charged. Quantifiable measures can be designed by regulators if they target wording, metaphor, and other presentation styles.

CONCLUDING REMARKS

Business news reporting affects stock prices, leads to frequent mini-bubbles, and cultivates long-run euphoria that surely will result in a marketwide crisis. The fundamental causality is that business news reporting has the capacity to generate or cogenerate an information monopoly. Mass media actually do stimulate information monopolies everyday in the form of their stock-related TV shows, newspaper columns, magazine articles, and web pages. Thus, such information monopolies are frequently used for manipulative trading or other profit-seeking activities. An exercise of this type of monopoly damages a fair and orderly market because it interrupts perfect competition with fairness and transparency. It frequently causes severe losses to uninformed investors who rely exclusively on business news reporting, and it has the potential to disrupt the security of the stock market. Breaking news of large, unexpected events can cause shocks to all investors. If the events have negative consequences, panic selling may follow immediately. Although we do not discuss the information monopoly of the breaking news reporting over investors in detail, earlier analysis shows the link.

In the spirit of antitrust and preventing conflicts of interest in the stock market, we have proposed eight principles for interested securities regulators to prevent generation of this type of information monopoly power, keeping it from becoming too powerful or too frequent. As media are not within the reach of securities regulatory agencies in all economies, principles, not implementable measures, are suggested. These principles, aimed at objectivity, fairness, transparency, and accountability, are expected to prevent or reduce the occurrence of mini-bubbles, prevent long-run manias, and mitigate panic selling, ultimately preventing marketwide crises.

Recognition of these principles by the relevant mass media and their journalists would indeed be a solid step forward, and would help to maintain an orderly and fair stock market. Most important, it would prevent stock market bubbles from the very beginning.

The investment culture will be improved on the basis of objective and fair business or nonbusiness news reporting employing a rational and responsible style. Not only will this benefit the investing public, it also will help construct a more scientific and healthier social environment. It will encourage more civilized behavior on the part of investors and others in the business culture.

NOTES

1. This chapter was presented at the Third Annual Meeting of the Academy of Behavioral Finance & Economics, UCLA, Los Angeles, September 21–23, 2011.
2. Credibility of the information source is also important. However, news reporting by a credible media outlet implies that the information source is credible. Thus, the media outlet's credibility is of great importance.
3. The historically severe earthquake in Japan on March 11, 2011, caused the Nikkei 225 index to plummet 1,390 points—or more than 14 percent—at one point in the session on the following trading day. In the end, the 10.6 percent closing marked the third-worst one-day plunge in the Nikkei's history (CNNMoney 2011).
4. Kolata, Gina. 1998. "Hope in the lab: A special report; a cautious awe greets drugs that eradicate tumors in mice." *New York Times,* May 3, 1:1. For the first 13 paragraphs, each paragraph having between 24 and 72 words, before EntreMed is first mentioned, Kolata uses comments such as "the first cancer patient will be injected with two new drugs that can eradicate any type of cancer, with no obvious side effects and no drug resistance—in mice," "the most exciting treatment that they have ever seen," "'the single most exciting thing on the horizon' for the treatment of cancer," "remarkable and wonderful," "very compelling," "they make tumors disappear and not return," "electrified," "People were almost overwhelmed," "the drugs are the only ones ever tested that can seemingly eradicate all tumors in mice." She enhanced the positive message by quoting James Watson, a Nobel Prize winner in medicine, who claimed that "(Dr. Folkman) is going to cure cancer in two years," and "Dr. Folkman would be remembered along with scientists like Charles Darwin as someone who permanently altered civilization." There are about six instances of cautionary words, but these are placed at the end of the paragraph or inserted among the positive comments. For investors who have no advanced training in cancer research, the message up to the first appearance of EntreMed paints a very rosy picture about the company's research—even though it offers no convincing proof using human samples up to today.
5. Journalists' personal goals include fame seeking and profit making from their reporting. Most journalists are assumed to obey the law. Since their pay is low relative to that of their PR colleagues, some of them engaged in manipulative trading by using the information monopoly power of their stock-picking columns or equity-related articles. These very few prosecution cases include Winans' conviction (Liu, Smith, and Syed 1990), Calandra's penalty (Chapter 8), and that of Hipwell and Bhoyrul (Murphy 2005; Tait 2005).
6. Private conversation with a business journalist in 2011.
7. Private conversation with a business journalist in 2011.
8. Private communication with a business journalist in 2011.
9. McChesney (2008) offers three regulatory solutions to the problems of media. The first possibility is that government intervenes to ensure that the

semi-monopolistic media provides a diverse range of views. The second alternative is to eliminate commercial media and create a large nonprofit, noncommercial media system, accountable to the public. The third alternative McChesney recommends is to accept the existence of corporate media giants, regulate broadcasters, and tax media giants to establish a parallel viable nonprofit and noncommercial media system.

10. If regulators of some markets find that the proposed principles are not implementable because of conflict with their freedom of the press, we suggest that they extract the spirit of our proposals to apply in their regulatory action. Research results in this chapter show that clear and present danger exists in some business news reporting that results in heavy losses by numerous investors and systemic risk to the market.

11. Occasionally, large unexpected business news, such as the bankruptcy filing of Lehman Brothers on September 15, 2008, can cause imminent marketwide panic. This type of news event is also included in the current study.

Bibliography

Abarbanell, Jeffery S. 1991. "Do analysts' earnings forecasts incorporate information in prior stock price changes?" *Journal of Accounting and Economics,* 14: 147–165.

Aboody, David, and Ron Kasznik. 2000. "CEO Stock Option Awards and Corporate Voluntary Disclosures." *Journal of Accounting Economics,* 29(1): 73–100.

Abramson, L. Y., G. I. Metalsky, and L. B. Alloy. 1989. "Hopelessness Depression: A Theory-Based Subtype of Depression." *Psychological Review,* 96: 358–372.

Aggarwal Rajesh K., and Guojun Wu. 2006. "Stock market manipulation." *Journal of Business,* 79(4): 1915–1953.

Ahern, Kenneth R., and Denis Sosyura. 2011. "Who Writes the News? Corporate Press Releases during Merger Negotiations." *AFA 2011 Denver Meetings Paper.* Available at SSRN: http://ssrn.com/abstract=1570530. Accessed February 28, 2011.

Ahnquist, Johanna, Peter Fredlund, and Sarah P. Wamala. 2007. "Is cumulative exposure to economic hardships more hazardous to women's health than men's? A 16-year follow-up study of the Swedish Survey of Living Conditions." *Journal of Epidemiology and Community Health,* 61: 331–336.

Aitken, Michael J., Jayaram Muthuswamy, and Kathryn L. Wong. 2001. "The impact of brokers' recommendations: Australian evidence." *Working paper,* University of Sydney.

Akerlof, George A. 1970. "The market for 'lemons': Quality uncertainty and the market mechanism." *Quarterly Journal of Economics,* 84(3): 488–500.

Alexander, Gordon J., and Mark A. Peterson. 2007. "An analysis of trade-size clustering and its relation to stealth trading." *Journal of Financial Economics,* 84 (2): 435–471.

Allen, Franklin, and Douglas Gale. 1992. "Stock-Price Manipulation." *Review of Financial Studies,* 3: 503–529.

Allen, Franklin, and Douglas Gale. 2007. *Understanding Financial Crises.* Clarendon Lectures in Finance. New York: Oxford University Press.

Allen, Franklin, and Richard Herring. 2001. "Banking Regulation versus Securities Market Regulation." *Working paper,* University of Pennsylvania.

Allen, Franklin, Lubomir Litov, and Jianping Mei. 2006. "Large Investors, Price Manipulation, and Limits to Arbitrage: An Anatomy of Market Corners." *Review of Finance,* 10: 643–691.

Amalgamated Bank et al. vs. Kenneth L. Lay et al. 2001. United States District Court for the Southern District of Texas, Houston Division (Civil Action No.

H 01-4198), December 5. Available at: http://securities.stanford.edu/1020/ENE01/2001125_o01x_014198.pdf. Accessed July 15, 2010.

Aman, Hiroyuki. 2010. "An Empirical Analysis of the Effect of Media Coverage on Stock Price Crashes: Evidence from Japan." *Asian Finance Association International Conference 2010,* 29 June–1 July, Hong Kong.

American Psychiatric Association. 1994. *Diagnostic and Statistical Manual of Mental Disorders, 4th ed. rev.* Washington, DC: American Psychiatric Association.

Amihud, Yakov. 2002. "Illiquidity and stock returns: cross-section and time-series effects." *Journal of Financial Markets,* 5(1): 31–56.

Anderson, Anders. 2007. "All Guts, No Glory: Trading and Diversification among Online Investors." *European Financial Management,* 13(3): 448–471.

Andreassen, Paul B. 1987. "On the social psychology of the stock market: Aggregate attributional effects and the regressiveness of prediction." *Journal of Personality and Social Psychology,* 53(3): 490–496.

Andreeva, E., S. Ermakov, and M. H. Brenner. 2008. "The Socioeconomic Aetiology of Suicide Mortality in Russia." *International Journal of Environment and Sustainable Development,* 7(1): 21–48.

Antweiler, Werner, and Murray Z. Herring. 2004. "Is all that talk just noise? The information content of internet stock message boards." *Journal of Finance,* 59 (3): 1259–1295.

Argyle, M. 1987. *The Psychology of Happiness.* London: Methuen.

Argyle, M. 1999. "Causes and correlates of happiness." In: Kahneman, Daniel, Ed Diener, and Norbert Schwartz. (Eds.) *Well-being: The Foundations of Hedonic Psychology.* New York: Russell Sage Foundation, pp. 353–373.

Aristotle. 2011. *Nicomachean Ethics.* Translated and edited by Robert C. Bartlett and Susan D. Collins. Chicago, IL: University of Chicago Press.

Askitas, Nikolaos, and Klaus F. Zimmermann. 2011. "Health and Well-Being in the Crisis." *IZA Discussion Paper No. 5601.*

Asquith, Paul, Michael B. Mikhail, and Andrea S. Au. 2005. "Information Content of Equity Analyst Reports." *Journal of Financial Economics,* 75(1): 245–282.

Automotive News Europe (ANE). 2009. "Porsche probe shows weakness of German market manipulation rules: Few are convicted for market manipulation." *Reuters,* August 23, 06: 01 CET. www.autonews.com/article/20090823/ANE02/308219971. Accessed September 15, 2009.

Avery, Christopher. 1998a. "Manipulation and herding."*Unpublished manuscript,* Harvard University.

Avery, Christopher. 1998b. "Manipulative trading and herding."*Unpublished manuscript,* Harvard University.

Avery, Christopher, and Peter Zemsky. 1998. "Multidimensional uncertainty and herd behavior in financial markets." *American Economic Review,* 88(4): 724–748.

Baber, W., P. Fairfield, and J. Haggard. 1991. "The effect of concern about reported income on discretionary spending decisions: The case of research and development." *The Accounting Review,* 66(4): 818–829.

Bagdikian, Ben H. 2000. *The Media Monopoly, 6th edition.* Boston, MA: Beacon Press.

Bagdikian, Ben H., and Den Emeritus. 2004. *The New Media Monopoly.* Boston, MA: Beacon Press.

Bainbridge, Stephen M. 1999. "Insider trading: An overview." Available at SSRN: http://ssrn.com/abstract=132529. Accessed July 13, 2010.

Baker, Russ. 1997. "The squeeze: Some major advertisers step up the pressure on magazines to alter their content. Will editors bend?" *Columbia Journalism Review,* September/October, 36(3): 30–36.

Ball, R. J., and P. Brown. 1968. "An empirical evaluation of accounting income numbers." *Journal of Accounting Research,* 6(1): 159–178.

Banerjee A. 1992. "A Simple Model of Herd Behavior." *Quarterly Journal of Economics,* 107: 797–817.

Barber, Brad M., Yi-Tsung Lee, Yu-Jane Liu, and Terrance Odean. 2009. "Just How Much Do Individual Investors Lose by Trading?" *Review of Financial Studies,* 22(2): 609–632.

Barber, Brad M., and Douglas Loeffler. 1993. "The 'Dartboard' column: Second-hand information and price pressure." *Journal of Financial and Quantitative Analysis,* 28(2): 273–284.

Barber, Brad M., and Terrance Odean. 2000. "Trading Is Hazardous to Your Wealth: The Common Stock Investment Performance of Individual Investors." *Journal of Finance,* 55(2): 773–806.

Barber, Brad M., and Terrance Odean. 2002. "Online investors: Do the slow die first?" *Review of Financial Studies,* 15: 455–487.

Barber, Brad M., and Terrance Odean. 2008. "All That Glitters: The Effect of Attention and News on the Buying Behavior of Individual and Institutional Investors." *Review of Financial Studies,* 21: 785–818.

Barraclough, B., J. Bunch, B. Nelson, and P. Sainsbury. 1974. "A Hundred Cases of Suicide: Clinical Aspects." *British Journal of Psychiatry,* 125: 355–373.

Barth, Mary E., John A. Elliott, and Mark W. Finn. 1999. "Market rewards associated with patterns of increasing earnings." *Journal of Accounting Research,* 37(2): 387–413.

Barton, J. 2001. "Does the use of financial derivatives affect earnings management decisions?" *The Accounting Review,* 76(1): 1–26.

Bartov, E. 1993. "The timing of assets sales and earnings manipulation." *The Accounting Review,* 68(4): 840–855.

Bartov, E., D. Givoly, and C. Hayn. 2002. "The rewards to meeting or beating earnings expectations." *Journal of Accounting and Economics,* 33: 173–204.

Bartov, E., and P. Mohanram. 2004. "Private information, earnings manipulations, and executive stock-option exercises." *The Accounting Review,* 79(4): 889–920.

Battalio, Robert H., and Richard R. Mendenhall. 2005. "Earnings Expectations and Investor Clienteles." *Journal of Financial Economics,* 77: 289–319.

Bauder, David. 2009. "Abrams Research Survey: Financial Journalists Say Media Dropped Ball on Crisis." Available at: www.huffingtonpost.com/2009/01/08/abrams-research-survey-fi_n_156369.html, January 8. Accessed March 13, 2011.

Bauer, R., M. Cosemans, and P. Eichholtz. 2008. "Option Trading and Individual Investor Performance." forthcoming in *Journal of Banking and Finance.*

Bauman, W. Scott, Sudip Datta, and Mai E. Iskandar-Datta. 1995. "Investment Analyst Recommendations: A Test of 'The Announcement Effect' and of the 'The Valuable Information Effect'." *Journal of Business Finance and Accounting,* 22 (5): 659–670.

Beatty, Anne, Sandra L. Chamberlain, and Joseph Magliolo. 1995. "Managing financial reports of commercial banks: The influence of taxes, regulatory capital, and earnings." *Journal of Accounting Research,* 33(2): 231–261.

Beaver, W. H. 1968. "The information content of annual earnings announcements." *Journal of Accounting Research,* 6(Suppl.): 67–92.

Beck, A. T. 1963. "Thinking and Depression." *Archives of General Psychiatry,* 9: 324–333.

Beck, A. T. 1967. *Depression: Clinical, Experimental and Theoretical Aspects.* New York: Harper & Row.

Beck, A. T. 1986. "Hopelessness as a Predictor of Eventual Suicide." *Annals New York Academy of Sciences,* 487: 90–96.

Beck, A.T., G. Brown, R. J. Berchick, B. L. Stewart, and R. A. Steer. 1990. "Relationship Between Hopelessness and Ultimate Suicides: A Replication with Psychiatric Outpatients." *American Journal of Psychiatry,* 147: 190–195.

Beck A. T., D. Schuyler, and I. Herman. 1974. "Development of Suicidal Intent Scales." In: Beck, A. T., H. L. P. Resnik, and D. J. Lettieri. (Eds.) *The Prediction of Suicide.* Bowie, MD: Charles Press.

Beck, A. T., A. Weissman, and M. Kovacs. 1976. "Alcoholism, Hopelessness and Suicidal Behavior." *Journal of Studies on Alcohol,* 37(1): 66–77.

Beneish, Messod D. 1991. "Stock Prices and the Dissemination of Analysts' Recommendations." *Journal of Business,* 64(3): 393–416.

Beneish, Messod D. 1999. "Incentives and Penalties Related to Earnings Overstatements That Violate GAAP." *The Accounting Review,* 74(4): 425–457.

Beneish, Messod D. 2001. "Earnings management: A perspective." *Managerial Finance,* 27(12): 3–17.

Beneish, Messod D., and Mark E. Vargus. 2002. "Insider trading, earnings quality, and accrual mispricing." *The Accounting Review,* 77(4): 755–791.

Bennett, W. Lance. 2005. *News: The Politics of Illusion, 6th edition.* New York: Longman.

Benson, Herbert, and Miriam Z. Klipper. 2000. *The Relaxation Response.* New York: Avon Books.

Bentham, J. 1996. *Introduction to the Principles of Morals and Legislation.* In Burns, J. H., and H. L. A. Hart. (Eds.) New York: Oxford University Press.

Beny, Laura N. 2005. "Do Insider Trading Laws Matter? Some Preliminary Comparative Evidence." *American Law and Economics Review,* 7(1): 144–183.

Berglund, Tom, Omar Farooq, and P. Joakim Westerholm. 2007. "Do Analysts Revise Their Recommendations to Facilitate Trading?" Available at SSRN: http://ssrn.com/abstract=968139. Accessed October 1, 2010.

Bergstresser, Daniel, and Thomas Philippon. 2006. "CEO Incentives and Earnings Management." *Journal of Financial Economics*, 80(3): 511–529.

Berkeley, Alfed R. 2001. "View from NASDAQ." In: Schwartz, Robert A. (Ed.) *Regulation of U.S. Equity Markets*. Boston, MA: Kluwer Academic Publishers.

Bernheim, Alfred L., and Margaret G. Schneider. (Eds.) 1935. *The Security Markets: Findings and Recommendations of a Special Staff of the Twentieth Century Fund*. New York: Twentieth Century Fund, Inc.

Betzer, André, and Erik Theissen. 2007. "Insider Trading and Corporate Governance—The Case of Germany."*CFR-Working Paper No. 07-07*, Center for Financial Research, University of Bonn.

Bhattacharya, Nilabhra. 2001. "Investors' Trade Size and Trading Responses Around Earnings Announcements: An Empirical Investigation." *The Accounting Review*, 76(2): 221–244.

Bhattacharya, Utpal, and Hazem Daouk. 2002. "The World Price of Insider Trading Risk." *Journal of Finance*, 57(1): 75–108.

Bhattacharya, Utpal, Hazem Daouk, Brian Jorgenson, and Carl-Heinrich Kehr. 2000. "When an Event Is Not an Event: The Curious Case of an Emerging Market." *Journal of Financial Economics*, 55(1): 69–101.

Bhaumik, Subir. 2002. "Broker held for Calcutta stock scam." BBC, Tuesday, December 3, 17: 31 GMT.

Bikhhchandani, S., D. Hirshleifer, and I. Welch. 1992. "A Theory of Fads, Fashions, Customs and Cultural Change as Informational Cascades." *Journal of Political Economy*, 100: 992–1026.

Bildik, R., and G. Gulay. 2004. "Price Limits: How Effective? Evidence from the Istanbul Stock Exchange." *Unpublished paper*.

Bilson, Christopher M., Timothy J. Brailsford, and Vincent C. Hooper. 2002. "The explanatory power of political risk in emerging markets." *International Review of Financial Analysis*, 11(1): 1–27.

Bittlingmayer, G. 1998. "Output, stock volatility, and political uncertainty in a natural experiment: Germany, 1880–1940." *Journal of Finance*, 53: 2243–2258.

Blanchflower, David G., and Andrew J. Oswald. 2004. "Wellbeing over time in Britain and the USA." *Journal of Public Economics*, 88(7–8): 1359–1386.

Bloom, David E., David Canning, and Dean T. Jamison. 2004. "Health, Wealth and Welfare." *Finance and Development*, March, 10–15.

Böhme, Rainer, and Thorsten Holz. 2006. "The Effect of Stock Spam on Financial Markets."*Working Paper,* Technische Universität Dresden.

Bok, Derek. 2010. *The Politics of Happiness.What Government Can Learn from the New Research on Well-Being*. Princeton, NJ: Princeton University Press.

Bolster, Paul, Emery Trahan, and Anand Venkateswaran. 2010. "How Mad Is *Mad Money*? Jim Cramer as a Stock Picker and Portfolio Manager." *Working paper,* Northeastern University.

Bonner, Sarah E., Arthur Hugon, and Beverly R. Walther. 2007. "Investor Reaction to Celebrity Analysts: The Case of Earnings Forecast Revisions." *Journal of Accounting Research*, 45(3): 481–513.

Bonner, Sarah E., Zoe-Vonna Palmrose, and Susan M. Young. 1998. "Fraud Type and Auditor Litigation: An Analysis of SEC Accounting and Auditing Enforcement Releases." *The Accounting Review,* 73(4): 503–532.

Booth-Kewley, Stephanie, and Howard S. Friedman. 1987. "Psychological predictors of heart disease: A quantitative review." *Psychological Bulletin,* 101: 343–362.

Bowe, Michael, and Daniela Domuta. 2004. "Investor herding during financial crisis: A clinical study of the Jakarta Stock Exchange." *Pacific-Basin Finance Journal,* 12(4): 387–418.

Bradshaw, Mark T. 2004. "How Do Analysts Use Their Earnings Forecasts in Generating Stock Recommendations?" *The Accounting Review,* 79(1): 25–50.

Bradshaw, Mark T., Scott A. Richardson, and Richard G. Sloan. 2003. "Pump and Dump: An Empirical Analysis of the Relation between Corporate Financing Activities and Sell-side Analyst Research." *Working paper,* Harvard Business School. May. Available at SSRN: http://ssrn.com/abstract=410521. Accessed August 5, 2010.

Bradshaw, Mark T., Scott A. Richardson, and Richard G. Sloan. 2006. "The relation between corporate financing activities, analysts' forecasts and stock returns." *Journal of Accounting and Economics,* 42(1): 53–85.

Brandes, Leif, and Katja Rost. 2009. "Media, Limited Attention and the Propensity of Individuals to Buy Stocks." Available at SSRN: http://ssrn.com/abstract=1342379. Accessed March 2, 2011.

Brav, Alon, Chris Geczy, and Paul Gompers. 2000. "Is the Abnormal Return Following Equity Issuances Anomalous?" *Journal of Financial Economics,* 56(2): 209–249.

Brav, Alon, and Paul Gompers. 1997. "Myth or Reality? The Long-Run Underperformance of Initial Public Offerings: Evidence from Venture and Non-Venture-Backed Companies." *Journal of Finance,* 52(5): 1791–1821.

Brav, Alon, and Reuven Lehavy. 2003. "An Empirical Analysis of Analysts' Target Prices: Short Term Informativeness and Long Term Dynamics." *Journal of Finance,* 58(5): 1933–1967.

Brenner, M. H. 1973. *Mental Illness and the Economy.* Cambridge, MA: Harvard University Press.

Brenner, M. H. 1976. *Estimating the Social Costs of National Economic Policy: Implications for Mental and Physical Health and Criminal Aggression.* (A study prepared for the Joint Economic Committee of Congress.) Washington, DC: Government Printing Office.

Brenner, M. H. 1979. "Mortality and the national economy: A review, and the experience of England and Wales, 1973–76." *The Lancet,* 314(8142): 568–573.

Brenner, M. H. 1984. *Estimating the Effects of Economic Change on National Health and Social Well-Being.* Joint Economic Committee of the U.S. Congress. Washington, DC: Government Printing Office.

Brenner, M. H. 2005. "Commentary: Economic Growth Is the Basis of Mortality Rate Decline in the 20th Century—Experience of the United States 1901–2000." *International Journal of Epidemiology,* 34: 1214–1221.

Brickey, Kathleen F. 2004. "Andersen's fall from grace." *Washington University Law Quarterly*, 81(4): 917–960.

Bris, Arturo. 2005. "Do insider trading laws work?" *European Financial Management*, 11(3): 267–312.

Brogaard, Jonathan. 2010. "High Frequency Trading and Its Impact on Market Quality." *5th Annual Conference on Empirical Legal Studies Paper*. Available at SSRN: http://ssrn.com/abstract=1641387.

Brooke, James. 1989a. "Check Bounces, and Brazil Shakes." *New York Times*, Tuesday, June 20.

Brooke, James. 1989b. "Brazil Indicts 11 People After Market's Crash." *New York Times*, Monday, August 14.

Brooks, Robert, and Huabing Wang. 2004. "The Securities Litigation Reform and Its Impact on Analyst Research." Available at SSRN: http://ssrn.com/abstract=606822. Accessed December 23, 2010.

Brown, Lawrence D., and Marcus L. Caylor. 2005. "A Temporal Analysis of Quarterly Earnings Thresholds: Propensities and Valuation Consequences." *The Accounting Review*, 80(2): 423–440.

Bruni, Luigino, and Pier Luigi Porta. (Eds.) 2005. *Economics and Happiness. Framing the Analysis*. Oxford, England: Oxford University Press.

Bruns, W., and K. Merchant. 1996. "The dangerous morality of managing earnings." *Management Accounting*, 72(1): 22–25.

Bryant, Jennings. 1986. "The Road Most Travelled: Yet Another Cultivation Critique." *Journal of Broadcasting and Electronic Media*, 30: 231–235.

Burazeri, G., A. Goda, G. Sulo, J. Stefa, and J. D. Kark. 2008. "Financial loss in pyramid savings schemes, syndrome in transitional Albania downward social mobility and acute coronary syndrome." *Journal of Epidemiology Community Health*, 62: 620–626.

Burgstahler, D., and I. Dichev. 1997. "Earnings management to avoid earnings decreases and losses." *Journal of Accounting and Economics*, 24: 99–126.

Bushee, B. 1998. "The influence of institutional investors on myopic R&D investment behavior." *The Accounting Review*, 73(3): 305–333.

Buss, David M. 2000. "The evolution of happiness. Evolutionary perspective on obstacles to achieving happiness." *American Psychologist*, 55(1): 15–23.

Cai, Fang. 2003. "Was There Front Running During the LTCM Crisis?" *FRB International Finance Discussion Paper No. 758*. Available at SSRN: http://ssrn.com/abstract=385560.

Cai, Zongqi. 2010. "CSRC exerts high pressure on insider trading: 15 investigations in two months." *China Securities Daily*, August 29. (in Chinese)

Cajueiro, Daniel O., and Benjamin M. Tabak. 2009. "Multifractality and herding behavior in the Japanese stock market." *Chaos, Solitons and Fractals*, 40(1): 497–504.

Cameron, Glen T., Lynne M. Sallot, and Patricia A. Curtin. 1997. "Public relations and the production of news: A critical review and a theoretical framework." In: Burleson, Brant R. (Ed.) *Communication Yearbook, 20*. Newbury Park, CA: Sage Publications, pp. 111–155.

Campbell, Angus, Philip E. Converse, and Willard Rodgers. 1976. *The Quality of American Life*. New York: Sage Foundation.

Campbell, John A. 2001. "In and out, scream and shout: An Internet conversation about stock price manipulation."*34th Annual Hawaii International Conference on System Sciences (HICSS–34), Volume 4*, pp. 4036–4045.

Cantril, Hadley. 1965. *The Pattern of Human Concerns*. New Brunswick, NJ: Rutgers University Press.

Caparrelli, Franco, Anna Maria D'Arcangelis, and Alexander Cassuto. 2004. "Herding in the Italian Stock Market: A Case of Behavioral Finance." *Journal of Behavioral Finance*, 5(4): 222–230.

Cardella, Laura, Jia Hao, and Ivalina Kalcheva. 2010. "The Floor Trader vs. Automation: A Survey of Theory and Empirical Evidence." Available at SSRN: http://ssrn.com/abstract=1650345. Accessed April 10, 2011.

Carhart, Mark M., Ron Kaniel, David K. Musto, and Adam Reed. 2002. "Leaning for the tape: Evidence of gaming behavior in equity mutual funds." *Journal of Finance*, 57: 661–693.

Carter, D. A., and B. J. Simkins. 2004. "The market's reaction to unexpected, catastrophic events: The case of airline stock returns and the September 11th attacks . . . " *Quarterly Review of Economics and Finance*, 44(4): 539–558.

Carvajal, Ana, and Jennifer Elliott. 2007. "Strengths and Weaknesses in Securities Market Regulation: A Global Analysis."*IMF Working Paper WP/07/259*, November, Washington, DC: International Monetary Fund.

Carvajal, Ana, and Jennifer Elliott. 2009. "The Challenge of Enforcement in Securities Markets: Mission Impossible?"*IMF Working Paper WP/09/168*, August, Washington, DC: International Monetary Fund.

Caspi, Avshalon, Karen Sugden, Terrie E. Moffitt, Alan Taylor, Ian W. Craig, HonaLee Harrington, Joseph McClay, Jonathan Mill, Judy Martin, Antony Braithwaite, and Richie Poulton. 2003. "Influence of Life Stress on Depression: Moderation by a Polymorphism in the 5-HTT Gene." *Science*, 301(5631): 386–389.

Catalano, Ralph, and David Dooley. 1983. "Health effects of economic instability: A test of economic stress hypothesis." *Journal of Health and Social Behavior*, 24(1): 46–60.

Chakraborty, A., and B. Yilmaz. 2004. "Manipulation in market order models." *Journal of Financial Markets*, 7: 187–206.

Chakravarty, Sugato, and John J. McConnell. 1997. "An Analysis of Prices, Bid/Ask Spreads, and Bid and Ask Depths Surrounding Ivan Boesky's Illegal Trading in Carnation's Stock." *Financial Management*, 26(2): 18–34.

Chan, K., L. K. C. Chan, N. Jegadeesh, and J. Lakonishok. 2006. "Earnings Quality and Stock Returns." *Journal of Business*, 79(3): 1041–1082.

Chan, Louis K. C., and Josef Lakonishok, 1993. "Institutional Trades and Intraday Stock Price Behavior." *Journal of Financial Economics*, 33: 173–199.

Chan, Louis K. C., and Josef Lakonishok, 1995. "Behavior of Stock Price around Institutional Trades." *Journal of Finance*, 50(4): 1147–1174.

Chan, W. S. 2003. "Stock Price Reaction to News and No-News: Drift and Reversal after Headlines." *Journal of Financial Economics*, 70: 223–260.

Chang, E. C., J. W. Cheng, and A. Khorana. 2000. "An examination of herd behavior in equity markets: An international perspective." *Journal of Banking and Finance,* 24: 1651–1679.

Chapman, Bruce, and Richard Denniss. 2005. "Using Financial Incentives and Income Contingent Penalties to Detect and Punish Collusion and Insider Trading." *Australian and New Zealand Journal of Criminology,* 38(1): 122–140.

Chemmanur, Thomas, and An Yan. 2008. "Product Market Advertising and New Equity Issues." *Journal of Financial Economics,* 92: 40–65.

Chen, Andrew H., and Thomas F. Siems. 2004. "The effects of terrorism on global capital markets." *European Journal of Political Economy,* 20(2): 349–366.

Chen, H. C., and J. R. Ritter. 2000. "The seven percent solution." *Journal of Finance,* 55(3): 1105–1131.

Chen, Ming-Hsiang, SooCheong(Shawn) Jang, and Woo Gon Kim. 2007. "The impact of the SARS outbreak on Taiwanese hotel stock performance: An event-study approach." *International Journal of Hospitality Management,* 26(1): 200–212.

Chen, Roger C. Y., Chao-Shi Wang, and Zhen-Yu Chen. 2008. "The Effect of Insider Trading on Stock Price." *Working paper,* National Kaohsiung First University of Science and Technology.

Chen, Y. M. 1993. "Price Limits and Stock Market Volatility in Taiwan." *Pacific-Basin Finance Journal,* 1: 139–153.

Cheng, Hongming. 2004. "A comparison of illegal insider trading in Canada and post-communist China: Globalized market economy and the role of law." *Ph. D. Dissertation,* May, Simon Fraser University.

Cheng, Qiang, and Terry Warfield. 2005. "Equity incentives and earnings management." *The Accounting Review,* 80(2): 441–476.

Cheng, S. 2004. "R & D expenditures and CEO compensation." *The Accounting Review,* 79(2): 305–328.

Cherian, Joseph A., and Robert A. Jarrow. 1995. "Market Manipulation." In: Jarrow, R. A., V. Maksimovic, W. T. Ziemba. (Ed.) *Handbooks in Operations Research and Management Science, Volume 9, Finance.* Amsterdam: Elsevier.

China Securities Regulatory Commission (CSRC). 2008. *Wang Jianzhong case.* (in Chinese)

China Securities Regulatory Commission (CSRC). 2009. www.csrc.gov .cn/n575458/n776436/n3376288/n3376382/n3418750/index.html. Accessed September 3.

China Securities Regulatory Commission (CSRC) and Press Bureau 2010. *Regulations of Information Dissemination about Securities and Futures by Print Media.* December 17. (in Chinese)

Chiyachantana, Chiraphol N., Pankaj K. Jain, Christine Jiang, and Robert A. Wood. 2004. "International Evidence on Institutional Trading Behavior and Price Impact." *Journal of Finance,* 59(2): 869–898.

Choe, H., B. Kho, and R. M. Stulz. 1999. "Do Foreign Investors Destabilize Stock Markets? The Korean Experience in 1997." *Mimeo,* Ohio State University.

Choi, Bobae, Doowon Lee, and Kooyul Jung. 2009. "Trading Behavior before the Public Release of Analysts' Reports."*Working paper,* University of Newcastle.

Choi, James J., David Laibson, and Andrew Metrick. 2002. "How does the Internet affect trading? Evidence from investor behavior in 401(k) plans." *Journal of Financial Economics,* 64: 397–421.

Choi, Stephen J., and Jill E. Fisch. 2003. "How to Fix Wall Street: A Voucher Financing Proposal for Securities Intermediaries." *Yale Law Journal,* 113(2): 269–346.

Choi, Stephen J., Karen K. Nelson, and A. C. Pritchard. 2009. "The Screening Effect of the Securities Litigation Reform Act." *Journal of Empirical Legal Studies,* 6(1): 35–68.

Chomsky, Noam, and Edward S. Herman. 2002. *Manufacturing Consent: The Political Economy of the Mass Media.* New York: Pantheon Books.

Christie, William G., and Roger D. Huang. 1995. "Following the Pied Piper: Do Individual Returns Herd around the Market?" *Financial Analysts Journal,* 51(4): 31–37.

Christophe, Stephen E., Michael G. Ferri, and Jim Hsieh. 2010. "Informed trading before analyst downgrades: Evidence from short sellers." *Journal of Financial Economics,* 95(1): 85–106.

Chung, J. R. 1991. "Price Limit System and Volatility of Korean Stock Market." In: Rhee, S. G., and R. P. Chang. (Eds.) *Pacific-Basin Capital Markets Research, Vol. 2.* North-Holland: Elsevier Science Publishers B.V., pp. 283–294.

Clardy, Alan. 2003. " ENRON: The Rise and Fall."*Working Paper 03-Clardy-03,* Human Resources Development Program, Towson University.

Clark, Andrew E., and Andrew J. Oswald. 1994. "Unhappiness and Underemployment." *The Economic Journal.* 104: 648–659.

Clark, Evans, Alfred L. Berheim, J. Frederic Dewhurst, and Margaret G. Schneider. (Eds.) 1934. *Stock Market Control: A Summary of the Research Findings and Recommendations of the Security Markets Survey Staff of the Twentieth Century Fund, Inc.* New York: D. Appleton-Century Company, pp. 107–126.

Clark, Gordon L., Nigel Thrift, and Adam Tickell. 2004. "Performing Finance: The Industry, the Media and Its Image." *Review of International Political Economy,* 11(2): 289–310.

Clark, Nicola, and David Jolly. 2008. "Societe Generale loses $7 billion in trading fraud." *New York Times,* Thursday, January 24.

CMEPSP. 2009. *Report by the Commission on the Measurement of Economic Performance and Social Progress.* Joseph E. Stiglitz, Amartya Sen, and Jean-Paul Fitoussi, IEP.

CNNMoney. 2011. "Tokyo stocks plummet as crisis deepens." March 14. Available at: http://money.cnn.com/2011/03/14/markets/japan_world_markets_tuesday/index.htm. Accessed March 31, 2011.

Coates IV, John C. 2007. "The Goals and Promise of the Sarbanes-Oxley Act." *Journal of Economic Perspectives,* 21(1): 91–116.

Coffee, John. 1986. "Understanding the Plaintiff's Attorney: The Implications of Economic Theory for Private Enforcement of Law through Class and Derivative Actions." *Columbia Law Review,* 86(4): 669–727.

Coffee, John C., Jr. 2003. "What Caused Enron—A Capsule Social and Economic History of the 1990s." *Cornell Law Review,* 89: 269–309.

Coffee, John C., Jr. 2006. *Gatekeepers: The Professions and Corporate Governance.* Oxford, England: Oxford University Press.

Cohen, D., A. Dey, and T. Lys. 2008. "Real and accrual based earnings management in the Pre and Post Sarbanes-Oxley periods." *The Accounting Review,* 83: 757–787.

Colledge, Malcolm. 1982. "Economic cycles and health: towards a sociological understanding of the impact of the recession on health and illness." *Social Science and Medicine,* 16(22): 1919–1927.

Collingwood, Harris. 2001. "The Earnings Game." *Harvard Business Review,* 79(6): 65–74.

Colombo, Ronald J. 2007. "Buy, sell, or hold? Analysts fraud from economic and natural law perspectives." *Brooklyn Law Review,* 73(1): 91–154.

Comerton-Forde, Carole, and Tālis J. Putniņš. 2009. "Measuring closing price manipulation." Available at SSRN: http://papers.ssrn.com/sol3/papers.cfm?abstract_id=1009001. Accessed December 29, 2009.

Cook, Chris. 2009. "The ABCs of Oil Manipulation." *Seeking Alpha,* July 27. http://seekingalpha.com/article/151480-the-abcs-of-oil-manipulation. Accessed August 21, 2009.

Cooper, Cary L., and Philip Dewe. 2004. *Stress: A Brief History.* Malden, MA: Blackwell Publishing.

Cooper, S., and D. Coxe. 2005. *An Investor's Guide to Avian Flu.* Montreal, Quebec: BMO Nesbitt Burns Research.

Cornell, Bradford, and Erik R. Sirri. 1992. "The Reaction of Investors and Stock Prices to Insider Trading." *Journal of Finance,* 47(3): 1031–1059.

Corsetti, Giancarlo, Paolo Pesenti, and Nouriel Roubini. 2001. "The Role of Large Players in Currency Crises." *NBER Working Paper No. 8303.*

Cotter, Julie, Irem Tuna, and Peter D. Wysocki. 2006. "Expectations Management and Beatable Targets: How Do Analysts React to Explicit Earnings Guidance?" *Contemporary Accounting Research,* 23(3): 593–624.

Cowen, Amanda, Boris Groysberg, and Paul Healy. 2006. "Which types of analyst firms are more optimistic?" *Journal of Accounting and Economics,* 41(1–2): 119–146.

Cox, James D., and Randall S. Thomas. 2009. "Mapping the American Shareholder Litigation Experience: A Survey of Empirical Studies of the Enforcement of the U.S. Securities Law." Available at SSRN: http://ssrn.com/abstract=1370508. Accessed December 5, 2010.

Crawford, John R., and Julie D. Henry. 2004. "The Positive and Negative Affect Schedule (PANAS): Construct validity, measurement properties and normative data in a large non-clinical sample." *British Journal of Clinical Psychology,* 43 (3): 245–265.

Creswell, Julie. 2010. "Speedy New Traders Make Waves Far from Wall Street." *New York Times,* May 16. Available at: http://www.nytimes.com/2010/05/17/business/17trade.html?_r=1&dbk. Accessed April 8, 2011.

Csikszentmihalyi, Mihaly. 1999. "If we are so rich, why aren't we happy?" *American Psychologist,* 54(10): 821–827.

Cui, Xing-Jai, and George E. Vaillant. 1996. "Antecedents and Consequences of Negative Life Events in Adulthood: A Longitudinal Study." *American Journal of Psychiatry,* 153(1): 21–26.

Cutler, David, F. Knaul, R. Lozano, O. Mendez, and B. Zurita. 2002. "Financial crisis, health outcomes and ageing: Mexico in the 1980s and 1990s." *Journal of Public Economics,* 84(2): 279–303.

Cutler, David, James Poterba, and Lawrence Summers. 1989. "What moves stock prices?" *Journal of Portfolio Management,* 15(3): 4–12.

D'Avolio, Gene, Efi Gildor, and Andrei Shleifer. 2001. "Technology, Information Production, and Market Efficiency." *Harvard Institute of Economic Research Discussion Paper Number 1929,* September. Cambridge, MA. Available at SSRN: http://ssrn.com/abstract=286597. Accessed July 8, 2010.

Daniel, Kent, David Hirshleifer, and Siew Hong Teoh. 2002. "Investor psychology in capital markets: Evidence and policy implications." *Journal of Monetary Economics,* 49(1): 139–209.

Das, Jishnu, Quy-Toan Do, Jed Friedman, and David McKenzie. 2009. "Mental Health Patterns and Consequences." *World Bank Economic Review,* 23(1): 31–55.

Das, Sanjiv, Asís Martínez-Jerez, and Peter Tufano. 2005. "eInformation" A clinical study of investor discussion and sentiment." *Financial Management,* 34(3): 103–137.

Davidson, Richard J., Klaus R. Scherer, and H. Hill Goldsmith. (Eds.) 2003. *Handbook of Affective Sciences,* Chapters 55–59: Emotions and Health. Oxford, England: Oxford University Press.

Davies, Howard. 2010. *The Financial Crisis: Who Is to Blame?* Cambridge, UK: Polity Press, pp. 197–201.

Davies, Nick. 2009. *Flat Earth News, An Award-Winning Reporter Exposes Falsehood, Distortion and Propaganda in the Global Media.* London: Vintage books.

Davis, Aeron. 2005. "Media Effects and the Elite Audience: A Study of Communication and the London Stock Exchange." *European Journal of Communication,* 20(3): 303–326.

Davis, James Allan, and Tom W. Smith. 2002. *General Social Surveys, 1972–2002.* Chicago, IL: National Opinion Research Center.

De Franco, Gus, Hai Lu, and Florin P. Vasvari. 2007. "Wealth Transfer Effects of Analysts' Misleading Behavior." *Journal of Accounting Research,* 45(1): 71–110.

De la Vega, Joseph. 1688. *Confusion de Confusiones.* New York: Marketplace Books, 1996.

De Long, J. Bradford, Andrei Shleifer, Lawrence H. Summers, and Robert J. Waldmann. 1990. "Positive Feedback Investment Strategies and Destabilizing Speculation." *Journal of Finance,* 45(2): 379–395.

DeAngelo, H., L. DeAngelo, and D. Skinner. 1996. "Reversal of fortune: Dividend signaling and the disappearance of sustained earnings growth." *Journal of Financial Economics,* 40: 341–371.

Dechow, Patricia M., Amy P. Hutton, and Richard G. Sloan. 2000. "The Relation between Analysts' Forecasts of Long-Term Earnings Growth and Stock Price Performance Following Equity Offering." *Contemporary Accounting Research,* 17(1): 1–32.

Dechow, P., and D. Skinner. 2000. "Earnings management: Reconciling the views of accounting academics, practitioners, and regulators." *Accounting Horizon,* 14 (2): 235–250.

Dechow, P., and R. Sloan. 1991. "Executive incentives and the horizon problem: An empirical investigation." *Journal of Accounting and Economics,* 14(1): 51–89.

Dechow, P., R. Sloan, and A. Sweeney. 1996. "Causes and consequences of earnings manipulation: An analysis of firms subject to enforcement actions by the SEC." *Contemporary Accounting Research,* 13(1): 1–36.

DeFond, M., M. Hung, and R. Trezevant. 2007. "Investor Protection and the Information Content of Annual Earnings Announcements: International Evidence." *Journal of Accounting and Economics,* 43(1): 37–67.

Degeorge, F., J. Patel, and R. Zeckhauser. 1999. "Earnings Management to Exceed Thresholds." *Journal of Business,* 72(1): 1–33.

Delort, Jean-Yves, Bavani Arunasalam, Maria Milosavljevic, and Henry Leung. 2009. "The Impact of Manipulation in Internet Stock Message Boards." Available at SSRN: http://ssrn.com/abstract=1497883. Accessed December 9, 2010.

Demirer, Rıza, Daigo Gubo, and Ali M. Kutan. 2007. "An Analysis of Cross-Country Herd Behavior in Stock Markets: A Regional Perspective." *Working paper,* Southern Illinois University Edwardsville.

DeNeve, Kristina M., and Harris Cooper. 1998. "The happy personality: A meta-analysis of 137 personality traits and subjective well-being." *Psychological Bulletin,* 124: 197–229.

Dewally, Michael. 2003. "Internet investment advice: Investing with a rock of salt." *Financial Analysts Journal,* 59(4): 65–77.

Di Tella, Rafael, and Robert MacCulloch. 2008. "Gross national happiness as an answer to the Easterlin Paradox?" *Journal of Development Economics,* 86(1): 22–42.

Di Tella, Rafael, Robert MacCulloch, and Andrew J. Oswald, 2001. "Preferences over Inflation and Unemployment: Evidence from Surveys of Happiness." *American Economic Review,* 91(1): 335–341.

Di Tella, Rafael, Robert MacCulloch, and Andrew J. Oswald. 2003. "The Macroeconomics of Happiness." *Review of Economics and Statistics,* 85(4): 793–809.

Diamonte, R., J. Liew, and R. Stevens. 1996. "Political risk in emerging and developed markets." *Financial Analysts Journal,* 52(3): 71–76.

Dick, Dennis. 2010. "HFT Market Making May Lead to a Crash." *Bright Trading LLC,* January 4. Available at: www.stocktrading.com/HFT.htm. Accessed April 9, 2011.

Diener, Ed, and Micaela Chan. 2010. "Happy people live longer: Subjective well-being contributes to health and longevity." *Journal of Applied Psychology: Health and Well-Being.* Forthcoming.

Diener, Ed, and R. J. Larsen. 1984. "Temporal stability and cross-situational consistency of affective, behavioral, and cognitive responses." *Journal of Personality and Social Psychology,* 47: 871–883.

Diener, E., and M. E. P. Seligman. 2002. "Very Happy People." *Psychological Science,* 13(1): 81–84.

Diener, E., and M. E. P. Seligman. 2004. "Beyond Money toward an Economy of Well-Being." *Psychological Science in the Public Interest,* 5(1): 1–31.

Diener, Ed, Eunkook M. Suh, Richard E. Lucas, and Heidi L. Smith. 1999. "Subjective Weil-Being: Three Decades of Progress." *Psychological Bulletin,* 125(2): 276–302.

Dohrenwend, Bruce P. 2000. "The Role of Adversity and Stress in Psychopathology: Some Evidence and Its Implications for Theory and Research." *Journal of Health and Social Behavior,* 41(1): 1–19.

Domowitz, Ian, Jack Glen, and Ananth Madhavan. 2001. "Liquidity, volatility and equity trading costs across countries and over time." *International Finance,* 4: 221–255.

Dooley, David, and Ralph Catalano. 1980. "Economic change as a cause of behavioral disorder." *Psychological Bulletin,* 87(3): 450–468.

Drakos, Konstantinos. 2004. "Terrorism-induced structural shifts in financial risk: Airline stocks in the aftermath of September 11th." *European Journal of Political Economy,* 20(2): 435–446.

Du, Julan, and Shang-Jin Wei. 2004. "Does insider trading raise market volatility?" *The Economic Journal,* October, 114(498): 916–942.

DuCharme, L. 1994. "IPOs: Private information and earnings management." *Ph.D. dissertation,* The University of Washington.

DuCharme, L. L., P. H. Malatesta, and S. E. Sefcik. 2001. "Earnings management: IPO valuation and subsequent performance." *Journal of Accounting, Auditing and Finance,* 16: 369–396.

DuCharme, L. L., P. H. Malatesta, and S. E. Sefcik. 2004. "Earnings Management, Stock Issues, and Shareholder Lawsuits." *Journal of Financial Economics,* 71(1): 27–40.

Dugar, Amitabh, and Siva Nathan. 1995. "The Effect of Investment Banking Relationships on Financial Analysts' Earnings Forecasts and Investment Recommendations." *Contemporary Accounting Research,* 12(1): 131–160.

Duhigg, Charles. 2009. "Stock Traders Find Speed Pays, in Milliseconds." *New York Times,* July 23.

Durkheim, E. 2006. *On Suicide* (translated by Robin Buss). New York: Penguin Books.

Dyck, Alexander, Adair Morse, and Luigi Zingales. 2009. "Who Blows the Whistle on Corporate Fraud?" *Journal of Finance,* forthcoming.

Dyck, Alexander, and Luigi Zingales. 2003. "The Media and Asset Prices." *Working paper,* Harvard Business School.

Dymke, Björn M., and Andreas Walter. 2007. "Insider Trading in Germany—Do Corporate Insiders Exploit Inside Information?" *Working paper,* University of Tüebingen.

Easley, David, Marcos Mailoc Lopez de Prado, and Maureen O'Hara. 2010. "The Microstructure of the 'Flash Crash': Flow Toxicity, Liquidity Crashes and the

Probability of Informed Trading." *Journal of Portfolio Management,* 37(2): 118–128.

Easley, David, Maureen O'Hara, and Liyan Yang. 2011. "Differential Access to Price Information in Financial Markets." Available at SSRN: http://ssrn.com/abstract=1787029. Accessed April 6, 2011.

Easterbrook, Frank H. 1986. "Monopoly, manipulation, and the regulation of futures markets." *Journal of Business,* 59(2), Part 2: S103–S127.

Easterlin, Richard A. 2003. " Explaining happiness." *Proceedings of the National Academy of Sciences,* 100(19): 11176–11183. A substantially expanded version is "Building a better theory of well-being," Chapter 1 In: Bruni, Luigino, and Pier Luigi Porta. (Eds.) 2005. *Economics and Happiness. Framing the Analysis.* Oxford, England: Oxford University Press.

Easterlin, Richard A. 2010. *Happiness, Growth, and the Life Cycle.* (Edited by Holger Hinte and Klaus F. Zimmermann.) New York: Oxford University Press.

Easterlin, Richard A., Laura Angelescu McVey, Malgorzata Switek, Onnicha Sawangfa, and Jacqueline Smith Zweig. 2010. "The Happiness-Income Paradox Revisited." *Proceedings of National Academy of Sciences of the United States of America,* 107(52): 22463–22468.

Easton, Mark. 2006. "Britain's happiness in decline." *BBC News Home Editor,* Tuesday, May 2, 20: 45 GMT 21:45 UK.

Eccles, Robert, and Dwight Crane. 1988. *Doing Deals: Investment Banks at Work.* Boston, MA: Harvard Business School Press.

Ehrhardts, J. J., W. E. Saris, and R. Veenhoven. 2000. "Stability of life-satisfaction over time." *Journal of Happiness Studies,* 1(2): 177–205.

Eisenberg, P., and P. F. Lazarsfeld. 1938. "The psychological effects of unemployment." *Psychological Bulletin,* 35(6): 358–390.

Elliott, J., D. Morse, and G. Richardson. 1984. "The Association between Insider Trading and Information Announcements." *Rand Journal of Economics,* 15(4): 521–536.

Ellis, Charles D. 2009. "Coming of Age: A Brief History of the Changing Role of the Securities Analyst." *The Investing Professional—The Journal of the New York Society of Security Analysts.* Available at: www.theinvestmentprofessional.com/vol_2_no_1/coming-of-age.html. Accessed September 6, 2010.

Emery, G. D., R. A. Steer, and A. T. Beck. 1981. "Depression, Hopelessness and Suicidal Intent Among Heroin Addicts." *Substance Use & Misuse,* 16(3): 425–429.

Engelberg, Joseph, and Chris Parsons. 2009. "The Causal Impact of Media in Financial Markets." *Journal of Finance,* forthcoming.

Engelberg, Joseph, Caroline Sasseville, and Jared Williams. 2006. "Is the Market Mad? Evidence from *Mad Money.*" *Working paper,* Northwestern University.

Eurobarometer. 2007. Database with all waves since 1973. Available from: http://ec.europa.eu/public_opinion/index_en.htm.

Fair, Ray C. 2002. "Events That Shook the Market." *Journal of Business,* 75(4): 713–731.

Fan, E. 2003. "SARS: Economic Impact and Implications."*ERD Policy Brief No. 15,* Economics and Research Department, Asian Development Bank, Manila.

Fang, Lily H., and Joel Peress. 2008. "Media Coverage and the Cross-Section of Stock Returns." *AFA 2009 San Francisco Meetings Paper.* Available at SSRN: http://ssrn.com/abstract=971202. Accessed April 15, 2011.

Farmer, J. D., L. Gillemot, F. Lillo, S. Mike, and A. Sen. 2004. "What really causes large price changes?" *Quantitative Finance,* 4: 383–397.

Fehle, Frank, Sergey Tsyplakov, and Vladimir Zdorovtsov. 2005. "Can Companies Influence Investor Behaviour through Advertising? Super Bowl Commercials and Stock Returns." *European Financial Management,* 11(5): 625–647.

Feng, L., and M. Seasholes. 2004. "Correlated trading and location." *Journal of Finance,* 59: 2117–2144.

Financial Services Authority (FSA). 2009. "FSA wins market abuse case against Winterflood." *FSA/PN/046/2009,* April 2. Available at: www.fsa.gov.uk/pages/Library/Communication/PR/2009/046.shtml. Accessed September 15, 2009.

Financial Stability Forum (FSF). 2000. *Report of the Working Group on Highly Leveraged Institutions.* April 5, Basel, Switzerland: Financial Stability Board.

Financial Times. 1987. "Insider trading." *Section I: Letters,* February 26, p. 21.

Finnerty, Joseph E. 1976. "Insiders and market efficiency." *Journal of Finance,* 31(4): 1141–1148.

Fisch, Jill E. 2007a. "Fiduciary duties and the analyst scandals." *Alabama Law Review,* 58(5): 1083–1102.

Fisch, Jill E. 2007b. "Does Analyst Independence Sell Investors Short?" *UCLA Law Review,* 39(1): 55–114.

Fisch, Jill E. 2010. *Private communication.*

Fisch, Jill E., and Hillary A. Sale. 2003. "The Securities Analyst as Agent: Rethinking the Regulation of Analysts." *Iowa Law Review,* 88: 1035–1098.

Fishel, Dan, and David Ross. 1991. "Should the law prohibit 'manipulation' in financial markets?" *Harvard Law Review,* 105: 503–553.

Fishman, M. J., and K. Hagerty. 1995. "The mandatory disclosure of trades and market liquidity." *Review of Financial Studies,* 8: 637–676.

Fong, Kingsley Y. L., David R. Gallagher, and Adrian D. Lee. 2009. "Who Win and Who Lose Among Individual Investors?" Available at SSRN: http://ssrn.com/abstract=1343519. Accessed February 15, 2009.

Forelle, Charles, and James Bandler. 2006. "The Perfect Payday." *The Wall Street Journal,* March 18.

Fox, J. 1997. "Learn to play the earnings game and Wall Street will love you." *Fortune,* March 31, pp. 77–80.

Francis, Jennifer, J. Douglas Hanna, and Donna R. Philbrick. 1997. "Management communications with securities analysts." *Journal of Accounting and Economics,* 24(3): 363–394.

Francis, Jennifer, and Donna R. Philbrick. 1993. "Analysts' Decisions as Products of a Multi-Task Environment." *Journal of Accounting Research,* 35(2): 216–230.

Francis, Jennifer, and Leonard Soffer. 1997. "The Relative Informativeness of Analysts' Stock Recommendations and Earnings Forecast Revisions." *Journal of Accounting Research,* 35(2): 193–211.

Francis, Jennifer, Mohan Venkatachalam, and Yun Zhang. 2005. "Do Short Sellers Convey Information about Changes in Fundamentals or Risk?" *Working Paper.* Available at SSRN: http://ssrn.com/abstract=815668. Accessed December 26, 2010.

Frankenberg, Elizabeth, Duncan Thomas, and Kathleen Beegle. 1999. " The Real Costs of Indonesia's Economic Crisis: Preliminary Findings from the Indonesia Family Life Surveys."*RAND Working Paper No. 99–04.* Santa Monica, California.

Freund, S., R. D. Fuerman, and L. Shaw. 2002. "Fraudulent audited annual financial statements in post-PSLRA private securities class actions: Determinants of auditor litigation." *Journal of Forensic Accounting,* 3(1): 69–90.

Frey, Bruno S., and Alois Stutzer. 1999. "Measuring Preferences by Subjective Well-Being." *Journal of Institutional and Theoretical Economics,* 155: 765.

Frey, Bruno S., and Alois Stutzer. 2002. "What can economists learn from Happiness research?" *Journal of Economic Literature,* 40(6): 402–435.

Frey, Bruno S., in collaboration with Alois Stutzer, Matthias Benz, Stephan Meier, Simon Luechinger, and Christine Benesch. 2008. *Happiness. A Revolution in Economics. Munich Lecture in Economics.* (Edited by Hans-Werner Sinn.) Cambridge, MA: The MIT Press.

Frieder, Laura, and Jonathan Zittrain. 2008. "Spam Works: Evidence from Stock Touts and Corresponding Market Activity." *Hastings Communications and Entertainment Law Journal (Comm/Ent),* 30(3): 479–520.

Friederich, Sylvain, Alan Gregory, John Matatko, and Ian Tonks. 2002. "Short-run Returns around the Trades of Corporate Insiders on the London Stock Exchange." *European Financial Management,* 8(1): 7–30.

Friedlan, John M. 1994. "Accounting choices of issues of initial public offerings." *Contemporary Accounting Research,* 11(1): 1–32.

Friedman, Jed, and Duncan Thomas. 2007. "Psychological Health Before, During, and After an Economic Crisis: Results from Indonesia, 1993–2000." *Policy Research Working Paper* 4386, World Bank.

Fuerman, Ross D. 2006. "Comparing the Auditor Quality of Arthur Andersen to That of the Big 4." *Accounting and the Public Interest,* 6(1): 136–161.

Fuller, Joseph, and Michael C. Jensen. 2010. "Just Say No to Wall Street: Putting a Stop to the Earnings Game." *Journal of Applied Corporate Finance,* 22(1): 59–63.

G-20. 2009. Available at: www.g20.org/. Accessed August 13, 2009.

Gaa, Charles. 2008. "Good News Is No News: Asymmetric Inattention and the Neglected Firm Effect."*Working Paper,* University of British Columbia.

Gabaix, Xavier, Parameswaran Gopikrishnan, Vasiliki Plerou, and H. Eugene Stanley. 2006. "Institutional Investors and Stock Market Volatility." *Quarterly Journal of Economics,* 121(2): 461–504.

Gadarowski, Christopher. 2002. "Financial Press Coverage and Expected Stock Returns." *EFMA 2002 London Meetings.* Available at SSRN: http://ssrn.com/abstract=267311. Accessed March 8, 2011.

Galbraith, John Kenneth. 1979. *The Great Crash of 1929.* Boston, MA: Houghton Mifflin Company.

Gallant, A. Ronald, Peter E. Rossi, and George Tauchen. 1992. "Stock Prices and Volume." *Review of Financial Studies*, 5(2): 199–242.

Gallup-Healthway mood data: www.gallup.com/.

Gan, L., and D. Li. 2001. "Using American Depository Receipts to Identify the Effect of Price Limits." *Unpublished paper.*

Ganzini, Linda, Bentson H. McFarland, and David Cutler. 1990. "Prevalence of mental disorders after catastrophic financial loss." *Journal of Nervous and Mental Disease,* 178: 680–685.

Garfinkel, Jon A. 1997. "New evidence on the effects of federal regulations on insider trading: The Insider Trading and Securities Fraud Enforcement Act (ITSFEA)." *Journal of Corporate Finance,* 3(2): 89–111.

Gasparino, Charles. 2002. "Merrill Lynch will negotiate with Spitzer." *The Wall Street Journal,* April 15, C1.

Gasparino, Charles. 2005. *Blood on the Street: The Sensational Inside Story of How Wall Street Analysts Duped a Generation of Investors.* New York: The Free Press.

Gaver, J., and J. Paterson. 1999. "Managing insurance company financial statements to meet regulatory and tax reporting goals." *Contemporary Accounting Research,* 16(2): 207–241.

Givoly, D., and D. Palmon. 1985. "Insider Trading and the Exploitation of Inside Information: Some Empirical Evidence." *Journal of Business,* 58(1): 69–87.

Glaberson, W. 1995. "Press." *New York Times,* May 1, D-9.

Global Financial Data (GFD). 2009. A comprehensive economic and financial time-series database covering 150 countries and 6,500 different data series.

Goedhart, Marc, Rishi Raj, and Abhishek Saxena. 2010. "Equity analysts: Still too bullish: After almost a decade of stricter regulation, analysts' earnings forecasts continue to be excessively optimistic." *McKinsey Quarterly*, April.

Golding, T. 2003. *The City: Inside the Great Expectations Machine, 2nd ed.* London: FT/Prentice-Hall.

Gomber, Peter, Björn Arndt, Marco Lutat, and Tim Uhle. 2011. "High-Frequency Trading." *Working paper,* Goethe Universität.

Goyal, Ashima. 2005. "Regulation and De-regulation of the Stock Market in India." Available at SSRN: http://ssrn.com/abstract=609322. Accessed October 3, 2009.

Graham, Carol. 2009. *Happiness Around the World. The Paradox of Happy Peasants and Miserable Millionaires.* Oxford, England: Oxford University Press.

Graham, Carol, and Stefano Pettinato. 2002. "Happiness and Hardship: Opportunity and Insecurity." In: *New Market Economies.* Washington, DC: Brookings Institute Press.

Graham, J. R. 1999. "Herding Among Investment Newsletters: Theory and Evidence." *Journal of Finance,* 54(1): 237–268.

Graham, J. R., C. R. Harvey, and S. Rajgopal. 2005. "The economic implications of corporate financial reporting." *Journal of Accounting and Economics,* 40(1): 3–73.

Greene, Jason, and Scott Smart. 1999. "Liquidity provision and noise trading: Evidence from the 'Investment Dartboard' column." *Journal of Finance,* 54(5): 1885–1899.

Greenspan, Alan. 2002. "Federal Reserve Board's semiannual monetary policy report to the Congress." *Testimony before the Committee on Banking, Housing, and Urban Affairs,* U.S. Senate, July 16.

Grinblatt, M., and M. Keloharju. 2000. "The investment behavior and performance of various investor types: A study of Finland's unique data set." *Journal of Financial Economics,* 55(1): 43–67.

Groysberg, Boris, Paul M. Healy, and David Maber. 2008. "What Drives Sell-Side Analyst Compensation at High-Status Banks?" *Working paper,* Harvard Business School.

Grullon, Gustavo, George Kanatas, and James P. Weston. 2004. "Advertising, Breadth of Ownership, and Liquidity." *Review of Financial Studies,* 17(2): 439–461.

Gunny, Katherine. 2005. "What are the consequences of real earnings management?" *Working Paper,* University of California at Berkeley.

Gurun, Umit G., and Alexander W. Butler. 2010. "Don't Believe the Hype: Local Media Slant, Local Advertising, and Firm Value." *AFA 2010 Atlanta Meetings Paper.* Available at SSRN: http://ssrn.com/abstract=1333765.

Hall, B., and J. Liebman. 1998. "Are CEOs Really Paid Like Bureaucrats?" *Quarterly Journal of Economics,* 113: 653–691.

Hamilton, James, and Joseph Kalt. 1987. *A Summary of the Report to the Foundation for American Communications and the Ford Foundation.* Cambridge, Massachusetts.

Hamilton, James T., and Richard Zeckhauser. 2004. "Media Coverage of CEOs: Who? What? Where? When? Why?" *Working paper,* Harvard University.

Han, Ki C., and David Y. Suk. 1996. "Stock prices and the Barron's 'Research Reports' column." *Journal of Financial and Strategic Decisions,* 9(3): 27–32.

Hand, J. 1989. "Did firms undertake debt-equity swaps for an accounting paper profit or true financial gain." *The Accounting Review* 64(4): 587–623.

Hart, Oliver D. 1977. "On the Profitability of Speculation." *Quarterly Journal of Economics,* 91(4): 579–597.

Harvard University Gazette. 2009. "Health, the Harvard Way." December 17, 2009–February 3, 2010.

Hasbrouck, Joel. 1991. "Measuring the Information Content of Stock Trades." *Journal of Finance,* 46(1): 179–207.

Hasbrouck, Joel, and Gideon Saar. 2011. "Low-Latency Trading." *Johnson School Research Paper Series No. 35–2010.* Available at SSRN: http://ssrn.com/abstract=1695460.

Hausman, J., A. Lo, and C. MacKinlay. 1992. "An Ordered Probit Analysis of Transaction Stock Prices." *Journal of Financial Economics,* 31: 319–379.

He, Zhongzhi (Lawrence), and Dongwei Su. 2009. " Price Manipulation and Industry Momentum: Evidence from the Chinese Stock Market." Available at SSRN: http://ssrn.com/abstract=1393505. Accessed December 1, 2010.

Healy, Paul M. 1985. "The Effect of Bonus Schemes on Accounting Decisions." *Journal of Accounting and Economics,* 7(1): 85–107.

Healy, P. M., and K. G. Palepu. 2003. "The Fall of Enron." *Journal of Economic Perspectives,* 17(1): 3–26.

Healy, P. M., and J. Wahlen. 1999. "A Review of Earnings Management Literature and Its Implications for Standard Setting." *Accounting Horizons,* 13: 35–384.

Hemingway, H., and M. Marmot. 1999. "Psychological factors in the aetiology and prognosis of coronary heart disease: Systematic review of prospective cohort studies." *British Medical Journal,* 318: 1460–1467.

Heninger, W. G. 2001. "The association between auditor litigation and abnormal accruals." *Accounting Review,* 76(1): 111–126.

Herbert, T. B., and S. Cohen. 1993. "Depression and immunity: A meta-analytic review." *Psychological Bulletin,* 113: 472–486.

Herrmann, D., T. Inoue, and W. Thomas. 2003. "The sale of assets to manage earnings in Japan." *Journal of Accounting Research,* 41(1): 89–108.

Hillier, D., and A. P. Marshall. 2002. "Are trading bans effective? Exchange regulation and corporate insider transactions around earnings announcements." *Journal of Corporate Finance,* 8(4): 393–410.

Hillion, P., and M. Suominen. 2004. "The manipulation of closing prices." *Journal of Financial Markets,* 7: 351–375.

Hiltzik, Michael. 2010. "Growth of electronic trading a major cause of stock market free fall." *Los Angeles Times,* May 9.

Hirshleifer, David, and Siew Hong Teoh. 2009. "Thought and Behavior Contagion in Capital Markets." Chapter 1 of *Handbook of Financial Markets: Dynamics and Evolution,* Schenk-Hoppé, Klaus Reiner, and Thorsten Hens. (Eds.) In: Ziemba, William. (Ed.) *Handbooks in Finance* series. New York: Elsevier/North-Holland, pp. 1–56.

Hittle, Byron D. 2001. "An Uphill Battle: The Difficulty of Deterring and Detecting Perpetrators of Internet Stock Fraud."*J.D. Dissertation,* Indiana University School of Law.

Holthausen, Robert, Richard Leftwich, and David Mayers. 1987. "The effect of large block transactions on security prices: A cross-sectional analysis." *Journal of Financial Economics,* 19: 237–268.

Hong, H., and J. Kubik. 2003. "Analyzing the analysts: Career concerns and biased earnings forecasts." *Journal of Finance,* 58(1): 313–351.

Hong, Harris, and Jeremy S. Stein. 1999. "A Unified Theory of Underreaction, Momentum on Trading, and Overreaction in Asset Markets." *Journal of Finance,* 54(6): 2143–2184.

Hong Kong Securities and Futures Commission (HKSFC). 2009. Available at: www .sfc.hk/sfcPressRelease/EN/sfcEnforceNewsServlet. Accessed August 23, 2009.

House, James S. 1987. "Chronic Stress and Chronic Disease in Life and Work: Conceptual and Methodological Issues." *Work and Stress,* 1(2): 129–134.

House, James S. 2002. "Understanding Social Factors and Inequalities in Health: 20th Century Progress and 21st Century Prospects." *Journal of Health and Social Behavior,* 43(2): 125–142.

Hribar, P., N. Jenkins, and W. Johnson. 2006. "Stock repurchases as an earnings management device." *Journal of Accounting and Economics,* 41(1): 3–27.

Hu, Bill, Thomas McInish, and Li Zeng. 2009. "The CAN-SPAM Act of 2003 and stock spam emails." *Financial Services Review,* 18: 87–104.

Huang, Yu Chuan, Roger C. Y. Chen, and Yao Jen Cheng. 2006. "Stock manipulation and its impact on market quality." *Working paper,* National Kaohsiung First University of Science and Technology, Kaohsiung, Taiwan, ROC.

Huberman, Gur. 2001. "Familiarity Breeds Investment." *Review of Financial Studies,* 14(3): 659–680.

Huberman, G., and T. Regev. 2001. "Contagious Speculation and a Cure for Cancer: A Nonevent That Made Stock Prices Soar." *Journal of Finance,* 56: 387–396.

Huddart, S., J. Hughes, and C. Levine. 2001. "Public disclosure and dissimulation of insider trades." *Econometrica,* 69: 665–681.

Hung, Mingyi, and Robert Trezevant. 2003. "Insider Trading and Corporate Governance Structure: Evidence from Southeast Asia." Available at SSRN: http://ssrn.com/abstract=374422. Accessed September 3, 2010.

Hunt, A., S. Moyer, and T. Shevlin. 1996. "Managing interacting accounting measures to meet multiple objectives: A study of LIFO firms." *Journal of Accounting and Economics,* 21: 339–374.

Hutcheson, F. 2002. *An Essay on the Nature and Conduct of the Passions and Affections.* (Edited by Aaron Garrett.) Indianapolis, IN: Liberty Fund.

Hutton, Amy P. 2002. "The Role of Sell-side Analysts in the Enron Debacle." *Tuck School of Business Working Paper No. 03-17.* Available at SSRN: http://ssrn.com/abstract=404020. Accessed August 7, 2010.

Hwang, Soosung, and Mark Salmon. 2001. "A New Measure of Herding and Empirical Evidence." *Working paper,* City University London.

Iati, Robert. 2009. "High Frequency Trading Technology," *TABB Group.*

Internet World Stats. 2010. Available at: www.internetworldstats.com. Accessed December 13, 2010.

IOSCO. 2000. "Investigating and prosecuting market manipulation." *Technical Committee.* Madrid, Spain: International Organization of Securities Commissions.

Irvine, Paul. 2001. "Do Analysts Generate Trade for Their Firms? Evidence from the Toronto Stock Exchange." *Journal of Accounting and Economics,* 30(2): 209–226.

Irvine, Paul. 2004. "Analysts' forecasts and brokerage-firm trading." *The Accounting Review,* 79: 125–149.

Irvine, P., M. Lipson, and A. Puckett. 2007. "Tipping." *Review of Financial Studies,* 20: 741–768.

Jackson, Andrew R. 2005. "Trade generation, reputation, and sell-side analysts." *Journal of Finance,* 60: 673–717.

Jackson, S., and W. Wilcox. 2000. "Do managers grant sales price reductions to avoid losses and declines in earnings and sales?" *Quarterly Journal of Business and Economics,* 39(4): 3–20.

Jacobs, Stevenson. 2010. "Letter: Lehman Accounting Tricks Possibly Illegal." *Associated Press,* New York, March 19.

Jaffe, Jeffrey. 1974. "The Effect of Regulation Changes on Insider Trading." *Bell Journal of Economics and Management Science,* 5(1): 93–121.

Jaggi, Bikki, and Judy Tsui. 2007. "Insider Trading, Earnings Management and Corporate Governance: Empirical Evidence Based on Hong Kong Firms." *Journal of International Financial Management & Accounting,* 18(3): 192–222.

Jagolinzer, Alan D. 2009. "SEC Rule 10b5-1 and Insiders' Strategic Trade." *Management Science,* 55(2): 224–239.

Japan Securities and Exchange Surveillance Commission (JSESC). 2009. Available at: www.sfc.hk/sfcPressRelease/EN/sfcEnforceNewsServlet. Accessed August 29, 2009.

Jarrell, G., and A. Poulsen. 1989. "Stock trading before the announcement of tender offers: Insider trading or market anticipation?" *Journal of Law, Economics, and Organization,* 5(2): 225–248.

Jarrow, Robert A. 1992. "Market Manipulation, Bubbles, Corners, and Short Squeezes." *Journal of Financial and Quantitative Analysis,* 27(3): 311–336.

Jensen, Michael C. 2005. "The Puzzling State of Low-Integrity Relations between Managers and Capital Markets" (PDF file of slides). *Harvard NOM Working Paper No. 06-04.* Available at SSRN: http://ssrn.com/abstract=783604. Accessed August 1, 2010.

Jiang, Xiao Q., and Mir A. Zaman. 2007. "Aggregate Insider Trading and the Predictability of Market Returns: Contrarian Strategy or Managerial Timing?" Available at SSRN: http://ssrn.com/abstract=970987. Accessed July 17, 2010.

John, K., and R. Narayanan. 1997. "Market manipulation and the role of insider trading regulations." *Journal of Business,* 70: 217–247.

Johnson, W., and R. F. Krueger. 2006. "How Money Buys Happiness: Genetic and Environmental Processes Linking Finances and Life Satisfaction." *Journal of Personality and Social Psychology,* 90(4): 680–691.

Joshi, Amit, and Dominique M. Hanssens. 2004. "Advertising Spending and Market Capitalization." *Working paper,* UCLA.

Kahle, Kathleen. 2000. "Insider trading and the long-run performance of new security issues." *Journal of Corporate Finance,* 6(1): 25–54.

Kahneman, Daniel, Ed Diener, and Norbert Schwartz. (Eds.). 1999. *Foundations of hedonic psychology: Scientific perspectives on enjoyment and suffering.* New York: Russell Sage Foundation.

Kahneman, Daniel, Alan Krueger, David Schkade, Norbert Schwarz, and Arthur Stone. 2004. "A Survey method of categorizing daily life experience: The day reconstruction method." *Science,* 306(5702): 1776–1780.

Kahneman, Daniel, Peter Wakker, and Rakesh Sarin. 1997. "Back to Bentham? Explorations of Experienced Utility." *Quarterly Journal of Economics,* 112(2): 375–405.

Kaiser. 2007. "Giving voice to the people of New Orleans: The Kaiser Post-Katrina Baseline Survey." *The Henry J. Kaiser Family Foundation.* May 2007.

Kaptchuk, Ted J., O.M.D. 2000. *The Web That Has No Weaver. Understanding Chinese Medicine.* Contemporary Books.

Karpoff, J. M. 1987. "The Relation between Price Change and Trading Volume: A Survey." *Journal of Financial and Quantitative Analysis,* 22(1): 109–126.

Karpoff, Jonathan M., and Daniel Lee. 1991. "Insider trading before new issue announcements." *Financial Management,* 20(1): 18–26.

Karpoff, Jonathan M., D. Scott Lee, and Gerald S. Martin. 2008. "The cost to firms of cooking the books." *Journal of Financial and Quantitative Analysis,* 43(3): 581–611.

Kasl, Stanislav, and Beth A. Jones. 2000. "The Impact of Job Loss and Retirement on Health." In: Berkman, L. F., and I. Kawachi. (Eds.) *Social Epidemiology.* New York: Oxford University Press, pp. 118–137.

Kasznik, Ron, and Maureen F. McNichols. 2002. "Does Meeting Earnings Expectations Matter? Evidence from Analyst Forecast Revisions and Share Prices." *Journal of Accounting Research,* 40(3): 727–759.

Ke, Bin, Steven Huddart, and Kathy Petroni. 2003. "What insiders know about future earnings and how they use it: Evidence from insider trades." *Journal of Accounting and Economics,* 35: 315–346.

Kedia, S., and T. Philippon. 2009. "The economics of fraudulent accounting." *Review of Financial Studies,* 22(6): 2169–2199.

Keim, Donald, and Ananth Madhavan. 1996. "The Upstairs Market for Large-Block Trades: Analysis and Measurement of Price Effects." *Review of Financial Studies,* 9(1): 1–36.

Keogh-Brown, M. R., and R. D. Smith. 2008. "The economic impact of SARS: How does the reality match the predictions?" *Health Policy,* 88(1): 110–120.

Keown, A., and J. Pinkerton. 1981. "Merger announcements and insider trading activity: An empirical investigation." *Journal of Finance,* 36: 855–869.

Kessler, Ronald C. 2006. "Overview of Baseline Survey Results: Hurricane Katrina Community Advisory Group." August 29. *Hurricane Katrina Community Advisory Group.* Available at: www.hurricanekatrina.med.harvard.edu. Accessed on September 17, 2010.

Khwaja, Asim I., and Atif Mian. 2005. "Unchecked Intermediaries: Price Manipulation in an Emerging Stock Market." *Journal of Financial Economics,* 78(1): 203–241.

Kiecolt-Glaser, J. K., L. McGuire, T. F. Robles, and R. Glaser. 2002. "Emotions, morbidity, and mortality: New perspectives from psychoneuroimmunology." *Annual Review of Psychology,* 53: 83–107.

Kim, Harold Y., and Jianping P. Mei. 2001. "What makes the stock market jump? An analysis of political risk on Hong Kong stock returns." *Journal of International Money and Finance,* 20(7): 1003–1016.

Kim, K. A., and S. G. Rhee. 1997. "Price Limit Performance: Evidence from the Tokyo Stock Exchange." *Journal of Finance,* 52: 885–901.

Kim, W., and S. Wei. 1999. "Offshore Investment Funds: Monsters in Emerging Markets." *NBER Working Paper No. 7133,* Cambridge, Massachusetts.

Kim, Yong H., and J. Jimmy Yang. 2004. "What Makes Circuit Breakers Attractive to Financial Markets? A Survey." *Financial Markets, Institutions & Instruments,* 13(3): 109–146.

Kindleberger, Charles P. 2000. *Manias, Panics and Crashes: A History of Financial Crises.* New York: John Wiley & Sons.

Kirchfeld, Aaron, and Tony Czuczka. 2009. "Porsche Raided on Suspicion of Market Manipulation (Update2)." *Bloomberg.* August 20, 12: 33 EDT. Available at: www.bloomberg.com/apps/news?pid=20601085&sid=a8sCW6BT5MQc. Accessed September 15, 2009.

Kirilenko, A., A. Kyle, M. Samadi, and T. Tuzun. 2010. "The Flash Crash: The Impact of High Frequency Trading on an Electronic Market." *Working paper,* University of Maryland.

Kiymaz, H. 1999. "The effects of 'stock market gossip' on stock prices: The ISE experience." *Iktisat, Isletme ve Finans,* 164: 20–29.

Kolata, Gina. 1998. "Hope in the lab: A special report; a cautious awe greets drugs that eradicate tumors in mice." *New York Times,* May 3, 1: 1.

Konana, Prabhudev, and Sridhar Balasubramanian. 2005. "The Social-Economic-Psychological (SEP) Model of Technology Adoption and Usage: An Application to Online Investing." *Decision Support Systems,* 19(3): 505–524.

Korczak, Adriana, Piotr Korczak, and Meziane Lasfer. 2007. "To Trade or Not to Trade: The Strategic Trading of Insiders around News Announcements." *Working paper,* Manchester Business School.

Krantz, D. S., and M. K. McCeney. 2002. "Effects of psychological and social factors on organic disease: A critical assessment of research on coronary heart disease." *Annual Review of Psychology,* 53: 341–369.

Kraus, Alan, and Hans R. Stoll. 1972. "Price Impacts of Block Trading on the New York Stock Exchange." *Journal of Finance,* 27(3): 569–588.

Krigman, Laurie, Wayne H. Shaw, and Kent L. Womack. 2001. "Why do firms switch underwriters?" *Journal of Financial Economics,* 60(2–3): 245–284.

Kumar, A., and C. M. Lee. 2006. "Retail investor sentiment and return comovements." *Journal of Finance,* 61: 2451–2486.

Kumar, Praveen, and Duane J. Seppi. 1992. "Futures manipulation with 'cash settlement.' *Journal of Finance,* 47(4): 1485–1502.

Kurtz, Howard. 2000. *The Fortune Tellers: Inside Wall Street's Game of Money, Media and Manipulation.* New York: The Free Press.

Kyle, Albert S. 1984. "A theory of futures market manipulations." In: Anderson, R. W. (Ed.) *The Industrial Organization of Futures Markets.* Lexington, MA: Lexington Books.

Kyle, Albert S. 1985. "Continuous Auctions and Insider Trading." *Econometrica,* 53(6): 1315–1335.

Kyle, Albert S., and S. Viswanathan. 2008. "How to Define Illegal Price Manipulation." *American Economic Review,* 98(2): 274–279.

Lakonishok, J., and I. Lee. 2001. "Are insider trades informative?" *Review of Financial Studies,* 14(1): 79–111.

Lam, K., W. K. Li, and P. S. Wong. 1990. "Price Changes and Trading Volume Relationship in the Hong Kong Stock Market." *Asia Pacific Journal of Management,* 7, Special Issue: 25–42.

Lang, Larry H. P. 2004. *Manipulation.* Beijing: Oriental Press. (in Chinese)

Lattman, Peter. 2010. "Reviewing the Druckenmiller Decades." *New York Times,* August 18.

Lauricella, Tom. 2010. "Market Plunge Baffles Wall Street—Trading Glitch Suspected in 'Mayhem' as Dow Falls Nearly 1,000, Then Bounces." *The Wall Street Journal,* May 7.

Layard, Richard. 2005. *Happiness: Lessons from a New Science.* New York: Penguin Press.

Lazarus, Richard S. 2001. "Relational Meaning and Discrete Emotions," Chapter 3 in: Sceerer, Klaus R., Angela Schorr, and Tom Johnstone. (Eds.) *Appraisal Process in Emotion.* New York: Oxford University Press.

Lease, David. 2010. "The Economics of Microcap Manipulation." *Senior Thesis:* Northwestern University.

Lee, Charles M. C. 1992. "Earnings news and small traders." *Journal of Accounting and Economics,* 15(2–3): 265–302.

Lee, Chi-Wen Jevons, and Chang Liu. 2008. "Financial Analysts and Speculative Bubble in Emerging Stock Market." *Working paper,* pp. 1–45.

Lee, S. B., and K. J. Kim. 1995. "The Effect of Price Limits on Stock Price Volatility: Empirical Evidence in Korea." *Journal of Business Finance & Accounting,* 22: 257–267.

Leinweber, D., and A. Madhavan. 2001. "Three hundred years of stock market manipulation." *The Journal of Investing,* 10(7): 7–16.

Lenihan, B. 2010. "Confidence in Action." *A speech given at the "Confidence in Media" conference,* Dublin, September 24.

Leuz, C., D. Nanda, and P. Wysocki. 2003. "Earnings management and investor protection: An international comparison." *Journal of Financial Economics,* 69 (3): 505–527.

Lev, Baruch. 2003. "Corporate earnings: Facts and fiction." *Journal of Economic Perspectives,* 17(2): 27–50.

Levitt, Arthur. 1998. "The Numbers Game." *Speech at New York University,* September 28.

Levitt, Arthur. 2001. *The Washington Post,* June 13.

Li, Wei, and Steven Shuye Wang. 2010. "Daily institutional trades and stock price volatility in a retail investor dominated emerging market." *Journal of Financial Markets,* 13(4): 448–474.

Li, Xi, and Hans G. Heidle. 2004. "Information Leakage and Opportunistic Behavior before Analyst Recommendations: An Analysis of the Quoting Behavior of Nasdaq Market Makers." *AFA 2004 San Diego Meetings.* Available at SSRN: http://ssrn.com/abstract=423840. Accessed September 23, 2010.

Liang, B. 1999. "Price pressure: Evidence from the 'Dartboard' column." *Journal of Business,* 72(1): 119–134.

Lie, Erik. 2005. "On the Timing of CEO Stock Option Awards." *Management Science,* 51(5): 802–812.

Lin, Hsiou-wei, and Maureen F. McNichols. 1998. "Underwriting Relationships and Analysts' Forecasts and Investment Recommendations." *Journal of Accounting and Economics,* 25(1): 101–127.

Lin, Luke, and Chau-Jung Kuo. 2007. "Stock Recommendations and Analyst Conflicts of Interest: Evidence from the Taiwan Stock Market." *Web Journal of Chinese Management Review,* 10(2): 1–24.

Linciano, Nadia. 2003. "The Effectiveness of Insider Trading Regulation in Italy. Evidence from Stock-Price Run-Ups around Announcements of Corporate Control Transactions." *European Journal of Law and Economics,* 16(2): 199–218.

Liu, Pu, Stanley D. Smith, and Azmat A. Syed. 1990. "Stock price reactions to *The Wall Street Journal." Journal of Financial and Quantitative Analysis,* 25(3): 399–410.

Lloyd-Davies, Peter, and Michael Canes. 1978. "Stock Prices and the Publication of Second-Hand Information." *Journal of Business,* 51(1): 43–56.

Loomis, C. J. 1999. "Lies, damned lies, and managed earnings: The crackdown is here." *Fortune,* 140 (August 2): 74–92.

Looney, Clayton A., Joseph S. Valacich, Peter A. Todd, and Michael G. Morris. 2006. "Paradoxes of Online Investing: Testing the Influence of Technology on User Expectancies." *Decision Sciences,* 37(2): 205–246.

Lopez, Antonio. 2000. "Do they really want to fix it? The will to change seems absent from the Philippine stock market." *AsiaWeek.* March 16.

Lopez, Thomas, and Lynn Rees. 2002. "The Effect of Beating and Missing Analysts' Forecasts on the Information Content of Unexpected Earnings." *Journal of Accounting, Auditing, and Finance,* 17(2): 155–184.

Lorie, James H., and Victor Niederhoffer. 1968. "Predictive and statistical properties of insider trading." *Journal of Law and Economics,* 11(1): 35–53.

Lou, Dong. 2009. "Attracting Investor Attention through Advertising." *Working paper,* London School of Economics.

Loughran, Tim, and Jay R. Ritter. 1995. "The new issue puzzle." *Journal of Finance,* 50(1): 23–51.

Loughran, Tim, and Jay R. Ritter. 1997. "The Operating Performance of Firms Conducting Seasoned Equity Offerings." *Journal of Finance,* 52(5): 1823–1850.

Lowenstein, Roger. 2000. *When Genius Failed: The Rise and Fall of Long Term Capital Management.* New York: Random House.

Lowenstein, Roger. 2004. *Origins of the Crash: The Great Bubble and Its Undoing.* New York: Penguin Press.

Lys, Thomas, and Sungkyu Sohn. 1990. "The association between revisions of financial analysts' earnings forecasts and security price changes." *Journal of Accounting and Economics,* 13(4): 341–363.

Ma, Yuanju, Jun Zhang, and Zhengzheng Du. 2009. "Review of insider trading and its regulations." *Economic Dynamics,* September. (in Chinese)

Mackay, Charles. 1841 (reprint 1996). *Extraordinary Popular Delusions and the Madness of Crowds.* New York: John Wiley & Sons.

Madrick, Jeff. 2001. "The business media and the New Economy." *The Joan Shorenstein Center on the Press, Politics and Public Policy Research Paper R-24.* John F. Kennedy School of Government, Harvard University.

Malmendier, Ulrike, and Devin M. Shanthikumar. 2007. "Do security analysts speak in two tongues?" *NBER Working paper.*

Manne, Henry G. 1966. *Insider Trading and the Stock Market.* New York: The Free Press.

Manne, Henry G. 1970, "Insider Trading and the Law Professors." *Vanderbilt Law Review,* 23: 547–590.

Markham, Jerry. 1991. "Manipulation: The Unprosecutable Crime." *Yale Journal of Regulation,* 8: 281–390.

Maslow, A. H. 1970. *Motivation and Personality.* New York: Harper & Row.

Mathias, James H. 1936. "Manipulative Practices and the Securities Exchange Act." *University of Pittsburgh Law Review,* 3: 7–32.

Mathur, Ike, and Amjad Waheed. 1995. "Stock Price Reactions to Securities Recommended in *Business Week*'s 'Inside Wall Street'." *Financial Review,* 30(3): 583–604.

Matsumoto, Dawn A., 2002. "Management's Incentives to Avoid Negative Earnings Surprises." *The Accounting Review,* 77: 483–514.

McChesney, Robert. 2008. "The New Theology of the First Amendment." In: *The Political Economy of Media: Enduring Issues, Emerging Dilemmas,* New York: Monthly Review Press, pp. 249–263.

McClelland, D. C., J. W. Atkinson, R. A. Clark, and E. L. Lowell. 1976. *The Achievement Motive.* Oxford, England: Irvington.

McGonagle, Katherine A., and Ronald C. Kessler. 1990. "Chronic Stress, Acute Stress, and Depressive Symptoms." *American Journal of Community Psychology,* 18(5): 681–706.

McGoun, Elton G. 2008. "The inherent manipulability of markets." *Accountancy Business and the Public Interest,* 7(2): 89–117.

McNally, W. J., and B. F. Smith. 2003. "Do insiders play by the rules?" *Canadian Public Policy,* 29(2): 1–20.

McNichols, M., and P. O'Brien. 1997. "Self-selection and analyst coverage." *Journal of Accounting Research,* 35 (Supplement): 167–199.

The Medical Classic of the Yellow Emperor. (The first classic of Traditional Chinese Medicine, translated by Zhu Ming.) 2001. Beijing: Foreign Language Press.

Mei, Jianping, Guojun Wu, and Chunsheng Zhou. 2004. "Behavior based manipulation—theory and prosecution evidence." *Unpublished manuscript,* New York University.

Menendez-Requejo, Susana. 2005. "Market valuation of the analysts' recommendations: The Spanish stock market." *Applied Financial Economics,* 15(7): 509–518.

Merced, Michael J. de la, Vikas Bajaj, and Andrew Ross Sorkin. 2008. "As Goldman and Morgan Shift, a Wall St. Era Ends." *New York Times,* September 21.

Meschke, Felix. 2004. "CEO Interviews on CNBC." *AFA 2003 Washington, DC Meetings.* Available at SSRN: http://ssrn.com/abstract=302602. Accessed August 23, 2010.

Metalsky, G. I., T. E. Joiner, T. S. Hardin, and L. Y. Abramson. 1993. "Depressive Reactions to Failure in a Naturalistic Setting: A Test of the Hopelessness and Self-Esteem Theories of Depression." *Journal of Abnormal Psychology,* 102(1): 101–109.

Meulbroek, Lisa K. 1992. "An Empirical Analysis of Illegal Insider Trading." *The Journal of Finance,* 47(5): 1661–1699.

Michaely, Roni, and Kent L. Womack. 1999. "Conflict of Interest and the Credibility of Underwriter Analyst Recommendations." *Review of Financial Studies,* 12 (4): 653–686.

Michaely, Roni, and Kent L. Womack. 2005. "Brokerage Recommendations: Stylized Characteristics, Market Responses, and Biases." In: Thaler, Richard. (Ed.) *Advances in Behavioral Finance II*. Princeton, NJ: Princeton University Press.

Michie, Ranald C. 2006. *The global securities market: A history*. New York: Oxford University Press.

Mikhail, Michael B., Beverly R. Walther, and Richard H. Willis. 2007. "When security analysts talk, who listens?" *The Accounting Review,* 82: 1227–1253.

Mill, J. S. 1998. *Utilitarianism*. (Edited by Roger Crisp.) New York: Oxford University Press.

Minkoff, K., E. Bergman, A. X. Beck, and R. Beck. 1973. "Hopelessness, Depression and Attempted Suicide." *American Journal of Psychiatry,* 130(4): 455–459.

Miron-Shatz, Talya, Arthur Stone, and Daniel Kahneman. 2009. "Memories of yesterday's emotions: Does the valence of experience affect the memory-experience gap?" *Emotion,* 9(6): 885–889.

Mitchell, Mark L., and J. Harold Mulherin. 1994. "The impact of public information on the stock market." *Journal of Finance,* 49(3): 923–950.

Montgomery, Robert H. (Ed.) 1933. *Financial Handbook, 2nd ed.* New York: The Ronald Press.

Moore, Aaron. 2003. "Entangling Alliances." *Columbia Journalism Review,* March/April: 64.

Morris, Michael W., Oliver J. Sheldon, Daniel R. Ames, and Maia J.Young. 2007. "Metaphors and the market: Consequences and preconditions of agent and object metaphors in stock market commentary." *Organizational Behavior and Human Decision Processes,* 102: 174–192.

Motta, Massimo. 2004. *Competition Policy: Theory and Practice*. New York: Cambridge University Press, pp. 442–454.

Murphy, Paul. 2005. "A tale of two City Slickers." *The Guardian,* December 12.

Murray, H. 2004. "Psychogenic Needs." Chapter 7, Trait Theory. In: Heffner, C. L. (Ed.) *Personality Synopsis*. Heffner Media Group, Inc. Available at: http://allpsych.com/personalitysynopsis/contents.html. Accessed May 23, 2011.

Musgrove, P. 1987. "The economic crisis and its impact on health and health care in Latin America and the Caribbean." *International Journal of Health Services,* 17: 411–441.

Myers, D. G. 1999. "Close relationships and quality of life." In: Kahneman, D., E. Diener, and N. Schwarz. (Eds.) *Well-Being: The Foundations of Hedonic Psychology*. New York: Russell Sage Foundation, pp. 374–391.

Myers, James N., Linda A. Myers, and Douglas J. Skinner, 2007. "Earnings Momentum and Earnings Management." *Journal of Accounting, Auditing and Finance,* 22: 249–284.

Myers, L., and Skinner, D. 1999. "Earnings momentum and earnings management." *Working paper,* University of Illinois at Urbana-Champaign and University of Michigan.

Nageswaran, V. A., and S. Krithivasan. 2004. "Capital market reforms in India and ASEAN: Avenues for co-operation." Paper presented at the *1st ASEAN-India Roundtable,* February 9–10, Singapore.

Narayanan, M. P., C. Schipani, and H. N. Seyhun. 2007. "The Economic Impact of Backdating of Executive Stock Options." *Michigan Law Review,* 105(8): 1597–1641.

National Credibility Index. 1999. *The National Credibility Index: Making Personal Investment Decisions Identifying Which Sources of Information the Public Believes When Evaluating Corporate Performance for Personal Investing.* Sponsored by the Public Relations Society of America Foundation and Supported by the Center for International Business Education, Columbia University Graduate School of Business and School of International and Public Affairs.

Nelson, Mark W., John A. Elliott, and Robin L. Tarpley. 2002. "Evidence from Auditors about Managers' and Auditors' Earnings Management Decisions." *The Accounting Review,* 77(S-1): 175–202.

New York Stock Exchange. 2009. Available at: www.nyse.com/about/history/timeline_1900_1919_index.html.

Newkirk, Thomas C., and Melissa A. Robertson. 1998. "Insider Trading—A U.S. Perspective." *Speech at 16th International Symposium on Economic Crime.* September 19, Cambridge, UK.

Nguyen, Bang Dang. 2009. "Is More News Good News? Media Coverage of CEOs, Firm Value, and Rent Extraction." *AFE/ASSA 2006 Boston Meetings.* Available at SSRN: http://ssrn.com/abstract=800746. Accessed March 16, 2011.

Nussbaum, M., and A. Sen. 1993. *The Quality of Life.* Oxford, England: Oxford University Press.

O'Flaherty, B. 2005. *City Economics.* Cambridge, MA: Harvard University Press.

Odean, Terrance. 1999. "Do Investors Trade Too Much?" *American Economic Review,* 89(5): 1279–1298.

Oh, Natalie Y., Jerry T. Parwada, and Terry S. Walte. 2008. "Investors' trading behavior and performance: Online versus non-online equity trading in Korea." *Pacific-Basin Finance Journal,* 16(1–2): 26–43.

Okun, M. A., W. A. Stock, M. J. Haring, and R. A. Witter. 1984. "Health and subjective well-being: A meta-analysis." *International Journal of Aging and Human Development,* 19(2): 111–132.

Ortony, A., G. L. Clore, and A. Collins. 1988. *The Cognitive Structure of Emotions.* New York: Cambridge University Press.

Palmrose, Zoe-Vonna. 1987. "Litigation and independent auditors: The role of business failures and management fraud." *Auditing: A Journal of Practice and Theory,* 6(1): 90–103.

Palmrose, Zoe-Vonna. 1988. "An Analysis of Auditor Litigation and Audit Service Quality." *The Accounting Review,* 63(1): 55–73.

Palmrose, Zoe-Vonna, and Susan W. Scholz. 2004. "The Circumstances and Legal Consequences of Non-GAAP Reporting: Evidence from Restatements." *Contemporary Accounting Research,* 21(1): 139–180.

Paltrow, S. J. 1999. "Are there cracks in Conseco's house of acquisitions?" *The Wall Street Journal,* March 23, at C1.

Pearlin, Leonard I., Elizabeth G. Menaghan, Morton A. Lieberman, and Joseph T. Mullan. 1981. "The Stress Process." *Journal of Health and Social Behavior,* 22: 337–356.

Pecora, Ferdinand. 1939. *Wall Street Under Oath: The Story of Our Modern Money Changers.* New York: Simon and Schuster.

Peress, Joel. 2008. "Media Coverage and Investors' Attention to Earnings Announcements." *Review of Financial Studies,* forthcoming.

Perminov, Sergey. 2008. *Trendocracy and Stock Market Manipulations: Trendocrats establish uptrends to sell you overvalued stocks. They capitalize on your greed and fear. Do you always recognize what is going on?* Lexington, KY: Stock Markets Institute.

Perold, Andre F., and Eric Sirri. 1998. "The cost of international equity trading." *Working paper,* Harvard University.

Petrie, K., and K. Chamberlain. 1983. "Hopelessness and Social Desirability as Moderator Variables in Predicting Suicidal Behavior." *Journal of Consulting and Clinical Psychology,* 51(4): 485–487.

Pettit, Dave, and Rich Jaroslovsky. 2002. *The Wall Street Journal Online's Guide to Online Investing: How to Make the Most of the Internet in a Bull or Bear Market.* New York: Three Rivers Press.

Phylaktis, K., M. Kavussanos, and G. Manalis. 1999. "Price Limits and Stock Market Volatility in the Athens Stock Exchange." *European Financial Management,* 5: 69–84.

Pieper, Ute, Dirk Schiereck, and Martin Weber. 1993. "Die Kaufempfehlungen des 'Effecten-Spiegel'. Eine empirische Untersuchung im Lichte der Effizienzthese des Kapitalmarktes." *Zeitschrift für betriebswirtschaftliche Forschung,* 45: 487–509.

Pincus, M., and S. Rajgopal. 2002. "The interaction between accrual management and hedging: Evidence from oil and gas firms." *The Accounting Review,* 77(1): 127–160.

Pindyck, Robert S., and Daniel L. Rubinfeld. 2001. *Microeconomics. 5th ed.* Upper Saddle River, NJ: Prentice Hall, pp. 327–367.

Piotroski, Joseph D., and Darren T. Roulstone. 2005. "Do insider trades reflect both contrarian beliefs and superior knowledge about future cash flow realizations?" *Journal of Accounting and Economics,* 39(1): 55–81.

Pirrong, Stephen Craig. 1995. "The self-regulation of commodity exchanges: The case of market manipulation." *Journal of Law and Economics,* 38(1): 141–208.

Pirrong, Stephen Craig. 1996. *The Economics, Law, and Public Policy of Market Power Manipulation.* Boston, MA: Kluwer Academic Publishers.

Plerou, Vasiliki, Parameswaran Gopikrishnan, Xavier Gabaix, and H. Eugene Stanley. 2002. "Quantifying Stock Price Response to Demand Fluctuations." *Physical Review E,* 66: 027104.

Pollock, Horatio M. 1935. "The Depression and mental disease in New York State." *American Journal of Psychiatry,* 91: 736–771.

Porteba, James. 2001. "The Rise of the 'Equity Culture': U.S. Stockownership Patterns, 1989–1998." *Working paper,* MIT.

Postman, Neil, and Steve Powers. 1997. "How to Watch Television News: What Can You Do?" In: Wells, Alan, and Ernest A. Hakanen. (Eds.) *Mass Media and Society.* Greenwich, CT: Ablex Publishing Corporation.

Presidential Task Force on Market Mechanisms (Brady Report). 1988. *Report of the Presidential Task Force on Market Mechanisms.* Nicholas Brady (Chairman), U.S. Government Printing Office.

Proimos, Alex. 2005. "Trust an analyst? An investigation of conflicts of interest in an Australian investment bank." *Journal of Investment Compliance,* 6(3): 59–70.

Putnam, Robert D. 2000. *Bowling Alone: The Collapse and Revival of American Community.* New York: Simon & Schuster.

Rangan, S. 1998. "Earnings management and the performance of seasoned equity offerings." *Journal of Financial Economics,* 50(1): 101–122.

Rayman, P., and B. Bluestone. 1982. "The private and social response to job loss: A metropolitan study." *Final report of research sponsored by the Center for Work and Mental Health,* National Institute of Mental Health.

Reilly, David. 2006. "Booming Audit Firms Seek Shield from Suits." *The Wall Street Journal,* November 1, p. C1.

Reingold, Dan. 2006. *Confessions of a Wall Street Analyst: A True Story of Inside Information and Corruption in the Stock Market.* New York: HarperCollins.

Reinhart, Carmen M., and Kenneth S. Rogoff. 2009. *This Time Is Different: Eight Centuries of Financial Folly.* Princeton, NJ: Princeton University Press.

Rendleman, Jr., R. J., C. P. Jones, and H. A. Latanie. 1982. "Empirical anomalies based on unexpected earnings and the importance of risk adjustments." *Journal of Financial Economics,* 10: 269–287.

Rezza, G., R. Marino, F. Farchi, and M. Taranto. 2004. "SARS: The epidemic in the press." *Emerging Infectious Diseases,* 10: 381–382.

Richardson, Scott A., Siew Hong Teoh, and Peter Wysocki. 2004. "The Walk-down to Beatable Analyst Forecasts: The Roles of Equity Issuance and Insider Trading Incentives." *Contemporary Accounting Research,* 21(4): 885–924.

Ritter, Jay. 2003. "Investment Banking and Securities Issuance." Chapter 5 in: Constantinides, George, Milton Harris, and René Stulz. (Eds.) *Handbook of the Economics of Finance.* Amsterdam: North-Holland.

Ritter, Jay, and Ivo Welch. 2002. "A review of IPO activity, pricing, and allocations." *Journal of Finance,* 57: 1795–1828.

Robertson, Jamie. 2008. "Stock markets in 2008: A year to forget or learn from?" *BBC World News.* December 29.

Ronen, J., and S. Sadan. 1981. *Smoothing income numbers: Objectives, means, and implications.* Reading, MA: Addison-Wesley Publishing Company.

Roseman, Ira. 2001. "A Model of Appraisal in the Emotional System. Integrating Theory, Research and Application." Chapter 4 in: Sceerer, Klaus R., Angela Schorr, and Tom Johnstone. (Eds.) *Appraisal Process in Emotion,* Oxford, England: Oxford University Press.

Roychowdhury, Sugata. 2006. "Earnings management through real activities manipulation." *Journal of Accounting and Economics,* 42(3): 335–370.

Roysamb, E., K. Tambs, T. Reichborn-Kjennerud, M. C. Neale, and J. R. Harris. 2003. "Happiness and health: Environmental and genetic contributions to the relationship between subjective well-being, perceived health, and somatic illness." *Journal of Personality and Social Psychology,* 85: 1136–1146.

Sabherwal, Sanjiv, Salil K. Sarkar, and Ying Zhang. 2008. "Online talk: does it matter?" *Managerial Finance*, 34(6): 423–436.

Sallot, Lynne M., and Elizabeth A. Johnson. 2006. "Investigating relationship between journalists and public relations practitioners: Working together to set, frame and build the public agenda. 1991–2004." *Public Relations Review*, 32(2): 151–159.

Sandvik, E., Ed Diener, and l. Seidlitz. 1993. "Subjective well-being: The convergence and stability of self-report and non-self-report measures." *Journal of Personality*, 61: 317–342.

Sant, Rajiv, and Mir A. Zaman. 1996. "Market reaction to Business Week's Inside Wall Street column: A self-fulfilling prophecy." *Journal of Banking and Finance*, 20(4): 617–643.

Sapolsky, Robert M. 2004. *Why Zebras Don't Get Ulcers, 3rd ed.* New York: Henry Holt and Company.

Saumya, Shubh, Jai Sinha, and Sudhir Jain. 2006. "Saving Sell-Side Research." Booz-Allen-Hamilton.

Sceerer, Klaus R., Angela Schorr, and Tom Johnstone. (Eds.) 2001. *Appraisal Process in Emotion*. Oxford, England: Oxford University Press.

Schack, Justin. 2001. "Should Analysts Own Stock in Companies They Cover?" *Institutional Investor*, 35 (April): 60–71.

Schiffrin, Anya. 2011. "The U.S. press and the financial crisis." In: Schiffrin, Anya. (Ed.) *Bad News*. New York: The New Press, pp. 1–21.

Schlumpf, Philipp M., Markus M. Schmid, and Heinz Zimmermann. 2008. "The First- and Second-Hand Effect of Analysts' Stock Recommendations: Evidence from the Swiss Stock Market." *European Financial Management*, 14(5): 962–988.

Schmitz, Philipp. 2007. "Market and Individual Investors Reactions to Corporate News in the Media." Available at SSRN: http://ssrn.com/abstract=1004488. Accessed October 19, 2010.

Schuster, Thomas. 2003. "Fifty-Fifty. Stock Recommendations and Stock Prices. Effects and Benefits of Investment Advice in the Business Media." *Leipzig University Working Paper No. 03-01*. Available at SSRN: http://ssrn.com/abstract=387341. Accessed September 20, 2010.

Schuster, Thomas. 2003. "Meta-Communication and Market Dynamics. Reflexive Interactions of Financial Markets and the Mass Media." *Leipzig University Working Paper No. 03-03*. Available at SSRN: http://ssrn.com/abstract=429303. Accessed March 13, 2011.

Schwager, Jack D. 1992. *The New Market Wizards: Conversations with America's Top Traders*. New York: HarperCollins.

Schwartz, Robert A. (Ed.) 2001. *Regulation of U. S. Equity Markets*. Boston, MA: Kluwer Academic Publishers.

Schwartz, Robert A., and James Shapiro. 1992. "The Challenge of Institutionalization for the Equity Markets." In: Saunders, Anthony. (Ed.) *Recent Developments in Finance*. New York: Business One Irwin, pp. 31–45.

Securities and Exchange Board of India (SEBI). 2007. *Order against Shri Ketan V. Parekh and his associated entities.* Available at: www.sebi.gov.in/cmorder/ketanorder1.pdf. Accessed August 26, 2008.

Securities and Exchange Board of India (SEBI). 2009. Available at: www.sebi.gov.in/Index.jsp?contentDisp=SubSection&sec_id=1&sub_sec_id=1. Accessed September 1, 2009.

Securities and Exchange Commission of the United States (SEC). 2004. "SEC charges Lucent Technologies Inc. and ten defendants for a $1.1 billion accounting fraud." *Litigation Release No. 18715,* May 17. www.sec.gov/litigation/litreleases/lr18715.htm. Accessed July 28, 2010.

Securities and Exchange Commission of the United States (SEC). 2006. *Annual Report.* Available at: www.sec.gov/about/secpar/secpar2006.pdf. Accessed August 25.

Securities and Exchange Commission of the United States (SEC). 2009. Available at: www.sec.gov/about/secstats2008.pdf. Accessed September 9, 2009.

Securities and Exchange Commission of the United States (SEC). 2010. Available at: www.sec.gov. Accessed July 25, 2010.

Securities and Futures Authority (SFA). 2000. "Disciplinary action against Nomura International PLC, Robert Mapstone and Gary Channon."*Board Notice 554,* September 26. London: The Securities and Futures Authority Limited.

Seligman, Martin E. P. 2002. *Authentic Happiness: Using the New Positive Psychology to Realize Your Potential for Lasting Fulfillment.* New York: Free Books.

Selye, Hans. 1956. *The Stress of Life.* New York: McGraw-Hill Book Company.

Seyhun, H. Nejat. 1986. "Insider profits, costs of trading, and market efficiency." *Journal of Financial Economics,* 16(2): 189–212.

Seyhun, H. Nejat. 1988. "The information content of aggregate insider trading." *Journal of Business,* 61(1): 1–24.

Seyhun, H. Nejat. 1992. "The Effectiveness of the Insider-Trading Sanctions." *Journal of Law and Economics,* 35(1): 149–182.

Seyhun, H. Nejat, and Michael Bradley. 1997. "Corporate bankruptcy and insider trading." *Journal of Business,* 70(2): 189–216.

Shanthikumar, Devin. 2009. "Consecutive Earnings Surprises: Small and Large Trader Reactions."*Working paper,* Harvard Business School, Cambridge, MA.

Shapira, Zur, and Itzhak Venezia. 2006. "On Timing and Herding: Do Professional Investors Behave Differently Than Amateurs?" *Working paper,* New York University and The Hebrew University.

Sheldon, Richard N. 1975. "The Pujo Committee 1912." In: Schlesinger, Arthur M., Jr., and Roger Burns. (Eds.). *Congress Investigates: A Documented History 1792–1974 (Volume 3),* pp. 2251, 2344–2346.

Shen, Chung-Hua, and Hsiang-Lin Chih. 2009. "Conflicts of Interest in the Stock Recommendations of Investment Banks and Their Determinants." *Journal of Financial and Quantitative Analysis,* 44(5): 1149–1171.

Shi, Yongdong, and Xianfeng Jiang 2004. "Insider trading, price volatility and information asymmetry: An empirical study based on China's stock markets." *World Economy,* 12(1): 1–25. (in Chinese)

Shi Ji (Historical Records). 1995. Written by Si Maqian in the Western Han Dynasty (206 BC–23 AD), modern translation by Wu Yun. 1995. Xian, Shaanxi Province: San Qin Press. (in Chinese)

Shiller, Robert J. 2000. *Irrational Exuberance*. Princeton, NJ: Princeton University Press.

Shivakumar, L. 2000. "Do firms mislead investors by overstating earnings before seasoned equity offerings?" *Journal of Accounting and Economics*, 29: 339–370.

Shleifer, Andrei. 2001. *Inefficient Markets: An Introduction to Behavioral Finance*. New York: Oxford University Press.

Shoemaker, Pamela J., and Stephen D. Reese. 1996. *Mediating the Message: Theories of Influences on Mass Media Content, 2nd ed.* White Plains, NY: Longman.

Siconolfi, Michael. 1992. "Under Pressure: At Morgan Stanley, Analysts Were Urged to Soften Harsh Views." *The Wall Street Journal,* July 14, at A1.

Siconolfi, Michael. 1998. "Out of sync: This securities analyst calls it as he sees it; That's the problem." *The Wall Street Journal,* May 18, at A1.

Silver, M. A., M. Bohnert, A. T. Beck, and D. Marcus. 1971. "Relationship of Depression to Attempted Suicide and Seriousness of Attempt." *Archives of General Psychiatry,* 25: 573–576.

Sina. 2009. "Thirty minutes on economy: Demystify the 'black mouth' Wang Jianzhong." December 17. Available at: http://finance.sina.com.cn/stock/stock aritcle/20091217/22377119916.shtml. Accessed July 19, 2010. (in Chinese)

Skinner, D. J., and R. G. Sloan. 2000. "Earnings surprises, growth expectations, and stock returns, or: Don't let an earnings torpedo sink your portfolio." *Working paper,* University of Michigan.

Sloan, Allan. 2002. "Is the boss dumping stock?" *Newsweek,* March 11, p. 30.

Sloan, R. 1996. "Do Stock Prices Fully Reflect Information in Accruals and Cash Flows about Future Earnings?" *The Accounting Review,* 71(3): 289–315.

Smith, Adam. 2008. *An Inquiry into the Nature and Causes of the Wealth of Nations.* (Edited by Kathryn Sutherland.) New York: Oxford University Press.

Smith, Adam. 2009. *The Theory of Moral Sentiments.* (Edited by Ryan Patrick Hanley.) New York: Penguin Books.

Smith, Dimity Kingsford. 2006. "Same Yet Different: Australian and United States Online Investing Regulation." *University of Toledo Law Review,* 37(2): 461–496.

Smith, Randall. 2004. "In signal from SEC, Bank of America is fined over a delay." *The Wall Street Journal,* March 11.

Smith, Richard D. 2006. "Responding to global infectious disease outbreaks: lessons from SARS on the role of risk perception, communication and management." *Social Science and Medicine,* 63(12): 3113–3123.

Snyder, Leslie B., and Chrystal L. Park. 2002. "National studies of stress reactions and media exposure to the attacks." Chapter 14 in: Greenberg, Bradley S. (Ed.) *Communication and Terrorism: Public and Media Responses to 9/11.* Creskill, New Jersey: Hamilton Press, Inc.

Solomon, William S. 1997. "The newspaper business." In: Wells, Alan, and Ernest A. Hakanen. (Eds.) *Mass Media and Society.* Greenwich, CT: Ablex Publishing Corporation.

Soros, George. 1995. *Soros on Soros: Staying Ahead of the Curve.* New York: John Wiley & Sons, p. 4.

Soros, George. 1998. *The Crisis of Global Capitalism: Open Society Endangered.* New York: PublicAffairs.

Specogna, Marino. 2003. *A Convicted Stock Manipulator's Guide to Investing.* Lincoln, NE: iUniverse, Inc.

Spiess, D. K., and J. Affleck-Graves. 1995. "The long-run performance following seasoned equity offerings." *Journal of Financial Economics,* 38(3): 243–267.

Stansfeld, Stephen. 2006. "Social support and social cohesion." Chapter 8 in: Marmot, Michael, and Richard G. Wilkinson. (Eds.) *Social determinants of health,* 2nd ed. New York: Oxford University Press.

Stark, John Reed. 2001. "EnforceNet Redux: A Retrospective of the SEC's Internet Program Four Years after Its Genesis." *Business Lawyer (ABA),* 57(1): 105–126.

Starkman, Dean. 2009. "Power problem: The business press did everything but take on the institutions that brought down the financial system." *Columbia Journalism Review,* May/June: 24.

Stice, Earl. 1991. "The Market Reaction to 10-K and 10-Q Filings and to Subsequent the *Wall Street Journal* Earnings Announcements." *The Accounting Review,* 66(1): 42–55.

Stiglitz, Joseph. 1974. "Alternative theories of wage determination and unemployment in L.D.C.'s. The Labor Turnover Model." *Quarterly Journal of Economics,* 88(2): 194–227.

Stiglitz, Joseph. 2002. "Information and the change in the paradigm in economics." *American Economic Review,* 92(3): 460–501.

Stiglitz, Joseph E. 2011. "The media and the crisis: An information theoretical approach." In: Schiffrin, Anya. (Ed.) *Bad News.* New York: The New Press, pp. 22–36.

Stone, A. A., and S. Shiffman. 1994. "Ecological Momentary Assessment (EMA) in Behavioral Medicine." *Annals of Behavioral Medicine,* 16(3), pp. 199–202.

Stuckler, David, Sanjay Basu, Marc Suhrcke, Adam Coutts, and Martin McKee. 2009. "The public health effect of economic crises and alternative policy responses in Europe: An empirical analysis." *The Lancet,* 374(9686): 315–323.

Summers, Scott L., and John T. Sweeney. 1998. "Fraudulently misstated financial statements and insider trading: An empirical analysis." *The Accounting Review,* 73(1): 131–146.

Swerling, Jerry, Chaiti Sen, Adam Bonefeste, Azita Rezvan, Daniel Lee, and Andy McHargue. 2010. "Report 3: Areas of Responsibility, Digital/Social Media, Evaluation."*Communications and Public Relations General Accepted Practices 2010. Sixth Communication and Public Relations Generally Accepted Practices (GAP) Study (Q4 2009 Data). GAP VI.* University of Southern California, Annenberg School of Communication and Journalism, Strategic Communication & Public Relations Center.

Szockyj, E. 1993. *The Law and Insider Trading: In Search of a Level Playing Field.* Buffalo, NY: William S. Hein & Co., Inc.

Tait, Nikki. 2005. "Case of the City Slickers and an 'optimistic, wacky traveler in cyberspace'." *Financial Times,* December 8.

Takkouche, B., C. Regueira, and J. J. Gestal-Otero. 2001. "A cohort study of stress and the common cold." *Epidemiology,* 12: 345–349.

Tambibi, Damian. 2008. "What is financial journalism for? Ethics and responsibility in a time of crisis and change."*POLIS,* London School of Economics.

Tan, Lin. 2005. "Empirical Analysis of Chinese Stock Market Behavior: Evidence from Dynamic Correlations, Herding Behavior, and Speed of Adjustment." *Ph. D. Dissertation,* Drexel University, Philadelphia, Pennsylvania.

Tan, Lin, Thomas C. Chiang, Joseph R. Mason, and Edward Nelling. 2008. "Herding behavior in Chinese stock markets: An examination of A and B shares." *Pacific-Basin Finance Journal,* 16(1–2): 61–77.

Teoh, S. H., I. Welch, and T. J. Wong. 1998a. "Earnings Management and the Long-Run Performance of Initial Public Offerings." *Journal of Finance,* 53(6): 1935–1974.

Teoh, S. H., I. Welch, and T. J. Wong. 1998b. "Earnings Management and the Underperformance of Seasoned Equity Offerings." *Journal of Financial Economics,* 50(1): 63–99.

Tetlock, Paul C. 2007. "Giving Content to Investor Sentiment: The Role of Media in the Stock Market." *Journal of Finance,* 62(3): 1139–1168.

Tetlock, Paul C., Maytal Saar-Tsechansky, and Sofus Macskassy. 2008. "More than words: Quantifying language to measure firms' fundamentals." *Journal of Finance,* 63(3): 1437–1477.

Thel, Steve. 1990. "The Original Conception of Section 10(b) of the Securities Exchange Act." *Stanford Law Review,* 42(385): 424–461.

Tomasic, R. 1991. *Casino Capitalism: Insider Trading in Australia.* Canberra: Australia Institute of Criminology.

Tsang, Donald. 1998. *Speech at the Hong Kong Trade Development Council in Frankfurt,* September 29.

Tumarkin, Robert, and Robert F. Whitelaw. 2001. "News or noise? Internet postings and stock prices." *Financial Analyst Journal,* 57: 41–51.

Turner, R. Jay, Blair Wheaton, and Donald A. Lloyd. 1995. "The Epidemiology of Social Stress." *American Sociological Review,* 60(1): 104–125.

Unger, Laura S. (Acting Chair, U.S. Securities & Exchange Commission.) 2001. *Written Testimony Concerning Conflicts of Interest Faced by Brokerage Firms and Their Research Analysts Before the Subcommittee on Capital Markets, Insurance, and Government Sponsored Enterprises, Committee on Financial Services United States House of Representatives.* July 31. www.sec.gov/news/testimony/073101tslu.htm. Accessed September 3, 2010.

U.S. Securities and Exchange Commission and the Commodity Futures Trading Commission. 2010. *Findings Regarding the Market Events of May 6, 2010.*

Valentine, Debra A. 1998. "Prepared Statement of Debra A, Valentine, General Counsel for the U.S. Federal Trade Commission on 'Pyramid Schemes' presented at the International Monetary Fund's Seminar on Current Legal Issues Affecting Central Banks, Washington, D.C., May 13, 1998." Available at: www.ftc.gov/speeches/other/dvimf16.shtm. Accessed December 29, 2010.

Vanderwicken, Peter. 1995. "Why the News Is Not the Truth: Review of *News and the Culture of Lying: How Journalism Really Works*" by Paul H. Weaver. The Free Press, 1994; *Who Stole the News: Why We Can't Keep Up with What Happens in the World* by Mort Rosenblum. John Wiley & Sons, 1993; and *Tainted Truth: The Manipulation of Fact in America* by Cynthia Crossen. Simon & Schuster, 1994." *Harvard Business Review,* May–June: 144–151.

Veldkamp, Laura L. 2006. "Media frenzies in markets for financial information." *American Economic Review,* 96: 577–601.

Vila, J. 1986. "The role of information in futures market manipulations." *Working paper,* Princeton University.

Vilardo, Mark F. 2004. "Online Impersonation in Securities Scams." *IEEE Security and Privacy,* May/June: 82–85.

Viscusi, W. Kip, John M. Vernon, and Joseph E. Harrington, Jr. 1995. *Economics of Regulation and Antitrust, 2nd ed.* Cambridge, MA: MIT Press.

Von Bommel, Jos. 2003. "Rumors." *Journal of Finance,* 58(4): 1499–1519.

Walker, Richard H., and David M. Levine. 2001. "ESSAY: 'You've Got Jail': Current Trends in Civil and Criminal Enforcement of Internet Securities Fraud." *American Criminal Law Review,* 38: 405–429.

Wang, Jiang. 1994. "A Model of Competitive Stock Trading Volume." *Journal of Political Economy,* 102: 127–167.

Wang, Q., T. J. Wong, and L. Xia. 2008. "State ownership, the institutional environment, and auditor choice: Evidence from China." *Journal of Accounting and Economics,* 46(1): 112–134.

Watson, David. 1988. "Intraindividual and interindividual analyses of Positive and Negative Affect: Their relation to health complaints, perceived stress, and daily activities." *Journal of Personality and Social Psychology,* 54: 1020–1030.

Watson, David, Lee A. Clark, and Auke Tellegen. 1988. "Development and validation of brief measures of positive and negative affect: The PANAS scales." *Journal of Personality and Social Psychology,* 54(6): 1063–1070.

Wecter, Dixon. 1948. *The Age of the Great Depression, 1929–1941.* New York: Macmillan.

Weissman, A. N., A. T. Beck, and M. Kovacs. 1979. "Drug Abuse, Hopelessness and Suicidal Behavior." *International Journal of the Addictions,* 14: 451–464.

Wells, Alan, and Ernest A. Hakanen. 1997. "Part V, News, Introduction." In: Wells, Alan, and Ernest A. Hakanen. (Eds.) *Mass Media and Society.* Greenwich, CT: Ablex Publishing Corporation, pp. 68 and 333.

Wetzel, R. D., T. Margulies, R. Davis, and E. Karam. 1980. "Hopelessness, Depression and Suicide Intent." *Journal of Clinical Psychiatry,* 47: 159–160.

White, Horace. 1909. "The Hughes Investigation." *Journal of Political Economy,* 17(8): 528–540.

Whitehouse, Kaja. 2011. "50 Cent millions: Rapper nets $8.7M on tweet feat." *New York Post,* January 11.

WHO (World Health Organization) Definition. 1948. *Preamble to the Constitution of the World Health Organization as adopted by the International Health Conference, New York, 19 June–22 July 1946; signed on 22 July 1946 by the representatives of 61 States* (Official Records of the World Health Organization, no. 2, p. 100) and entered into force on 7 April 1948.

WHO (World Health Organization). 2009. "The financial crisis and global health." *Report of a high-level consultation.* Geneva, Switzerland.

Wijmenga, R. Th. 1990. "The Performance of Published Dutch Stock Recommendations." *Journal of Banking and Finance,* 14(2–3): 559–581.

Wilkinson, Richard, and Michael Marmot. (Eds.) 2003. *Social Determinants of Health: The Solid Facts, 2nd ed.* World Health Organization.

Williams, R. B., and N. Schneiderman. 2002. "Resolved: Psychosocial interventions can improve clinical outcomes in organic disease (pro)." *Psychosomatic Medicine,* 64, 552–557.

Wilson, N., G. Thomson, and O. Mansoor. 2004. "Print media response to SARS in New Zealand." *Emerging Infectious Diseases,* 10: 1461–1464.

Winkelmann, Liliana, and Rainer Winkelmann. 1998. "Why are the unemployed so unhappy? Evidence from panel data." *Economica,* 65: 257, pp. 1–15.

Wisniewski, Tomasz Piotr, and Brendan John Lambe. 2010. "The Role of Media in the Credit Crunch: The Case of the Banking Sector." Available at SSRN: http://ssrn.com/abstract=1696105. Accessed March 28, 2011.

Wolfers, Justin. 2003. "Is Business Cycle Volatility Costly? Evidence from Surveys of Subjective Well-Being." *International Finance,* 6(1): 1–26.

Womack, Kent L. 1996. "Do brokerage analysts' recommendations have investment value?" *Journal of Finance,* 51(1): 137–167.

World Values Survey: www.worldvaluessurvey.org/.

Wysocki, Peter D. 1999. "Cheap talk on the web: The determinants of postings on stock message boards." *Working paper,* University of Michigan.

Xie, H. 2001. "The mispricing of abnormal accruals." *The Accounting Review,* 76: 357–373.

Xu, Jin. 2008. "New Evidence on the Effects of the Insider Trading Sanctions Act of 1984." Available at SSRN: http://ssrn.com/abstract=1100641. Accessed July 8, 2010.

Yazici, Bilgehan, and Gülnur Muradoglu. 2002. "Dissemination of Stock Recommendations and Small Investors: Who Benefits?" *Multinational Finance Journal,* 6(1): 29–42.

Yermack, D. 1997. "Good timing: CEO stock option awards and company news announcements." *Journal of Finance,* 52(2): 449–476.

Zang, Amy Y. 2007. "Evidence on the Tradeoff between Real Manipulation and Accrual Manipulation." Available at SSRN: http://ssrn.com/abstract=961293. Accessed July 6, 2010.

Zhang, Xin, and Hongmei Zhu. 2003. "Economic analysis of insider trading." *China Economic Quarterly,* 3(1): 71–96. (in Chinese)

Zhang, Yi-Cheng. 1999. "Toward a Theory of Marginally Efficient Markets." *Physica A,* 269: 30–44.

Zheng, Hongtai, and Shaolun Huang. 2006. *History of Hong Kong Stock Market: 1841–1997.* Hong Kong: San Lian Shu Dian. (in Chinese)

About the Editors

Lawrence R. Klein, Benjamin Franklin Professor Emeritus of Economics of the University of Pennsylvania; Ph.D., Economics, Massachusetts Institute of Technology (1944); Nobel Laureate in Economics (1980). Dr. Klein has published widely, as well as edited numerous books. Some of the most current books that he has edited and to which he has contributed articles are *Recent Financial Crises* (2006, Edward Elgar) and *The Making of National Economic Forecasts* (2009, Edward Elgar). Dr. Klein is the intellectual father of Project LINK, established in 1969, a global consortium of national economic forecasting, coordinated partly by the United Nations Department of Economic and Social Affairs. Dr. Klein is a Founding Trustee of the Economists for Peace and Security, serves on the Finance Committee and the Human Rights Committee of the National Academy of Sciences (U.S.), and serves on various committees of the American Philosophical Society, among others. Dr. Klein served as a member of the board of directors of W. P. Carey & Co, an investment banking company.

Viktoria Dalko, Ph.D., Economics, University of Pennsylvania (1992). Dr. Dalko is a Global Professor of Finance at Hult International Business School and an instructor at Harvard University, as well as being listed as a VIP of Who's Who Cambridge. Dr. Dalko served as Advisor to the President of the National Bank of Hungary and Chief of Staff of the Committee of Budget, Tax, and Finances of the Hungarian Parliament. She provides executive training and consulting on finance worldwide, including training for the National Association of Corporate Directors. She was Visiting Professor in numerous countries, and received several teaching awards. Dr. Dalko is coauthor of the Blue Ribbon Commission Report on Health Insurance Reform and a contributor to the *Handbook of Mergers and Acquisitions,* published by the Oxford University Press.

Michael Hao Wang, Ph.D., Mechanical Engineering, University of Illinois at Urbana-Champaign. Dr. Wang is cofounder, Vice President, and since 1999, has been Director of Research of the Boston-based think tank Research Institute of Comprehensive Economics. Prior to his current position, Dr. Wang concentrated on life and health insurance (at New York Life) and accident prevention (at Ford). Dr. Wang has served on the board of directors of an international nonprofit organization, aiming to improve the overall health and wellbeing of people through the study and promotion of pioneering research in life science, natural science, and social science.

Index